Mrs. Trollope

Frances Milton Trollope, by Auguste Hervieu (1832). The National
Portrait Gallery, London.

Mrs. Trollope:
The Triumphant Feminine
in the
Nineteenth Century

Helen Heineman

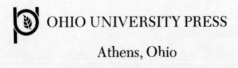 OHIO UNIVERSITY PRESS

Athens, Ohio

Library of Congress Cataloging in Publication Data

Heineman, Helen, 1936-
    Mrs. Trollope : the triumphant feminine in the nineteenth century.

    Bibliography: p.
    Includes index.
    1.   Trollope, Frances Milton, 1779–1863—Biography. 2. Authors,
English—19th century—Biography.
PR5699.T3Z715   823'.7 [B]   78-9940
ISBN 0-8214-0354-0

to my husband and my family

Contents

List of Illustrations   ix

Acknowledgments   xi

1. Beginnings   3

2. The Trollopes at Harrow and La Grange   19

3. Years of Crisis: To Nashoba and Beyond   37

4. The Cincinnati Bazaar and Afterwards   59

5. Good Yankee Stories: *Domestic Manners of the Americans* and *The Refugee*   79

6. Some Works of Imagination and a Bitter Reality   107

7. Mrs. Trollope as Traveler   121

8. Social Consciousness and the Repulsive Subject   143

9. The Strong Woman Theme: The Barnaby Novels   157

10. *Michael Armstrong*: Fiction with a Purpose   169

11. Productive Years   186

12. Frances and Anthony   196

13. Emergence of the Feminine Consciousness   206

14. Contentment, Change, and Loss   226

15. The Triumphant Feminine   240

16. Endings   250

Abbreviations Used in Notes   260

Notes   261

Bibliography
    Manuscript Sources   299
    Works by Frances Trollope   302
    Published Books and Articles   304
    List of Periodicals Cited   312

Index   313

Illustrations

Frontispiece:
Frances Milton Trollope, by Auguste Hervieu (1832)

Fig. 1. Julians Hill

Fig. 2. The farm house at Harrow Weald

Fig. 3. Portrait of Frances Wright

Fig. 4. Nashoba, Auguste Hervieu's illustration for *Domestic Manners* (1832)

Fig. 5. Contemporary caricature of the Trollopes in Cincinnati

Fig. 6. Conjectural Restoration of the Bazaar

Fig. 7. Contemporary print of the Bazaar

Fig. 8. Riverfront view of Cincinnati in 1840

Fig. 9. The separation of the sexes in a Cincinnati Ballroom, Auguste Hervieu's illustration for *Domestic Manners* (1832)

Fig. 10. Evening at a boarding house, Auguste Hervieu's illustration for *Domestic Manners* (1832)

Fig. 11. Portrait of Frances Trollope, from Auguste Hervieu's frontispiece for the 5th edition of *Domestic Manners* (1839)

Fig. 12. "A loose, slatternly woman," American caricature of Mrs. Trollope

Fig. 13. "Tail Piece," American caricature of Mrs. Trollope

Fig. 14. Frances Trollope's two sons: Thomas Adolphus and Anthony

Fig. 15. Factory boys competing with the pigs, Auguste Hervieu's illustration for *Michael Armstrong* (1840)

Fig. 16. The widow Barnaby in the United States, John Leech's illustration for *The Barnabys in America* (1843)

Fig. 17. The widow Barnaby reads her book on America,
          John Leech's illustration for *The Barnabys in
          America* (1843)
Fig. 18. Frances Trollope's two sons: Thomas Adolphus
          and Anthony

Acknowledgments

CURATORS OF library collections across this country and abroad have been helpful: Alexander Wainwright, Morris L. Parrish Collection, Princeton University; Mrs. Mary Ciebert, University of Illinois; Miss Elfrieda Lang, Lilly Library, Indiana University; J. H. W. Norwood, Harrow School; Dr. Brooke Whiting, University of California; Margaret McFadden, University of Chicago; James E. Mooney, Historical Society of Pennsylvania; Mrs. Elmer S. Forman, Cincinnati Historical Society; Mrs. Phyllis S. Pestieau, Lafayette Collections, Cornell University; Christian M. Hanson, Yale University; Mr. R. J. Lee, County Borough of Reading Library; W. H. Kelliher, British Museum Library; Mr. James Lawton, Boston Public Library; Francis O. Mattson, New York Public Library; Mr. Rodney Dennis, Houghton Library, Harvard University; Carole Rawcliffe, Royal Commission on Historical Manuscripts. I also wish to thank the librarians of the Widener, Schlesinger, and Houghton Libraries at Harvard, for kindly assisting me in my research.

Owners of private collections have been generous: Robert H. Taylor, Princeton University; Virginia Murray, Murray Archives; Dr. Cecilia Payne-Gaposchkin and her daughter, Mrs. Katherine Haramundanis.

Directors and staffs of Public Record Offices have given me much assistance. Particular thanks belong to Mr. W. J. Smith, Head Archivist of the Greater London Record Office, for his splendid, detailed, and generous replies to my many lists of questions and "supplementaries"; to the Bristol Archives Office, which directed me to the treasures of the Greater London Council; to Brian S. Smith, County Record Office, Gloucester.

For information and assistance I am indebted to Mr. Robert Cecil, Mrs. Trollope's great-great-grandson; Mrs. Isla Brownless, wife of the present vicar of Heckfield; G. V. Bennett, Librarian of New College, Oxford; Dr. Robert Lee Wolff, Harvard University; Mrs. Guest Perry; and Mrs. Jo Phillips.

A special note of gratitude is due Dr. Cecilia Payne-Gaposchkin, to whose rich collection of family letters I was directed, over ten years ago, by Donald A. Smalley, who vaguely recollected a "Russian-sounding name" and a fascinating woman astronomer at Harvard. Given these hints, I was able to track down both the correspondence and the lady, who has been to me over the years helper, inspiration, gentle critic, and finally, valued friend. Dr. Gaposchkin's great-grandmother, Julia Garnett Pertz, was one of Mrs. Trollope's closest friends and a life-long correspondent.

I wish to express special gratitude to the Radcliffe Institute for the fellowship (1973-75) that gave me the money and room of my own so necessary to the writing of this book. Special thanks to Susan Storey Lyman and Hilda Kahn. I wish to thank my mother for her assistance and my four sons for their good behavior and interest in my work.

Finally, I would like to thank those who carefully read my manuscript, adding their editorial wisdom to my efforts. Dr. Cecilia Payne-Gaposchkin made pertinent comments on the text and did valuable research for me concerning baptismal, marriage, and residential records during several of her trips to London and Bristol. To her belongs the distinction of finding Mrs. Trollope's accurate date of birth. Mr. John Bright-Holmes has edited the manuscript with intelligence and care. My husband, Dr. John L. Heineman, has encouraged and helped me at every stage of this work. Whatever praise this book may receive is his to share in full.

Mrs. Trollope

1

Beginnings

A very lively, pleasant young woman

THE MONTH of March 1779 began with a prevailing cloudiness and ended with heavy showers, but the tenth was "very bright night and day."[1] Appropriately on such a day Frances Milton was born near Bristol. In her twenty-ninth year, she married a rising young lawyer, Thomas Anthony Trollope, and settled into the life of a conventional English matron, raising a large family in pleasant country surroundings. Twenty years later, as a woman of forty-nine, she was abruptly propelled, by circumstances and the needs of her own nature, into an activity that resulted in her lasting fame as world traveler, social critic, and best-selling author of thirty-four three-volume novels and six books of travel. Her youngest son Anthony was to become one of the literary giants of his time, beginning his long and prolific career even as his mother was at the peak of hers.

Frances's father was the Rev. William Milton, born in 1743 in Bristol of a merchant family and educated at Winchester. On 31 March 1762, he matriculated at St. John Baptist College, Oxford, was admitted as a probationary fellow, and two years later became a full fellow of New College, Oxford. There his talents were generally recognized to be somewhat exceptional, though not perhaps those expected of a young man preparing for the ministry. One of the heads of New College remembered him as "a person of considerable mechanical genius." Like many country clergymen of his time in whom "enthusiasm was not the order of the day," William Milton was not noted for his piety.[2] He was more the amateur scientist than the vicar, always full of schemes, the most practical of which arose from his interest in and intricate knowledge of the port of Bristol.

By the end of the eighteenth century, Bristol had become the second city in the kingdom, and the greatly increased amount of shipping required improvement in the tortuous channel of the Avon River. The Society of Merchant Venturers of Bristol (one of whose masters was William Milton's friend John Garnett) pressed for a new cut to relocate the river bed and make the old channel a permanent floating harbor. In

1792 William Milton submitted his own proposal for consideration by a joint committee of the Society and the city. Although his plan was politely rejected as "not of sufficient Importance to justify such an increased Expenditure," Mr. Milton continued to work on the plan and doggedly published suggestions for the "improvement and enlargement of the Port and Harbour of Bristol." Even when he assumed full responsibility as vicar of Heckfield, his mind and energies were never solely employed by these duties.[3]

His favorite private invention was a set of dinner plates studded with silver pieces to prevent the nasty sound of knives contacting porcelain. He also concocted a device to prevent stage coaches from upsetting—a patent wheel, in connection with which his shed at Heckfield was in later years full of models illustrating the principles of traction. In 1814 and 1818 the *Gentleman's Magazine* printed accounts, descriptions, and diagrams of his ideas, whose complicated detail reveals the prolixity of the Reverend Milton's knowledge. Here again, he took to print and published in 1810 a well-written tract, "The Danger of Travelling in Stage Coaches, etc., A Remedy Proposed," and long before the later safety coaches came into vogue, a coach after his model was built by the proprietors of the Reading Stage. These many inventions all had a special quality. More than mere eccentricities, the "brain-stimulating hobbies and amusing inventions" with which many country parsons enlivened their existences, his revealed an ingredient of firm practicality and a concern with the minutiae of daily life, traits which in time came down to his daughter Frances. He also passed on a remarkable playfulness, good humor, cleverness, and ingenuity. His descendants recalled him as charming, "a very popular man, a good scholar with decidedly scholarly tastes, much of a mathematician, a genuine humorist, with a sort of Horatian easy-going geniality about him."[4]

On 23 June 1774, when he was thirty one, William Milton married Mary Gresley by license in the Church of St. Thomas in Bristol. Little is known about Mary except that she came from a prosperous Derbyshire family with good connections. She was the sole surviving child of Francis and Cecilia Gresley, and no doubt her family was not overly enthusiastic about her union with the son of a Bristol saddler who was preparing for ordination and obliged to resign his fellowship upon marrying. His eventual benefice, the living of Heckfield cum Mattingly, was of but middling value financially.[5] While the family lived in Bristol, four children were born to the Miltons: Mary (1776), Cecilia (1778, died in infancy), Frances (1779), and Henry (1784). About the eldest daughter little is known. Not especially close to her family, at the age of forty-two she married Charles Clyde, a captain in the Royal Navy. Henry Milton's accomplishments were considerable, and he was personable and popular with the ladies. He was sent to Winchester, like his father, and destined for New College. In later years he combined an administrative and legal career with artistic tastes. Perhaps spurred by his sister's subsequent achievements, he even tried his hand at writing novels, with moderate success.[6]

Shortly after Henry was born, Mary Gresley Milton died, leaving her husband to teach the children and shape their destinies as best he could. Frances, who like so many female writers of this century, grew up without a mother, flourished precociously under her father's tutelage. By the time she was in her twenties, she read Italian and French, knew contemporary literature and poetry, and had more than a casual familiarity with the plastic arts. Her earliest lifelong friends were intelligent and cultured, especially the Garnett family of Bristol, Marianne Gabell, daughter of the headmaster of St. Mary's College, Winchester, and Doctor Nott, a prebendary of Winchester Cathedral. These associations suggest that Frances might have, for a time, attended some school in one of these cities. But very little detail is known of the first twenty years of her life.

In 1801 William Milton, then in his fifty-eighth year and remarried to Sarah Partington, decided to take up full-time residence at the Heckfield vicarage. It may be that the Gresleys stopped aiding the family financially after Mary's death or that Mr. Milton had been prompted by the recent decree requiring vicars to spend more than half their time in residence. But henceforth, he lived the life of a country parson, seeing to it that the church was kept clean and neat, reading the service twice on Sunday, and celebrating the Sacrament at least three times a year. He was respectable and kindly, kept the parish records conscientiously (occasionally crossing through his curate's errors and correcting them himself), and saw to it that things were done with propriety.[7] Probably he performed his duties to his fellow man, visiting the poor and relieving them as far as possible and admonishing those he considered unworthy. He apparently worked hard at preparing learned sermons, which his daughter Frances suspected went unappreciated by all but a handful. Although none of them have survived, their latitudinarian tone was doubtless similar to one preached during those years in a nearby village:

Shame to those teachers of a severe and gloomy creed . . . . Look there my children, examine your own hearts, they will teach you, that the great end of your existence is to be happy yourselves, and to contribute to the happiness of your fellow-creatures. . . . Be active in your several occupations; be contented with your lot in life; be not envious of those that are above you. . . . love God as the Father of mercies; and enjoy those innocent pleasures which are within your reach, for this is the attribute most acceptable to your Creator. Be happy here. . . .[8]

This sturdy philosophy and healthy outlook on life were to become Frances Milton's own deepest religion, and they were manifested by what both her sons were to remember as a sunny disposition and a joviality that was "all for others." Anthony recalled:

> She could dance with other people's legs, eat and drink with other people's palates, be proud with the lustre of other people's finery. Every mother can do that for her own daughters; but she could do it for any girl whose look, and voice, and manners pleased her. Even when she was at work, the laughter of those she loved was a pleasure to her. She had much, very much, to suffer. . . . but of all people I have known she was the most joyous, or, at any rate, the most capable of joy.[9]

Frances emerges from the obscurity of these early years during a social gathering at the mansion and park of Lord Rivers at Heckfield, attended by the mother of her lifelong friend, Mary Russell Mitford. Mrs. Mitford found much to notice about Mr. Milton, his wife, and two daughters,

> the youngest of whom, Miss Fanny Milton, is a very lively pleasant young woman. I do not mean to infer that Miss Milton may not be equally agreeable, but the other took a far greater share in the conversation, and, playing casino great part of the evening with Mr. S. Lefevre, Mr. Monck, and your old Mumpsa, it gave me an opportunity of seeing her in a more favourable light than her sister.[10]

The scene is tantalizing, suggesting a certain amount of daring in its glimpse of the young girl boldly playing cards with the men and an older woman. It was certainly not the kind of behavior which Mrs. Ellis, that subsequent arbiter of female manners, would recommend to young ladies of a later period. The young Frances, brought up in the freedom of the late eighteenth century and accustomed to enjoy the company of men, would many times run afoul of the feminine proprieties during her long writing career that extended well into the reign of Queen Victoria.

Her enjoyment of such society suggests that Frances was becoming somewhat restless. At first, she did not miss Bristol and was enthralled by Heckfield's beautiful location, its Norman church standing on a small hill with all Hampshire spread to the south and west. The vicarage itself was a fine house, Tudor in origin, with some brick and beam and a very old garden wall. The country was agricultural, with cottage and laboring people for the most part, living busy and hard-working country lives, enlivened occasionally by trips to the alehouse. There were two big houses, Highfield Park, and Heckfield Place, but life centered on the church and vicarage. Frances loved the walks along paths winding between deep banks and through rich coppices. (One lane leading by the side of a green cool meadow turned suddenly by a large old farmhouse and a quaint water mill; a quarter of a mile further was a fine avenue of elms.) She was a horsewoman too and enjoyed rides through such lanes of magnificent trees. There were fresh air, genteel country life, and occasional visits to Reading,[11] but in general cultural activities were rare.

Eventually such simple delights began to pall. Also, there were undoubtedly few eligible young men of her position in Heckfield; most were laborers, farmers, wheelwrights, smiths, or bakers. For a young lady who read Dante and enjoyed Molière, Heckfield was stifling. Her father, preoccupied with increased pastoral duties and a second wife, could no longer be the friend and tutor of her childhood. Moreover, the vicarage was really not big enough for three adult women. Her father's second marriage, while not painful to her, nevertheless made Frances feel uneasy. And while she probably enjoyed talking French with her stepmother, who taught the neighborhood children, no real warmth ever developed between them and she always called her stepmother Mrs. Milton. Under such circumstances, it is not surprising that she and Mary were anxious for some opportunity to leave, even though neither girl as yet had those prospects for marriage which were the usual means of escape. Her brother, however, had already made his decision.

In 1803, Henry Milton accepted a clerkship at the War Office, rented a house in Keppel Street, and invited his two sisters to live with him. It was a fortunate move. For the next five years, Frances thrived in London, even on the insignificant allowance permitted to Mary and herself (£50 a year) by Mr. Milton. With gusto, she visited the museums and theaters and read extensively.[12] She enjoyed the house, its pretty backyard garden, and the manifold cultural life of London. Then, on a summer day in 1808, a few months after her twenty-ninth birthday, Henry Milton introduced his sisters to Thomas Anthony Trollope, a thirty-four-year-old barrister, born of good family in the parish of Cottered in Hertfordshire, son of Anthony Trollope, a clerk in Holy Orders, and the younger son of a baronet. The Milton and Trollope backgrounds were remarkably similar. Quickly, Thomas Anthony began to notice the lively, pleasant young woman who clearly overshadowed her older sister.

Like many attractions of the heart, this one sprang up between two personalities of very different kinds—the fun-loving, talkative, impulsive, and lively Frances and the stern, taciturn, reserved, and conservative Thomas Anthony. In later years, he became abnormally disputatious and irritable, but in the autumn of 1808, he seemed a suitor endowed with many advantages, for not only was he a moderately

successful lawyer, but he could also expect in time to inherit the ample
Herfordshire estate Julians from his mother's old and childless brother
Adolphus Meetkerke.[13] Frances found Thomas Anthony learned, cul-
tured, and serious. Almost at once, the ritual of courtship began.

In a series of letters (commencing on 19 July 1808), Thomas Anthony
took as his first subject the problems of translating Latin odes into
English.[14] In a few months time, he had enlivened these polite intellectual discussions with some clumsy jokes about a forgotten umbrella, to
which Miss Milton appended a brief, polished reply, including her
brother's invitation to dinner. Afterwards, Miss Milton recommended
for Mr. Trollope's perusal Maria Edgeworth's short tale, *The Modern
Griselda*, a story of a too-indulgent husband who pets his wife into selfish
unrestraint. Strictly enjoined to read the tale before they next met, the
enamored Thomas Anthony finished it in a single night while "sitting
without a fire after a walk home thro' the snow," not so much, in his own
admission, from "the entertainment the elegant pages of Miss Edgeworth afforded" as from "some secret apprehension" that he not finish in
time to comply with Miss Milton's instructions.[15]

In August, Thomas Anthony wrote proposing marriage. His letter
began with a note of stuffy pedantry, as he cloaked his intention behind
an academic question: "Is it most expedient for a man to make an avowal
of his attachment to a lady viva voce (*anglice* in a tête à tête), or by
epistolary correspondence?"[16] Too timid to ask the question in person,
he admitted that for many months now his chief delight had been her
"society and conversation"; with a delicacy born of trepidation, he
offered her three weeks to consider "this serious, this final step." His tone
was formal and controlled, rather lacking in emotion for a marriage
proposal. He stressed the importance of pecuniary stability in language
more appropriate to a lawyer discussing a case with one of his clients,
recommending to those who would marry "those necessaries and
comforts of life to which they have been accustomed, and which are
commonly incident to the rank and situation they hold in society." He
spelled out his own circumstances. He earned £900 per annum, but
should he marry, he would drop his Oxford fellowship, thus losing some
£200. He was subject to "certain incumbrances" which were, however,
"gradually wearing away." Uncomfortable himself with his tone, he was
nevertheless sure that Frances would understand his motives for offering
these particulars because—and then he drew abruptly back, roughly
apologizing for even seeming to flatter: "But let me avoid compliments,
which were always my detestation—fit tools only for knaves, and to be
employed against fools."

In this parenthetical remark lay much of the tragedy of Mr. Trollope's personality. Even as he was making to Frances a "declaration which [he] could no longer conceal," his temperamental reserve made him unable to show comfortably the love he felt. He hoped she would understand his rejection of "the flippant nonsense . . . commonly used on occasions of this nature." His pathological inability to employ the graces and amenities even in courtship letters is a remarkable prefiguring of his subsequent failure to achieve and express human relationships. By his own admission, the letter's "manner and style . . . so little adapted to its subject," reveal a man struggling with an emotion so intense that he could not safely utter it. Mrs. Trollope's first biographer perceived in the letters a "subterranean fire" spurting out "from beneath the iron-bound crust with which the wooer has chosen to cover it." This acute perception is indeed a key to all Mr. Trollope's subsequent failures and disappointments. Over a lifetime, his rugged, rough-edged frankness, contentiousness, and inability openly to demonstrate his affections alienated clients, friends, and even his family. After his death, his oldest son sadly recalled:

> Happiness, mirth, contentment, pleasant conversation, seemed to fly from before him as if a malevolent spirit emanated from him. And all the time no human being was more innocent of all malevolence towards his fellow creatures; and he was a man who would fain have been loved, and who knew that he was not loved, but knew neither how to manifest his desire for affection nor how to conciliate it.[17]

But Frances Milton herself did not set great store upon an outward show of affection. She knew her own feelings, and was confident of the depth of his. Disdaining his offer of a three week's waiting period, and disregarding contemporary notions of feminine gentility, she replied on the following day. Adopting a stiff formality foreign to her nature, she tried to reply in kind, describing her own financial situation—a fortune independent of her father of £1300 and an annual allowance of £50 a year—and offering him time to consider his offer in the light of her information. She was less successful than Thomas Anthony in concealing emotion.

> I have not, nor can I, express myself quite as I wish. There is something of cold formality in what I have written, which is very foreign to what I feel,—but I know not how to mend it.[18]

On the following day, he asked for that permission to call which they both knew would result in an engagement to marry. One month later, Frances left for Heckfield to make the final marriage arrangements and to prepare her trousseau. Thomas Anthony stayed in London or was on circuit, and between December 1808 and May 1809, some thirty letters passed between them.

Once arrived at Heckfield on 2 December, the impulsive Fanny ignored etiquette by writing first. Always teasing the stolid Thomas Anthony, she warned him: "if you do not mean that I should undertand you are *shocked* at my doing so, you will let me have a line from you *Tuesday*." She signed herself at first "Fanny" Milton, but then playfully scratched out the nickname, substituting and underlining *Frances*. In his reply, he addressed her as *Fanny*, and underlined it, thus breaking down all notions of formality. Frances emerges as already somewhat satirically inclined. Once, while writing her lover, she described a visitor, "the most disagreeable of created beings, by name Col. Addinbrook" who was meanwhile "talking in an animated strain of eloquence to Mrs. Milton, frequently seasoning his discourse with the polished phrase, 'blood and thunder ma'am.' " Roguishly, Frances warned Thomas Anthony: "if I happen to *sware* a little, before I conclude, be so good as to believe that I am accidently writing down what he is saying."[19]

Following Fanny's lead, Thomas Anthony slowly began to try humor. She had described her embroidering work on a baby's cap "to the great hazard of [her] eyes." He remonstrated: "I have another plan still, which I had much rather see adopted than that you should injure your eyes about it—Burn the cap at once.—" Fanny reported that his "hasty directions about the cap made Mrs. Milton laugh so heartily that she could eat no breakfast." She was pleased over this "*fantasticality*" and continued the banter: "Are you serious? I can hardly believe you so, though you say it so gravely." In turn, he now began to make witticisms about the marriage settlements, concerning which he had been so deadly serious just a few weeks earlier.[20] He learned that Fanny was entitled "to a property which you have hitherto omitted to mention to me—Indeed I apprehend that you meant to reserve it snugly for a little secret pin-money—I mean 1/8th of the patent coach, which Mr. Milton tells me he has made over to you." In her next she joked: "And so you have found me out! *I did hope* that *my share* of the patent coach would have supplied all my little private extravagances and you have been never the wiser."[21]

Their equality was obvious from the start. When Thomas Anthony received an offer of £2000 for his Keppel Street house, he immediately asked for her opinion. She replied:

'Pray write me now about every thing' say you—and so here I am, pen in hand, gravely going to give you my *opinion* and *advice* on points on which it is *just possible* you may be the best judge yourself—however it is your own fault—if you will give a female encouragement to *discuss*, depend upon it she will profit by it—

Although she advised him to "sell your great house and buy one, in size, about mid-way between that, and our small one," the decision was postponed, in his words, "till we can have some conversation about it." He was, however, "extremely obliged" to her "opinion and good advice, as I trust I shall ever be in all things."[22] Here, in words as solemn as those of the marriage ceremony itself, was the stance he would ever adopt toward his Fanny. She would always have an important voice in all the major decisions of their life.

During these first months, the respective families exchanged visits and greetings, and Fanny went to meet Uncle Adolphus Meetkerke at Julians, where she spent two weeks and loved everything she saw. She told Thomas Anthony: "I felt no sensations whilst at Julians but those of pleasure, and I might more than once have said with Miranda, 'I am a fool to weep for what I am glad of.' "[23] Later, she and her sister Mary, who had accompanied her, found Heckfield "a bit somewhat *piano* after the cheerful circle at Julians." She who had enjoyed the card-playing at Lord Rivers's great house and who found Julians exciting, sought repeatedly to recreate such surroundings, full of elegance, prosperity, and interesting, fun-loving people. Here she differed from her husband-to-be. For him, she was always brightness and society enough. But her yearnings would take her to London, Harrow, La Grange, Nashoba, Cincinnati, the Lake Country, Paris, and at the end, Florence, where she finally found, as a very old lady, the paradise of social and intellectual activity she had all her life been seeking.

When Thomas Anthony asked for a description of her occupations at Heckfield, she was amused, for life there seemed to her dull indeed. She wrote:

> You say my pursuits are not uninteresting to you—This is better than a fine speech my dear friend, but has a little the effect of one, for it certainly makes me vain . . . fancy you could be amused by my telling you how we went to Nanny Cain's and gave our opinion of her great pig, then returned and ate bread and butter, made a pocket handkerchief, and concluded the day by studying the bible in order to find texts by which to puzzle you—but this with the mixture of a little *roast beef*, and a little Dante on some of his brethren is the account of every day's occupation.

She envied him the life of the town and wondered "how often *you* think of *me* and whether you ever fancy you might like to exchange a little of your London gaiety for the quiet of Heckfield Vicarage."[24] And while her family were far from country bumpkins—Mrs. Milton following with Frances the debate over the authenticity of Rowley's poems, and the Reverend Milton pursuing his inventions and preaching from two pulpits—Frances was not satisfied in the country.

She had to be involved in varied activities and seemed happiest when engaged in a mixture of domestic and intellectual pursuits, embodied in the letters in her alternate occupations of "hemming sheets and reading Dante." Thomas Anthony seemed faintly uncomfortable with his wife-to-be's unflagging energies. He who was already plagued by rheumatism, back pains, bad colds, an eye inflammation, and persistent headaches, worried himself further lest she tire herself with her round of activities. While noting her many "pretty employments," he fretted: "you must *not indulge* yourself." She replied frankly: "What else would you have me to do?" He wanted her to take advantage of the rest that "these fine days in the country must afford. Indeed I am happy to find by your last letter that the sheets and Dante do sometimes give way for excursions in Lord Rivers' Park." Her answer was characteristic. She would make a disciple of him: "*You positively must read Dante.*"[25]

He repeatedly wished to be reassured that she was feeling fine.

> The knowledge of your being unwell will always be a subject of uneasiness to me, and the concealment of it on your part therefore may certainly prevent that uneasiness; but what is this to be compared to that general anxiety which must be the consequence of such a habit of concealment?

Once Fanny somewhat impatiently wrote: "I know you will expect a bulletin of *my health. I am perpetually well I thank you.*" Her greatest physical ailment during these months was the lancing of her gums to admit the entrance of "the last shoot of my hitherto dormant *wisdom.*" Always roguish, she protested, "If I go on at this rate, I shall be a perfect *shark*," and warned her lover "to take the opinion of the learned before you proceed any farther—imagine the extreme unpleasantness of finding yourself unexpectedly bitten in two!"[26]

For courtship letters, the correspondence so far had been remarkably devoid of sentiment. Thomas Anthony's sister, in a kind letter, had tried to prepare Frances for her brother's undemonstrative ways. Fanny relayed the report to her lover, jokingly.

> She speaks of *flattering*, and says, "My brother always contends against it, in any garb, & I always tell him he can use it in a neat style as well as others, & perhaps he renders it still more forcible by the half concealment"—I

shall certainly endeavour to profit by this hint, and do all I can to be on my guard against your *sly ways.*

Following their first misunderstanding—regarding some long-over-due letter— he tried to explain his reticence to his less inhibited sweetheart.

You say that I had never said how often I wished you to write, and that you was afraid . . . that I might think you wrote oftener than I expected. You then tell me that this is the effect of a little *female feeling,* which perhaps I may not comprehend . . . . I confess that it never had occurred to me to tell you that the oftener I heard from you the more I should be pleased, and that if you should write more frequently than I had expected your letters would only be the more grateful to me. Perhaps I was wrong in fancying that you must know all this.[27]

Then, midway in the letters, he began a practice which both of them continued intermittently. After their little contretemps, some three days intervened during which Thomas Anthony heard nothing from Fanny. Troubled, fearing that he had truly offended her, Thomas Anthony sent another brief missive, setting out his specific locations over the next week and begging a reply. Wrestling with the problem of a suitably affectionate closing, even while distrusting the language of lovers, he hit upon the notion of using French. His reserve dropped all at once, and he wrote, "Adieu. Aime moi toujours." Her reply gratefully took up the request. "Aime toi toujours? I believe I must—for I cannot help it, even tho you do scold me when I dont deserve it—and so, I am yours ever, Fanny Milton." In his next, as though released, he further expanded his closing, "Adieu—amie du mon coeur—mon âme est toute pleine de toi." Reassuringly, her reply came back: "Il ne *faut pas* que je vous dise tout ce que je suis pour vous mais—au moins—je suis la votre."[28]

The courtship was winding down into its final days. In April, she teased Thomas Anthony about a ball he would be attending in town. "Do not, *if you can help it,* fall in love with Miss Foot." Disturbed in her writing by some fascinating male visitor, she told him, "Do you not marvel how I could tear myself [away] to write to you? Even now I hear the sweet sound of his voice in the next room—and yet I stir not—Oh wonderful power of constancy! Remember this when you see Miss Foot."[29] But as the month of May opened, a new note of seriousness appeared. The Reverend Milton had decided not to perform the marriage ceremony himself, preferring instead "being the *father.*" Stirred by the discussion of such details to thoughts of the awesome ritual which was rapidly approaching, Fanny dropped her usual playfulness, and mused:

It is a solemn business, my dear friend. Does not the near approach of it almost frighten you? I tremble lest you should love me less a twelve-month hence than you do now. I sometimes fear you may be disappointed in me, that you will find me less informed, less capable of being a companion to you, than you expect, and then—

But she shook herself out of the passing mood: "but I am growing very dismal—this will never do. I must go and sun myself a little upon the heath." Thomas Anthony perceived that he had been responsible for her mood. Anxiously, he strove to reassure her of his love.

My dearest love, are you still to learn my character and sentiments? Still to be made acquainted with my lifeless manners, my stone-like disposition? Are you yet to be informed in what detestation I hold all ardent professions & in what admiration actions that want not the aid of declamation, but boldly speak for themselves? When I see a man vehement in his expressions without any apparent or sufficient cause I am always inclined to suspect him—If he states to me a plain fact and takes unnecessary pains to inforce the truth of it, I immediately conclude it to be false . . . . it may not be improbable that I often seem to be too cautious of making use of [what] might be considered a natural and becoming warmth in my declarations; but I confess . . . I always feel afraid of raising doubts to the prejudice of my own sincerity by professing too much or declaring myself in too vehement a manner—Besides if our professions are only consistent with our actions where is the necessity for them? If they go beyond them, they are evidently not to be trusted in.[30]

Her reply, although wistful, shows her mature acceptance of her lover for what he was.

You are an odd mortal but you call *yourself* so many names (*lifeless*, *stonelike* etc.) that I *forbear* I think. —What you say of professions, is very just, nay I think it is great and noble—but yet one cannot help being pleased (at least women I believe cannot) with *expressions* as well as *proofs*, of tenderness from those they love—vehement professions, I think I detest as much as you can & indeed vehemence tho' it may express passion, can never express tenderness, which is the only affection I could ever wish to inspire—but I own my heart welcomes a look or a word of fondness from those who are dear to me as cordially as it does more unequivocal proofs of attachment.

Then, realizing abruptly that her argument was turning round upon itself, she resolved to be content:

Do not mistake me, however, I entreat you, and fancy I wish to have 'Soft nothings whispered in my ear.' I think I never could have loved a man who gave a reason to suppose he thought me a fool . . . . You are certainly right & the quietest expression of *good will* as you manage, goes deeper than whole volumes of love from other people.[31]

He was pleased to think that they had finally achieved mutual understanding, that she could "entirely coincide . . . in certain sentiments I expressed in my last letter, and which must be the corner stone of that confidence I spoke of."

From 11 May until the concluding letter, dated 18 May, their pages are filled mainly with superficialities, the external hustle and bustle surrounding last-minute wedding preparations. All Heckfield was excited about this first wedding from the vicarage, and a week before the actual event many "left their usual work . . . that they might see the wedding." Fanny was amused, commenting how the villagers eagerly awaited Thomas Anthony each Sunday, wondering if the wedding would take place on the following Monday. There were lists for invitations and the all-important wedding cake, which had to be large enough for pieces to be sent to those who could not attend the ceremony. Thomas Anthony was so busy and flustered that for the first time Fanny found four or five words in his letter which she could not read. She complained: "they have tormented my eyes and my curiosity sadly." For the last time, she signed off in French: "Adieu mon ami a voile mon dernier *billet doux*."[32] He attended to last-minute details in town and told Fanny:

> My time is wholly occupied with business in chambers, workmen in the city, attendance upon Sir John and my land at the West End of the town, and necessary preparations in Keppel St.—I have given orders for the blinds, for the grates to be put in—the cellar to be done and the pole to be made for curtains in the dining parlour. In erecting this last . . . I found myself greatly at a loss—the first question the makers put to me *threw me on my back* and I was obliged to leave it entirely to himself.[33]

The carpet had come and the furniture was almost ready. He had removed most of his books to Keppel Street so that his bookcases could be varnished. A dressing-case was being made for him, at Fanny's suggestion, and Sir John Trollope, in town, expressed the wish to present the couple with some silver forks. Thomas referred the question to Fanny,[34] explaining that "if I had you at my elbow I might find you of some assistance, but at present, *being all alone by myself*, I am perfectly at a loss what to think of." He could not be admitted to Heckfield before "*the* Tuesday morning, being considered as a very improper guest till that time," but suddenly he and Harry Milton prepared to come by the Reading coach on the preceding Saturday and take "a very humble apartment . . . at the Vicarage instead of . . . at the Inn."

The last word in the courtship letters belongs to Fanny. She made further depositions as to the distribution of the cake and mentioned that Mrs. Milton had seen his gig in Reading being varnished, which she heartily approved. Fanny happily awaited his arrival on Saturday. "The three wheeled equipage will await you—Expect a jumble." Impulsively, she added, "I would you could be here tomorrow." Five days before her wedding, she went off to see the prisoners of war at Odiam perform one of Molière's plays. Mirthful to the last, she asked once more after the ubiquitous Miss Foot: "How did *your* heart stand Miss Foot's attractions all Sunday?" Typically, she had much to do—"four letters to write and a great deal of work to do this morning—so addio." She mentioned an "immense present" from Uncle Adolphus, who had obviously bestowed it upon the young girl he liked so much merely because she had admired it. She protested that his generosity would "make me for ever afraid of mentioning any thing." Her concluding words epitomize the personality she brought to her marriage on 23 May. "All well here," she wrote confidently.[35]

And so, with a sentimental flair, Frances and Thomas Anthony were united on his thirty-fifth birthday, and their married life commenced at 16 Keppel Street. During much of the first year, life went along evenly. That summer, while Thomas Anthony was away on circuit, Frances went to stay first at Julians and then at Heckfield. He continued to dote upon his new wife, worrying over her health and well-being almost pathologically. Because she had complained about a slight stomach ailment, she had to write her "Antonio mio" *by appointment* to report everything about her condition. She had constantly to reassure him—it was as though he feared that his happiness was too great to last. She wrote: "and now my dearest friend adieu—I am going to be very busy— but you may rely upon my taking good care of myself—As long as I am valuable to you, you need not fear my doing otherwise." Her feelings for him were equally intense: "Love me half as well as I love you, and I will be contented." She reported all well at Julians—the air was incredibly fresh after the stuffy city, his "good aunt" was very kind to her, and, as she told him, "if you were with me I should be very happy." She waited for his letter for, as she explained, "my best beloved, it is the best medicine I can take."[36]

On 29 April 1810 their first child, a son, was born. He was named after his father and Uncle Meetkerke: Thomas Adolphus. That summer, Thomas Anthony decided to buy a farm. From on circuit at Bedford, he described his efforts to his wife, who had gone with her new infant to Heckfield.[37] He was happy to know that "all's well and Tom and his mamma are enjoying themselves in the country." He had been to look over Well End Farm, finding the "country . . . remarkably beautiful but the land not near as good" as he had expected. But after two hours of inspection, he sent his agent back to town with a commission to bid £3550. Because the owner wanted more, Thomas Anthony was unsuccessful. Afraid that he would be disappointed at the loss on her account, Frances wrote: "If the place you went to see is *only* pretty, I am not very sorry you have not got it—The profit of such a purchase must I should think be precarious." Nothing could make Frances unhappy. She was reveling in the delights of first motherhood. Her letter was full of Tom, his beauty, his great cleverness ("it is really wonderful how quietly his intelligence increases from day to day"), and the fun they were both having with old Reverend Milton, who was enjoying with equal relish the pleasures of his first grandchild.

> Every day after dinner [he] plays some new trick to try his sagacity. Yesterday he put two glasses, the one empty, and the other full, before him,—the former, the young tippler eyed with perfect indifference, the latter he tryed all his little powers to get possession of, and at last drew it to his mouth. The experiment was frequently repeated. Were I not *too wise* to be vain, I should certainly become so here. Everybody exclaims that my darling is the loveliest creature they ever beheld, and most add (now pray endeavour to be as wise as I) that he is very like his father. I screw my features into all possible forms, that I may not look as delighted as I feel.[38]

Indeed, motherhood and child-bearing were to be her chief occupation and joy over the next eight years, during which seven children were born to the Trollopes. After Thomas Adolphus came Henry (1811), Arthur William (1812), Emily I (b. and d. 9 December 1813), Anthony (1815), Cecilia (1816), and Emily II (1818).[39] Of these, Arthur William lived to be twelve, the second Emily to be eighteen, Henry, twenty-three, and Cecilia, thirty-three. Only her eldest and youngest sons survived their mother. There was, of course, in this sensible middle-class menage, a nurse, several servants, and even a liveried footman who later seemed to Thomas Adolphus somewhat ludicrous, serving a family by no means rich, for whom "two tallow candles . . . supplied the whole illumination of the evening. . . ."[40] While Mrs. Trollope was rearing the family, Thomas Anthony worked hard in his Lincoln Inn chambers, often not returning home until five o'clock.

Within this bustling household, there was much freedom for the older boys, who often took "long exploring walks" throughout London to

watch the Piccadilly coaches start or arrive or see the great ships passing
through the dock gates. Thomas Adolphus recalls being dazzled by the
thought that the passengers on deck "would absolutely touch land no
more till they stopped at far Bombay on the other side of the world." No
doubt Mrs. Trollope shared her sons' "longings for the unattainable,"
even while she prepared rather regularly for the birth of yet another
addition to the family.[41]

The Trollopes entertained many visitors. Lady Dyer came, and
Doctor Nott, their Winchester friend and elegant Italian scholar who
supervised the restoration and repair of the Cathedral and had been a
tutor of Princess Charlotte. General Pepe, subsequently the hero of the
hopeless defense of Venice against the Austrians, dropped in frequently
and treated the young Trollopes to "dried Neapolitan figs and Mandarin
oranges." There were frequent excursions to the theater. The entire
family went to see Mrs. Siddons as Lady Macbeth and stood in the queue
for six hours! There were trips to Exeter to see Mrs. Trollope's aunts,
Fanny and Mary Bent. Once, on the return trip, Tom persuaded his
mother to ride on the box of the coach, while he sat behind. Afraid at
first, she ended by admitting "that she had never enjoyed a journey
more."[42] Her hardy willingness to try something new and her apparent
imperviousness to the rigors of travel in those days would one day stand
Mrs. Trollope in good stead.

It was a fun-loving, easy, and contented household. The family ate
dinner together at five, without the elegance of napkins but with port
and sherry after the cloth was withdrawn. She was interested in the
children's education and taught Tom to read at an early age, using
ingenious pedagogical methods.

> She had a great number of bone counters with the alphabet in capitals and
> small letters on either side printed on them; then having invited a charming
> little girl. . . who was just my own age, she tossed the counters broadcast
> over the floor, instituting prizes for him, or her, who should, in crawling
> races over the floor, soonest bring the letter demanded.[43]

To Fanny Trollope, learning was meant to be fun. And when she tucked
the children in their beds at night, even her lullabies were unconventional, as she regaled them by singing all the verses of the story of the
"unfortunate Miss Bayly."

2

The Trollopes at Harrow
and La Grange

He shall and may lawfully peacefully and quietly
have hold occupy possess and enjoy the said hereby
demised premises.

MR. TROLLOPE was soon doing well enough in his law practice to consider once again, as he had in 1810, the purchase or renting of a farm near London. The wars against Napoleon and the attendant revolution in agriculture had produced a situation in which large fortunes could be made by farming. With an annual income of over £700, Thomas Anthony was already in the ranks of the rich; he hoped to achieve additional prosperity with a well-situated, steadily producing farm. His good financial prospects were further guaranteed by the expectation of the Meetkerke inheritance and farming would prepare him for a career as a country gentlemen.[1]

In 1813 he found the land he desired, and arranged to rent "Illots Farm," 160 acres near the center of Harrow, from John Lord Northwick, who had recently enlarged his family's holdings and now owned over 1,300 acres in that area. The farm ideally suited Thomas Anthony's purposes by being only an hour's ride from his chambers in London and included a small but comfortable house just south of the great park and only a short stroll from the village. There were extensive barns and stables, fine yards and gardens, an acre of orchard near the house, 21 acres of plowed fields suitable for a variety of crops, and 138 acres of meadow lands, used principally for hay. Years later, after the Trollopes had enlarged it, Anthony captured the spirit of what his mother called "my pretty little cottage" in his fictional Orley Farm.

> When first inhabited . . . the house was not fitted for more than the requirements of an ordinary farmer, but [had been gradually] added to, and ornamented till it was commodious, irregular, picturesque, and straggling. . . . It consisted of three buildings of various heights, attached to each other, and standing in a row. The lower contained a large kitchen, which had been the living-room of the farm-house, and was

surrounded by bakehouse, laundry, dairy, and servants' room, all of fair dimensions. It was two stories high, but the rooms were low and the roof steep and covered with tiles. The next portion had been added . . . when [the owner] first thought of living at the place. This also was tiled, and the rooms were nearly as low; but there were three stories, and the building therefore considerably higher. [Later there was] built a good dining-room, with a drawing-room over it, and bedroom over that; and this portion of the edifice was slated.

The whole stood in one line fronting onto a large lawn which fell steeply away from the house into an orchard at the bottom. This lawn was cut in terraces, and here and there upon it there stood appletrees of ancient growth; for here had been the garden of the old farm-house. . . . The face of the house from one end to the other was covered with vines and passion-flowers, for the aspect was due south; and as the whole of the later addition was faced by a verandah, which also, as regarded the ground-floor, ran along the middle building, the place in summer was pretty enough. As I have said before, it was irregular and straggling, but at the same time roomy and picturesque. Such was Orley Farm-house.

All in all, Anthony concluded, it had the "unmistakeable appearance of an English gentleman's country house."[2]

For this extensive farm, Trollope agreed to pay £660 annually (£4 per acre), a high rent but one in keeping with currrent inflationary trends. Convinced that he could make a good profit, he took possession in September 1813 with a lease of twenty-one years (with a guaranteed renewal at the same rate for thirty-one years). It appears that he did not originally intend to use the farm as his principal residence, but in the agreement he insisted upon provisions that would permit him to build a suitable residence in the future. Obviously, he and his family would continue to live in Keppel Street until the acquisition of the Meetkerke inheritance would permit building their own mansion nearer London. In the meantime, a bailiff and tenant were installed at Illots Farm.[3]

Several months later, Mrs. Trollope lost her first daughter, Emily, who was born and died on 9 December 1813. This fourth pregnancy in as many years was hard on the mother, and prompted by its tragic outcome, Thomas Anthony became even more zealous about his wife's health, bringing the family during the summers to the farm, where Frances could engage in those splendid country walks upon which her husband had insisted in the days preceding their marriage. During the next three years, while his older sons welcomed the freedom of the London streets, the father became more ill-tempered and preoccupied in his lawyer's work, so that Frances welcomed the summer interludes. At first she had gone to Heckfield, but as the children multiplied such visits grew more difficult. They interrupted Mrs. Milton's orderly schedule, and now the vicar, in his seventieth year, had retired to a smaller residence in Reading.[4]

Shortly after the birth of Anthony (April 1815), Frances became pregnant again, and it was obvious to her worried husband that he would need a larger establishment for his growing family. For her part, Frances hoped that the country would soothe and quiet the nerves of her overworked husband. Sometime late that year, Thomas Anthony decided to move the family permanently to Harrow. The family vacated their London home and moved into the quaint farmhouse.[5]

Although Thomas Anthony now had to commute daily for more than an hour each way to his chambers, the situation seemed an improvement. Frances fell in love with the cottage. Her husband, however, almost immediately turned to the pressing problem of how to provide better quarters. His uncle Meetkerke was over sixty years old and would probably not last very much longer. Already Trollope and his oldest son had been "shown to the tenantry [at Julians] as their future landlord," and it seemed proper that the presumptive heir to a large establishment should rear his own family in more genteel surroundings. Knowing the circumstances of his tenant, Lord Northwick approached Thomas Anthony with a suggestion to build a spacious new house upon a corner of the rented farm. Although its view would command the fields and meadows of the original farm, the new house would be surrounded by its own gardens and thus would not suffer from closeness to the farm buildings. It would be located in a neighborhood of large homes also on this corner of the Northwick estates.[6]

Aware of the advantages that this construction would bring to his own holdings in the area, Lord Northwick proposed to reduce the annual rent on the farm by £240 in order to cover Trollope's cost for the interest and principal on a construction mortgage of £3,000. With this sum— exceeding $50,000 in current value—Thomas Anthony knew he could raise a handsome house in which he and his family could live in effect rent free, since his original rent for the farm would not be increased. When the lease expired either a new one would be negotiated or Lord Northwick could assume full ownership of the house. By then, Trollope's mortgage would have been paid off through the reduction in rent, and he would be free from all encumbrances. It was a mutually beneficial proposal. Thomas Anthony was all the more receptive because he knew that within the period of the lease, he and his family would inherit Julians in Hertfordshire. If necessary, they could move there and profitably rent the new house, for which he would undertake no capital outlay. Far from being an extravagant speculation, Trollope's scheme was shrewd and advantageous.[7]

Sometime in 1818, Thomas Anthony resolved to pursue Lord North-wick's suggestion, secured the required mortgage, and engaged the carpenters and masons. Soon a stately brick mansion rose four stories above its Harrow environs, commanding a magnificent view of distant London. Although large, its proportions were graceful. The arched and becolumned entrance was prominent and friendly; the several chimneys promised a hospitable warmth indoors, while many balconies bespoke a love of the cultivated outdoors. From the spacious windows, one could breathe freely that country air the Trollopes had come seeking. Facing south, contrasting nicely with the starkness of the main house, lay two gracefully curving wings, whose mullioned doors led on to a rolling green lawn, inviting leisurely walks or croquet. Indeed, the house they created was splendid in every way.

Almost from the first, however, Trollope underestimated the building costs, and an even greater sum went into the physical improvements surrounding the house. To give it a proper setting, he persuaded Lord Northwick to purchase acres at the foot of the hill, and at his own expense relocated the roadway, installed new fences, planted new shrubbery, and drained ponds. Having just delivered Mr. Trollope still another child, a second daughter Emily, Frances threw herself into the new project with her usual enthusiasm. When lawsuits and a balking neighbor threatened the whole project, she herself wrote to Lord Northwick to describe their plans "for bringing this bit of rude ground into cultivation and beauty."

Will Your Lordship excuse my troubling you with the ideas which have suggested themselves to me respecting the improvements proposed in the front of our house. The possessing this ground has been so long an almost hopeless wish, that now it is obtained, I confess I feel very eager on the subject. It appears to me, my Lord, that to make the approach to our house at all handsome, our primary object must be to throw the newly acquired ground into a paddock, which we shall hope in time to bring into the highest possible order, by draining and dressing. The form of this must be irregular, but if belted by shrubs, not ungraceful; the bounding which the hill forms on the North side, when planted, will certainly be very hand-some. . . .

Another improvement which I thought was absolutely essential to throw-ing our little valley into anything like beauty, was the filling up that very ugly pond at the foot of the hill, which to me has always had the appearance of a large hole, and which would be exactly a bird's eye view from our projected road. My eagerness for this made it one of the first points we attacked, and before your Lordship's last letter reached Mr.

Trollope, the ground beneath the hill, i.e. around the pond, was nearly leveled. . . . I have little doubt however that on seeing the ground from the line of the projected road, your Lordship will approve of the alteration. . . . [8]

There was in all this activity a characteristic verve and an interest in beauty and external harmony. Her husband was more than a little proud of this side of his charming wife and freely underwrote the costs, which turned out to exceed his budget by nearly £1,000, a great amount of money toward which he could expect no help at all from Lord Northwick. Still, if Fanny were happy and the house were the better for it, the future remained bright.

When the house was finished, Frances and her family took possession, and because one of the fields leased was locally known as Julians, the family christened their new house "Julians," no doubt regarding the coincidental echoing of the Meetkerke property in Hertfordshire as a happy omen.[9] They looked upon their residence in Harrow as permanent. From there they would send their four boys to the famous school to study under Lord Byron's old schoolmasters. Joyful prospects for the boys seemed logical, but both Thomas Adolphus and Anthony hated the schooling from which Mrs. Trollope expected so much and recalled their years there as the bitterest of their lives. Nevertheless, the boys were educated. In 1820, Thomas Adolphus completed Harrow and fulfilled his father's dream by enrolling at Winchester. Henry followed in 1821. In 1823, Arthur and Anthony entered Harrow. It was a busy and productive time.

Almost immediately, however, the family fortunes suffered the first of many severe strokes which would—but for the indomitable qualities of a great woman—have ruined them. Soon after the building of Julians, Adolphus Meetkerke, still a fine figure, unexpectedly married a young woman, who immediately and most unaccomodatingly began to produce a healthy progeny. Realizing that his future had been destroyed, Thomas Anthony took some necessary economic steps. After all their work on the new house, he and Frances agreed that it must be rented, if possible at a profit. He put on as good a face as he could, writing Lord Northwick: "The continued ill state of my health has induced me with the advice of my medical friends to return to my residence in town. I have it in contemplation therefore to let my house at Harrow, and to fit up the farm house for the summer vacation and other occasional visits to my farm." Although he added in the same letter that Frances was still making a "few improvements" and asked Northwick's permission to "cut down two or three elm trees that are grown in the hedge row between the orchard and the adjourning field, for the purpose of opening a better view towards Primrose Hill," the Trollopes were now primarily concerned with making the farm house habitable. They spent £500 to enlarge and improve it, thereby providing the irregular shape that Anthony remembered. The house would be very comfortable and still have the same handsome view. In the hopes of looking a malicious fortune squarely in the face, they bravely named it Julian Hill. Mrs. Trollope told friends that her favorite had always been the pretty cottage. This house, in which the family would live for nearly ten years, Frances regarded as her home forever.[10]

In this house, the children grew up; in this house, Frances entertained her friends, spending sometimes more than she rightly should, and held the amateur theatricals that were her chief joy outside her children and that served as an outlet for her creative powers. Often she invited neighbors to play charades, ebulliently making the arrangements, placing all the young ones on the front room sofa, which would easily hold "five little ones," whose "heads will be in the way of no one." When the large Drury family came for an evening, the unflustered hostess added, "it will be quite charity to give us a full pit." Herself an avid partygoer, she thoroughly enjoyed herself at London dinners and gatherings where her vivacious personality made her a welcome guest. At the Merivales' in 1822 she so impressed the party with her conversation and dramatic "Siddonian glances" that one guest noted that Mrs. Trollope had appeared "in her deepest blue stockings."[11] She would have laughingly conceded the characterization, for she reveled in the company of the cultured and eagerly followed the happenings of the world around her, not the least of which was the controversy of the day at Harrow-on-the-Hill concerning the great Lord Byron.

When his illegitimate daughter Allegra died in April 1822, he requested that she be buried in Harrow churchyard. Scandalized by his request to have an inscription raised above the grave, the clergy of the area refused. Irate over this treatment of her favorite English poet, Mrs. Trollope set down her thoughts in a long satirical poem "Salmagundi Aliena,"[12] which displays much of the cleverness and sharp satiric thrust she would later employ in her fiction. Privately circulated, the poem was appreciated, and her son Anthony later provided a glossary of the events and a running commentary on the great ones of Harrow School who had fallen victim to his mother's pen.

The poem began with Mrs. Trollope asking her Muse to help her sing a song, not to the "worn out Goddesses of old," but to a new one, "of late enrolled/Beneath the wide Pantheon of the sky, Almighty *Cant*." Mischievously, she sketched various Harrow personages and masters, identified by name, in attitudes of worship to this goddess. All protested the raising of a tablet for poor Allegra, and Mrs. Trollope lamented their slavish subservience to popular opinion:

> Why does thou bend so low when rank is near?
> Why are thy better feelings set to sleep?
> Should Lord or Bishop frown,—what dost thou fear?
> Thy mind can soar, then let not thine heart creep.—
> Seek not to all in power to appear
> Bound to their cause with such devotion deep.
> Abandon once for all the canting plan,
> Value thy self and dare to be a man.

Culminating the procession of notables came Mrs. Trollope's favorite target, the Reverend Cunningham, "the mild-eyed vicar," who was "the Goddess' darling son."[13] Cunningham worried about leading "the school boys into vice." This part of the poem was no fiction. A note by Anthony confirmed Cunningham's fear that a tablet raised to the memory of Allegra Byron might "teach the boys to get bastards." Abruptly the poetess drew to a halt, with nothing really resolved. The whole affair, she protests, "is nauseous, I can write no more/These are the orgies Cant that thou dost claim." Her son, in a note, agreed. "There is quite enough already and to spare. Had it been condensed it could have been better— the latter part about the masters is very clever—true—and well put." Always at her best when angry, Frances Trollope had now found her satiric voice.[14]

But while Mrs. Trollope herself seemed full of bounce and life, the family's prospects were not good. Thomas Anthony still suffered from his persistent headaches and brooded over the loss of his inheritance. Moreover, his law practice was beginning to deteriorate, partly as a result of his own quarrelsome disposition. It seemed unlikely that he could maintain his apartment and chambers much longer. The farm, too, was turning into a great liability. He had contracted the indenture at the height of an inflation when prices reached a level unsurpassed until 1946. He reckoned upon the earnings of that farm to help supplement his income, but falling prices drove profits downward, so that by 1823 they stood at only 60 percent of the 1813 level. The disaster of the Trollopes at Harrow was a by-product of this downward spiral, not the outgrowth of an ill-advised scheme. Neither Mr. Trollope's incompetence at farming nor his fiscal ignorance were responsible, but his declining health and mental state made coping effectively with the situation that much more difficult.[15]

Mercifully, as the year 1823 opened, future tragedies were as yet hidden from her. Mrs. Trollope believed that in time good fortune would return to Julian Hill and to the family and friends who still occupied all her attention.

She was known to her neighbors as a knowledgeable, witty, vivacious, yet still domesticated woman whose interests were mainly personal and local. For her, the biggest event of that year was the religious controversy then electrifying Harrow. The local vicar, Dr. J. W. Cunningham, whose book *The Velvet Cushion*, attacking the aristocratic pretense of Anglicanism, had earned him the epithet of "Velvet Cunningham," had won over a large portion of the town to his gloomy brand of evangelical enthusiasm. He was opposed by the clergy of Harrow school and Mrs. Trollope's particular friends, the Drurys. Mrs. Trollope was repelled by the vicar's emotionalism and pharisaical prudery, no doubt in part because this "villain" now lived in her beautiful Julians.[16]

In a playlet entitled "The Righteous Rout," written for enactment by her children and houseguests, she made a clumsy yet biting attack upon evangelicalism. In doggerel verse, she dramatized the issues and at the same time presented an important aspect of her personal faith—there was more salvation in joy than in fear. The brief drama culminated in a scene where a group of pious men and women revel in the glories of suffering. Mrs. Trollope's hero rejects this concentration on the pains of Hell.

> Did he, who for thy feet cool verdure spread,
> And arched his azure vault above thy head;
> He who has left no sense without its joy
> Did he create thee, only to destroy?

When his host cries out, "beware!" Mrs. Trollope's hero replies, "Come what may/I shall not stay to hear my God blasphemed."[17] Like that of her hero, Mrs. Trollope's own religious creed could never accept a philosophy that did not emphasize life's joy.

Indeed, she tried to instill this sense of joy in her family, and sought to provide them with an atmosphere in which the world's best pleasures—art, literature, culture—were easily accessible. She took her children to London for theater and museum outings, and invited playwrights, artists, and literary people to her home. An unemployed French painter was engaged to give the children drawing lessons, and she herself taught them Italian so they could read Dante in the original. But all these activities, and the amateur theatricals from her own scripts, were primarily the efforts of a well-read, cultivated hostess and mother, who as yet had no thoughts of any professional career of her own.[18]

Toward the end of the year, however, her life began to change, while still seeming substantially unaltered. In late August 1823, after moving to their new home and beginning the more austere budget upon which her husband insisted, Frances persuaded Thomas Anthony to take her on a holiday trip to France. The sons were at school, and the girls safely tended by relatives. Frances traveled to Paris to meet once again a group of old friends, and there she formed a new circle of relationships which was to influence the whole course of her life.

First and central to this circle were old friends of the Miltons, the family of John Garnett, the Bristol merchant with scientific tastes. Educated and widely traveled, John Garnett was an amateur mathematician and made contributions to navigation and astronomy. He had served as a member of the prestigious Bristol corporation for ten years and was elected sheriff in 1783 and master of the Society of Merchant Venturers in 1794. He was a close friend of the Rev. William Milton and encouraged the latter's investigations in harbor improvements; he tutored the Milton children in mathematics and science. In common with many, Garnett believed that great disturbances were coming and, disenchanted with English life, in 1796 he requested advice from an old friend, Gen. Horatio Gates, then a member of the Continental Army and resident of the United States:

> I have very old prejudices (as you may call them) in favor of America, 1 boy and 4 girls to fix in life with about 25 or 30 thousand pounds to divide among them makes me anxious where to settle them. I would look at America. I would ask your advice as my former 'mentor.' . . . I love an active useful country life, and the manners and language of Free Men. Give me then a line to say, if a good climate, rational society, and a field for honest industry, are to be found near you.[19]

Apparently satisfied with his friend's assurances, Garnett brought his family to America, where he renewed acquaintance with Charles Wilkes, subsequently president of the Bank of New York. There he purchased Whitehouse Farm, near the town of New Brunswick, on the banks of the Raritan River, and established his utopia. Fine furniture and a good library had been brought from England, and an observatory was built for Garnett's favorite studies. But his aim was to become a gentleman farmer. In one short spring, he planted "near eight-hundred Apple trees besides Cherries and other trees," and after another year, he could write with a tinge of romanticism: "I am proud to see the construction of my Barn . . . and every Beast I have enjoying his separate Den."[20]

Physical labor alternated with intellectual pursuits. A governess, Sophia Hay, came with the family to teach French, literature, and classical translating, as well as the more "feminine" art of the piano and writing a fine copperplate hand. The son Henry was duly sent to Princeton, while for his daughters John Garnett provided at home the education that society did not furnish. The girls, especially the two youngest, Julia and Harriet, were encouraged to study astronomy and even to raise religious matters in a spirit of open investigation. Continuing his own career, Garnett was elected to the American Philosophical Society, contributing numerous papers, and was credited with discoveries ranging from methods of finding altitudes to observations of double stars. He was awarded the Magellanic Prize of the society for his accomplishments in astronomy.[21]

Throughout this period, the Garnetts remained in touch with their friends in England, and especially with William Milton and his son Henry, who subsequently managed the family's English landholdings. Shortly after the second peace of Paris, the Garnetts visited Europe, seeing friends in Bristol and London, and renewed ties with Frances Milton Trollope. Then in 1820, John Garnett suddenly died in New Brunswick. When his widow and children counted their assets, they discovered that the visionary had not really made the farm a paying concern and that his investments had failed to produce their expected earnings. After two years of trying to hold the farm together, they sold the property at a loss and returned to England where, in 1823, Mrs. Garnett and her unmarried daughters settled in Paris, as the only place they could live "respectably" on a limited income.[22]

When Mrs. Trollope arrived in Paris on 2 September, her first engagement was to dine with Mrs. Mary Garnett, and her daughters Julia, Harriet, and Fanny. There she met again another element in this new circle of relationships, the striking personality Frances Wright, the wealthy young Scotswoman, orphaned at three, who had embarked upon a reformer's career in the face of opposition. Always proud and rashly imperious, full of exalted theories, Frances Wright seemed to some an angel, to others possessed of a demon. Like John Garnett, Fanny Wright had been attracted to the possibilities of America. Inspired by a reading of Botta's history of the Revolution, she considered this nation "the theatre where man might first awake to the full knowledge and the full exercise of his powers."[23] In 1818 at the age of twenty-three, bearing introductions to some prominent families, she had sailed for a visit to America with her younger and more docile sister, Camilla, and soon entered the enlightened paradise of John Garnett.

The Wright sisters passed many weeks at Whitehouse Farm, and affection among the girls quickly blossomed. Within a short time, Julia and Harriet Garnett and Fanny and Camilla Wright swore an eternal friendship. In her subsequent book, *Views of Society and Manners in America* (1821), Frances Wright wrote of her deep devotion to John Garnett and remained in correspondence with the family after her own return to Europe in May 1820.[24] Later that year, she told them of her plans to emigrate:

> If you then continue in America, I shall seek you there & follow the bent of my heart in becoming a citizen of the only country to which I acknowledge an attachment. . . . Here all is *retrograde*. England had once public spirit, she had dignity, she had, to a certain degree, freedom;—where is all this now? In the lower classes there is discontent because there is misery, there is a considerable body among the middling classes where you will still find principle; but these chosen bands seem to be forsaking their country in disgust, & planting their domestic hearths in the wilds of your America.

But her own visit to the United States had revealed a flaw even in that dream—slavery:

> My Harriet I love your feelings toward your country. You may well be proud of it; you may well exult in its prosperity & its freedom, & you may well too sigh when you throw your eyes Southward, & see liberty mocked & outraged & that by a race of free men, who while they have her name in their mouths, ay and her energy in their souls, grasp the chain of oppression in their hands, denying to the wretched sons of Africa that holy birthright which they themselves declare man holds of God. When my thoughts turn to America the crying sin of her slavery weighs upon my heart; there are moments when this foul blot so defaces to my mind's eye all the beauty of her character that I turn with disgust from her & in her from the last & only nation on the globe to which my soul clings with affection, pride & hope. From a misanthrope I then find myself a Cynic; my heart is at war with man, I loathe his nature & his name & attribute his creation to a malignant demon, rather than to a beneficent God.

> Reflection, however, makes me draw back the curse with the acknowledgment of my own injustice, I remember that the better half of those great republics are unprofaned by this crying sin—this reconciles me to the name of the United States. I recollect that some of the *free* were once *slave*

states—this reconciles me in part with my species, & makes me hope that other states will follow this example, & that all those republics, nay that all that great Continent, *North & South*, may exhibit the perfection of freedom.[25]

These private feelings, which would soon ripen into a plan to help free the slaves, were kept from the public. The appearance of her book, with its enthusiastic praise for the United States, made Frances Wright a minor celebrity, especially among advocates of reform. She was summoned into the presence of Jeremy Bentham, to whom she lectured for hours despite the fact that he was now nearly deaf. When the Garnetts decided at last that they would return to Europe, they sought the assistance of Henry Milton; through him Frances Wright (who was also helping in the arrangements) met Frances Trollope. They soon became fast friends, and Mrs. Trollope introduced Miss Wright to her own circle of intellectuals in Harrow and London.[26] In the autumn of 1823, Frances Wright was in Paris, visiting the Lafayettes and the newly returned Garnetts, and Frances Trollope looked forward to renewing their friendship.

This visit made the matronly Mrs. Trollope suddenly aware of her lack of experience and accomplishment. Always a "special friend of all the young girls" at Harrow,[27] at forty-four she saw in these younger women (Julia was thirty, Harriet twenty-nine, the Wright sisters twenty-eight and twenty-seven) who had seen the world and even, in the case of Fanny Wright, written books, an exciting dimension missing from her own sheltered life. She had reared five children, and the youngest was now at school. She was ripe for something new.

Another important figure completed this circle. When Frances Wright had published her book on America, General Lafayette expressed a desire to meet the author. On 16 July 1821, Fanny Wright had replied to the flattering invitation:

> I anticipate the moment which will give to me one of the earliest and fondest wishes of my youth, and place me in the presence of the generous assistor of the liberties of America, of France, and of mankind.

In five months' time, she was calling him "the best and greatest man that lives . . . my friend—my father," and herself "the child of [his] affection, the child of [his] adoption."[28] All these people were united by old connections, family ties, and deep affection, but partly too by an ever-increasing fascination with the possibilities of life in the New World. General Lafayette was to be the catalyst as he entertained the circle. Here were planted the seeds of much that was to come—of much that none of the principals could have dimly foreseen as the Trollopes arrived, "very tired by dust and sun," at the Garnetts' home in the Rue St. Maur. Resisting their entreaties to "join the party in their salon, of which Mr. Washington Irwin [*sic*] made one," they drove to their lodgings and retired for the night.[29]

The next day they breakfasted with the Garnetts and plunged into a whirl of aesthetic and cultural activity. Perhaps in concession to the husband's interest, the Trollopes' first day began with a visit to the Exposition on Art and Industry at the Louvre. Although Mrs. Trollope dutifully recorded that the display "must lend greatly to the encouragement of science and ingenuity," she had not another word to say about it in her detailed journal of these Paris days. She devoted greater space to art exhibits, where she was obviously more in her element. In the Luxembourg galleries and at the Louvre, opinions poured from her pen.

> . . . A head of the Pope . . . I thought good. . . . A holy family by A. del Sarto—a female by Guido—a Christ by Titian—and a Madonna's head by Correggio are I think the finest pictures in this collection—the mixture of French artists much injures the general effect of it.

Two days later the Trollopes and Fanny Wright visited a private gallery, where Mrs. Trollope's enthusiasm for Canova's "Magdelen Penitent" bespoke the serious critic, not the casual traveler.

> It is beyond all comparison the finest modern statue I ever saw—and I think the most interesting of any age.—It stands alone in a small salon hung with olive brown silk—the window and door way are curtained by the same—and the sombre light thus admitted adds to the charm of this exquisite figure—young and delicately lovely, it has the appearance of being reduced to extreme bodily weakness by the intensity of mental agony—yet the deep but mild woe of the sweet face is evidently not hopeless.

Her proclivity for committing to writing personal reflections and emotional reactions and her tendency to see static art in dramatic terms reveal even here something of the incipient novelist, but she did not at the time regard her jottings seriously.

The Trollopes visited the Louvre five times and were admitted to several fine private collections, including Count Denon's assemblage of Egyptian and Japanese art, and another collection of Spanish masterpieces. In the evenings, there was theater, opera, or ballet. Throughout, Mrs. Trollope occupied the foreground of the scene. Her energies were unflagging, while her husband, on at least one occasion, kept to his bed

with a severe, day-long headache. In his absence, Mrs. Trollope indulged a poetical fancy to visit the monument of Abelard and Heloise,
but found "nothing beautiful or very impressive about it."

In a flurry of sightseeing, the Trollopes traveled to Versailles, where
again Mrs. Trollope's observations on the architecture and decoration
reveal a tendency to stress the human and dramatic element.

> The Palace and gardens exceeded in magnificence everything I ever saw
> or could have imagined—and impressed me with a profound conviction
> that Louis le Grand was the vainest, the most lavish and the most selfish of
> men—the eternal repetition of his own figure is at once ludicrous and
> disgusting.

She asked to see the "private door through which Marie Antoinette fled
to the king's chamber on the memorable 10th August—also the spot on
which her faithful guard lost his life in defending her apartment." For
pure pleasure, they attended a splendid fête at St. Cloud, and Mrs.
Trollope indulged in some shopping, buying Paris lace and noting a visit
to a "stay-maker."

Except perhaps in scale and scope, such cultural activities were not
new for her. She had often attended London plays and was a regular
visitor to the National Gallery of Art, no stranger to "the pleasure which a
good picture is capable of bestowing."[30] But her renewed acquaintance
with the Garnetts and the Wrights prompted a vague sense of personal
dissatisfaction with her own life-style. These Paris friends moved easily
in a circle which included Washington Irving, Fenimore Cooper,
Prosper Mérimée, Benjamin Constant, the Swiss historian Sismondi, and
Henri Beyle (Stendhal). Mrs. Trollope could boast nothing comparable
in her Harrow set.

After two weeks in Paris, Frances Wright arranged that General
Lafayette invite the Trollopes to la Grange, his country estate some forty
miles outside Paris. Because of last-minute complications, she herself
remained in Paris, planning to join the group later. The journey to the
country estate was hot, dusty, and uncomfortable, but not so much so to
make Mrs. Trollope insensible to the great personal charm of the
general, with whom, for the first time, the Trollopes were alone. In her
journal, she noted "the delightful conversation of our illustrious fellow-
traveller—We talked much of [General] Pepe—of Fanny Wright—of
the revolution—of the various scenes in which he had himself been a
principal actor." Mrs. Trollope's effusive account of Lafayette's conversation reveals how deeply she was impressed with "this illustrious man—
great and simple in his manners—open and unconstrained in giving his
opinion—gentle and unassuming in listening to the opinion of others. He

talked with ease and frankness of the most interesting events of his life."

Perhaps more important were Lafayette's comments on his experiences during the French Revolution. To many of Mrs. Trollope's class and position, the very mention of the word *revolution* was fearful. Lafayette deplored the "want of policy in the republicans," which had prompted them to behead Louis XVI:

> Had they, said he, instead of falsely accusing him as one of the worst of men, proclaimed him as he really was, one of the best of kings, they might have shown to demonstration that even such were dangerous to the liberty and happiness of the people, and without injustice and without crime he might have been removed in safety and honor from a country no longer in a condition to submit to the yoke.

Had Lafayette consciously wished to indoctrinate the impressionable Mrs. Trollope with the rectitude of liberal ideals, he could not have done better. Again and again, his stories illustrated how reform and change could be achieved and demonstrated that republicans were not to be feared. In recalling an incident during his five-year imprisonment in Austria, he told how "the inhabitants of a town they passed through requested permission of their guards 'to look at the wild beasts they were conducting.' " But when Lafayette spoke to the villagers of his position and "all the sorrow he felt," his auditors exclaimed with surprise that he was the first republican they had ever heard who spoke compassionately about the poor king. Hearing these stories from the mouth of the general himself, Frances noted in her journal: "I should think my journey to France well repaid were this afternoon passed in his society the sole result of it."

La Grange itself was splendid, lying haunting and beautiful in the pleasant and fertile valley of the Yeres River. The estate had been saved from confiscation during the revolution by Madame de Lafayette, whose property it originally was. When Lafayette returned from his prison at Olmutz in 1808, it became the family retreat and, with the restoration of 1815 and the return of aristocrats, almost a symbolic shrine of liberalism in France. The building itself was surrounded by an extensive lawn, beautifully planted "with woods of oak and beech—branch[ing] off into vistas stretching as far as the eye can reach." On her first evening there, Frances Trollope wandered out on the lawn "till we had no light than that of a bright moon." Afterwards, she returned to her apartment but did not go immediately to bed. Full of all she had seen and heard, she romantically set herself at the window to sketch the venerable turrets of the chateau, stopping only when a violent thunderstorm interfered.

The style of life at La Grange was rich, easy , refined, cultured, and elegant. Dinners were ample, consisting of "many courses, fine wine," and coffee handed round by butlers. The Trollopes' suite of rooms was "charming, the bed was covered with heavy crimson satin quilts, and curtains of the same vivid color lined the windows." A smaller room contained another bed which in a polite way Mrs. Trollope learned was "for Monsieur if it were preferred." There was nothing to do but improve the mind and tastes at leisure. Vistors read papers, wrote letters, and listened to M. de Segur read tragedies. One was in verse, on the subject of Clytemnestra, and although he read "very finely," the fun-loving Frances confessed to her journal that "I should have preferred another play." Lafayette's daughters sang and played duets, and the party was entertained by a young pianist who had taken first prize at the French Academy. During long and beautiful walks, Mrs. Trollope discussed the relative merits of French and English literature with Mde. de Maubourg and Mlle. de Lasteyrie. One day, she drew a silhouette of "the dear General which all the party declared to be very like him." She vowed to keep it "as long as I live as one of my most valued possessions." Frequently, she detailed hour-long conversations with the general, and always her accounts ended in praise of him. "Wisdom and goodness mark every word he utters—and his sweet gentle kind unassuming manner make it delicious to listen to him."

One day, the general decided on an outing, called his Russian carriage, and took the Trollopes to a "fête du village," which Frances described in slightly condescending tones:

> The scene in front of a pretty little rustic church was enchanting. It was delightful to watch the good man, looking like the father of the hamlet dispersing his smiles around. All the young people from the Chateau joined in the dance. Trollope danced with them.

Probably the general mentioned to the Trollopes his proposed plan to make a tour of the United States in the following year. As she watched these young rustics, who "performed their quadrilles" so stylishly, perhaps she believed she was partaking, albeit at arm's length, of the nature of egalitarianism. Yet even here in such picturesque and protected surroundings, she drew a little back, leaving her husband to join more actively. The experience would prove but poor preparation for the rough equality of backwoods America, whither in four years Mrs. Trollope would be drawn by a combination of factors, not the least of which was her increasing attraction to liberal ideas and her admiration for that fervent reformer, Frances Wright.

In many ways, although Frances Wright was physically absent, her spirit dominated Mrs. Trollope's stay at La Grange. She discussed Miss Wright with the general at length on the journey out; they were free to speak of her in more glowing language than had she been present. When the post brought letters "announcing [Frances Wright's] intention of arriving by the Guigne Diligence, the Russian carriage was ordered to go for her." In a gesture measuring the extent of her fascination, Mrs. Trollope insisted on riding in the carriage for the journey of several hours to meet her friend. "But alas! the diligence arrived without bringing her—I brought back this sad intelligence to our dear General who came into my room to lament it with me." The next day, Mrs. Trollope persuaded her husband to join her in yet another drive, to Rossay, but to no avail. Nevertheless, Frances Wright had made her presence felt, particularly through her book on America which, for the first time, Mrs. Trollope read at La Grange. In the pages of that eloquent defense of the New World, Mrs. Trollope had a glimpse of the intellectual accomplishments of her friend—the traveler, writer, and activist woman.

As she concluded her La Grange journal of impressions, she recalled her last evening in Paris, spent in the company of "the dear General" and the Wright sisters. Of him, she wrote: "Never did I meet with a being so every way perfect. . . . The recollection of him will remain with me as long as I have life." Speaking in a general way of the total experience, Mrs. Trollope recorded her already deep sense of loss:

> The last half hour of this last evening was very painful—I know not where to find so intellectual, so amiable a set of beings as those I have been living amongst here.

This society of important friends, quite eclipsing her provincial Harrow acquaintance, her magnificent memories of La Grange, and a growing attraction to the promise that was the New World would all soon combine to impel Mrs. Trollope herself toward America, when other factors made her life in England intolerable.

Mr. Trollope, a somber background figure throughout the visit, seems largely unaffected by this Paris vacation. His wife was the more dynamic personage. The pair must so have struck Washington Irving, who, when he recorded his 1823 Paris meeting with the Trollopes at the Wilkes home, recalled them in an order so uncustomary as to indicate his impression of their relative significance: "Call on Payne then on Mr. Chas. Wilkes—see Miss Wright there—tall thin talking woman—Mrs. Trollop & husband." General Lafayette too had been taken with Mrs.

Trollope, writing his impressions of her "agreeable and amiable qualities" to Fanny Wright.[31]

From their marriage in 1809 until the present moment, Mr. Trollope
had shaped and dominated the family's fortunes. After 1823, he receded
into an increasingly hazy background. Prompted by forces over which
she had at first no control, his wife was soon to occupy center stage as
over the next three years a series of events released the forces, desires,
and motivations that had been deeply, if ever so obscurely, born within
her on that crucial visit to La Grange.

3

Years of Crisis:
To Nashoba and Beyond

Allez toujours

UPON HER return to Harrow, Mrs. Trollope resumed her domestic concerns. Tom's accomplishments in particular were a great joy to her. Convinced that he would become the scholar of the family, she thanked him for the pleasure his academic honors had given her.

> The talents and industry of a son may inspire a pride perfectly innocent, and therefore I have indulged myself in telling my friends how happy you have made me.[1]

Perhaps with an eye to one day introducing her sons to her French acquaintances, she began writing large parts of her letters to them in French and Italian.

But motherhood brought deep sorrows too. In the summer of 1824, on a visit to his grandfather in Reading, her frail, twelve-year-old son Arthur suddenly sickened and died. This loss, combined with her fears about the similar physical weakness of Henry, Cecilia, and Emily, made her draw back from completely submerging herself in her children. Loving them all deeply, she nevertheless learned early not to cling to them too tightly or depend too heavily upon them.

In that same summer, Mrs. Trollope lost her father. But his had been a long and happy life, and she did not feel intense grief. Julia Garnett wrote to offer condolences on the deaths of Arthur and the Reverend Milton. Mrs. Trollope's reply, the first in a series of letters that illuminates her life for the next twenty years, reveals a stern refusal to be crushed by a mother's sorrows and a determination not to dwell on losses. Resiliently, she concentrated on the living, her husband, about whom she betrayed an undertone of anxiety. Would his heart, like her own, learn the great lesson of yielding? That it did not was perhaps to prove his undoing. Unlike so many who wallow in private sufferings, Mrs. Trollope sought instead "the balm of society," "the kindness of old and valued friends," especially that of Frances Wright, whose fascination did not wane, although she had recently been the target of scandalous rumors when she planned to accompany the aging General Lafayette on another visit to America. Members of the general's family were sufficiently concerned about his affectionate relationship with the young Scotswoman to prevail upon him to sail alone, but Fanny and her sister followed on the next ship. Of Fanny's impulsive decision, Mrs. Trollope had at first disapproved, but the peculiar magic of the woman's personality overcame her objections. Society's rules didn't apply to this "angel friend": "The very acts that in all other women we should deem wrong— are in her a great, or over-powering duty."[2]

Since letters from America were rare and costly, communications from Fanny were often shared between the Garnetts and Mrs. Trollope. In one exchange, Julia complained to Fanny Wright that their lengthened separation had left a void. Miss Wright's answer was a stern call for women to hinge their lives to the firmness of an occupation.

> Without some fixed and steady occupation of labor—of business—of study—something which keeps in habitual exercise our physical or mental energies and the better when it is both, it is impossible to make our existence glide smoothly—We must know moments nay hours of vexation and lassitude. It is this which makes the pretty universally marked difference between men and women, that gives to the former good health and good nerves & fits them more or less to taste the enjoyments of life without being dependent upon any & to bear or brave its ills with a resisting spirit. I remember an observation of your father's—that geometry had been his best friend & consoling companion. Rousseau said the same of botany—Gibbon of historical research & composition & every poet has said or sung the same of his muse. . . . Seek cultivate & enjoy the talents which nature has so bountifully bestowed—Consult . . . on a good apportionment of time & take up some one pursuit or occupation with persevering determination. I can truly declare that I have never enjoyed tranquility but when my time has been steadily employed.[3]

So increasingly Mrs. Trollope propelled herself into more active occupation. Her house continued to be a center of gaiety, filled with amateur theatricals, parties, entertainments, and a constant stream of guests,[4] but she now set out to encourage and aid those of her acquaintance who were engaged in artistic or literary careers. Mary Russell Mitford, who wrote to support her family, was trying to break in as a playwright; Mrs. Trollope volunteered to intercede with the famous actors Kean and Macready to persuade them to appear in Miss Mitford's *Rienzi*. Confident that she could flatter and cajole her old friend Macready into starring, she wrote Miss Mitford:

When I am talking to 'William,' I always feel quite enough inclined to pet him, and moreover, I know he would make a glorious 'Rienzi'—Trust me, dear William would rather eat his heart than see Kean appear in *Rienzi*.

At the same time, she pursued Kean, inviting him to Harrow. She confessed to being temporarily thwarted: "I never saw anything to equal the ice-case into which he retreats the instant a word is uttered relative to his profession." Nevertheless she was indomitable: "Before he leaves town, however, he shall have a letter from me, which he must read, you know, and which I suppose he will answer." Ultimately appointed mediator in Miss Mitford's negotiations with Macready, Mrs. Trollope continued to encourage her friend, offering her some advice which would become her own watchword in days to come.

Allez toujours is what those who know the world best always say to the happy ones of the earth, who are sailing before the wind. *Allez toujours* and you will reach a station which no woman has ever reached before. You will have possession of the stage.[5]

She had taken under her wing the French artist Auguste Hervieu. Even as a young boy, he had shown decided artistic talent, but his father, a colonel in Napoleon's army, had prepared him for a military career. After his father's death in the retreat from Moscow, Hervieu left school and embarked on the study of painting. But his training was interrupted by the overthrow of Napoleon and the restoration of the Bourbons. Along with other student activists, the young Hervieu was drawn into the antimonarchical movement. To escape imprisonment and fines, he fled to England, where he worked at the Royal Academy for a while and tutored privately to support himself. When Mrs. Trollope engaged him to teach the children at Julian Hill, their long friendship began. Soon the dashing Hervieu, fifteen years younger than Mrs. Trollope, was an established member of the Harrow household.[6]

Mrs. Trollope did her best to assist him in his career. She wrote Miss Mitford and others:

If I have any knowledge of what is meant by the phrase *a man of genius*, I conceive it to belong to him—but he is totally and entirely *alone*, and unknown. . . . It would make your gentle heart ache if I were to tell you one quarter of what he has endured since he took refuge among us. How he has contrived to live I know not, but he has now a few pupils, and this has enabled him (by sometimes going without his dinner to buy colours) to paint a picture, which has been received by the committee at Somerset House. It is not *my* judgment alone that I give you, when I say that this picture is *most admirable*; but I well know its merits will never be felt without the aid of the public press. I know you have influence enough with Mr. Walter to get it spoken of in the *Times*, and perhaps in some other publications. All I would ask is to direct attention to it; for I am *quite* sure that, if it is hung where it can be seen, it cannot be looked at without admiration. The picture will be called in the catalogue, 'Love and Folly,' by A. J. Hervieu. . . .[7]

When the exhibition failed to bring Hervieu the recognition he had sought, Mrs. Trollope blamed the picture's placement: "les acade-miciens *have* hung it in such a place, that had they hung it the front to the wall it would have made no difference." Dramatically, she described his plight:

Imagine a being full of lofty aspirations—conscious of high powers, yet dragged to earth by the pitiful necessity of earning his daily morsel. — Whilst painting this picture he has more than once gone without his dinner, that he might buy colours—he hoped this picture would make him known—[8]

She could not have dreamed, as she tried to help the young artist, that he would endure more than going without dinner before his fortunes were made, nor that she would be his benefactor in a way neither could have envisioned. When, in a few years' time, she came before the public as an author, those whom she helped in their need did not forget her. Hervieu's support and unique illustrations for her first book, combined with Miss Mitford's letter of introduction to the publisher Whittaker, were repayment for her early devoted efforts in their behalf.

In 1826, the Trollopes again visited Paris, continuing their association with the great ones of the world, meeting Benjamin Constant, Sismondi, Fenimore Cooper, the Garnetts, and Lafayette, who had returned to France from his triumphant American tour. Conversation naturally turned to the absent Frances Wright, who had embarked on her life's work. While in the United States, Miss Wright had visited New Harmony, Indiana, and resolved to duplicate for the blacks of America the experiment in communal living that Robert Owen and his son Robert Dale had initiated. To General Lafayette's dismay, she had remained in western Tennessee to establish her utopian experiment Nashoba, by means of which she hoped to improve the condition of black slaves in the United States. She had purchased about twenty slaves to work a piece of land (several hundred acres in all, of which only a small portion was cleared and suitable for cotton). Miss Wright reasoned that slave labor would produce a surplus of money that would support the project and eventually repay her expenses. The surplus would also pay for eventual resettlement of the freed slaves in some country other than the United States. During that period of labor, the slaves would be educated and eventually made enlightened citizens.[9]

In September 1826, Mrs. Trollope read Fanny's first idyllic account of the progress of her establishment.

> Our people are now singing in chorus—We have a tolerable fiddle among them, and I shall bring from Harmony a flute for another—We have already a large room where they dance twice a week, and so heartily after a hard days work of hewing and chopping that I could wish myself one of them. Thus far I am amazed at our success—We were told of difficulties and apprehended many—Truly as yet we have found none worthy of the name.—[10]

To Mrs. Trollope this scene, like the stories from Whitehouse Farm and the fondly remembered La Grange, seemed far out of reach, for back at Harrow, serious financial worries were multiplying. For the first time, Mrs. Trollope mentioned stringent economies. Describing the assiduous repair of old garments, she put on a brave front, flattering herself "that they will turn out something worthy of a very good tailor." On one occasion, she sent Tom some spending money with an excuse for its being so little. "Half a crown from Papa,—a proof at once of poverty and kindness. Without the former it would be more, without the latter it would be nothing." Mr. Trollope's law practice was steadily deteriorating, and his farming fared no better. "All the world are poor as Job,—and, rather poorer, for Job put none of his sons to public school, and had no clients who did not pay him. Next year I fear we shall be poorer still, for assuredly there will be *no hay*."[11] Early in 1827, Mr. Trollope sadly informed his wife that serious retrenchment was necessary. She could no longer succor artists, dash up to London to importune Macready, or feature her lavish entertainments. Indeed, she would even have to give up her Harrow home and move to a small, undistinguished cottage miles from her friends and acquaintances.

In addition to these woes, Mr. Trollope's health was steadily worsening. As his eldest son later recalled:

> He had suffered very distressingly for many years from bilious headache, which gradually increased upon him during the whole of his life. . . . the common practice was to treat such complaints with calomel. He was constantly having recourse to that drug. And I believe that it had the effect of shattering his nervous system in a deplorable manner. He became increasingly irritable; never with the effect of causing him to raise a hand against any one of us, but with the effect of making intercourse with him so sure to issue in something unpleasant that, unconsciously, we sought to avoid his presence, and to consider as hours of enjoyment only those that could be passed away from it.

My mother's disposition, on the other hand, was of the most genial, cheerful, happy, *enjoué* nature imaginable. All our happiest hours were spent with her; and to any one of us a *tête-à-tête* with her was preferable to any other disposal of a holiday hour. But even this, under all the circumstances, did not tend to the general harmony and happiness of the family circle. For, of course, the facts and the results of them must have been visible to my father, and though wholly inoperative to produce the smallest change in his ways, must, I cannot doubt, have been painful to him. It was all very sad.

Apparent even to the children was a widening rift between husband and wife. As she struggled to be cheerful, active, and doing, he fell ever more deeply into pain and moroseness.[12]

In the summer of 1827, Mrs. Trollope bravely prepared for a family reunion of sorts. It was to be one last fling, for Julians Hill was to be rented at the turn of the year. All the boys planned to be home from school, and Mrs. Trollope looked forward to arranging French plays, other "drolleries," and berry-hunting trips. One has the sense of somewhat frenzied activity; it was always better to be doing than thinking these days. Feeling in need of female and sympathetic company, she invited Julia Garnett to visit. Earlier that spring, she had written: "Oh how I wish for you! How completely you have spoiled me for everybody else—strange that you should be the only friends (you and Harriet) to whom I can venture to say just everything I think upon every subject—yet so it is."[13]

But Julia's invitation came also in the spirit of matchmaking. In her "motherly" way, Mrs. Trollope suspected that Georg Heinrich Pertz, a rising young Hanoverian historian, and Julia had fallen in love. They had met frequently in the winter of 1826 in Paris but had been separated when Pertz left to do research in England without making a final declaration of his intentions. Julia had given him a letter of introduction to Mrs. Trollope, who at once guessed the secret.

> I shall treat him accordingly.—but don't be frightened. I will *not* seize his hand the moment I see him, and with a tender squeeze exclaim "Lover of my Julia, welcome!" No—I will only pump his heart a little—and it shall be done so gently, that he shall not even be conscious of what I am at—[14]

Now she invited both to join the family at Harrow. Although Pertz continued to work in the British Museum for the next six weeks, he came to Harrow every weekend.

Mrs. Trollope worked hard in Julia's behalf. With an eye to sealing the relationship, she utilized one of her special dramatic evening entertainments to feature Julia. Subsequently, Dr. Pertz recalled the effect.

> I had to marvel at Julia, in English speech and dress, in the role of Roscolana in the *Malade Imaginaire*. I had waited to declare myself until my position was decided, but as a powerful bud, illuminated by the sun of July, breaks its casing and unfolds its priceless blossom, so did my love break through this last boundary, and on the 3rd of August she made me the happiest man by acknowledging her love for me.

Long years later, Dr. Pertz gratefully recalled the "marked friendliness" and the "hospitable roof" under which their "loving hearts were united to each other for ever."[15] Characteristically, in the midst of her own troubles, Mrs. Trollope had helped a pair of lovers.

In that summer when Julia was staying at Harrow, the first really unpleasant rumors about Fanny Wright and Nashoba began. Her original ideals had become confused with principles of free love and free thinking about religion, which she had decided to test in her colony.[16] Miss Wright set forth these innovations in an account of her undertaking which she planned to publish in England. She sent a copy to Mrs. Trollope, who agreed with her husband that it would be "utter madness to print it here—contempt, ridicule, and reprobation would be the result. . . . Dear, noble, single-hearted Fanny dreams not of the light in which her declared opinions against religion would be viewed— *I* think her perfectly right in her idea that religion should never be tampered with, by lawmakers or schoolmasters—but what is my opinion?" Still, Mrs. Trollope told Julia, she would not desert her friend because of society's ill-natured misinterpretations.

> I dare no more venture to give breath to my opinions, than I would set fire to the castle at Windsor—all this makes society very flat stale and unprofitable—Heaven knows I do not want to be talking . . . radicalism—nor infidelity—but I should like to live among human beings who would not look upon reason as crime, nor on free discussion, as treason and blasphemy.[17]

The eventual publication of the prospectus set off just such a flurry of controversy as the Trollopes had predicted, heightened, perhaps, by Fanny's own return to Europe in the autumn of 1827 to recuperate from a particularly severe variety of the American "fever." When she arrived, her uncle, the prominent Glasgow professor Dr. James Mylne, refused to see her and even tried to conceal their relationship. He wrote Julia (who probably informed Mrs. Trollope) a terse and impassioned criticism of the Nashoba scheme. The picture of outraged (albeit affectionate) propriety, he begged Julia to talk to his

> poor and infatuated niece who, having returned, had left her younger and weaker sister Camilla to encounter all the horrors of forest solitude, and of a solitude abated only by the society of negroes in all the debasement of ignorance and slavery: or if of whites, of whites whose intellects seem to be destroyed and whose moral feelings are I fear ruined by the absurd principles of her senseless system—left there to manage and control an establishment which she had set up on the doctrines of property-non-responsibility—atheism—and an intercourse of the sexes unrestrained except by choice of the parties.

Julia, betrothed to the respectable Pertz, believed that Fanny Wright was "now incapable of judging for herself. Mr. Owen's system took possession of her mind when under the effect of a brain fever—it has never left her & she speaks as one incapable of seeing the consequences of the principles she advocates. . . ."[18] Mrs. Trollope reserved judgment.

Miss Wright's return to Europe had been only partially prompted by ill health. She planned to visit friends and prominent Europeans in hopes of interesting them in her project. She had been encouraged to seek recruits from the old world by Robert Dale Owen, who had accompanied her:

> The more I see of the old world the less I feel inclined to remain in it. But I should like to rescue out of it a few rational beings who are too good for it & would be much happier in the woods.[19]

Earlier attempts to attract the Garnetts had failed; Robert Dale suggested Mary Shelley as a suitable female companion for the founder of Nashoba. Invoking the names of Mrs. Shelley's illustrious parents and husband, Fanny Wright forcefully painted the glories of her colony and offered Mrs. Shelley a role in its growth. The latter, no doubt somewhat tired of idealistic schemes, politely declined the invitation, revealing the reservations with which she regarded such experiments.

> If you feel curiosity concerning me, how much more . . . must I not feel for yourself—a woman, young, rich & independent, quits the civilization of England for a life of hardship in the forests of America, that by so doing she may contribute to the happiness of her species. Her health fails in the attempt, yet scarcely restored that, she is eager to return again to the scene of her labours, & again to spend the flower of her life in arduous struggle &

beneficient, self-sacrificing devotion to others. Such a tale cannot fail to inspire the deepest interest, & the most ardent admiration. You do honour to our species, & what perhaps is dearer to me, to the feminine part of it.— and that thought, while it makes me doubly interested in you, makes me tremble for you. Women are so particularly the victims of their generosity & their purer & more sensitive feelings render them so much less than men, capable of battling the selfishness, hardness & ingratitude which is so often the return made, for the noblest efforts to benefit others. But you seem satisfied with your success, so I hope the ill-fortune which too usually frustrates our best views, will spare to harm the family of love, which you represent to have assembled at Nashoba.[20]

The search for a female companion had so far failed. Julia was looking forward to marriage, Harriet had failed to persuade her mother and sister to join Fanny in America, and Mrs. Shelley declined. Miss Wright asked:

I must return without a bosom intimate? . . . our little circle has mind, has heart, has right opinions, right feelings—cooperates in an experiment, having in view human happiness. Yet I do want one of my own sex to commune with & sometimes to lean upon in all the confidence of equality and friendship.[21]

At the same moment, Mrs. Trollope was preparing for another visit to Paris.

Financial difficulties had raised serious obstacles for the education the Trollopes had planned for their children. When their second son Henry did poorly at Winchester, his disappointed father withdrew him from the school in which grandfather, father, and brother Tom had excelled, and decided to apprentice him to a counting-house. A sole concession to his wife was to select a firm in Paris where Henry might enjoy himself and, with the assistance of Mrs. Trollope's friends, see a little of the world. But after a few months, Henry was unhappy with his confining apprenticeship, and while his parents pressed him to perfect his French, he implored them for a dancing and gymnastics master.[22] It was concern for Henry that brought Mrs. Trollope to Paris in the fall of 1827. She came alone while her husband stayed behind to supervise the harvest. She was thus free to accept an invitation to visit the recuperating Fanny Wright at La Grange. While Mrs. Trollope unburdened herself about Henry's unpromising future and the unhappy state of affairs at home, Miss Wright spoke rapturously of America and its glorious potential. She suggested that Henry take a position at Nashoba as a teacher and that Mrs. Trollope assume the role of her female companion and confidante.

Once more caught up in the spell of her friend, Mrs. Trollope was determined to go.

But when she returned to Harrow in early October, Henry remained in Paris at his desk. Mr. Trollope would first have to be convinced, and for this purpose, she brought with her the eloquent Miss Wright. Mrs. Trollope was fully convinced that she would ultimately secure her husband's approval, for her enthusiastic letter to Harriet Garnett indicates a wholehearted conversion to the Nashoba experiment.

Never was there I am persuaded such a being as Fanny Wright—no never—and I am not the only one who thinks so—some of my friends declare that if worship may be offered, it must be to her—That she is at once all that woman should be—and something more than woman ever was—and I know not what beside. . . . Will it be possible to let this "angel" . . . will it be possible to let her depart without vowing to follow her? I think not. I feel greatly inclined to say 'where her country is, there shall be my country.' The more I see of her, the more I listen to her, the more I feel convinced that *all* her notions are right.—she is pointing out to man a short road to that goal which for ages he has been in vain endeavoring to reach. Under her system I believe it possible that man may be happy—and we have had proof enough that he can not be so under any of those already tried. Does poor dear Henry still continue to dream of Fanny Wright and Nashoba? More improbable things have happened than that his wish should be listened to—but I dare not tell him so as yet— as his father has by no means made up his mind on the subject.[23]

At the close of the letter, she was already seeking further recruits herself. "Do something to amuse and comfort yourself," she told Harriet: "Next year perhaps we shall be amusing each other at Nashoba."

Mrs. Trollope's motives for joining Miss Wright were several. For nearly eighteen years, she had made an occupation of being mother, wife, and hostess. With the death of Arthur, she had determined not to confine herself to the vocation of motherhood. Moreover, Mr. Trollope's worsening illness and withdrawal made him increasingly hard to live with. Faced with the need to bring their expenditures into line with his dwindling income, he planned to remove the family to an old farmhouse at Harrow Weald. There the rooms were small and dingy, and his unrelieved presence—and the worries which justifiably troubled him— would be the more difficult to bear. The prospect of leaving her pretty cottage in Harrow and the social whirl that had helped her escape these conflicts came as the final blow. With Tom and Anthony safely in school and Henry at work, although unhappily, in Paris, Frances and the girls faced an existence framed by constant mental turmoil.[24]

She explained her thinking to the Garnetts:

My final determination to accompany Fanny to Nashoba was brought on
by Mr. T's telling me on my return to Harrow that he was determined upon
letting our house there, for the purpose of retrenching our expenses. He
proposes one or two plans of retirement—at which my heart sickened—
and I used all my power to persuade him that a year or two passed at
Nashoba would repair our affairs more completely than any other.[25]

The Garnetts were well aware of the other, equally important motivation behind Mrs. Trollope's decision. Miss Wright's eloquent talk had
touched the imaginative side of her nature. Anthony also knew that his
mother was poetic and idealistic as well as practical, as he later
speculated on her voyage:

Her life, I take it, though latterly clouded by many troubles, was easy,
luxurious, and idle, till my father's affairs, *and her own aspirations* sent her
to America.[26]

When arrangements were completed Mr. Trollope moved into two
rooms of the Harrow Weald farm, while continuing to maintain his
chambers in Lincoln's Inn. His wife, Henry, and the two girls, accompanied by two servants and all the rest of the furniture, sailed to
America. Clearly, she planned a lengthy stay, and one of her English
friends wrote: "It looks like a little settlement there."[27]

To most of her contempories, her decision to join the Nashoba colony
seemed extraordinary. General Lafayette wrote of his astonishment to a
friend:

You will be not a little surprised to hear that Mrs. Trollope, after a full
explanation of the Nashoba experimental system has with the assent of her
husband determined to become, with her daughters and son, members of
the society and to give up the habits and comforts to which I thought her
peculiarly attached.[28]

Her closest friends were shocked because she had chosen to disregard
the aura of scandal that had increasingly clouded the name of Nashoba.
When Henry was recalled from Paris, Mrs. Mary Garnett could only
comment disapprovingly: "Will wonders never cease!" Mrs. Trollope
said goodbye to no one, leaving only a brief note for her Harrow acquaintances, representing her journey as a visit to friends in New York
and Nashoba, a trip to see Niagara, and an attempt to place her children
in new schools. Only the Garnett circle of friends knew that her destination was the infamous Nashoba, and she left "all Harrow . . . in amaze

at her sudden departure."[29] In their eyes, her decision was irrevocable; they would find it difficult to welcome her back. Harriet wrote:

> I can scarcely yet believe that Mrs. T. is actually on her way and Trollope alone in his old age in London. How can he bear the reports that must at last reach him of Nashoba. The horror that that community will excite in every country, and most in America. What things will be said and written on such a field for slander and ill-nature. And we must bear all in silence— for we cannot defend such a system. Principle and propriety both equally oppose our defending it. . . . But the step once taken there is no return, at least for a woman. The gates of the most rigid convent are not so insurmountable a barrier betwixt the world and the nun they enclose as public scorn makes against a woman who has joined such a community as Nashoba.

And while the Garnetts sympathized with Mr. Trollope, in their hearts they condemned him for failing to prevent this wild expedition: "Her poor husband with all his oddities doted on Fanny. How could he consent for consent he did. . . . Nothing can be said in extenuation of her conduct. . . ."[30]

The Nashoba venture was clearly and totally Mrs. Trollope's own idea, spontaneous and daring, with an eleventh-hour urgency about it. Her husband had opposed it to the last. The Garnetts, upbraiding Frances Wright for not having revealed her plans to include Mrs. Trollope, received a description of the last-minute flurry.

> My reason for not writing you [of my departure] or rather of F[rances] T[rollope] sooner was that she requested me not to do it. My own was only positively settled 24 hours before I was on shipboard and her's only 5 days. . . . She expected always something would prevent her voyage and wished it therefore not known or talked about.[31]

The further decision to have Mrs. Trollope's protégé Auguste Hervieu accompany the party was a well-guarded secret. He boarded on the night they weighed anchor, swept along on this expedition into the unknown by the enthusiastic determination of two powerful women. He had little to lose; the breakup of the Harrow household eliminated the living and working accommodations so generously provided by his patroness. Despite the inferences some have drawn, they were not lovers but devoted friends. Still, they could not be unaware of the talk that would circulate once the young artist was found to be among the group sailing for America, and so they left like hasty criminals.[32]

Most previous commentators have viewed this American venture as primarily a financial speculation. In these interpretations, Nashoba was only a way station to the final destination, the commercial metropolis of Cincinnáti, where the failing family fortunes were to be revived. But none of the contemporary letters about the trip refer to a speculation, and none even mention Cincinnati or hint at plans for marketing European fancy goods. As for improving the manners of the Americans, that was to be effected at Nashoba.[33] Indeed, so successful was Mrs. Trollope in later hiding her movements and associations with the Nashoba community, that not until the present moment, with the discovery of the Garnett correspondence, has the full story emerged.

Mrs. Trollope found the Atlantic crossing long and fatiguing (they had left England on 4 November), but she was not one to complain. On Christmas day the party was on board the *Edward* in the Mississippi:

> Here I am with my two girls beside me, and our Fanny vis a vis! I can hardly believe it—The arrangement was so sudden that at times I still fancy that I dream—had I time and paper I would explain to you at large all the motives that have led me to wish, and Mr. Trollope to consent to this expedition—but I can *now* only tell you th[at] some pecuniary claims which came upon us quite unexpectedly, made it very necessary that we should leave our pretty place and large establishment for a year or two at least—and where, or with whom, could I pass that interval so much to my satisfaction as in the home,and in the society of our Fanny? *You*, at least my Julia will not wonder at my choice—Henry's very earnest wish to visit Nashoba was another strong reason for my going thither—I have left the people making great eyes at me—but I care but little for this. I expect to be very happy, and very free from care at Nashoba—and this will more than repay me for being the object of a few 'dear me's'![34]

As they sailed up river to Nashoba, Mrs. Trollope noticed her fellow voyagers' bad manners, their incessant spitting, the way they ravenously devoured their dinner; still, she reasoned, things would be different at Nashoba. Her shock at the first sight of the settlement she subsequently recorded in her book of American experiences. Frances Wright had emphasized the potentiality and the ideal; Frances Trollope saw the somber reality. Her experience jolted into consciousness her previous doubts about Miss Wright. In a letter written less than a year later, she vividly expressed her new insights:

> I was a very poor creature during the voyage and persuaded myself repeatedly that it was my weakness that made me deem Fanny too eccentric, when I saw her sitting upon a coil of rope in the steerage, reading to a sailor occupied in patching his breeches, on another some of the wildest doctrines of equality and concubinage that pen ever traced on

paper.—Writing such, and reading them aloud, was her chief occupation during the voyage—and I often recurred to the idea that had tormented us at Paris, that she was not in her right senses.

In her published account she was more generous, suggesting that Miss Wright's mind "was so exclusively occupied by the object she had then in view, that all else were worthless, or indifferent to her."[35]

Upon her arrival, Mrs. Trollope had found Nashoba

so infinitely more dreadful than I ever imagined possible that I almost immediately decided upon not suffering my children to breathe the pestilential atmosphere more than a day or two—it is impossible to give you an idea of their miserable and melancholy mode of life while I was there. Whitby and his wife both look like spectres from fever and ague. Lolotte the New Orleans washerwoman and her three children, full of wretched regret and repining. This was the whole community, except the slaves—whom we only saw when they brought logs for the fires. The food was scanty and far from wholesome—no milk or butter—bad water— very little bread—and no meat but pork.—In short I left them in ten days.

Hervieu, who had been told that he would be teaching art, found "the schools of Nashoba consisted of 3 yellow children running wild in the swamps." His subsequent sketches caught that mournful desolation stressed by Mrs. Trollope. A few poorly constructed cabins, some zigzag fences, a clearing in the wilderness, several slaves, and all around the dense, fever-ridden forest—this was Nashoba.[36]

Although Mrs. Trollope later described it as a place she had meant only to visit, and herself and her children as observers of this great egalitarian experiment, this account was only a pose. One of her American contemporaries who knew the truth was Timothy Flint, a Cincinnati acquaintance who, angered by her later attack on America, described, with smug delight, her blighted hopes:

She came to this country, induced to the step . . . by the eloquence of Frances Wright, who was about at that time to bleach out the Ethiopian tinge of the negroes, by her own peculiar process, change their bumps, and make them free, wise, and etc. as the French say *toute de suite* at Nashoba. In Mrs. Trollope's teeming and imaginative brain, the dreary forests of Nashoba, with its huge tulip trees and sycamores, and its little log cabins, with their dirty and halfclad negro tenants . . . was a sort of splendid hall, with columns and arcades, where she could see the aforesaid process of bleaching passing under her eyes, and where Her- vieu . . . could paint it. . . .[Once she had seen the reality of the place], she came, as fast as steam could waft her, to Cincinnati, where she arrived without a line of introduction to any individual, and where our acquaintance with her commenced.[37]

When she abandoned her Nashoba plans, she had to wait ten days or so while the trustees made arrangements to grant her a loan so that she could take herself and her household to more compatible surroundings. The Nashoba journal recorded

a loan of $300 to Mrs. Trollope to assist her in removing from Nashoba to some place in the western world better suited to her future plans for herself and her children.

The last mention of her in the record occurs on 27 January 1828. "Frances Trollope and family with their manservant William Abbot and Esther Rust, her maid, and Auguste Hervieu, left us for Memphis."[38]

After sending Henry to the more established colony of New Harmony on the Wabash, Mrs. Trollope arranged for repayment of the Nashoba loan. Her first concern, "notwithstanding the unequalled abundance and cheapness of this place," was money. Earlier, Frances Wright had designated her friend, the New York banker Charles Wilkes, to handle the Trollopes' financial investment in Nashoba. From Cincinnati, Mrs. Trollope wrote Wilkes, throwing herself upon his kindness "in consideration of the forlorn situation into which this wild goose expedition has thrown me."

. . . I certainly do not believe that it was [Frances Wright's] intention to deceive me, when she gave such a discription [*sic*] of her Nashoba, as induced us to fix upon it as a residence for a year or two during which, from motives of economy, we had decided upon residing abroad.—but most assuredly we were altogether deluded by the picture her imagination drew . . . you will understand the impression made by Nashoba, when I tell you that we left at the end of ten days.[39]

She asked that Wilkes advance her some money and secure further sums from Mr. Trollope.

Loath to detail her forlorn and misplaced hopes, Mrs. Trollope did not write her close friends for over a year. Only to Wilkes did she confess her most recent conclusions about Miss Wright's health: "Poor Fanny Wright! I own to you that my firm conviction is, that the brain fever which attacked her last year, has affected her intellect. There is no other mode of accounting for her words or her actions."[40]

The Garnetts were bewildered by Mrs. Trollope's silence, when in March they first heard rumors of her departure and further travels.

Think . . . of Mrs. Trollopes having absolutely left Nashoba after ten days residence. She has written to Mr. Wilkes that the climate is so bad that she is gone with her children to Cincinnati to wait for her husband. . . . Mrs. Trollope went with her eyes open and now so suddenly to change. . . . How strange! Mrs. T. with her family established at Cincinnati—having left Nashoba ten days after her arrival.[41]

The rapid change in plans seemed utterly unaccountable.

The more I think of it—of her enthusiasm in the cause—of all the sacrifices she made to accompany Fanny—of the difficulties she conquered—of the public opinion she braved—the more astonishing does it seem to me that she should so soon have been discouraged [by] the difficulties she encountered there.[42]

After arriving in Cincinnati, "the metropolis of the West," on 10 February 1828, Mrs. Trollope immediately wrote her husband, but by May, nine letters had gone unanswered. Almost frantic, she asked her son Tom the cause of this implacable silence.

Is your father ill? Is he dead? have his affairs fallen into such confusion that he has not been able to procure the money necessary to send us a remittance? . . . I entreat you to write to me immediately. Our situation here would be dreadful, were it not for M. Hervieu's grateful, and generous kindness. It is more than a month that we have not had a mouthful of food that he has not paid for.[43]

The Nashoba loan was long gone, and Mr. Trollope's failure to send money for a return passage or even write a line made her resolve to make her way alone. For the first time in her life, she was on her own, in a strange land with children to support and no immediate means of livelihood at hand.[44]

Everything seemed to be going wrong at once; Henry, overworked at New Harmony, begged to be recalled, and with Hervieu's help, she managed to pay his fare to Cincinnati. Hoping to capitalize on her son's knowledge of Latin, she advertised his services as tutor on 28 March in the Cincinnati *Gazette*.

Mr. Henry Trollope, having received a completely classical education, at the royal college of Winchester, (England) would be happy to give lessons in the Latin language to gentlemen at their own houses. By an improved method of teaching, now getting into general use in Europe, Mr. H. Trollope flatters himself he shall be able to give a competent knowledge of the Latin tongue in a much shorter space of time than had hitherto been considered necessary. Terms: Fifty cents for lessons of one hour. Apply to Mr. H. Trollope, Hollingsworth Row, Race street.[45]

But Henry's skills drew no buyers. Mrs. Trollope wondered what services would sell in this bustling frontier city of 20,000.

In April, Hervieu opened a drawing school in his lodgings, near the Western Museum. Through him, Mrs. Trollope met the recently appointed director, Joseph Dorfeuille, a French naturalist. In 1823 the Museum's holdings were listed as

100 mammoth and Arctic elephant bones, 50 Megalonyx bones, 33 quadrupeds, 500 birds, 200 fishes, 5000 invertebrates, 1000 fossils, 3500 minerals, 325 botanical specimens, 3125 medals, coins and tokens, 150 Egyptian and 215 American antiquities, 112 microscopical designs, views of American scenery and buildings, tattooed head of a New Zealand chief and about 500 miscellaneous specimens of the fine arts and an 'elegant organ.'[46]

But the level of scientific knowledge in Cincinnati could not sustain the museum as a serious effort, and by 1828 it was practically bankrupt. To encourage attendance, Dorfeuille began to combine his scientific displays with shows featuring oddities and freaks. He devised exhibitions in which, as Tom Trollope later recalled, "he collected anything and everything that he thought would excite the curiosity of the people and induce them to pay their quarter dollars for admission." He hired the young and as yet unknown sculptor Hiram Powers to make wax figures. But despite such displays as "the celebrated Indian Chief Tecumseh . . . completely dressed in the Indian garb," and "a superb allegorical representation, in wax, of the Death of George Washington," the museum continued to show a deficit budget.[47]

Mrs. Trollope, herself striving to survive in Cincinnati, realized with the genius of the outsider that the citizens were uninterested in such commonplace scenes, and gave Dorfeuille the idea for a new attraction. She proposed the creation of an oracle, surrounded by mysterious decorations to be created by Hervieu, from which would come a voice, ready to answer the questions of the spectators in a variety of languages, some real, some imaginary. Henry's linguistic talents, so recently rejected, would form the basis of a new exhibition, marking an upswing in the fortunes of the Western Museum of Cincinnati.

The first dramatic announcement of the "Invisible Girl" appeared in

the *Gazette* on 12 April 1828, and from its melancholy introductory
verses, to its air of offering something impressive from an older culture,
bore the mark of Mrs. Trollope's own pen:

THE INVISIBLE GIRL

"Sweet spirit of mystery: how I could love,
In the wearisome ways I am fated to rove,
To have you forever invisibly nigh,
Inhaling forever your song and your sigh;
Mid the crowds of the world and the murmurs of care,
I might sometimes converse with my nymph of the air,
And turn with disgust from the clamorous crew,
To steal in the pauses one whisper from you."

The proprietor of the WESTERN MUSEUM is now able to tender to the
public, the gratification of receiving the responses of the '*Invisible Girl.*' As
he has spared no expense in preparing this most interesting philosophical
experiment, he relies upon his fellow citizens for a fair demonstration of a
disposition to remunerate him for an attempt to present to the world, a
subject in which science and taste have been equally consulted.

In addition to the pleasure to be expected from the mysterious responses
of the '*Invisible Girl*' herself, it is but fair to state that her chamber of
audience has been fitted up in such a style, as to afford great interest to the
classical and refined mind. In this the proprietor of the Museum has been
aided by the taste and skill of one of the most accomplished artists who has
ever visited our country. The room is made to resemble one of those
theatres of probations, in the Egyptian Mysteries, in which the candidate
for initiation was subjected to his incipient trials: the genius and pencil of
Mr. Hervieu have given to it an effect truly impressive: Shakespeare has
been put in requisition, and the gloomy chamber, in addition to many
other appropriate devices, exhibits an admirable group of the '*Weird
Sisters*' returning to the cauldron of Hecate, with the various ingredients of
her horrible incantation. In the centre of the room is a cloud, perfectly
pervious to the sight, from which a female arm projects, holding gracefully a small glass trumpet; the whole is entirely unconnected with any part
of the wall or ceiling.

This slight sketch of a part of the interesting subjects of the dark chamber,
is sufficient to give an idea of the labor and attention its preparation has
cost. . . .

Parties of 12 persons, and no more, can be admitted at a time to the
presence of the Oracle—and each visitor allowed to propound three
questions, if other visitors are present, or six, if no one else should be in

waiting. The *profoundest silence* to be observed during the delivery of the responses—[48]

The show was a tremendous success. Henry, proficient in Latin and knowing some French, German, and Italian, made such an impressive display that one observer later recalled that the marvellous oracle spoke at least seven languages! With a flair born of necessity, Mrs. Trollope had brought to the backwoods of the Ohio Valley the mystical and the occult. Not surprisingly, she never mentioned her pivotal role in the creation of this pseudo-circus. Even so, her participation did not earn large sums of money, and she had to devise further methods of assuring the family's subsistence in America.

In June 1828, she vaguely began to think of writing. Rummaging about in her past experience for something marketable, she hit upon the idea of bringing out a little volume on her travels to Paris and her conversations with Lafayette, whose Cincinnati reputation had been high since his visit there in 1825. The city even sustained a Lafayette Lodge. But she was unsure of herself and asked Charles Wilkes if such an idea might prove feasible, sending him a sample of the manuscript of her journal of a visit to La Grange.

I enclose to you a few pages of the little volume I mentioned to you and also a list of the persons noticed in the subsequent pages. Perhaps the best plan would be to put them into the hands of the publisher you mention, and take his opinion as to the *finishing up*, and *writing fair* the remainder, as I should not like to take even thus much trouble, if he were not likely to publish it, when it was done.[49]

Her plans never materialized. Later that month she thought of making use of her present-day Cincinnati experiences. Ever since 1823, she had continued the habit of keeping notes and wrote to Tom,

I amuse myself by making notes, and hope some day to manufacture them into a volume. This is a remote corner of the world, and but seldom visited and I think that if Hervieu could find time to furnish sketches of scenery, and groups, a very taking little volume might be produced.

She could discuss climate, local customs, and scenery, while Hervieu made the expected picturesque sketches of the city and its environs.[50] This project was abandoned almost at once for a more immediately remunerative one in Dorfeuille's service. But when she returned to her notes more than a year later, after profound disappointments and serious ill-health, she found that she had quarried a dramatic story, a travel book quite different from the "very taking little volume" she had originally visualized.

The enterprise which for a time drove thoughts of a book from her mind came about quite casually. One night, in the spring of 1828, as she chatted with Hiram Powers, whom Dorfeuille had by now engaged as factotum and general manager of his establishment, she suggested getting up "a representation of one of Dante's *bolgias* as described in the *Inferno*. The nascent sculptor . . . caught at the idea on the instant. And forthwith they set to work, [Frances] explaining the poet's conceptions, suggesting the composition of "tableux," and supplying details, while Powers designed and executed the figures and the necessary mise en scene."[51] Her idea subsequently became famous as the "Infernal Regions," and a Bostonian who visited the production soon after its initial staging in July, described the main attractions of this popularized display.

In the centre is seated his Infernal Highness 'as large as life.' This diabolical personage sits on a throne of darkness of sufficient elevation to give him a commanding view of the abyss on either side. His body is clad in a sable robe, which, however, discloses that all-essential appendage—a 'cloven foot.' In his left hand he holds a pitchfork, like a weaver's beam; while his right is pointed towards an inscription directly in front, '*Whoever enters here leaves hope behind!*' His head is adorned with a huge crown, and his face, (which by the way is not the most pleasant) is woefully ornamented with a hoary beard, made of horses' tails! To give importance to this King of Hell, his neck is so constructed as to admit of his giving a nod of recognition to the spectator; and his glaring eye-balls are made to roll most horribly by means of some machinery in the room below. . . .

On the right hand of the devil above described, and on the left of the spectator, is seen one department of this hell, which is denominated the *hell* of ice; a most heretical place, where the damned, instead of being burned in fire and brimstone, are *frozen* in eternal death! This department is filled with wax figures representing persons of all ages and conditions—and among others, I observed a beautiful child, represented as in the greatest agony, frozen fast to the foot of the infernal throne. But what added much to the *effect*, was the condition of a poor old negro just entering upon a state of perpetual freezing; a sad predicament, truly, for one so constitutionally fond of a warm climate! In the corners of *this* part of hell, were to be seen several *imps* waiting the orders of his Majesty, 'grinning ghastly a horrible smile' at the miseries of their unfortunate subjects.

On the left of the devil, which is to the right of the beholder, is the *hell of fire*. In this department, are seen the skeletons of persons, thrown into various positions, the sockets of their eyes, their nostrils &c. &c. filled with some bright substance resembling fire; presenting to the eye one of the

most loathesome and disgusting scenes that imagination can portray!
While the heart is pained with beholding these representatives of misery,
the ear is saluted with a subterranean noise, produced by some instru-
ments of discord in the apartment below, resembling the imaginary
groans of the damned! Taken all together, it presents a scene well
calculated to alarm weak minds. . . .[52]

Mrs. Trollope wrote the explanatory translations and supervised the
selection of scenes, Hervieu did the graphic art (the transparencies), and
Hiram Powers formed the wax figures, coming "as near what might be
imagined the reality as one could come," in the words of one observer.[53]
As in the Invisible Girl project, Mrs. Trollope always remained faintly
ashamed of her connection with this enterprise and later acknowledged
no responsibility for what she later described as a pandemonium,
incorporating

all the images of horror that his fertile fancy could devise; dwarfs that by
machinery grow into giants before the eyes of the spectator; imps of
ebony with eyes of flame; monstrous reptiles devouring youth and beauty;
lakes of fire, and mountains of ice; in short, wax, paint and springs have
done wonders. 'To give the scheme some more effect,' he makes it visible
only through a grate of massive iron bars, among which are arranged wires
connected with an electrical machine in a neighbouring chamber; should
any daring hand or foot obtrude itself within the bars, it receives a smart
shock, that often passes through many of the crowd, and the cause being
unknown, the effect is exceedingly comic; terror, astonishment, curiosity,
are all set in action, and all contribute to make 'Dorfeuille's Hell' one of the
most amusing exhibitions imaginable.

In her book, she wrote condescendingly about that creature born of her
own lively imagination.

Cincinnati has not many lions to boast, but among them are two museums
of natural history; both of these contain many respectable specimens,
particularly that of Mr. Dorfeuille, who has moreover, some highly
interesting Indian antiquities. He is a man of taste and science, but a
collection formed strictly according to their dictates, would by no means
satisfy the western metropolis. The people have a most extravagant
passion for wax figures, and the two museums vie with each other in
displaying specimens of this barbarous branch of art. As Mr. Dorfeuille
cannot trust to his science for attracting the citizens, he has put his
ingenuity into requisition, and this has proved to him the surer aid of the
two.[54]

Despite this later pose, Mrs. Trollope never forgot how she had taught

Dorfeuille the way to catch the fancy of the public, and her association with the Western Museum had an important effect on her next, more ambitious undertaking in Cincinnati.

4

The Cincinnati Bazaar and Afterwards

"God knows what will become of us all"

MRS. TROLLOPE had been gone from England for almost a year. Surely, her friends thought, it was time for her to return. She had averted social ostracism by her swift departure from Nashoba. Mr. Trollope, although bitter about both the expedition and its results, decided to sail for America on the first of September 1828. When he heard that even Fanny Wright had "thought it best Mrs. Trollope should leave Nashoba," he commented: "it is a pity she had not thought the same before she induced Mrs. Trollope to go with her." But he was too cautious to state definitely that he would bring his wife and children back.[1] After all, she had gone alone and did not need him to fetch her. She had urged him to come for reasons of her own. Although he told no one, Mrs. Trollope was pressing him for funds and for permission to remain still longer in America. New prospects and plans, recently evolved after her brief stay in Cincinnati, had seized her imagination.

While still working on the "Infernal Regions" project, Mrs. Trollope conceived the idea for what has subsequently become famous as the bazaar, a building in downtown Cincinnati that would house both commercial and artistic activities. She described her project as "a very elegant building—here it will be the chief lion of the city. . . . The lower part will be let out as a bazzaar [*sic*]; the upper rooms, as exhibition, lecture, and reading rooms—on the top is a rotunda for a Panorama."[2] Sensing the possibilities of success in this "extraordinary city," Mrs. Trollope proposed building, superintending, and collecting the rents of such a structure. She was sure the citizens of Cincinnati would patronize an establishment designed to enliven their drab western existence with the unusual, the strange, and the exotic. Dorfeuille had linked the artistic with the sensational in a relatively small-scale endeavor; she would mix art, entertainment, and commerce in so large and elegant a way that even that old showman Dorfeuille could not have imagined it.

During her first year in Cincinnati, Mrs. Trollope noted a cultural and recreational void in the life of the city. What were treated by Cincinna-

59

tians as major intellectual events seemed to her either boring or unfortunate. Dr. Caldwell's lectures on phrenology were at best second-hand
for Mrs. Trollope, who had herself heard Dr. Spurzheim, whom
Caldwell ("the American Spurzheim") had only studied. His talks
inspired the formation of a Phrenological Society of Cincinnati, which
"hardly survived beyond the third meeting." There was certainly
nothing new to Mrs. Trollope in Fanny Wright's Cincinnati lectures on
the nature of true knowledge. Nashoba was about to be dissolved, and
Miss Wright had decided to devote herself to the editorship of the New
Harmony *Gazette* and public lecturing. If Mrs.Trollope had been a
foolish enthusiast flinching at the first sight of unpleasant reality, how
much more reprehensible was Miss Wright, who had tired of the day-to-
day living out of her high ideals and had abandoned ship, as described
by her adoring sister in a passage of confession and rationalization.

> She thought it would be a poor appropriation of her talents to sit down and
> devote herself to the emancipation of a few slaves, besides its being an
> employment for which she was altogether and in every respect incompe-
> tent.[3]

Miss Wright's appearance in Cincinnati excited much astonishment and
flurry, and Mrs. Trollope attributed the fuss to the simple fact of sex, for
in America "women are guarded by a seven-fold shield of habitual
insignificance." She rather scornfully reduced the talks, which she
attended, to their common denominator: "Fanny appears in good
spirits, and anticipates confidently the regeneration of the whole human
race from her present exertions. . . ." A seven-day, fifteen-session
debate on the existence of God between the Rev. Alexander Campbell
and Mr. Owen of Lanark and New Harmony "could only have happened in America. I am not quite sure that it was very desirable it should
have happened any where." She later rather caustically summarized its
result: "at the end of the 15 meetings the numerical amount of the
Christians and the Infidels of Cincinnati remained exactly what it was
when they began. . . ."[4]

For learned societies and associations, there was the shortlived Semi-
Colon Club, which suffered from upper-class pretentiousness, and a
young men's temperance society. In general, ladies did not participate.
One club even required that papers written by women be read by a male
member.[5] Frances would later expostulate in her book about this
destructive sheltering of women from the intellectual and social life of
the community. Also, there were few public places, it seemed to her,
where Cincinnati's citizens could enjoy elegant leisure and intelligent
amusement. In these observations, Frances Trollope was ahead of her

time, and she would pay the price that those who attempt to be innovative often do: condemnation, ridicule, and eventual failure.

Since she had come to America, she had offended in at least three crucial areas. Her position as a married woman had been faintly anomalous; she traveled without her husband and, even worse, in the company of a French artist. Her "very eccentric" connection with this "French compagnon de voyage" would have operated "against her being taken notice of by respectable ladies, or treated as one herself." Her subsequent association with other male artists and entrepreneurs weakened an already poor reputation. In America, men associated in public even "with their wives as little as may be." For women to socialize with men would "break down the barriers of chastity which is the peculiar ornament and virtue of women, and the true source of their delicacy and refinement."[6] In stepping outside the narrow circle of domestic life and dependence, Mrs. Trollope violated the separation of the male from the female that de Toqueville so approvingly noted as fundamental to American society. He wrote:

> In no country has such constant care been taken as in America to trace two clearly distinct lines of action for the two sexes and to make them keep pace one with the other, but in two pathways which are always different.—American women never manage the outward concerns of the family, or conduct a business, or take a part in political life. . . .[7]

Finally, although she was not ostensibly political, her association, short as it was, with a project for the emancipation and education of blacks and her outspoken views on slavery would obviously hinder her acceptance by the elite of the city. Fearful of the increasing immigration of southern blacks, some Cincinnatians had banded together just two years before to form the Cincinnati Colonization Society, dedicated to relocating freed blacks outside the United States. Like most border towns in the nation, Cincinnati was a quietly racist society, a fact which lay dormant until the summer of 1836 when two days of mob destruction and race riots brought to a head the antiblack sentiment that had been growing in the Ohio Valley through the decade. Mrs. Trollope's unfamiliarity with the unspoken agreement to ignore the problem of the blacks in America was doubtless the basis of much later criticism of her social blunders and unpleasantly coarse frankness.[8]

Later, some of her Cincinnati critics claimed that Mrs. Trollope had never been received in the better circles because she lacked refinement, fine clothing, and acceptable manners. "After seeing how she behaved in market," one dowager recalled, "no one could think of asking her inside a drawing room." Outspoken, learned, cultured, and bold-mannered, she emphasized her independence by long, unaccompanied walks, even in the roughest weather, often dressed in an unusual green calash with a plaid cloak dragging at her heels and taking "those collossean strides unattainable by any but Englishwomen." Working to support her family, she failed to keep her home immaculate and tidy, thus giving "practical illustration of the contempt she confesses for the domestic virtues of American females." All this evidence of "unfeminine" behavior and indifference toward Cincinnati proprieties persuaded the townspeople to consider her eccentric. But in attempting to write Mrs. Trollope off lightly as "a wandering huzzy who . . . chose to build bazaars and lose money," critics masked a deep matrix of suspicion and fear. Her major flaw was a failure to fit into the pattern of American female domesticity.[9]

When she embarked on her ambitious enterprise, realizing that she needed to improve her social position, Mrs. Trollope had recourse to that necessary amenity of nineteenth-century life, the letter of introduction. Through the kindness of General Lafayette, who responded to her plea for such letters, she managed to gain entrance to several of Cincinnati's better houses. Without such help, the obstacles to residence and further achievement in the city would have been all but insurmountable. She wrote Tom, "Such an introduction is worth something in this country," adding that Lafayette's letter contained "*in fact*, the first certain assurance that we are not a set of very accomplished swindlers!"[10] In an area of marginal urban development, social lines were more sharply drawn than in older, more firmly settled societies. The frontier, out of a sense of insecurity, preserved more rigid forms of society than any in Europe. Mrs. Trollope's disregard for such pretensions seriously injured her efforts.

In September 1828 her husband and Tom arrived, ostensibly to bring Mrs. Trollope and the family home. Her friends saw no alternative. "Mrs. Trollope has paid for her rambling—Mr. T. goes for her in August." Harriet exclaimed to Julia, "How imprudent it will be in poor Mrs. Trollope should she remain in America and let her husband return without her!"[11] But when Mrs. Trollope described her new idea, her husband reluctantly agreed. The bulk of the money, after all, was to come from his wife's recent inheritance from her father. His own funds had been exhausted. Mrs. Trollope described their arrangements to Harriet:

Mr. Trollope has entered into an equal division with Henry of all profiits proceeding from this institution till he shall be of age—after which he is to have the whole, as long as he choses [*sic*] to remain here to superintend it—

When he leaves it, which he hopes to do in ten years, Mr. Trollope hopes to sell it to advantage.[12]

Mrs. Trollope proposed staying in America out of motives both financial and personal. Nearly all commentators on her American trip and the bazaar have insisted that she sought only to restore the family fortunes by means of a daring speculation. But she seemed more interested in making a safe investment of the remaining family capital. Then she and the children could live pleasantly in America for a time, placing no further strain on Mr. Trollope's already heavy financial burdens. She explained this primary factor to Harriet:

> We are now living upon about one-fourth of [our income] and our incumbrances will we think all be removed by the time I have fixed as that of our intended return.

She had still not abandoned her hope of finding Henry some secure and profitable profession.

> *My* plan (to which Mr. Trollope makes no objection) is to remain here with Henry for about two years—by which time we think he will be settled in the establishment in which his father is now engaged in placing him.

Once the bazaar was operating successfully, she planned to travel with her girls, visiting "the eastern cities—seeing Niagara of course," and afterwards the continent: Paris and her "most ardent wish," Italy. She envisioned no immediate return to Harrow. In a rare and revealing moment, she confided a personal reason behind her extended plans:

> I will not deny that this scheme is the more agreeable to me because it promises me frequent intervals of tranquility [*sic*] in the absence of Mr. Trollope.—He is a good honourable man—but his temper is dreadful— every year increases his irritability—and also, its lamentable effect upon the children.[13]

A painful awareness of Mr. Trollope's psychological problems had partially prompted her trip to America; this new project also sprang from her reluctance to return to that strained family situation.

Mrs. Trollope's scheme was not as preposterous as some have implied. Much of the rhetoric with which subsequent travelers and commentators have embellished the bazaar has only obscured its original concept. One must go back to its prospectus, as set forth in the

Directory of the City of Cincinnati for the year 1829, to recover both its functions and the favorable sense with which the citizens looked forward to that "remarkable enterprise" at its inception.[14]

First, the prospectus commented on the exotic title, which "carries the imagination directly to Constantinople, so celebrated for Mosques, Minarets, Caravanseras, and Bazaars," clearly stipulating that only a "small proportion of its ample area is to be appropriated to its legitimate uses as a constant *mart*." Had she merely wished to sell goods, she might well have rented a little shop somewhere in the downtown district.[15] Her superstructure was a daring idea, far ahead of its time. She saw the bazaar as a cultural emporium, and since its primary function was to be "Henry's institution of fine arts," the very style of the architecture should be distinguished. The resulting edifice was certainly unusual. "Its freestone front exhibited a rich and beautiful specimen of arabesque style, combining the airy lightness of the Grecian with the sombrous gravity of the gothic tastes. . . . The rear of this unique and multifidous edifice, presents a noble facade of Egyptian Columns, which will vie in magnificence and novelty, with the Arabian windows that decorate its front. . . . The whole arrangement and architectural device of this superb building, reflects great credit upon the taste and skill of . . . the architect." To contemporaries in an age not distinguished for its attention to purity of style, the bazaar was an admirably designed building. To be sure, its style was eclectic and heavily influenced by Mrs. Trollope's own tastes. She had expressed admiration for the Egyptian art which she had seen in Paris and knew that buildings in that style were then in vogue in Europe. Contemporary prints of the bazaar reveal grace and tastefulness, contrasting with later descriptions by its detractors. Certainly, in mid-century Cincinnati it may well have been, as Mrs. Trollope claimed, "the chief lion of the city."[16]

Within the walls of this spacious structure, Mrs. Trollope planned to provide elegant rooms for eleven different activities, only the least of which was shopping. There was to be a coffee house, a bar room, and some basement apartments for general commercial business. Over the basement was the bazaar, "where it is presumable, every useful and useless article, in dress, in stationery, in light and ornamental household furniture, chinas, and more pellucid porcelains . . . from the sparkling necklace of 'Lady fair' to the Exquisite's *safety chain*, will be displayed and vended." The shops would be akin to today's museum shops, featuring exotic books, sculptures, cards, and jewelry. The structure itself was a predecessor of today's modern shopping malls, most of which feature elaborate eclectic architecture, fancy goods stores, art theaters, and, in general, space for elegant leisure, entertainment, and shopping. In the rear was an elegant saloon "where *Ices* and other refreshments, will lend their allurements to the fascinations of architectural novelty." While sipping their ices, citizens could walk out on to one of the several balconies that Mrs. Trollope thought one of the most distinctive features of her project. Indeed, she had placed her building precisely in such a spot, "on the very slope where the palisades of old Fort Washington used to stand . . . with balconies looking out toward the Kentucky hills . . . hard by the beautiful River."[17]

Beyond the balcony was an exhibition gallery for Hervieu's "superb picture of Lafayette's landing at Cincinnati." Here too the best that local painters could produce would be displayed. Above the bazaar was the "magnificent Ball Room, the front of which, looking upon the street, will receive the rays of the Sun, or emit the rival splendors of its gas-illuminated walls, by three ample arabesque windows, which give an unrivalled lightness and grace to the festive hall. The walls, and the arched and lofty ceiling of this delectable apartment are to be decorated by the powerful pencil of Mr. Hervieu." In the rear of the ball room was a separate orchestral gallery, suitable for the performance of musical entertainments, and behind it yet another saloon, issuing onto yet another balcony. There were rooms for private parties on this level, and atop the whole

a circular structure, of exceedingly light and beautiful proportions, which is intended for Panoramic exhibitions. . . . Around it is constructed, in concentric circle, an airy Corridor from whence the eye that has been already delighted to satiety, by the exhibitions of art, may recreate itself amid the varied beauties and blandishments of nature.

Surely it was something less than understatement for a recent commentator to describe Mrs. Trollope's project as "a boutique, to sell gew-gaws, bric-a-brac, and imitation jewelry to the benighted inhabitants of Cincinnati."[18]

But despite her thorough conception of the building, its functions, and its artistically executed exterior, the project was an immediate disaster. In part, it failed because Cincinnati had never really accepted Mrs. Trollope.[19] Given the chance to boycott her innovative idea, the citizens were secretly glad to find the means of expelling her from their midst. Still, the indomitable woman might even yet have succeeded had it not been for bad luck and miscalculation. Analyses of the bazaar's failure have emphasized its location, somewhat removed from the commercial district, and the poor quality of the marketed goods. Since the building was to serve primarily as an artistic and cultural center—for which the location selected was very good—its failure cannot be attributed to its distance from other buildings. Moreover, the evidence supports Mrs. Trollope's version of events, in which she placed the blame on her husband's misunderstanding of her original idea:

> When Mr. Trollope was with us, he agreed to advance 6000 dollars for the purpose of erecting a building in which Henry and Mr. Hervieu were to be engaged in partnership. . . . Mr. T. thought that to this plan he would add that of a *Bazaar*, the letting the stands of which, he calculated would be very profitable. It was objected that the people having never seen such a thing, would not be likely to take to it.—To this he replied that he would *teach them* what it was, by sending out things to fit out the room at first.— This frightened me, as I knew we none of us understood anything of buying and selling—but he was determined on making the experiment.—I then entreated him to limit his purchase to £150 and I made out a list of such articles as I thought would be easily disposed of, in some manner or other—he went to England engaging to send out the funds for the building—He did send 2000 dollars, and the building proceeded rapidly— and then (imagine my dismay) he sent out 4000 dollars worth of the most trumpery goods that probably ever were shipped.—Mr. C. Wilkes to whom they were consigned, assured him further that they never could sell for as much as the duties upon them amounted to.—Mr. Trollope wrote at the same time, to say that he had exerted himself extremely to procure those goods, and that he flattered himself they would sell well, and speedily, and *so enable me to pay for the completion of the building.*— Meanwhile *this* had been finished on *credit*, and the workmen were becoming clamorous for payment.—The sight of those dreadful and utterly unsalable [*sic*] goods, and the consciousness of the money to be paid, was *certainly* the cause of the fever which seized me a few days after their arrival.—I was eleven weeks in my room, and a great part of the time delirious.—Poor Henry was obliged to sell these things, or most of them at auction for what he could get, in order to pacify the workmen.—The bills came in, infinitely higher than we calculated upon—and after an ineffectual attempt to let the bazaar, *every thing* was seized by the creditors. . . .[20]

Mrs. Trollope too had contributed to this disaster. Her supervision of the building had been from the first faulty. Her decision to include such expensive novelties as gas-lighting and her naive trust in unscrupulous contractors helped to add to the financial stress. At the opening, the gas pipes emitted nothing but "an unpleasant smell" and some smoke. She was often overcharged, even for something as ordinary as bricks. "In fine," one Cincinnatian concluded, "she was a tempting subject, and things took their natural course"; she was "snuffed like carrion by every rogue within cheating distance." When she lay helplessly ill, the goods were disposed of, "some sold at fourth price, some *given away*, and some shipped for another market."[21] Construction debts, however, remained, and there was no hope of further help from England.

Next, the expected income from renting the halls and rooms for entertainments failed to materialize. Advertisements for the bazaar's events sounded a desperate note. One praised "the enterprising individuals who have spent so much money in our town in the erection of a splendid building" and urged that they "ought to be encouraged by receiving back from the citizens, some portion of it, and this we trust will be the case." When Hervieu advertised his painting of Lafayette's landing, again the announcements barely concealed pleas for patronage.

> [The painting] has been the labour of about 12 months and represents General Lafayette, with a large group of citizens who were present on that occasion. So far as we can judge, this painting is well executed, for which Mr. Hervieu deserves to be encouraged.

But in three short months these valiant efforts at recuperation had failed. Auguste Hervieu, who had scheduled a regular Thursday evening entertainment of "painting, poetry, and music" in the great room of the bazaar, had to admit his defeat in a public notice. "On Thursday evening last, half a dozen gentlemen from a steam boat, were all who presented themselves. He therefore respectfully withdraws the attempt."[22] Within six months from the date of its opening, the building itself was put into receivership, and even Mrs. Trollope's personal belongings were seized to pay the outstanding debts. The Trollope family in America was literally destitute. Indeed, "had not Hervieu's labour," she wrote later, "enabled him to furnish us with money to live upon—I know not how we should have escaped *starving* in that land of plenty."[23]

Frances Trollope's Cincinnati venture was in ruins. Creditors had seized the goods, yet bills still remained. The original owner of the land proposed a joint stock company to provide for the "considerable part of the money expended in erecting and fitting up the building [which was] yet due and owing to the workmen & others employed in or about the same." Thomas Anthony agreed to turn over the building to a group of trustees (himself and ten creditors) who would operate the bazaar, making a return to the investors whenever possible. Thus he at least escaped liability for the debts incurred. Since the building was worth a great deal of money (it was officially appraised at $7,000 in 1833) and Mr. Trollope's original investment was between $4,000 and $6,000, all was not yet lost, although he could not hope for any return from it for many years.[24]

For the time being, however, Mrs. Trollope was desperate. Recovering from her illness "very much thinner—and very much older," she had no money or means of support. She had to confess to her friends that her plans had been crushed.

> The building we have been erecting (which certainly is highly beautiful) has cost so much more than the Architect estimated, that years must pass before one cent of rent can return to us—if indeed the whole property be not swallowed up to pay what yet is due.

Then Henry, who during his mother's illness had tried to run the bazaar, suffered a serious relapse in health. Mrs. Trollope told her problems to Julia:

> No sooner was his physician dismissed and we thought him recovered, he fell ill again worse than ever—again we recovered him, and after about six weeks interval, he took the ague and fever so severely that he soon looked like a walking corpse. Every one said that his native air was all that was left to try for him.

She determined to get him back to England, but had no resources of her own:

> Guess what I must have suffered at finding that all the pecuniary efforts poor Trollope has been making to place him well, and permanently, at Cincinnati, were utterly thrown away! I only wonder that I have stood it as well as I have done.[25]

The final blow was news from England that Thomas Anthony's own financial state was so precarious that he did not have enough funds to bring them home or to return to America as he had planned. He told his wife that she must provide her own travel funds. With Hervieu's help, Mrs. Trollope somehow raised the money for Henry's return, "leaving myself and my dear girls with less than sufficient to pay what few bills I had in the town," and prepared to leave Cincinnati. When she thought of her prospects and those of Henry (who in a few short years would die of tuberculosis), she refused to admit the worst, forcing herself into her customary optimism: "I certainly must be composed of very elastic materials for spite of sickness, embarrassment and sorrow, I still am in good spirits and full of hope for the future."[26]

Although still "far from steady," Henry sailed alone for England, to restore his health and "apply with diligence to the law." Thomas Adolphus described his brother's extraordinary arrival on 19 April 1830, noting what a severe experience the trip had been for that "delicate lad of 18," who, "having suffered hardships and sickness in a foreign land,

and just arrived after a tedious voyage across the Atlantic Ocean in a sailing-ship," did not have enough money to complete his journey but had to walk the sixteen miles home from London, where the Liverpool coach had deposited him.[27] More grave was the plight of his mother, still in America, now relying for financial support solely upon Hervieu, "the well-tried friend." She would never forget his aid, unselfishly given at the lowest point in her fortunes. One day, as a famous author and traveler, she would take the staunch Hervieu with her as companion and illustrator. With him she shared the glory, prosperity, and comfort she had deservedly earned.

When Hervieu had exhausted the market for itinerant portrait painters in the immediate Ohio Valley area, he resolved to move to Washington. Anxious herself to shake the dust of Cincinnati from her heels, Mrs. Trollope accompanied him. She had suffered much in Cincinnati, and she would describe the city caustically in her book *The Domestic Manners of the Americans*. Ironically, her account put Cincinnati on the map. Captain Hamilton, who visited the city even as Mrs. Trollope's work was appearing, described with tongue in cheek the sudden and perhaps unwelcome celebrity which the "Queen City" owed to Mrs. Trollope:

> For nearly 30 years, Cincinnati had gradually been increasing in opulence, and enjoying a vulgar and obscure prosperity. Corn had grown, and hopes had fattened; men had built houses, and women borne children; but in all the higher senses of urbane existence, Cincinnati was a nonentity. It was "unknown, unhonored, and unsung." Ears polite had never heard of it. There was not the glimmering of a chance that it would be mentioned twice in a twelve-month. . . . But Mrs. Trollope came, and a zone of light has ever since encircled Cincinnati. Its inhabitants are no longer a race unknown to fame. Their manners, habits, virtues, tastes, vices and pursuits, are familiar to all the world; but, strange to say, the marketplace of Cincinnati is yet unadorned by the statue of the great benefactress of the city! Has gratitude utterly departed from the earth?[28]

With letters of introduction to the president and some members of Congress, Hervieu now hoped to make money by exhibiting his picture of Lafayette's landing and painting the portraits of Washington notables. Because Mrs. Trollope could not afford to live in Washington, she took lodging in Virginia at Stonington, home of "the oldest friend she had in the world," Anna Maria Stone, Julia's eldest sister. Mrs. Stone too had fallen on hard times and regretted the necessity of charging her old friend a weekly boarder's fee, which the ever-loyal Hervieu paid. She told Harriet of her new temporary residence.

With her [Mrs. Stone] I hope to remain until something can be arranged for our future plans. I fear that our means, crippled as they have been by the loss at Cincinnati, will not allow us to live *decently* in England until some return from the property there can help us to do so.[29]

The future was shrouded in uncertainty. She was waiting to hear whether her husband planned to come for them, or whether he would again commit them to Hervieu's care to convey them back to Europe. She knew they could not resume their former style of living. The yearly expenses of the boys at school ran very high. She talked of living economically with her girls either in Germany (whither she had been invited by her old friend Lady Dyer) or in France with the Garnetts. She preferred these plans to living "among the people who used to see us and in different circumstances." But a deep longing for home sometimes broke through this brave front. To Julia she wrote:

My heart swells with so much pleasure at the idea of returning to Europe that I can hardly remember that we have lost much money and that our affairs are embarrassed—God grant that my lot may place me where I may sometimes see you.[30]

As long ago as January 1829, the thought of writing had first crossed her mind, only to be forgotten among other projects more immediately related to financial survival. She had casually mentioned to Mary Russell Mitford the urge to put into writing some of her experience, but had disclaimed it.

O! my dear friend, had I but the tenth of an inch of the nib of your pen, what pictures might I draw of the people here!—so very queer, so very unlike any other thing in heaven above or earth below!—but it may not be. I can look, and I can laugh, but the power of describing is not given to above half a dozen in a century.

Still, she had kept notes of her Cincinnati adventures; her impressions had not vanished into the vague and irretrievable past. To some little notebooks, makeshift volumes for which during the first twenty-five months of her stay in America she seemed to have no specific purpose other than diversion and the unburdening of her own powerful feelings, she confided many of her reactions. Distracted by the dramatic events surrounding the failure of the bazaar, her notes lay forgotten until, shortly after leaving Cincinnati, she resolved upon a new project.[31]

Turning to her journals, Mrs. Trollope found that they contained an embryonic account of life in the western United States. Bolstered by this discovery, she resolved to write a book which she would call *The Domestic Manners of the Americans*. With the determination and enthusiasm which always accompanied her actions, she boldly proclaimed her new career:

> As soon as I had decided that Henry could not continue in Cincinnati, I determined to leave it myself, as soon as possible; it is in no respect an agreeable residence, and I have long ago written every thing about it that I think worth putting in *my book*.—And most rejoiced am I to have left it, for every thing I have seen since I began to climb the Alleghany mountains has delighted me—and to confess the truth it is the first time I have been delighted since I came to America.—The whole of the 90 miles that we travel over the mountain is one continued series of exquisite scenery—but I will not waste paper in description—besides I feel sure that you will read my book.[32]

The immediate catalyst in her literary inclination was probably the appearance of Captain Basil Hall's *Travels in North America*. First published in 1829, the book was a rather unfavorable description of his American tour, which reportedly had "put the Union in a blaze from one end to the other."[33]

Mrs. Trollope did not procure her own copy of Hall's book until late June 1830 when she made a trip to Philadelphia to hear Frances Wright lecture. While in the city, she even visited Hall's publisher to discuss the captain's method of composition. She recorded the meeting in her notebooks.

> Lea, the Philadelphian publisher, told me that Capt. Hall told him the method he pursued in the composition of his work on South America was as follows: He made copious minutes of all he saw—he brought home fifteen volumes of notes. He had them all written fair by a copier. He employed his brother and brother-in-law to read them, and to mark with a number every passage according to its value, then to select two volumes full, beginning with all the number ones and going on till they had got enough. He said these voyages had been written over five times.[34]

Mrs. Trollope apparently tried to incorporate some elements of this method into her own work; in her notebooks, she penciled general subject headings across passages concerning Cincinnati adventures, and wrote topical headings at the top of sections written after this Philadelphia visit.

Besides suggesting a technique of composition, Mrs. Trollope's reading of Hall gave her a focus, as well as an awareness of the potential value of her own scribblings. She now believed that a book about life as

she had seen it in America would not be repetitious. Indeed, she wrote
Miss Mitford of Captain Hall's lack of objectivity and her wider range of
experience.

> It appears that the 'agreeable captain' was under writing orders as surely as
> he ever was, or hopes to be again, under sailing orders. He would have
> done quite enough service to the cause he intends to support if he had
> painted things exactly as they are, without seeking to give his own eternal
> orange-tawny colour to every object. His blunders are such as clearly to
> prove he never, or very rarely, listened to the answers he received—for we
> must not suppose that he knew one thing and printed another. Do not
> suppose, however, that I am coming home fraught with the Quixotic
> intention of running a tilt with Captain Hall. My little book will not be of
> him, but of all I have seen, *and of much that he did not*.

Her book would be pervaded by a woman's spirit, for she believed that
the study of manners, "and the minutiae of which it is composed, suits
better the minute and lynx-like optics of the female. . . ."[35]

She began seriously to hope that she might earn money by writing a
book about America. Many critics, stressing the monetary motivation
behind *Domestic Manners*, have made it the decisive factor in determin-
ing the nature of the book. But the nature of her journal entries over the
past twenty-five months, and not the necessity of writing a best-seller,
determined the kind of book *Domestic Manners* would become, both
structurally and otherwise. Because her personal journals contained
vivid experiences and deep feelings, her book became chatty and
intimate in style and gossipy in manner. As she told her friend Miss
Mitford, she would not claim more: "My book is gossiping, and without
pretension, most faithfully true to the evidence of my senses, and written
without a shadow of [previous] feeling for or against the things described." She used first impressions, from which she sometimes reasoned
back from effects to causes, but her primary concerns were the minutiae
of everyday life and their effect on Frances Trollope and family.
Domestic Manners was an essentially personal account.[36]

The notebooks tell much of her attitudes toward the work as it
progressed and grew into a book proper. Mixed in with notes on
American habits ("If a distinguished man is at table, he is helped before
the ladies—") are entries of rent records ("April 24, 1830 board began at
Stonington 8/25 per week. . . .") and rough drafts of letters. Medicines
for dysentery ("Laudenum, and lavender, and spirits of hartshorn in
equal quantities—80 to 100 drops to an adult to children in proportion.
Shake the bottle well—") and a formula to prevent the spoilage of meat
alternate with notes that she eventually incorporated into the book,

almost verbatim. Not until well into the second notebook (there are
three in all, and the third is small in size) did the idea come to transform
the material into a book; midway, then, an elaborate outline shows Mrs.
Trollope organizing her material into chapters. The one subject she
wished to erase even from her own memory—Nashoba—does not
appear at all in the notebooks.

But on all else she was very frank. At one point in the second
notebook, after a description of Dorfeuille's pandemonium, she
scribbled a private emotion at the bottom of a page. "I am certain that no
one who has not experienced the suffering produced by American
spitting can imagine what it is. Not one moments's interval! Never can
the mind forget that the body is a nasty incumbrance." Organizationally,
the thought was out of place. But from the writing of it, no doubt, she
derived some solace.

After deciding to convert her notes into a book, she had still much to
do and suffer before a return to England could be effected. First came
the pressing need for further travel. If her book was to compete with
others of its kind, it must treat of more than just Cincinnati. Hervieu's
exhibitions of the Lafayette painting had not proved successful, but his
portrait commissions would enable them to see Niagara, without which
she feared her book "will seem very imperfect." While there, she met
another traveling Englishman, Captain Hamilton, who was also visiting
Niagara in preparation for a proposed book about America. He subsequently described Mrs. Trollope to his cousin as "a very eccentric
person."

> She was then travelling with her 2 daughters, merely girls, and a French-
> man. In what capacity the latter attended her, Hamilton could not make
> out, but from the odd appearance of matters, and her apparent poverty,
> which hardly admitted her and her daughters being decently dressed, it
> was conclusive against her being taken notice of by respectable ladies, or
> treated as one herself.[37]

Indeed, their poverty was so great that her girls were without shoes.
Their clothes were mended and remended, for they could afford to buy
nothing. "As to other articles of dress, we should any of us as soon think
of buying diamonds!" She herself needed nothing new: "I sit still and
write, write, write,—so old shoes last me a long time." Her thoughts now
focused on her book.

> Hope—that quits us the last, perhaps, of all our friends—tells me that it is
> *possible* my book may succeed. It will have great advantages from
> Hervieu's drawings. If it *should* succeed, a second book would bring

money. If I can but get home next spring, I feel as if I should still find the means of being happy and comfortable.[38]

In the autumn of 1830 the American fever "again knocked [her] up," and she was forced to leave the frame house at Stonington to seek a change of air at Alexandria, "a pretty town at the distance of about 15 miles, which had the reputation of possessing a skillful physician." A manuscript in hand, she was longing for home, but Mr. Trollope had declared,

> he had no more money to send—That he was ruined by the transaction which *we* had managed wretchedly—That he felt himslf under the greatest obligations to Hervieu, and that he should be glad to see us home, as soon as we could find the means of coming! . . . Mr. Trollope constantly continued to write very kindly, but always assuring us he had *no* money to send—With all the exertions Hervieu could make, he never could get enough before hand, to realize a sum sufficient to bring us home. I wrote to Mr. Trollope and told him that for my dear girls sake I was *determined* upon returning to England—and that if he was unable to furnish me with the means, I would apply to his family for them—This brought eighty pounds.[39]

Anticipating her homeward voyage with "feverish impatience," she sustained her spirits with thoughts of her book. She told Julia:

> I think you know I have *written a book*.—It will make Harriet angry—and perhaps you will shake your dear little head, but I have described things exactly as I have seen them and have only omitted what I thought it invidious, and ill natured to mention—never any thing, that could be admired and approved. Such as it is, however, it shall win its way to you; provided I and it, win ours in safety to London.

From Miss Mitford she begged assistance in getting it accepted by a publisher.

> You know, I believe, that I have looked and listened since I have been here with a view to publication, and you know also, dear friend—for how can you help it?—that I am as utterly unknown in the world of letters as your dog May was before you immortalized him. What I would ask is such a letter of introduction to your publisher as would enable me to present myself before him without feeling as if I had dropped upon him from the moon. . . .[40]

At last, combining a reluctant remittance from Mr. Trollope with the last of Hervieu's resources, they sailed for home, arriving at Woolwich on 5

August 1831; shortly thereafter she was reunited with her family at Harrow.

She found the situation far worse than the one she had sacrificed energy, reputation, and money to escape. Mr. Trollope's affairs were in total disarray, and even the letting of Julian Hill had proved inadequate. With heavy commitments to Lord Northwick, he had even failed to profit from Harrow Weald. In the summer of 1830, just after he had unwisely sunk the last remaining capital in the Cincinnati venture, the bottom dropped out of the hay market, and farmers throughout Middlesex and other farming communities went bankrupt. With his costly lease, Trollope suffered more than most, but the general picture was dismal.[41]

Because of his education and legal training, Thomas Anthony was approached by a number of Lord Northwick's tenants and asked to draft a petition begging for some reduction in rents because of the poor price situation. Hay had fallen to £2, 10s per load, while expenses remained the same. Moreover, since the poor rates "have been more than doubled within a few years," it "would indeed take four times the produce to pay them." He and the others were compelled, nevertheless, "to comply with the demands of [our laborers] to preserve our Stocks from the flames." Concluding the petition in rather impudently strong language, Trollope wondered that Northwick would "wish to continue to put large sums of money into [his] own pocket, which have never been the produce of [his] own prosperity, and which can only be raised, not only at the expense, but by occasioning the ultimate ruin of [his] tenants."[42]

Faced with this squeeze, by December Thomas Anthony found he could not pay the half-year's rent (which had fallen due in October), and Lord Northwick's agent issued a distress against him. Since so many of the tenants were in arrears, Lord Northwick eventually granted a 15 percent reduction in rents, but specifically excluded Trollope, whom his agents considered the instigator of the petition. On 28 December Trollope, ill in bed with another of his severe headache attacks, was served notice that if the full sum were not paid in five days, his crops and household goods would be seized and sold to pay the rent. Trollope complained of the injustice by which he was singled out for punishment, and while Lord Northwick admitted the charge, he refused to make any reduction. Eventually, Trollope paid off the rent in installments, but he never recovered from this blow. Thus, while Mrs. Trollope had been struggling to make ends meet in America, Mr. Trollope was really in no position to help her. Loss of his crops and property would have resulted in imprisonment and the complete destruction of the family's fortunes.[43]

Upon her return, Mrs. Trollope realized the true state of affairs. Ill and imbued with an irritability born of defeat, Mr. Trollope was now living at a miserable house on the Harrow Weald farm. He was even more morose than she had remembered. Although Tom was doing well at Oxford, his education could not long continue unless more money were found. Henry and Anthony were "perfectly without destination," equipped with Latin and Greek but unable to earn anything thereby.[44]

Despite this dismal homecoming, Mrs. Trollope set about preparing her manuscript for a publisher and trying to send the girls away from these reduced and unhealthy surroundings. She asked Julia to let Cecilia pay her a visit in Hanover. They had not even been home a month and already the straitened conditions of the farm were making life impossible. Her book was placed "in the hands of a publisher"; it was the one hope she had left. At fifty-two years of age, when she contemplated the future that lay dreary and forbidding before her, she could not stifle an exclamation of utter despair: "Here we are.—God knows what will become of us all!"[45]

In September 1831, Mrs. Trollope's manuscript of her American tour, received by the firm of Whittaker on the recommendation of Mary Russell Mitford, was being read by Captain Basil Hall, whom Mrs. Trollope thought "almost *too* good a judge of the subject." But his flattering remarks and strong recommendations gave Mrs. Trollope new self-confidence. Far from seeing her age and position in life a detriment to beginning a literary career, she realized the incalculable value of her experiences. When she heard that a girl of nineteen had just published "*a very fine tragedy*" she was understandably scornful and incredulous. "To me this appears like a joke—a girl of 19 write a fine tragedy! Do you believe this possible? I do not."[46]

In the difficult days that lay ahead, while waiting for the publication of the book, Mrs. Trollope's family and friends were loyal and supportive. It has been said that a woman, in order to write fiction, must have "money and a room of her own." The first was a commodity impossible for anyone but Mrs. Trollope herself to provide; the latter was the single quantity which her family could contribute. In the Harrow Weald Farm, a room was set aside for Mrs. Trollope's special use, and her children— with a mixture of fun and devotion—christened it "The Sacred Den of Harrow." Mr. Whittaker offered Mrs. Trollope half the profits of a first printing of 1,250 copies. If that sold, she would earn some £270 "which in these bad times would be an important sum to us." She realized that such arrangements were less than perfect, but knew "this is as favourable an offer as a person so utterly unknown can expect."[47]

Indeed, her hope of earning money by this book was foremost in her mind during these days as she frankly acknowledged to Julia.

If the delays of the law are tormenting, those of booksellers are at least equally so.—Capt. Basil Hall to whom my little volumes were sent for *judgement*, has been most kind and serviceable to me, and by his means the thing is now *en route*—I remember the time dearest, when if I had made such an attempt my only thought would have been "what will be said of it?" but now Alas! my only anxiety is, what will be paid for it?— This same poverty has a mighty lowering effect upon ones sublimities.[48]

Even if her book were successful, further effort would be necessary; Mrs. Trollope had already almost completed a second manuscript and was contemplating a third. In an atmosphere of financial urgency, she reused her American experiences to fashion a novel of American life which she first thought of calling "The American Exile," but subsequently released as *The Refugee in America*. By February of 1832, in a feat of sheer doggedness she had completed the first volume. Once, while passing two days with a Harrow friend, she was surprised to find that others "hoped I should be *ready* with something else. Now, as I have never mentioned this intention . . . I was well pleased to find it had occurred to them as the natural and proper result of the encouragement I have received." She hoped also to begin another travel book, and told Julia.

If my book should take, and *if* it should be favorably reviewed in the quarterly (The *Edinburgh*, if it does any thing, must abuse it) I should offer the publisher to travel into Germany—to visit the watering places etc. and to write a volume of gossip of all I should see—Hervieu, whose 24 beautiful lithographs will be the best recommendation of my present experiment would give the modes, manners, and features.[49]

Already, she manifested the indefatigable energy that would make her the second most prolific novelist of her generation.

There was always something of the incipient wanderer in Mrs. Trollope. Even at the time of her worst troubles in America, she had written:

For myself I can truly say, that I had much rather have seen all I have, and all I still hope to do . . . notwithstanding all contretemps, than to have remained in Harrow.

No sooner settled again at home than she thought again of traveling. Indeed, much of her life would reveal an innate restlessness. Even though extensive journeying seemed at this point "only moonshine," still, she told herself, "when one is rather in the dark . . . even such borrowed light is worth something."[50]

Her letters during the winter of 1831–1832 reveal family difficulties and preoccupations with the unsettled political scene. When she looked to the great world, she saw "the agitation of the times, with the Bristol and Manchester riots" and the madness surrounding the first submission of the Reform Bill of 1832. The cholera was at Edinburgh, "but not violent as yet." When Hervieu fell ill with a complaint fearfully resembling that disease, it was Mrs. Trollope who nursed him. Indeed, Harrow Weald farm seemed a microcosm of the troubles of the world. There were violent scenes between Mr. Trollope and the children, making his wife "so shaken and agitated as to be obliged sometimes to have recourse to a dose of laudanum to procure a night's rest!" When Mr. Trollope buried himself in antiquarian research, Frances was relieved that he had found "an occupation" to distract him from present worries. His application for a London magistracy, however, was unsuccessful. Mrs. Trollope stolidly accepted still another defeat: "I shall not be disappointed." Even Hervieu, who had brought them through their trying days in America, began to succumb to despair. He told Tom, "your poor Mamma has been floating about from incertitude to incertitude, cholera morbus and revolution spread their wings over everything we meet,—yes, we must all go to the devil at last! That is my firm opinion."[51]

Then, on 19 March 1832, nine days after Mrs. Trollope's fifty-third birthday, *The Domestic Manners of the Americans* appeared. She told Julia triumphantly, "The book is out, is highly praised in the *Quarterly*, and the sale is going on well."[52]

5

Good Yankee Stories: *Domestic Manners of the Americans* and *The Refugee*

*She saw many things which no refined English-
woman would have seen, or seeing would have
understood—still less have written and published.*

MRS. TROLLOPE'S account of America was an instant success, an unexpect-ed best-seller that quickly exhausted its first edition and subsequently ran through many printings, translations, and pirated editions. It is still one of the most readable accounts of the English pilgrimage to the new world, with a popular appeal and more enduring excellences that made it the most famous travel book of the century.

Domestic Manners is a chronologically arranged account of Mrs. Trollope's stay of almost four years in the United States. In her first preface (which she subsequently discarded) she was careful to stipulate that she did not pretend to give complete information on America:

> I greatly doubt if my book contains much valuable instruction; nay I
> should not be much surprised if it were called trifling; for to tell the honest
> truth I suspect that it is . . . gossiping. But I have seen and heard so many
> queer things that wiser people may have never seen nor heard that without
> intending to tell one quarter of it I still may find enough respectable to fill
> 500 pages. . . . There is, in fact, so much in America that English ladies
> and gentlemen know nothing about; the people are so strangely like, and
> so strangely unlike us; the connection with us is so close, yet the disunion so
> entire; speaking the same language, yet having hardly a feeling in com-
> mon, that I am clearly of opinion there is still much untold that is worth
> telling.

> I really do not believe that I have any particular talent to qualify me for the
> undertaking, but nobody seems to choose to visit America who has. As to
> Capt. Hall, he is altogether too wise for the sort of business I have
> undertaken. . . . How is a man whose thoughts are fixed on the philo-
> sophy of government to find time for such tiny observations as my notes
> are filled with? And yet the world is made up of atoms, and though I may

dole them out one by one, they are still part and parcel of the great machine we are all so fond of examining.[1]

She held fast to this resolve; *Domestic Manners* contains little of a deep, philosophical nature about American society. What it does offer is countless particulars—scenes, events, characters, conversations. She recorded everything: the rude, suspicious landlords, the hogs implacably clearing the streets of refuse, the professedly "literary" evenings. The lasting appeal of her work lies in this brilliant selection of detail and its transformation into representative and amusing vignettes of nineteenth-century American life.

The anecdote was the building-block of her style, one intimately related to her penchant for keeping notebooks, jotting down scenes, and recording conversations. In the first half of the book, she included brief narratives of her everyday life in Cincinnati. Hervieu's sketches faithfully followed her conception; his illustrations were vivid caricatures of American traits and not the conventional city or scenic views. The anecdotal technique was right for Frances Trollope. She had certain natural abilities essential to good storytelling and could catch both the absurdities and the essentials of scenes and characters. She was interested in people and able to describe them with that exaggerated outline that made them at once colorfully individual and broadly representative. She had a skilled ear for the accents, inflections, and vagaries of vocabulary and phraseology, and from her notebook collection of "American Phrases," she included in her book several samples of "Yankee talk" (pp. 112–14, 371–72). Her Cincinnati critic Timothy Flint was later to recall her as a "most accomplished mimic."[2] She was aware of her ability to reproduce language and later advised her son Tom against publishing a volume on Germany because "your not speaking the language . . . would rob you of that sort of racy originality which the remarks, and even the phrases of the people among whom you travel, can *alone* give to such a work."[3]

Although she frequently insisted upon her documentary accuracy— "whenever I give conversations they were not made *à loisir*, but were written down immediately after they occurred, with all the verbal fidelity my memory permitted" (p. 53)—all her dialogues are included at strategic points and carefully support her themes.

When the Englishwoman declined to lend a servant an article of dress, the girl's reply, first recorded in the notebook, became a study of the national paranoia.

Well, I never seed such grumpy folks as you be; there is several young ladies of my acquaintance what goes to live out now and then with the old women about the town, and they and their gurls always lends them what they asks for; I guess you Inglish thinks we should poison your things, just as bad as if we was Negurs. [p. 53]

Similarly, when she wanted to describe polite and literary society in Cincinnati, Mrs. Trollope reproduced her conversation with a "serious old gentleman" about the great men of English literature. As he spoke scornfully, waving a pocket handkerchief to punctuate his outrageous critical judgments, Mrs. Trollope thought his gesture worthy of "Paul to the offending Jews," its unspoken meaning: "I am clean." She presented his views dramatically. He considered Pope "entirely gone by"; to her mention of "The Rape of the Lock" he muttered with an indignant shake of the handkerchief, "The very title!" Shakespeare was "obscene," Gray "has had his day," and Chaucer and Spenser were "no longer intelligible." Mrs. Trollope concluded with the understated point of the anecdote: "This was the most literary conversation I was ever present at in Cincinnati" (pp. 91–93).

Mrs. Trollope was more than just a good storyteller. She reproduced incidents not primarily because they were entertaining but rather because they were, in her view, representative of American life. Frequently, she reasoned from particulars to large conclusions, making close observations of Cincinnati a microcosm of life in western America. A forest farm became "a specimen of backwoods independence." The rapid rise in a woodcutter's career and the proud discontent of domestic servants illustrated conflicting aspects of an egalitarian society (pp. 120–21, 52 ff.).

The generalizations which inevitably follow her anecdotes have unusual force, for she paid great attention to the smallest details. She rarely attempted the panoramic view; her focus was sharpest at close range. When she visited a revival meeting, her description began with a cursory view of the entire congregation and meeting-place. Next she concentrated on the two most important characters, depicting the preachers, one with perspiring, foam-covered lips, the other adept at the hypnotic style:

Come then! . . . come to us, and tell us so, and we will make you see Jesus, the dear gentle Jesus, who shall save you from [hell]. But you must come to him! You must not be ashamed to come to him! This night you shall tell him that you are not ashamed of him; we will make way for you; we will clear the bench for anxious sinners to sit upon. Come, then! come to the anxious bench, and we will show you Jesus! Come! Come! Come! [p. 79]

Finally, she concentrated on a single young girl, who in response to the preacher's entreaties, moved up.

Her face was pale as death; her eyes wide open, and perfectly devoid of
meaning; her chin and bosom wet with slaver; she had every appearance
of idiotism. I saw a priest approach her, he took her delicate hand, "Jesus is
with her! Bless the Lord!" he said and passed on. [p. 80]

The progression from an overall to an almost myopically close view is
characteristic of *Domestic Manners*. The particulars of the scene are so
well delineated that the reader treats the subsequent generalizations
with respect.

The broad conclusions are also forceful because Mrs. Trollope wore
the cloak of authority well. Although she shunned ideology or politics,
she claimed to be an expert in her chosen field—the minutiae of
American domestic life. Here she dogmatically made numerous judgments, from the merits of peaches to the physical "violence" of hand-
shaking. And when she and her family finally left the city, she paused for
a last time to emphasize her complete knowledge:

We quitted Cincinnati the beginning of March 1830. . . . We had seen
again and again all the queer varieties of its little world; had amused
ourselves with its consequence, its taste, and its ton, till they had ceased to
be amusing. Not a hill was left unclimbed, nor a forest path unexplored. . . . [p. 181]

Time and again she stressed the length and quality of her personal
observation. Today her accuracy is generally conceded, and even Mark
Twain appreciated the expertise of "Dame Trollope," dubbing her work
"photography."

She lived three years in this civilization of ours; in the body of it—not on
the surface of it, as was the case with most of the foreign tourists of her
day. She knew her subject well, and she set it forth fairly and squarely,
without any weak ifs and ands and buts.[4]

Knowing that Americans had reacted violently to the mildly critical
statements of Captain Hall and other travelers, Mrs. Trollope anticipated such objections and claimed eyewitness familiarity to buttress her
remarks, so much more astringent than those of previous visitors.

'That is because you know so little of America,' is a phrase I have listened
to a thousand times, and in nearly as many different places. *It may be so*—
and having made this concession, I protest against the charge of injustice in
relating what I have seen. [p. 16]

She was always careful to specify any bit of information or story that came from hearsay evidence. The line of demarcation was clearly drawn.

Yet Mrs. Trollope's book is not all of a piece. What has been said so far applies primarily to the Cincinnati section (to p. 181). *Domestic Manners* is really two books, with two distinct kinds of style and material. When she headed East, Mrs. Trollope became an ordinary traveler. She maintained her sharp eye for observation, her ability for characterization, and her ear for reproducing speech patterns, but she no longer had any special knowledge about what she saw. Nor did she continue to see the same things. The change in her material is at once apparent. In the Cincinnati section, she recorded the problems of getting domestic help and buying eggs. In Baltimore, she reported impressions of national monuments, the Catholic Cathedral, St. Mary's College, and an infant school. In the Cincinnati section she described dinner parties, table manners, and the visits of inquisitive neighbors. In Philadelphia, she recorded her impressions of the United States Bank, Washington Square, and the Pennsylvania Academy of the Fine Arts. In Washington, she visited the Patent Office, the office of the secretary of state, and the Bureau of Indian Affairs. Like other travelers, she attended a debate in the House of Representatives and visited the Senate chamber. Instead of the intimate revelations of the well-informed English homemaker and businesswoman in painful confrontations with American egalitarian society, the book becomes a conventional account, dedicated to the inspection and description of famous scenes. The lively stories and casual style disappear, replaced by more formal information transmitted in a stilted and unnatural manner.

Now the conscious author, Mrs. Trollope journeyed to Niagara to include the appropriately "sublime" passage on that American marvel: "It has to me something beyond its vastness; there is a shadowy mystery hangs about it which neither the eye nor even the imagination can penetrate . . ." (p. 381). Instead of caustic accounts of the palpable truths of American life, her superficial eastern tour produced mainly poetic and sentimental raptures: "We seemed to enter the harbour of New York upon waves of liquid gold, and as we darted past the green isles which rise from its bosom, like guardian sentinels of the fair city, the setting sun stretched his horizontal beams farther and farther at each moment, as if to point out to us some new glory in the landscape" (p. 336). She traveled to West Point, through the Mohawk Valley, and through the Erie and Morris canals. Her book became a compilation of facts, figures, exclamations of delight and awe, and overwrought "pretty" descriptions of nature:

The magnificent rhododendron first caught our eyes; it fringes every cliff, nestles beneath every rock, and blooms around every tree. The azalia, the shumac, and every variety of that beautiful mischief, the kalmia, are in equal profusion. . . . Oak and beech, with innumerable roses and wild vines, hanging in beautiful confusion among their branches, were in many places scattered among the evergreens. The earth was carpeted with various mosses and creeping plants, and though still in the month of March, not a trace of the nakedness of winter could be seen. [p. 195]

This section is redeemed only by accounts of stopovers at the inns, when Mrs. Trollope coped with the old problems of Cincinnati days. Her surest and best artistic stimulants seem to have been physical discomfort and annoyance. When she was pleased with scenery, with American flora and fauna, her work was lifeless and artificial; rose-covered cottages were not her best material. But at the inns, when she bristled at hardship and rudeness, at boastful Americans who liked to spit, at the ever-present odors of tobacco and whiskey, at brash servant girls who muttered about the difficulty of "fixing English folks," the scenes rallied once again into life.

Only the pages describing her experiences in Virginia (pp. 236–57) compare favorably with those on Cincinnati, because Mrs. Trollope lived for several months with her old friend Mrs. Stone and thus came to know well the people of the area. There she had her first unpleasant encounter with the institution 'of slavery. She made no general remarks on the subject, but, characteristically, related an anecdote concerning a little slave girl who, because of a young white's negligence, had mistakenly eaten arsenic. While others stood back aghast, watching the girl suffer, Mrs. Trollope went to help, even while she noted a bystander's casual exclamation which, better than any abstract discussion, epitomized nineteenth-century southern attitudes: "My! If Mrs. Trollope has not taken her in her lap and wiped her nasty mouth! Why I would not have touched her mouth for two-hundred dollars!" (p. 248). Here in Virginia, she again had time to visit, talk, record speech and incident, and see her experiences as symbolic of the deeper dynamics of human society.

The later sections of *Domestic Manners* contain her most extraordinary exaggerations.[5] "I never saw an American man walk or stand well; not withstanding their frequent militia drillings, they are nearly all hollow chested and round shouldered" (p. 301). The amount of hearsay evidence increased. She reported that an Englishman, long resident in America, "had never overheard Americans conversing without the word DOLLAR being pronounced between them" (p. 301). She said that theaters were unpopular because Americans were "totally divested of gaiety; there is no trace of this feeling from one end of the Union to the other. They have no fêtes, no fairs, no merry-makings, no music in the streets, no Punch, no puppet-shows" (p. 209). Her statements become so extreme as to lose the air of documentary accuracy pervading the earlier part of the book. Lacking the colorful material of personal experiences, she had recourse to an anthology of American literature (pp. 317 ff.) and an American annual (pp. 321–26); she even published the prospectus of a boarding school (p. 341). Indeed, had the entire book resembled the travel section in style and matter, *Domestic Manners* would have remained just another journal of nineteenth-century travel, outdated, unread, and forgotten.

Mrs. Trollope's book contained, however, a controversial theme which unified its diverse parts. Believing the spirit of a nation could be deciphered in the details of its daily living, she was the first to make "domestic manners" the significant subject of a book. Puzzling over her experiences, she decided that the quality of American life had been determined not by political arrangements but by the relationship between the sexes. She discovered a fact which has been only recently recognized: the status of women in any society shapes as well as reflects the essence of that society's values and institutions. Relentlessly documenting what she called "the lamentable insignificance of the American woman" (p. 285), her book proclaimed a daring solution: "the American people will not equal the nations of Europe in refinement till women become of more importance among them."[6]

She originally became aware of this subject through Frances Wright's earlier glowing descriptions of the high place accorded women in America:

> It strikes me that it would be impossible for women to stand in higher estimation than they do here. The deference that is paid to them at all times and in all places has often occasioned me as much surprise as pleasure.[7]

Such sentiments were bound to appeal to a woman who customarily moved freely among men as an equal. But Nashoba and Cincinnati had shown Frances Trollope the real truth. In her book, she exposed the protectiveness of the American male, claiming that "women are guarded by a seven-fold shield of habitual insignificance" (pp. 47–48), relegated to a position of inferiority in education, and lacking influence in political, public, and economic areas. American ladies even seemed to lack "any command of ready money." A surprised Mrs. Trollope noted: "I have been a hundred times present when bills for a few dollars, perhaps for one, have been brought for payment to ladies living in perfectly easy circumstances, who have declared themselves without money, and referred the claimant to their husbands for payment" (p. 305).

At the heart of her analysis lay her observation that in America the sexes were inflexibly separated, the men working in their businesses during the day, the women remaining at home to care for families. Surprisingly, these arrangements persisted even in their amusements, interests, and leisure hours. Basil Hall too had commented on this interesting phenomenon. At a Charlestown ball

> the ladies were planted firmly along the walls, in the coldest possible formality, while the gentlemen, who, except during the dance, stood in close column near the door, seemed to have no fellow-feeling, nor any wish to associate with the opposite sex. In the ordinary business of their lives—I mean their busy, moneymaking, electioneering lives—the Americans have little or no time for companionship, that I could ever see or hear of, with the women, still less for any habitual confidential intercourse.[8]

Mrs. Hall, too, remarked in private letters to her sister: "There appears to be no sort of sympathy between the sexes. They have no subjects of conversation in common and at a dinner table, for instance, instead of sitting alternately even if there be but three or four of them to a dozen gentlemen, all get together." But the Halls never questioned the effect of these conditions beyond their own annoyance: American society was "a very great bore."[9] It remained for Mrs. Trollope to describe the situation and analyze its debilitating effects.

She traced the cause to male preference, not economic necessity. Throughout her book, Mrs. Trollope documented a hostility to women lying under the surface of American life. In one way or another, all her famous subjects—spitting, the servant problem, revivals and camp meetings, indecent postures at the theater, boarding-house existences, the rough egalitarianism of Americans, the lack of gaiety—although somewhat ramblingly treated, had a relationship to this large central issue. She refused to consider exaggerated courtesy as a substitute for participation in active community life and was somewhat at a loss to know why women tolerated such exclusion, which, she knew, was not part of any cosmological order but a cultural decision by those in power.[10]

In her view, those arrangements limited the potential social development of both sexes. Without a coming-together for enrichment, communication, and sharing of experiences, there could be no society worthy of the name. In one scene (which most critics have regarded as merely an attack on the American habit of spitting), Mrs. Trollope pointed out the stultifying effect of such separation.

> Whatever may be the talents of the persons who meet together in society, the very shape, form, and arrangement of the meeting is sufficient to paralyze conversation. The women invariably herd together at one part of the room, and the men at the other; but, in justice to Cincinnati, I must acknowledge that this arrangement is by no means peculiar to that city, or the western side of the Alleghanies. . . .
>
> The gentlemen spit, talk of elections and the price of produce, and spit again. The ladies look at each other's dresses till they know every pin by heart; talk of Parson Somebody's last sermon on the day of judgment, on Dr. T'otherbody's new pills for dyspepsia, till the "tea" is announced, when they all console themselves together for whatever they may have suffered in keeping awake, by taking more tea, coffee, hot cake and custard, hoe cake, johnny cake, waffle cake, and dodger cake, pickled peaches, and preserved cucumbers, ham, turkey, hung beef, apple sauce, and pickled oysters than ever were prepared in any other country of the known world. After this massive meal is over, they return to the drawing-room, and it always appeared to me that they remained together as long as they could bear it, and then they rise *en masse*, cloak, bonnet, shawl, and exit. [p. 58]

The heavy meal, described with Dickensian gusto, stood for her judgment on the atrophy of American society. And, while she sometimes attributed coarse manners and ungentle private habits to political equality, her book mainly emphasized another cause: the exclusion of women from the mainstream of American life:[11]

> I am led to mention this feature of American manners very frequently, not only because it constantly recurs, but because I consider it as being in a great degree the cause of that universal deficiency in good manners and graceful demeanour, both in men and women, which is so remarkable. [p. 156]

Because "all the enjoyments of the men are found in the absence of the women," the ladies had naturally withdrawn to the domestic sphere, leaving society in the hands of men who dine, play cards, have musical meetings, suppers, and large parties,

> but all without women. Were it not that such is the custom, it is impossible but that they would have ingenuity enough to find some expedient for sparing the wives and daughters of the opulent the sordid offices of household drudgery which they almost all perform in their families. Even

in the slave states, though they may not clear-starch and iron, mix puddings and cakes one half of the day, and watch them baking the other half, still the very highest occupy themselves in their household concerns, in a manner that precludes the possibility of their becoming elegant and enlightened companions. [p. 156]

Here were subversive words. Most writers of the time on female conduct insisted on female domesticity. "Her heart must be at home. She must not be on the look-out for excitement of any kind, but must find her pleasure as well as her occupation in the sphere which is assigned to her. St Paul knew what was best for woman when he advised her to be domestic. He knew that home was the safest place, home her appropriate station."[12] Mrs. Trollope rejected this limiting concept. She cared about women who had to run households, bear children, and still find time and energy to become fully developed human beings. Aware that some special societal arrangements were necessary if American women were to emerge from their domestic incarceration, she could only recommend the use of servants. Critics have misread her many scenes showing the difficulty of getting and holding reliable servants in America and failed to appreciate the reasoning behind her complaints:

Such being the difficulties respecting domestic arrangements, it is obvious, that the ladies who are brought up amongst them cannot have leisure for any great development of the mind; it is, in fact, out of the question; and, remembering this, it is more surprising that some among them should be very pleasing, than that none should be highly instructed. [pp. 57–58]

As she observed the relegation of women to the domestic sphere, she noted the effects on the lower-class laboring poor, the middle-class shopkeeper, and the prosperous professional class. For the American cottager's wife, domestic drudgery took the form of hard physical labor:

The life she leads is one of hardship, privation, and labour. It is rare to see a woman in this station who has reached the age of 30, without losing every trace of youth and beauty. You continually see women with infants on their knee, that you feel sure are their grandchildren. . . . Even the young girls, though often with lovely features, look pale, thin, and haggard. [pp. 117–18]

Such women paid a terrible price in helping their husbands achieve the much-vaunted "rugged independence" of Americans. While appreciating their indomitable strength, Mrs. Trollope underlined the personal waste inherent in lives of such unremitting toil. Still, these women at least "seemed content," for they knew they were useful and necessary members of the family. When she turned to the middle-class woman, Mrs. Trollope found more serious problems.

Freed from the exigencies of physical labor but excluded from assisting their husbands in the business or public world, these ladies led boring and useless lives. Many settled into a "boarding-house existence." While men could "hurry to their occupations," women had nothing better to do than "clear-starch a little, and iron a little, and sit in a rocking-chair, and sew a great deal." The permissible female activity of this class was elaborate needlework. Mrs. Trollope "always observed that the ladies who boarded wore more elaborately worked collars and petticoats than any one else. The plough is hardly a more blessed instrument in American than the needle. How could they live without it?" (pp. 284 ff.). She condemned this life style because it seemed an effectual contrivance "for ensuring the insignificance of a woman." She could not imagine

> a life of more uniform dulness for the lady herself; but this is certainly a matter of taste. I have heard many ladies declare that it is "just quite the perfection of comfort to have not a thing to fix for oneself." Yet despite these assurances I always experienced a feeling which hovered between pity and contempt, when I contemplated their mode of existence. [p. 283][13]

She followed this description with the kind of generalization which was so provoking to her nineteenth-century critics: "It is not thus that the women can obtain that influence in society which is allowed to them in Europe, and to which both sages and men of the world have agreed in ascribing such salutary effects" (p. 285).

In the evenings, when the separation of the sexes should have ended, Mrs. Trollope saw the couples go out to walk ("after a silent meal"), and again they separated by mutual consent. They walked together

> as far as the corner of the street, where his store, or his office is situated, and there he will leave her to turn which way she likes. As this is the hour for being full dressed, of course she turns the way she can be most seen. Perhaps she pays a few visits; perhaps she goes to chapel; or, perhaps, she enters some store where her husband deals, and ventures to order a few nothings, and then she goes home again. . . . The gentlemen were generally obliged to go out every evening on business, and, I confess, the arrangement did not surprise me. [pp. 285–86]

Unlike many, Mrs. Trollope remained undeceived by America's impressive educational institutions for young ladies, with their long lists of curricula. "A quarter's mathematics, or two quarters political economy, moral philosophy, algebra, and quadratic equations," will not, she wrote, enable the female scholar "to lay in such a stock of these sciences as would stand the wear and tear of half a score of children and one help." When the social structure did not support woman's development, a fancy and abstract education was not enough:

> It is in vain that "collegiate institutes" are formed for young ladies, or that "academic degrees" are conferred upon them. It is after marriage, and when these young attempts upon all the sciences are forgotten, that the lamentable insignificance of the American woman appears. [p. 285]

Finally, in a devastating rendition of "a day in the life of a Philadelphia Lady," Mrs. Trollope illustrated the effects of enforced domesticity upon the life of upper-class ladies who in Europe would have exercised considerable influence upon society and manners. The picture here was different.

> This lady shall be the wife of a senator and a lawyer in the highest repute and practice. She has a very handsome house, with white marble steps and door-posts, and a delicate silver knocker and doorhandle; she has very handsome drawing-rooms, very handsomely furnished, (there is a sideboard in one of them, but it is very handsome, and has very handsome decanters and cut glass water-jugs upon it); she has a very handsome carriage, and a very handsome free black coachman; she is always very handsomely dressed; and, moreover, she is very handsome herself.
>
> She rises, and her first hour is spent in the scrupulously nice arrangement of her dress; she descends to her parlour neat, stiff, and silent; her breakfast is brought in by her free black footman; she eats her fried ham and her salt fish, and drinks her coffee in silence, while her husband reads one newspaper, and puts another under his elbow; and then, perhaps, she washes the cups and saucers. Her carriage is ordered at eleven; till that hour she is employed in the pastry-room, her snow-white apron protecting her mouse-coloured silk. Twenty minutes before her carriage should appear, she retires to her chamber, as she calls it, shakes, and folds up her still snow-white apron, smooths her rich dress, and with nice care, sets on her elegant bonnet, and all the handsome *et caetera*; then walks downstairs, just at the moment that her free black coachman announces to her free black footman that the carriage waits. She steps into it, and gives the word, "Drive to the Dorcas society." Her footman stays at home to clean the knives, but her coachman can trust his horses while he opens the carriage door, and his lady not being accustomed to a hand or an arm, gets out very safely without, though one of her own is occupied by a work-basket, and the other by a large roll of all those indescribable matters which ladies take as offerings to Dorcas societies. She enters the parlour appropriated for the meeting, and finds seven other ladies, very like herself, and takes her place among them; she presents her contribution,

which is accepted with a gentle circular smile, and her parings of broad cloth, her ends of ribbon, her gilt paper, and her minikin pins, are added to the parings of broad cloth, the ends of ribbon, the gilt paper, and the minikin pins with which the table is already covered; she also produces from her basket three ready-made pincushions, four ink-wipers, seven paper-matches, and a paste-board watch-case; these are welcomed with acclamations, and the youngest lady present deposits them carefully on shelves, amid a prodigious quantity of similar articles. She then produces her thimble, and asks for work; it is presented to her, and the eight ladies all stitch together for some hours. Their talk is of priests and of missions; of the profits of their last sale, of their hopes from the next; of the doubt whether young Mr. This, or young Mr. That should receive the fruits of it to fit him out for Liberia; of the very ugly bonnet seen at church on Sabbath morning, of the very handsome preacher who performed on Sabbath afternoon, and of the very large collection made on Sabbath evening. This lasts till three, when the carriage again appears, and the lady and her basket return home; she mounts to her chamber, carefully sets aside her bonnet and its appurtenances, puts on her scolloped black silk apron, walks into the kitchen to see that all is right, then into the parlour, where, having cast a careful glance over the table prepared for dinner, she sits down, work in hand, to await her spouse. He comes, shakes hands with her, spits, and dines. The conversation is not much, and ten minutes suffices for the dinner; fruit and toddy, the newspaper and the work-bag succeed. In the evening the gentleman, being a savant, goes to the Wister society, and afterwards plays a snug rubber at a neighour's. The lady receives at tea a young missionary and three members of the Dorcas society.—And so ends her day. [pp. 280–82]

Beneath the bright and tranquil exterior of this life were submerged elements that Mrs. Trollope emphasized with images of restriction, uselessness, uniformity, limited interests, boredom, and lack of communication. At day's end, when both parties by silent agreement fled each other's company for more congenial atmospheres, one recognizes a situation that still troubles American society and limits the quality of its life. Mrs. Trollope's nineteenth-century America, with its polite facades and denied lives, calls to mind T. S. Eliot's twentieth-century English wasteland, where the relationship between the sexes, while having come physically closer, has remained mechanical. Mrs. Trollope foresaw the deep troubles accompanying even material prosperity should this problem not be resolved.[14]

Since men monopolized the political and economic spheres in America, and restricted even the domestic activities of ladies, the latter's sole outlet was religion. Elizabeth Sandford, in her *Woman in Her Social and Domestic Character* (1831), saw religion as a great tranquilizer for women's undefined longings: "Religion is just what woman needs. Without it she is ever restless or unhappy, ever wishing to be relieved from duty or from time." Most important, "the domesticating tendency of religion . . . especially, preposseses men in its favor" (pp. 35, 41, 43). A clergyman's daughter, Mrs. Trollope rejected the idea that religion was merely a female opiate. Exposed in America to a new kind of evangelical hysteria—a variety of religious enthusiasm she had already confronted in Harrow—she was struck at once by an obvious connection. Female absorption in these religious activities was primarily an escape from emotionally sterile lives. Nothing in her own past had prepared her for this phenomenon, and she was as shocked as her critics by the sexual undertones present in the camp meetings and revivals of America. The language of *Domestic Manners* frankly implied this sexual substitution. Watching the "prostrate penitents" receive "whispered comfortings," coaxings, and "from time to time a mystic caress," Mrs. Trollope included the indelicate particulars. "More than once I saw a young neck encircled by a reverend arm. Violent hysterics and convulsions seized many of them." Without being sensational, she emphasized the dangerous effects upon society when women "in the gay morning of existence" were thus seized upon, "horror struck, and rendered feeble and enervated for ever" (pp. 77 ff.). Mrs. Trollope's explanation for the appeal of this brand of religious fanaticism was a social one:

> I think that it is from the clergy only that the women of America receive that sort of attention which is so dearly valued by every female heart throughout the world. With the priests of America, the women hold that degree of influential importance which, in the countries of Europe, is allowed them throughout all orders and ranks of society, except, perhaps, the very lowest. [p. 75]

By forcing women to such religious extravagances, the American male, Mrs. Trollope concluded, inadvertently penalized his own society.

> Did the men of America value their women as men ought to value their wives and daughters, would such scenes be permitted among them? It is hardly necessary to say that all who obeyed the call to place themselves on the "anxious benches" were women, and by far the greater number, very young women. The congregation was, in general, extremely well dressed, and the smartest and most fashionable ladies of the town were there; during the whole revival the churches and meeting-houses were every day crowded with well dressed people. . . . For myself, I confess that I think the coarsest comedy ever written would be a less detestable exhibition for the eyes of youth and innocence than such a scene. [p. 81]

In the "cult of true womanhood," prevailing in American life at that time, delicacy and purity were the handmaidens of piety.[15] Mrs. Trollope compiled many examples of American women's exaggerated sensitivity on subjects dealing even peripherally with sex or the body. A young gentleman is condemned for pronouncing the word *corset* before a group of ladies (p. 136). A woman walks into a room and is surprised to find herself alone in male company. Covering her eyes, she runs out screaming "A man! a man! a man!" (p. 137). A girl meets a boy of fourteen on the stairs and collapses, panting and sobbing, until "the boy . . . swung himself up on the upper banisters, to leave the passage free" (p. 137). In Cincinnati's rose garden was a sign

representing a Swiss peasant girl, holding in her hand a scroll, requesting that the roses might not be gathered. Unhappily for the artist, or for the proprietor, or for both, the petticoat of this figure was so short as to show her ankles. The ladies saw, and shuddered; and it was formally intimated to the proprietor, that if he wished for the patronage of the ladies of Cincinnati, he must have the petticoat of this figure lengthened. The affrighted purveyor of ices sent off an express for the artist and his paint pot. He came, but unluckily not provided with any colour that would match the petticoat; the necessity, however, was too urgent for delay, and a flounce of blue was added to the petticoat of red, giving bright and shining evidence before all men of the immaculate delicacy of the Cincinnati ladies. [p. 137]

Mrs. Trollope shocked her contemporaries by finding in such delicacy deeply buried prurience about sex, suggestive of a limited life:

I was sometimes tempted to suspect that this ultra refinement was not very deep seated. It often appeared to me like the consciousness of grossness. Occasionally, indeed, the very same persons who appeared ready to faint at the idea of a statue, would utter some unaccountable sally that was quite startling. [p. 137]

When ladies tittered about antique statuary, refused to sit down on the grass with men at a picnic, fled from the ballet shocked at the pirouette, or shuddered at the thought of sea bathing in the presence of men (called "*tête à tête* immersion" in a neat circumlocution), American women revealed to Mrs. Trollope their insecurity about sex which would remain part of the national character long after its nineteenth-century manifestations had disappeared.

By attacking the "cult of true womanhood" Mrs. Trollope had touched upon themes highly charged with emotion for the century. The theme of the rights, role, and position of women in society was danger-

ous; just as her unwittingly offensive behavior had antagonized Cincinnatians and jeopardized the success of her bazaar, so too the book which
rose from the ashes of that defeat enraged most Americans and many
Englishmen.

One by one, the reviewers tried to contradict or disprove her
assertions, and their main line of attack was character assassination.
Associating prurience with her call for the sexes to come into closer
contact, the *Illinois Monthly Review* abusively linked Mrs. Trollope and
Basil Hall:

> It is a pity that this accomplished pair could not have met, while they were
> in the United States, and given us a specimen of those agreeable flirtations,
> which, it appears, form so great a portion of the delight of European
> manners. Insensible as the Americans are to amusements, the gravest
> among them could hardly fail to be amused by witnessing a meeting
> between those distinguished personages—a meeting, in which their
> philanthropy might induce them to give an example of that refined
> intercourse between the sexes, that forms such a striking display of English
> superiority. We can hardly imagine a scene that would be more amusing
> than the sight of such an interview, between Mrs. Trollope, decked out in
> the tawdry finery worn by her on extraordinary occasions, put on with a
> degree of taste so near to that displayed by the native Indians of our
> country, as to cause a doubt, whether she was really what she pretended to
> be, either in sex or descent—with that draggled look that was peculiar to
> her, and which gave at once the idea of her name being a *soubriquet*—and
> with that self-possessed, easy bearing of her *outre* appearance, which
> made it seem so very natural, and Captain Hall, with his cold, self-
> conceited air of importance, and dignified disdain of every thing around
> him, which appeared to as great advantage in his manners as in his book.[16]

Seizing upon her friendship with Hervieu, some reviewers called her
"a profligate woman." The *New Monthly Magazine* noted that "she
would no doubt be excellent at a flirtation," while the *Edinburgh Review*
began its notice of the book with direct reference to her "irregular"
personal life.

> The scene opens with a matron, her son, and two daughters. On looking
> narrowly into the background, whom else do we discover? No Mr.
> Trollope, the centre of a family group. . . . First appears her friend, a
> Mr. H. This is pretty good for a beginning. After that—farewell to the
> virtue of common sense, whatever other discretion may be retained.

A contemporary letter from a cousin of Captain Hamilton repeated the
rumors which were then circulating:

I understand Mrs. Trollope is a woman of very good family & education, & I believe of good character, notwithstanding her connection with Miss Wright, & her French Compagnon de voyage at Niagara—I have been told her Father is Rector of Bristol, and that she has a Brother very high in one of the Government offices—Her husband is some kind of a Lawyer, & a near relation of Sir John Trollope a rich Leicestershire Baronet, but he had run himself into difficulties, & his wife went to the United States with Miss Wright on some absurd speculation or another—They soon parted company, & Mrs. Trollope I understand went to Cincinnati, & entered into some wild scheme of building an Hotel or Bazaar there. In this she failed, & I suppose quarrelled with every body, & became disgusted with every thing, and now vents her spite, or spleen, upon the whole country, in place of herself, from her folly, ignorance & presumption.—I am told she has many more anecdotes & observations to make public, but as even she considers them too strong, & piquant to be published in her travelling observations, she is going to embody them in a Novel, which she is now preparing for the press.[17]

Her remarks on religion earned spiteful attacks in both England and America. The writer for the *New Monthly Magazine* found

the most outrageous, malicious, and inexcusable portions of these volumes . . . those which relate to religion. It is difficult to conceive of any real reverence for religion existing in a mind capable of treating even the fanatical extravagances of its misguided followers with heartless levity. On these points, Mrs. Trollope's facts are exceedingly suspicious; her *comments* absolutely indecent and revolting. . . . she gives way to a pert, coarse, and prurient style of innuendo and description, which is as inconsistent with delicacy as it is with fairness and candour.

Concluding his angry remarks, he professed to be "largely indebted to our female writers," in works characterized by "all that is chaste, lovely, and beautiful in the female mind." The *Athenaenum* claimed that when she described scenes of religious fanaticism "she puts her hands before her face, so as she may see thru her fingers, and cries, 'O fie! I am afraid you are naughty girls; how can you do such things?' " That journal reprinted in full Mrs. Trollope's famous description of the camp meeting.

But how am I to describe the sounds that proceeded from this strange mass of human beings? . . . Hysterical sobbings, convulsive groans, shrieks and screams the most appalling, burst forth on all sides. . . . Many of these wretched creatures were beautiful young females. The preachers moved about among them, at once exciting and soothing their agonies. I heard the muttered "Sister! dear sister!" I saw the insidious lips approach the cheeks of the unhappy girls; I heard the murmured confessions of the poor victims, and I watched their tormentors, breathing into their ears consolations that tinged the pale cheek with red. Had I been a man, I am sure I should have been guilty of some rash act of interference.

One "very pretty girl," calls out

"Woe! woe to the backsliders! hear it, hear it, Jesus! when I was 15 my mother died, and I backslided, oh Jesus, I backslided! take me home to her, for I am weary!" . . . and after sobbing piteously behind her raised hands, she lifted her sweet face again, which was as pale as death, and said, "Shall I sit on the sunny bank of salvation with my mother? my own dear mother? Oh Jesus, take me home, take me home!"

Who could refuse a tear to this earnest wish for death in one so young and lovely? But I saw her, ere I left the ground, with her hand fast locked, and her head supported by a man who looked very much as Don Juan might, when sent back to earth as too bad for the regions below.

The reviewer found it offensive that Mrs. Trollope had dared even describe such a scene: "We must lift up our voice like this gentle backslider, and exclaim, 'Oh Mrs. Trollope! Mrs. Trollope! we hope when this was going on that you remembered you were *an old woman.*' "[18]

But nothing matched the vituperativeness of the response to her remarks on American prudery. How could Jonathan's women be "prudes, but indelicate," the *Edinburgh Review* asked triumphantly, accusing Mrs. Trollope of an unhealthy "relish" in recounting her many prudery stories. The *New Monthly Magazine* called the "texture of her mind . . . essentially gross. There are stories in her book which offend modesty, and in her spite against prudery she indulges in something far less to be endured." At least one reviewer thought that she "saw many things which no refined Englishwoman would have seen, or seeing would have understood—still less have written and published."[19]

Ironically, one American review confirmed the accuracy of Mrs. Trollope's observations. She had told of the "horror and dismay" occasioned to "the morals of the Western world" by the sight of two ballet dancers—"very indifferent figurantes" (pp. 134 ff.)—who had made their appearance at Cincinnati. The *North American Review* found it remarkable that

females not lost to shame should be found to perform [the ballet] on the stage; and second, that they should find men and women of character to countenance the exhibition in the boxes. The *pirouette*, in a word, is a movement, in which a woman, dressed as we have described, posing herself on one limb, extends the other to its full length, at right angles, and in this *graceful* attitude spins round, some eight or ten times, leaving her drapery, "transparent" and short as it is at the best, to be carried up, by the centrifugal force imparted to it by the rapid revolution of the dancer, as far as it will go. This we believe is an unexaggerated description of that scene, which Mrs. Trollope sneers at the ladies of Cincinnati for regarding with horror. Is there a father, or a mother, a husband or wife, a brother or sister in Christendom, "If damned Custom had not brazed them so," who would view it with any thing but horror?[20]

Her remarks on the affected delicacy of American ladies were considered the most dangerous part of her book. Most reviewers singled out this theme. The *North American Review* noted: "Our readers will bear in mind, how much is said in the work which bears this lady's name, of the insignificance of the women in America, the neglect of their education and their depressed state in society." But the reviewer could only lamely respond that the British had no better attitude toward their women. And indeed, English reviewers, while glad to discuss the positive or negative facets of egalitarianism or the effect of the frontier, were similarly sensitive about Mrs. Trollope's remarks on women. European culture had concurred with America in reaching a consensus on women's proper place. The *Edinburgh Review*, in castigating Mrs. Trollope's report, specifically compared it to the imaginary ones that might have been received "not merely from Hannah More, and Mrs. Fry, but from Miss Edgeworth, and Miss Aikin, Mrs. Hamilton and Mrs. Markham, or from a hundred others, of whose *feminine* virtues and accomplishments the modern literature of England is so justly proud!"[21]

The *Illinois Monthly Magazine* believed the book a dangerous attempt to remove from the female sex the "restraints of religion and morality," and it launched a personal attack on Mrs. Trollope, Frances Wright ("her patroness"), and Robert Owen, all of whom had tried to convert "the natives to atheism."[22]

While some reviewers called her theme subversive, an attempt to introduce "that coarse, forward, masculine style of manners" that would relieve the young American ladies of "what she considers insipidity of character," others simply made light of her findings. The *American Quarterly Review* found her observations on women unimportant to any larger analysis of American society:

Her chief topics of complaint . . . are apt among all reasona-ble . . . people, to provoke a smile. They are mostly evils of the tea-table and the toilet—subjects, we grant, of infinite importance among the young and budding of her sex, but, we should think, not exactly such as should very greatly provoke the anger, or occasion the severe censure of an ancient and intelligent personage of Mrs. Trollope's dimensions.[23]

Others claimed that women had no right to discuss such subjects at all. The *New Monthly Magazine* believed that in so doing, Mrs. Trollope had stepped out of her proper sphere "by rejecting those proprieties with which she can never dispense without deducting largely from her legitimate influence." Repeatedly, the charge of "unladylike" was lodged against her. "Robust and masculine," one critic called her. "There are some things in this volume . . . which we cannot think that she or any other lady (not to say gentleman) could have written." This view came to its logical conclusion when the *North American Review* claimed that not Mrs. Trollope but rather "the men-editors of this farrago" had written *Domestic Manners*. Evoking the whole gamut of emotional associations surrounding womanhood, the writer appealed: "Were we wrong in averring, that Mrs. Trollope did not write this? She is a woman and a mother."[24]

She was frequently called "amazonian" in the common rhetoric for a woman who had overstepped her feminine limits. And the *Illinois Monthly Magazine* called her the very personification of the idea conveyed by her name in its vulgar acceptation:

> The appellations of 'the old woman,' and 'the Englishwoman,' which her neighbors employed in speaking of Mrs. T., and of which she complains so frequently, were probably used by them from mere delicacy, and were the result of their rustic, native politeness. Her name, as we have said, appeared to them so characteristic, that they felt as if it would appear insulting to use it in her hearing; and her style of dress and masculine stride in walking, made them think that it would be complimentary to designate her by any term that would show that they did not consider her a descendant of our aborigines; the females of which race—owing to our prejudices of education— are in much worse odor among us than even female cockney philosophers and witlings.[25]

No harmless collection of gossiping anecdotes could have called forth this outcry against her evidence and conclusions: it was her theme that had offended. She had investigated the "condition of that half of society over which the other half has power." Tried by this test, America failed. Whatever hope there might be for the future would come only when both sexes changed. First, men would have to abandon their conviction, deeply held "to the very centre of their hearts and souls, that women were made for no other purpose than to fabricate sweetmeats and gingerbread, construct shirts, darn stockings, and become mothers of possible presidents." Women, too, would have to throw off their protective chains. "Should the women of America ever discover what their power might be, and compare it with what it is, much improvement might be hoped for" (p. 280).

The subject of America and the interest in women would return in her later novels. She wrote five major novels on American themes, spaced fairly evenly over the remaining thirty-three years of her life, and the woman theme became a preoccupation to which she returned with increasing originality and seriousness in the last decade of her writing career when, free at long last from financial and familial cares, she could explore at leisure the many facets of the strong female in a male-dominated society. Those who say she wrote *Domestic Manners*, made her money, and then forgot the subject, know little of Frances Trollope or her later career.[26]

For the immediate future, however, this "dangerous" theme and the barrage of attacks that followed served one purpose: the book sold well. Moreover, the political atmosphere in England, on the verge of the First Reform Bill of 1832, occasioned great interest in the state of affairs in America and the political democracy which was in operation there. To capitalize on this preoccupation, Mrs. Trollope dropped her original preface and wrote a new one which rather disingenuously claimed that her major interest was "to shew how greatly the advantage is on the side of those who are governed by the few, instead of the many." Although her book in fact contained very little on politics, her new preface insisted: "The chief object she has had in view is to encourage her countrymen to hold fast by a constitution that ensures all the blessings which flow from established habits and solid principles. If they forego these, they will incur the fearful risk of breaking up their repose by introducing the jarring tumult and universal degradation which invariably follow the wild scheme of placing all the power of the state in the hands of the populace."[27] This obvious effort to boost sales may have disguised the real thrust of the book, but the two favorable reviews in English journals did not ignore the woman's angle. The *Quarterly* (in a review by Captain Hall) praised the book as touching topics which "only a female eye could correctly appreciate, or a female pen do justice to in description," and *Fraser's* called it "acute and amusing," adding that the United States was "a tarnation country for a lady to travel in."[28]

Even today, the book is instructive. Utilizing what she herself called "the lynx-like eye of the female" and professing herself satisfied with a domain of "all that constitutes the external of society," Mrs. Trollope also provided an original and provocative explanation of an important weakness of American society. This combination distinguished her book from the run-of-the-mill accounts of the day. All who seek to recover that elusive sense of "the way things were" in these early years of the American Republic cannot neglect *The Domestic Manners of the Americans*—"the old woman's book."[29]

Three days after her book's appearance, Mrs. Trollope described the "happy termination of my troublesome publishing business." She had already seen the bad reviews and defended herself in a letter to Julia Pertz:

> Murray says that Washington Irving declares it is all an abominable fabrication got up in London by someone who has never visited America. I suppose that I shall be most heartily abused by all who hold the theory that America is a pattern country. . . . I have selected nothing as *fact*, which I do not know to be such. . . .

Undiscouraged by poor notices, she stressed the favorable ones which, as she dryly added, "will certainly help the sale."[30]

Domestic Manners achieved a success almost unheard of for a first attempt by an unknown author. In 1832 alone it went through four English and four American editions. In 1838 there was a fifth American edition, and in 1839 a fifth English edition in Bentley's *Standard Library of Popular Modern Literature*. Within a few years it appeared in Spain (*Costumbres familiares de los americanos del Norte*), Germany (*Leben und Sitte in Nordamerika*), France (*Moeurs domestiques des Americains*), and the Netherlands (*Zeden, Gewoonten en Huisselijk Leven der Noord-Amerikanen*). The author received £250 for the first edition, which immediately sold out, and £200 for the second, with which she renounced future rights in an arrangement common for the time. In all, with foreign royalties included, she probably earned some £600. Never was money more sorely needed or quickly expended. The items she purchased were practical and met the family's most immediate and pressing needs: "half a year's rent and taxes paid in advance"; coal, candles, "a sopha, and a chest of drawers bought at a sale"; tuition fees for the boys; and "a good bed" with pillows and bolster. She also bought a cow and malt for brewing and spent over £70 on fixtures, in a valiant attempt to renovate the poor house at Harrow Weald. Her son Tom later recalled that the success of *Domestic Manners* brought about a change "in the condition and circumstance of affairs at home which resembled the transformation scene in a pantomime that takes place at the advent of the good fairy."[31]

She gave Hervieu £100, one-half the proceeds of the second edition, a proportion which Frances Eleanor Trollope, in her later biography of her mother-in-law, thought "excessive," considering his share of the work. But Mrs. Trollope credited Hervieu's unusual drawings with playing a large part in the book's success and was grateful for his generous and unfailing help in America. Given the chance to repay him handsomely, she did not count the pennies, badly as she herself needed them.[32]

Many wrote congratulatory letters: Miss Mitford, the Gabells, Captain Kater, and even Captain Hamilton, who had been so scandalized by Mrs. Trollope's irregular "menage" at Niagara. But not all her friends received the book favorably.[33] In this respect, they shared the opinion of the reviews, most of which were bad. The Garnetts did not like it and called her "well-paid for her abuse of America." Harriet thought Mrs. Trollope had achieved success at "the sacrifice of principle," and Julia, always frankest of all, openly disagreed with the book's conclusions. General Lafayette, who had known about Mrs. Trollope's early enthusiasm for America, saw her conversion to more conservative views with cynical disdain. He believed that "her abuse of the American character and American manners, in a published book and daily conversations has not a little contributed to make her very fashionable in the fine circles in England." Hereafter, the general would no longer receive Mrs. Trollope. The Garnetts' friend Sismondi admitted that Mrs. Trollope had much wit and talent but found the book full of "a very violent and sometimes very unjust prejudice against the Americans." These criticisms she shrugged off, for she was learning to look at herself merely as a person "what makes books." This craftsmanlike and dispassionate view of writing she passed on to her son Anthony, who was later to shock a generation of aesthetes by comparing his own trade to that of a shoemaker.[34]

Mrs. Trollope had not sought personal fame. Her ambition was to use her talents to achieve economic security for her threatened family. The immediate beneficiary of this income was Henry, her embattled companion at Nashoba, New Harmony, and Cincinnati. Although he was frail and ill-suited to demanding studies, Mrs. Trollope used the proceeds of her book to launch him on a legal career by enrolling him at the Temple. She had equal ambitions for the others and at once began to cast about for further sources of revenue. She asked Miss Mitford: "What does one do to get business with the mags and annuals? Does one say, as at playing ecarte, 'I propose,' or must one wait to be asked? Remember dear, that I have five children."[35] She took time to counsel Tom who, inspired by his mother's literary success, was somewhat overanxious to begin the career of authorship himself. His mother advised caution and more study: "A good degree will aid you at first setting out, beyond anything else whatever. Be firm to this object."[36]

She went to London for the season to promote the sale of the book, taking a lodging for Cecilia and herself in Thayer Street, Manchester

Square. Although she swiftly became the toast of London, she never lost sight either of her real position or of the limits of her talents in that social whirl which she described to Tom with the humorous perspective she always maintained towards attempts to aggrandize her achievements. "You would laugh did you know to what an extent I am lionized." Captain Hall generously played the mentor, introducing her to high society and bringing her to the salon of the bluestocking Miss Berrys. There she was told by the Countess of Morley that

> If I drove through London proclaiming who I was, I should have the horses taken off and be drawn in triumph from one end of town to the other! The Honourable Mr. Somebody declared that my thunderstorm was the finest thing in prose or verse. Lady Charlotte Lindsay *implored* me to go on writing—never was anything so delightful. Lady Louisa Stewart told me that I had quite put English out of fashion, and that every one was talking Yankee talk. In short I was overpowered![37]

But not quite: immediately following this breathless rendition, she returned to reality. "But all this must help the sale of the next book whatever may happen after." In fact, she grudged the time required by her newly won fame. She struggled to "find an hour in each day" to complete her first novel, *The American Exile* (subsequently renamed at Captain Hall's suggestion *The Refugee in America*), and felt excessively fatigued. She wrote to Tom, "God bless you and preserve the brain of your venerable mother through this whirl." She spent her days writing and her nights socializing and felt always busy, rushed, and interrupted. She hoped "that the time I have given to engagements is not lost, speaking professionally."[38]

Before the season ended and she faced another return to Harrow Weald, she sought a place to spend the winter, her object simply "to be a few months very quiet and very happy—where my children could be taking lessons, and I could be writing at *very* little expense." She seized upon Julia Pertz's long-standing invitation to visit Hanover where, combining business with pleasure, she looked forward to using some of the profits from her American book "in order to begin my German one."[39] She dreaded a disappointment in these plans "for I know not how I should bear it." But rather than "pass through a country visited by the cholera and threatened by war," she reluctantly abandoned the project even as her restless mind turned in other directions:

> As I am disappointed in this scheme (at least for the present) I mean if possible to get back to my dear Julian Hill (you love that house dearest Julia as well as I). It will *I hope* be vacant at Michaelmas and I think that

with my little *gains* and steady economy we may be able to get on there
again very well. All the dear children wish it, and though they will not be
able to have the lessons I had intended for them in Germany, they will
have a comfortable and quiet room to study in.[40]

She persuaded Mr. Trollope to terminate the profitable sublease of
Julian Hill and move the family back to their former home. This
somewhat precipitate step, inconsistent with Mrs. Trollope's usual good
sense, would eventually have dire consequences.

At once she began negotiations for her completed novel. Because she
believed that Whittaker had not been generous enough with the royalties
from the subsequent editions of *Domestic Manners*, she seriously
considered changing publishers for *The Refugee*. But Basil Hall, whom
she consulted, advised otherwise:

Unless Messrs. Whittaker and Co. shall fail in any of their engagements to
you, I conceive it would not only be very imprudent, but not quite correct,
to think of any other person as the Publisher of your novel. Such steps are,
indeed, sometimes taken by authors, but none, I think, without loss. . . . I
strongly advise you therefore not to think of any such change; for I am well
convinced that Messrs. Whittaker & Co. will deal with you fairly and on
many accounts more to your satisfaction than any one else. It would sorely
hurt [future sales of *Domestic Manners*] to carry your novel to another
publisher, unless you had reason to think ill of your first publishers.[41]

So in July 1832 she signed an agreement with Whittaker: £400 for
1,250 copies. Awaiting the publication, she readied herself for possible
failure:

I carefully restrain my hopes. . . . Should my little fame expire directly
and no further returns reward my labours, I shall burn my pen, and
immediately seek a situation where I may earn something. In families of
distinction women of my age are often highly paid for superintending
masters and directing a course of study. I trust it will not come to this; but
the word of my Maecenas, one from Miss Gabell in the same warning tone,
and Miss Milman's laughing words, 'You must not expect to make a
thousand pounds *every* year!' have set me thinking a little upon the
uncertain nature of literary success. And I have therefore made up my
mind to do without it.[42]

But such renunciations were unnecessary. The profits from *The Refugee
in America* helped reestablish the Trollopes at Julian Hill by September of 1832.

It would seem that Mrs. Trollope had rightly interpreted the success of *Domestic Manners* as proof that readers were ready for another book on America. "I have not yet given all my good yankee stories to the public," she had written to Julia, and these found their way into the novel. Although "the personages are imaginary," the book had a solid grounding in its "sundry sketches from the life."[43] A curious mixture of smugglers and fugitive English aristocrats, the book also featured an assortment of vulgar American types that Mrs. Trollope had culled from *Domestic Manners*, along with details of setting and route. The plot is unbelievable, the narrative occasionally lifeless, and the book interesting only when she describes experiences, settings, and characters she herself had observed.[44] These include sketches of Americans who are silent at dinner and whose whole cultural nourishment consists of "several newspapers, a volume of the 'Eloquence of the United States,' a book of receipts, and two numbers of the *American Quarterly*." The characters are calculating and boastful; one asks of foreigners: "just to own that we are first and foremost; and after that, we grant him freedom to keep the rest of his thoughts to himself." Landladies overcharge, and young ladies are "accomplished" and rich in "quarters" in the arts and sciences. One is a patriot; her whole duty "to let the English see what an American woman could be." To these alarming exemplars of American womanhood, Mrs. Trollope adds the usual number of boardinghouse gossips whispering about the "suspicious" English.[45]

Several minor characters she drew with deep feeling, in a rare fictional use of her Nashoba experience. M. de Clairville is an unsuspecting and idealistic European who comes to America to join a Utopian colony named "Perfect Bliss." Once there, he is assigned the task of cutting trees to make fences. Mrs. Trollope commented: "the poor Frenchman, whose visions had been of scientific lectures, amateur concerts, private theatricals, and universal philanthrophy, was startled. . . ." Eventually, de Clairville dies in despair and frustration; Auguste Hervieu, at least, had been more fortunate.[46] There were, of course, a few "good" Americans, safely conscious of their inferiority. The heroine, an infinitely adaptable girl, sees with little prodding the inestimable advantages of being born English. Dazzled by the English family's grace, breeding, and elegant speech, she becomes a quick pupil, rapidly dropping her more obvious "Americanisms." Once reformed and enlightened, she marries the English lord who brings her safely to England where, as Mrs. Trollope made it abundantly clear, such rejuvenated characters rightly belonged.[47]

The sales of *The Refugee* did not disappoint Mrs. Trollope; the first edition briskly disappeared. "I got £400 for the first edition of the refugee," she wrote Julia, "and I am told there is not a copy to be got—so I hope I shall have a second." Such was the measure of her success that

Mary Russell Mitford herself now asked the fledgling author for help. Earlier, she had assured Mrs. Trollope that "reputation will afterwards bring money." Now she sent an advance copy of her latest effort, *Our Village*, asking Mrs. Trollope to review it. After careful inquiries, however, Mrs. Trollope learned "that no woman has ever written for the *Quarterly*" (her sole contact in the publishing world), and she shrewdly offered to write the review "*gratis* and to the very top of my power," should Miss Mitford use her own connections to get the article placed. The new professional was already trying hard to gain further recognition, even while offering to help a friend.[48]

This first novel was not, however, greeted with praise by the reviewers. Mrs. Trollope was especially disturbed to see that the *Quarterly Review*, which had so enthusiastically praised *Domestic Manners*, now roundly condemned *The Refugee*:

> It is the established faith of these days, that any one who has written anything, can write a novel. If a traveller has acquired a little notoriety by some lively sketches of a distant country, his next step is infallibly to publish a novel. . . . It seems to be imagined that nothing more is required for this purpose, than to couple together a pair or two of out-of-the-way sirnames, or a well-sounding title or so, for the heroes and heroines—to throw in among them a little random love—to conjure up in their way two or three good set villains for the sake of difficulties and escapes—then to scrape together a lot of things called mottoes . . . and at length, after a reasonable quantity of description, sentiment, and small-talk, to punish the bad and 'happify' the good, by the most unscrupulous and arbitrary contrivances.

Calling the characters "wire-drawn common-places," and the whole book "absurd nonsense from beginning to end," the reviewer confessed that "nothing but the reputation of the authoress could induce us to throw away a line upon it."[49]

Mrs. Trollope believed a rumor that Basil Hall had written the *Quarterly*'s attack. Directly, she inquired the truth and Hall disclaimed responsibility, even as he offered her some advice:

> You must be aware that having written such a book as your travels you necesarily raised an immense host of vindictive vulgar active enemies, and this is but one of thousands of envenomed shafts which you must expect to have shot at you.

In a series of letters at the beginning of 1833, Hall reiterated this theme: she must learn to be "amused" by such black calumny and "borrow a little of [his] philosophy and accept all such things as compliments to

[her] talents and testimonies to [her] truth." She must regard the "sneers and censures of persons who differ" as "the surest compliments of all."[50]

But had she heeded Captain Hall, Mrs. Trollope might never have advanced beyond these clumsy beginnings. While regarding personal attacks with detachment, she was not impervious to criticism and could not afford to ignore her public. Her later novels show that she paid careful heed to these early reviews, especially noting the mention of her alleged strong points. Even the *Quarterly* had praised her satirical talents, and the *Gentleman's Magazine* liked the "broad caricature" of the book's American characters. The *Westminster Review* appreciated her ability to raise a laugh and liked the relatively unimportant but comical boardinghouse scenes, seeing in the characters a certain universality which "may be matched in every particular in every market-town of England." While most reviewers found the English high-life characters foolish boobies, they appreciated "the talent with which [Mrs. Trollope] exhibits the foibles and follies of some of the middle ranks of society which belong as much to this country as to America. Here her success is as complete as her failure is decisive when she comes to put in motion the aristocracy of her own country."[51] Soon Mrs. Trollope would move more markedly in these directions, as she grew artistically mature and self-confident. But for the next few years, while she so desperately needed financial success, she continued to rely heavily upon older models and more established fictional formulas.

6

Some Works of Imagination
and a Bitter Reality

A mixture of good and evil in her life

MRS. TROLLOPE's next novel, *The Abbess: A Romance*, was in the gothic tradition of "Monk" Lewis and Mrs. Radcliffe, whose *Mysteries of Udolpho* had been a part of young Fanny Milton's reading. She confessed to Julia that she was working on an old idea: "I am now writing with a very different object and feeling a romance which I shall call *The Abbess*. It is a story, or rather a character that I have had in my head for a long time, but I know not if I shall be able to make any thing of it."[1] Unlike Mrs. Radcliffe, however, Mrs. Trollope did not leave the reader in suspense very long about this character. Her abbess, mysterious only for a brief chapter or two, is soon revealed as a secret Protestant, condemned at an early age by a weak and superstitious father to enter a convent. A nun in name only, she rose quickly (ostensibly on the strength of her pure Protestant faith) to achieve a high position. Her arch-enemy was the monk Isadore, who in his machinations resembles a hoard of other scoundrel monks so common to this genre. Earlier, Isadore became unhappy with Count D'Albano's marriage to a Protestant; he poisoned the wife and devoted his life to pursuing the daughter Geraldine, now the abbess, of whom he is vaguely suspicious. To this tale of pursuit, Mrs. Trollope added the familiar theme of innocent youth and defenseless beauty subjected to evil—the Abbess's niece, whose father has also destined her for the convent but who finds the protection of her aunt until the central action of the book traps them. Exploiting fully the horror and wickedness so dear to the gothic mode, Mrs. Trollope has the abbess and her niece attempt the rescue of a pregnant nun who has been condemned to a live burial. The fact that she is really a nobleman's wife in disguise adds little to the plot, which proceeds according to formula to emphasize the theme of imprisonment so perennially dominant in the castles and convents of romantic novels. Along the way, Mrs. Trollope provides black-hooded inquisitors, great, flaming crucifixes, myriads of candles, and the breathless voice of gothic horror:

107

Who in those days but had heard of that living death? —its hideous preparation? —its maddening stillness? —its dark, cold, lingering agony? Who had not heard that the young, the lovely, and the gentle, had been laid a conscious corse, within a loathsome tomb . . . .[2]

The *Spectator*, in its largely favorable review, praised *The Abbess* as

manufactured by a not unskilful bookmaker: the taste of the circulating library is remarkably well hit; there is no doubt but that it will extremely well suit the wants of the ladies who have been long pining for a genuine bit of romance, such as they used to be supplied with in the days of their youth—those 'deep' times when Mrs. Radcliffe made them hide their heads under the bed-clothes, and converted every sound into a warning and every sight into a ghost.

And although the whole was "wrought of hackneyed materials,—though there is no incident for which we could not give chapter and verse in the circulating library, —though the dialogue is altogether artificial, and the sentiment from the great book of commonplace," still, the reviewer found Mrs. Trollope "something of an artist."

There are scenes not deficient in that effect which is produced by a tolerably fair talent at calculation. We should say, were a board of novelists set down to be examined like a parcel of Cambridge students, without any assistance but such as pen, ink, and paper could afford, and the problem ran thus: describe a baronial castle of the middle ages, set forth a trial in the vaults of the Inquisition, poison a heretic, mix up a particularly foul plot, immure an erring nun in a living grave with all proper ceremony—in such an examination Mrs. Trollope would on the spot do her part as well perhaps as any of our scribblers.[3]

But running alongside the traditional gothic tableaus were minor scenes in which nuns appeared not as thrilling subjects of high sanctity or lascivious evil but as ordinary human beings who relieve the longueurs of convent life with a little wine, some story-telling, jokes, and gossip. In several episodes, gullible nuns listen wide-eyed to a servant's fantastic stories of lovers seduced by the devil, ladies falling in love with towers, and haunted bedrooms. When the nuns appear as chattering busybodies, when they say extra *Credos* for the courage to sleep in a haunted castle, when they innocently sing a catchy but ribald Latin song, they are transformed into homely, recognizable females, betraying their creator's interest in low-life realism and humour. In such a ponderous, stilted novel as *The Abbess*, this is all the more remarkable evidence of Mrs. Trollope's real talent. For even in these clumsy and derivative efforts, her depictions of "the middle ranks of society" rose like cream to the surface. Reviewers of her work during these years, while usually condemning her high-life characters, noted these small successes in describing "the ridiculous, the petty, and the vain. . . . Only let her eschew law, and lords, and villainy on the romantic scale, and entertain us with the people she evidently knows."[4] Soon she would come into her own as a social satirist of respectable abilities: the vicar of Wrexhill and the widow Barnaby were waiting in the wings.

Despite the mixed reviews, *The Abbess* was a success. Through her remarkable diligence, Mrs. Trollope had in 1833 published two financially profitable novels; *The Refugee* even went into a second edition, and there appeared a fourth edition of *Domestic Manners*. It was an age of ascendancy for women in the field of literature. Miss Mitford's books were best-sellers; her plays were mounted on the London boards. Harriet Martineau had become the hit of the season with her "delightful illustrations of political economy." The Garnetts admired her pluck. She was "the daughter of a merchant at Norwich who failed," and although penniless girls had customarily "gone out as governesses," Miss Martineau, deaf to boot, had "turned her talents to better account." Lord Brougham had taken notice of her work, claiming that this "little ugly, deaf girl is doing more good to her country than all the men in it." Even the shy Harriet Garnett was trying to enter the field with translations and a little novel, which Mrs. Trollope attempted to place with a publisher.[5] For the present, Mrs. Trollope was satisfied that her books were earning money, and she began to turn them out with regularity.

With *The Abbess* completed, Mrs. Trollope planned to "start for some watering place on the Rhine with the commission *to make a book*." She was not eager to leave her "dear cottage . . . so lately recovered," as she ruefully noted, but "*poverty* is the greatest despot existing," and while the returns from her first books had helped pay some bills and add to the family's comfort, they had done nothing to decrease or even alleviate the ever-mounting debts arising from the disastrous rental arrangements at Harrow with Lord Northwick.[6] By late May, she, Henry, and Hervieu were on the Rhine, "looking about on its banks in all directions." Mr. Trollope stayed behind, ill with influenza. Once his wife nearly returned home. Then she "heard from him giving a very good account of himself" and planning to meet them at Hanover to visit Julia and her family. They could not indulge in a lengthy visit, for, as Mrs. Trollope explained to Julia, "I *must* be ready with my book by November and as yet I have merely notes." By 24 September she was home again, assembling her German travel notes and beginning her third novel, *Tremordyn Cliff*.[7]

Almost at once, she discovered disturbing news.

I have had great reason to believe that Mr. Whittaker printed a second edition of the *Refugee* without my knowledge—and for his own exclusive benefit. My reason for such suspicion was this—Just before I set off for Germany he came here to dine with us, and said that he had got into a bad scrape by forgetting to send a copy of the *Refugee* to the stationers company, as ordered by act of parliament—"They never would have thought of it," said he, "had they not found it was out of print—and then they sent for it." He said it had given him a vast deal of trouble for he had *beat the town through* for a copy, but in vain—but his clerk at last got a circulating library to sell a copy at a premium, which he got newly bound to conceal its worn condition, and stopped their mouths with it. —About a month after I went out of the country, all the shops again exhibited the *Refugee* in their windows—though it was impossible to prove the cheat, it was impossible to doubt it. . . .[8]

Distressed by Whittaker's duplicity, she determined to approach the prestigious John Murray, who had been kind enough to say that her "little book on America was one which [he] would have liked to publish." While remembering that he had added: "I should not feel equally certain of the success of any other work," Mrs. Trollope nonetheless offered him her new travel book. She told Julia that "he received the manuscript very graciously, and sent it to Mr. Lockhart for judgment—who spoke highly [of] it." To assist his decision, in January she sent more of the manuscript, together with her "scratched" and "very freely" marked copy of "Sir Arthur Brooke Faulkner's abominable volumes" on Germany, which had recently appeared.[9] She wanted Murray to realize that hers was a different kind of travel book. In February she came to town determined to wring a positive decision from Murray. Unwilling to promote her works on the plea of being her family's sole support, as did some other women of this period, she spoke rather of her position in the literary world. In her long publishing career she rarely alluded to private necessity in negotiating terms of publication. She claimed she was earnest for a decision because "the publication was expected *this spring* both in Germany and at home— and . . . there was no time to lose."[10]

When they finally talked of terms, "this autocrat of Albermarle Street . . . offered *half profits*." The personal difficulty such arrangements would cause she related only to Julia.

I particularly wished a payment in ready money on account of Tom's taking his degree next month at Oxford—at which time all arrears are paid—I stated my difficulty—or rather my objection to this mode of dealing—but he assured me that for many years past he had practiced no other—I then asked him frankly if [he] would let me return to him in case

Mr. Whittaker's offer did not content me—He said "*most certainly*, and will do my very best to forward the success of the work." Whittaker offered £200—I refused it and sent the manuscript again to Murray—this is a fortnight ago today—and I have not yet heard from him on the subject—so know nothing as to estimate, time of publication, or any thing else. Is not this bungling business of mine a torment? You will say and feel that it is—yet you can hardly guess how much so.[11]

Her subsequent letter to Murray, which firmly repeated her objections to the half-profits system, provides a glimpse of the helpless and exposed position of the author in those days:

Having sent the manuscript and drawings, I received a week afterwards the following offer—namely £100 down for 750 copies, and £75 for every 500 printed afterwards. On this I desired my son to call for the manuscript and inform Mr. Whittaker that I declined his proposal. He then informed my son that he was willing to pay £200 for 1000 copies, and £50 . . . for all printed after, declaring he had made *a mistake* in his note respecting the sum offered for the subsequent copies. He also proposed half-profits—and finally begged that the question might be left open.

I would by no means ask you to give me any opinion on this sort of proceeding—but I think you will hold me justified for preferring half profits from Mr. Murray to entering into any farther engagements in Ave Maria Lane.[12]

Ten days later Mrs. Trollope wrote again, still stressing professional advancement and not personal need:

The vexatious uncertainty respecting the manner of publication has already so much retarded the work that I feel very anxious lest any farther delay should arise, the consequences of which would indeed be most injurious to me.[13]

Only in July did Murray agree to publish the book, but Mrs. Trollope could have felt no triumph. By that time, her whole being was caught up in the collapse of her family's way of life.

The winter of 1833–1834 had been marked by severe influenza attacks, and the spring came in cold and biting. There had been little time for letter-writing, and Mrs. Trollope explained her long silence to Julia:

I have never had so much sickness in my family as this year—For about ten days we were very seriously alarmed for Anthony—and since that more seriously still for my poor Henry who has been, and yet is, very ill—He is grown pale and thin beyond what you can imagine and has a cough that tears him to pieces. But our medical man assures me that *as yet* he perceives no danger and that if he will not leave the house till the east winds are over, and warm weather settled in, he thinks he will recover the attack upon his lungs. All this has certainly kept me in a state of mind not favorable to writing.[14]

It was just a little over ten years since Arthur's death, and both Henry and Emily were displaying alarming symptoms of the consumptive disease that would eventually kill them both. The frail Cecilia was another worry, and Mr. Trollope, ill with influenza and constant headaches and aging rapidly, could not help with the nursing of invalids, which soon became Mrs. Trollope's major duty.

All these problems, however, seemed insignificant beside what now burst upon them. Agricultural conditions in Harrow had become increasingly disastrous, compounded by an excessive poor rate which—in the words of Trollope's landlord Lord Northwick—"spread ruin and desolation throughout the land, reducing industrious inhabitants of all classes . . . to a mass of insolvent debtors." Ever since his dismaying brush with Lord Northwick in 1830, Thomas Anthony had fallen behind in his rents. Despite generous reductions (12 percent in 1834) Trollope was no longer able to meet his regular payments and negotiated a series of delays. In October 1833 he had not been able to pay his monthly bills, and when he eventually settled the last two accounts, his personal draft bounced. Lord Northwick threatened legal action. Many farms came under foreclosures in that winter of 1833, but Trollope could take little comfort in knowing that he was not alone in his distress. He scraped together as much money as he could borrow in London, but in December could pay only £25.[15]

Stubbornly proud, he had not given his wife any inkling of his real financial state. Exertion and worry wore him out. When Northwick's agent called on the day after Christmas, he found Trollope in bed, and for the first time, Frances learned of the large arrears for which Lord Northwick was demanding immediate settlement. As she later told Julia:

We had no idea that a years rent of the *pernicious* farm which for twenty years has been so losing a concern for him, was due to Lord Northwick—*I* could have paid this at almost any other period since my first publication—but now it was impossible—my last summer's tour was very costly and my five children's private expenses as well as my own have swallowed the rest of what remained from furnishing Julian Hill.[16]

There was simply no money left, and a few days later, the agent reported:

> I have been waiting until this moment, 3 o'clock, before I could hear from Mr. Trollope and now I find he could not receive any money on Saturday but he is promised to be paid this week sufficient to take up the first bill. This he promised last week and many times before, which makes me have no confidence in him, and what would be best to do with him I know not.
>
> He don't appear to me to have but very little stock dead or alive, and how he is to pay the second bill and the rent of the last half year I cannot imagine.

The picture was grim. Somehow, Trollope came up with £37 to cover the last of his previous bills, but more than £210 was outstanding. There was little likelihood that he could ever recover this amount from his farming profits. For the land on which Trollope was paying £4 per acre, Lord Northwick could now obtain less than £2.[17]

Thomas Anthony's affairs were beyond salvation. His one hope was help from America, where he was still the major stockholder of the bazaar, but during this same winter the Cincinnati venture finally collapsed. When the local trustees fell into arrears, Nicholas Longworth, who held the original mortgage with an unpaid balance of $1,612.99, secured a court order to seize the building. Despite an appraised value of $7,000, the sheriff offered the bazaar at public auction, where it was knocked down for a high bid of $4,667. Subtracting the outstanding debts, the net return to the eleven stockholders was somewhat in excess of $3,000. Even this money failed to reach Thomas Anthony at the moment of his greatest need.[18]

By February, Northwick's agent urged action, since "Mr. Trollope is in a very bad situation." Yet months passed, and in April the agent again reported:

> I have made many and repeated applications to Mr. Trollope for payment of the large arrears due from him to your lordship. In my last application he stated that it was totally out of his powers at present to discharge your lordship's demand, but that he was willing to let the farm or to act in any way your lordship might think best, to secure the ultimate payment of your lordship's claim.
>
> I am fearful that Mr. Trollope's affairs are in sad disorder, but as he has not now nor for a long time past any live or dead stock upon his premises, I think the most prudent course to pursue will be to seize at the proper time and sell the present growing crops and permit Mr. Trollope to let his farm

from Michaelmas next by which means I should hope your lordship will realize all that is and will then be due to him.[19]

Nothing could have brought the Trollopes out of these ever-increasing debts: they now owed Lord Northwick more than £500. When Henry Milton discovered the real state of things, he made some desperate but overdue efforts to put Thomas Anthony's financial affairs in order, securing a separate account for Mrs. Trollope's earnings, safe from her husband's creditors.

Mrs. Trollope now stepped in to take charge of her family's fortunes. In Cincinnati she had lost everything; she would not let it happen again. Anticipating a seizure, she determined to rescue some of her possessions before they were put under the hammer. First, Frances delivered her furniture—most of it newly purchased from literary profits—to a neighbor, Colonel Grant, who promised to ship it out of the country for her. By the time the transaction came to the attention of Northwick's agent, only a fraction of the house furnishings were left. Next, she packed her husband off to Ostend, where her friend Mrs. Fauche promised to find him lodgings. Northwick's agent was appropriately suspicious of the activity at the household and had heard alarming reports.

> Mr. Trollope told me today that he was going to Chittenham [sic, Cheltenham] for three or four weeks to recruit his health, but I understood Coln. Grant that he was gone to London in order to go a Broad [sic] which your lordship may depend upon is most likely the truth—[20]

Northwick's broker moved in to seize what remained: "furniture and three horses, 5 carts, brewing utensils, faggots, etc." The agent calculated that "what is now left on the premises . . . will sell for about £90 or thereabouts."[21] Julians Hill, which had become the visible sign of Mrs. Trollope's success, now stood occupied by bailiffs. She and the girls, aided by the Grant daughters, braved the local officials in a dramatic scene later described by Anthony, who had been summoned to assist:

> The house and furniture were all in charge of the sheriff's officers . . . a scene of devastation was in progress. . . . My mother, through her various troubles, had contrived to keep a certain number of pretty-pretties which were dear to her heart . . . some china, and a little glass, a few books, and a very moderate supply of household silver. These things, and things like them, were being carried down surreptitiously through a gap between the two gardens onto the premises of our friend Colonel Grant. My two sisters, then 16 and 17, and the Grant girls, who were just younger, were the chief marauders. To such forces I was happy to add myself for

any enterprise, and between us we cheated the creditors to the extent of our powers, amidst the anathemas, but good humored abstinence from personal violence of the men in charge of the property.[22]

While the sheriff's men stood by, Lord Northwick's agent abruptly terminated the theft, for he could not "permit Mrs. Trollope to have the remainder of the goods to be given to her (because I considered that she and Coln. Grant had robbed your lordshp sufficiently by so clandestinely taking away to his house that portion of furniture that should have come to the Hammer)." Halting the procession, he summoned the auctioneer to appraise the articles and demanded £12, after payment of which Anthony and the girls were permitted to continue. Such was the sad conclusion of Mrs. Trollope's residence at Harrow, as she bargained for her last few "pretty-pretties" with Lord Northwick's angry agent.[23] Indeed, events moved so swiftly to their conclusion that Mrs. Trollope had to leave England before she could sign the formal agreement for her German travel book. Still proudly determined to conceal her personal woes, she lied to Murray about these events.

> Mr. Trollope having decided upon taking his family abroad for some time, I fear I shall not have the satisfaction of signing the agreement with you before my departure—I have therefore to request that you will have the kindness to send the estimate of the expenses of publication, and the terms of agreement to my brother, Henry Milton . . . who is authorized to execute the agreement for me.

Mrs. Trollope did not even have time to correct the proofs, a difficult task which her brother kindly undertook.[24] In the flurry of their whirlwind departure there was confusion, and Murray omitted to print Mrs. Trollope's preface and some of Hervieu's plates.

After sending Cecilia and Anthony (who had failed to win an expected Oxford scholarship) to join their father, Mrs. Trollope remained with the Grants to make final arrangements. Afraid that the climate in Belgium might be too severe for Henry, she made a fatiguing trip to Devonshire where she left him in the care of her aunt, Fanny Bent. Because Tom was preparing for his final examinations, she deliberately kept him in ignorance of all these events. The Garnetts grieved over Mrs. Trollope's new troubles: "What will she do with such a family and their expensive habits! It is dreadful to think of it . . ."[25]

And indeed, it was a desperate assortment of troubled characters who finally settled into their "new banishment" at Bruges, a location chosen for its cheapness and proximity to London. The best description of the family circle was recorded by young Anthony:

My brother Henry . . . was ill. My younger sister was ill. And though as
yet we hardly told each other that it was so, we began to feel that the
desolating fiend, consumption, was among us. My father was broken-
hearted as well as ill, but whenever he could sit at his table he still worked
at his ecclesiastical records. My elder sister and I were in good health, but I
was an idle desolate hanger-on, that most hopeless of human beings, a
hobbledehoy of 19, without any idea of a career, a profession, or a
trade. . . . Now and again there would arise a feeling that it was hard
upon my mother that she should have to do so much for us, that we should
be idle while she was forced to work so constantly; but we should
probably have thought more of that had she not taken to work as though it
were the recognised condition of life for an old lady of 55.[26]

In the face of these seemingly impossible circumstances, Mrs. Trollope
refused to be broken. In a letter to Julia she was determined and bravely
optimistic.

But, as it often happens . . . evil has brought forth good. For years I have
been endeavoring to persuade Mr. Trollope to let us reside on the
continent where every guinea goes as far, or farther than two in England
and this event has brought him to it at last—He has given up his farm into
the hands of Lord Northwick, and made the best settlement of his affairs
that circumstances would allow—My settlement (oh! what a blessed thing
is a settlement!) affords an income sufficient to support us in perfect
comfort here—and if in addition to this, I continue able to gain money by
my pen, we shall be much richer than we have ever been—Even now, I
feel a thousand times more at my ease than I have done for years. Mr.
Trollope permits me to receive our little revenue—every thing is paid for
before it is consumed—and should I again make money by my pen we
shall be *rich*.[27]

She resolved that her family would rise from the ashes of this second
major catastrophe, and her resolve required from her self-discipline and
unremitting work which, without rhetoric or fanfare, she engaged upon
with an unobtrusiveness and joy which her son Anthony recalled in later
years with open admiration.

Of the mixture of joviality and industry which formed her character, it is
almost impossible to speak with exaggeration. The industry was a thing
apart, kept to herself. It was not necessary that any one who lived with her
should see it. She was at her table at four in the morning, and had finished
her work before the world had begun to be aroused. But the joviality was
all for others.[28]

Her energetic spirit she communicated to her family, as she busied them and herself with the numerous tasks of everyday life, which were always her therapy for despair and regrets. "Plotting and planning from morning to night how to make one table and two chairs do the work of a dozen," she set about making their new rented lodgings as comfortable as possible. "Each of us have already learned to fix ourselves in some selected corner of our different rooms, and believe ourselves at home.— The old desks have found new tables to rest upon, and the few favorite volumes that could not leave us, are made to fill their narrow limits in orderly rows that seem to say—'here we are to dwell together.' " And although she permitted herself a moment's mention of "how the change pinches most"—in the loss of dear friends—she was quick to reassure her old neighbors that her hours were not passed in repining. She had no leisure "like Jacques, to be 'melancholy and gentlemanlike'—on the contrary I am almost as active and busy as when my Helps ran away from me in America. . . ."[29]

When the weather turned warmer, Henry returned from Devonshire, and Mrs. Trollope planned to use her expected income from the German travel book to send him on a West Indies trip under Tom's care.

> This I am assured will give him the best, if not the only chance of recovering from the severe affection on his chest. He has just joined us from Devonshire, looking wretchedly ill, but clinging to the idea of this voyage, which I trust in God I shall have the power to obtain for him.

But in July she was still waiting to learn both the terms and the time of her book's appearance.

> It is living in hot water—but I know great men must not be plagued— [Murray] tells me that Mr. Lockhart has sent the manuscript to his wife, and that it is approved—This is comfort, nevertheless, I wish the business were settled. I have had two *strong* nibbles from other publishers—but John the Great is—John the Great.[30]

When at last the good news came, and Murray liberally proposed an "early period of settling," it was too late. The proposed trip had been a wild scheme, totally unsuitable for the weak and ravaged Henry. In the fall of 1834, Mrs. Trollope returned to London to seek further medical advice and was frankly told there was no hope. Indeed, for Emily too there was but little. When the party returned to Belgium, Tom recalled a feeling that he was parting for the last time from his brother.

Mrs. Trollope arranged to send Cecilia away from contagion with her uncle Henry Milton at Fulham. She procured a London appointment at the Post Office for Anthony through her friend Mrs. Francis Freeling.

Excused from his unsuccessful tutorship at William Drury's Bruefield
school, he left at once to share Tom's London lodgings. Her travel book,
expanded by her unexpected experiences, became *Belgium and
Western Germany* and proved greatly successful; Murray, contrary to
his usual practice in such matters, paid Mrs. Trollope "a considerable
sum of money" in advance of a total sale. Later, she thanked the
publisher for his "*premature* payment" which had rendered the last
weeks of Henry's life as comfortable as they could be. The Garnetts
followed her present struggles with sympathy:

> A letter from Mrs. Trollope tells us no hope for poor Henry, but that he
> may yet linger some time from great natural strength. Her eldest son is
> going Tutor with a family for three years to Italy and Germany and her
> younger one is appointed to a good place in the post office and that a *rising
> one*, all owing, she adds, to her American book. Her Belgium is going
> through another addition [*sic*] and a very profitable work it proves—Thus
> she says is a mixture of good and evil in her life—[31]

She settled down to face the long winter of nursing the mortally ill
Henry, aided only by two part-time Belgian housemaids and faced with
subsequent prospects of a dying husband as well. At the same time, she
worked to complete her novel, *Tremordyn Cliff* the financial returns
from which were already desperately needed.

Better than anyone else, Anthony realized the strain of the compart-
mentalization that was necessary if she was to succeed at both tasks.
Surely his own subsequent steady writing habits and well-known ability
to divide his time between the requirements of Barsetshire and the Post
Office were born as he watched his mother in the Chateau d'Hondt in
that winter of 1834.

> From that time forth my mother's most visible occupation was that of
> nursing. There were two sick men in the house, and hers were the hands
> that tended them. The novels went on, of course. We had already learned
> to know that they would be forthcoming at stated intervals,—and they
> always were forthcoming. The doctor's vials and the ink-bottle held equal
> places in my mother's rooms. I have written many novels under many
> circumstances; but I doubt much whether I could write one when my
> whole heart was by the bedside of a dying son. Her power of dividing
> herself into two parts, and keeping her intellect by itself clear from the
> troubles of the world, and fit for the duty it had to do, I never saw equalled.
> I do not think that the writing of a novel is the most difficult task which a
> man may be called upon to do; but it is a task that may be supposed to
> demand a spirit fairly at ease. The work of doing it with a troubled spirit
> killed Sir Walter Scott. My mother went through it unscathed in strength,

though she performed all the work of day-nurse and night-nurse to a sick household;—for there were soon three of them dying.[32]

In the midst of these trials, she continued to encounter difficulties in her publishing career. Following her dispute with Whittaker over suitable payments, she had found few takers for her new books. Manuscripts sent to publishers remained unread or were returned after inordinate delays with comments about the ruinous expenses of publishing books just then. John Murray would not even consider her new novel, and she finally turned to Richard Bentley, a publisher of popular works, for whom she agreed to provide a thousand-page novel by January. But this deadline she would not meet, for nursing Henry was an exhausting task. He suffered from oppressive chest pains, and everything he ate caused discomfort. He kept to his upstairs room and slept but irregularly. She had to wait for his periods of fitful rest to "scribble away" and drank strong coffee to stay awake on alternate nights. When Tom remonstrated with his mother on this spartan regime, she reassured him. "I *do* take care of myself, dear Tom. All the more because my children wish it. My working nights are far from disagreeable, and I sleep the night after like a top."[33]

Tremordyn Cliff, with its strong heroine and weak young earl dying of hemorrhaging, surely bore the traces of Mrs. Trollope's current preoccupations. The story involves a modern Lady Macbeth, the only surviving daughter of seven, whose claim to succeed to her father's estate and titles is suddenly displaced by the birth of a son. Mrs. Trollope's dominating, determined, and clever heroine is better qualified to rule than the young earl, who proves to be tender, soft, girlish, and poetic. Even the boy's subsequent bride notes: "It is a pity she and her gentle brother cannot make an exchange; she would be the most lordly knight that ever buckled on a sword, and he would be . . . the very prettiest damsel in the world" (1:45–46). In a clumsy and involved conspiracy, Augusta seeks to murder her brother and disinherit his wife. Thwarted by an improbable mistake, she conveniently throws herself off Tremordyn Cliff to end the novel.[34]

The sole interest of the book lies in its unusual reversal of the traditional sex roles. All the male characters are feeble, contemptible, and easily ruled. From this novel on, the women are the equals of men, and more often their superiors. Herself the family nurse and breadwinner, Mrs. Trollope found the traditional heroine—weak, lovely, and soft-eyed—uncongenial to her own womanhood. She had no patience with ladies "formed of that softest, purest, and most plastic clay, of which the great majority of woman kind are fabricated" (2:81–82), and displayed nothing but contempt for them. From her subsequent fine portrait of the self-made woman, the widow Barnaby, to the clever ladies of her late fiction, Mrs. Trollope's heroines are mostly strong women who achieve success on their own.

As Christmas approached, Henry's condition rapidly worsened. On 23 December 1834, he died, and Mrs. Trollope recalled her absent children with an unusual cry for help: "We have suffered greatly." Tom hurried back to Bruges and stayed with his mother until April 1835, when the novel written under these painful conditions appeared.[35] Most of the reviewers, while critical of *Tremordyn Cliff* as a whole, found her strong heroine intriguing. The *Athenaeum* liked the idea of a high-born and ambitious girl who wanted to keep the family honors and influence in her own hands, and even the *Times*, disappointed in the improbable plot, remarked that "the character of the Countess of Tremordyn is sketched with considerable dramatic power." As in her two earlier novels, the reviewers emphasized her inability to draw convincing pictures of fashionable life and good society. Claiming that her pictures of nobility lacked "airiness, ease, and truth," her best bits being "descriptions of furniture," The *Spectator* isolated Mrs. Trollope's fictional talent.

> In *showing-up* the half genteel society of a provincial town, our author is at home. Her dialogues, representing the vulgar tittle-tattle and the spiteful scandal of "Broton in Gloucestershire," though by no means essential to advancing the story, and somewhat literal in themselves, are very good. Mrs. Trollope may desire grandeur; she may admire, with the ladies in the *Vicar of Wakefield*, "Shakespeare, high life, and the musical glasses," and may even school herself into loving them; but in painting the vulgar, the half-bred, or better still, the under-bred, she seems to luxuriate with a congenial zest.[36]

Though familiar with such criticisms, Mrs. Trollope was not yet ready to take them seriously, for she was already planning a new excursion and another travel book: she explained to the publisher Richard Bentley, "Though my novels are read, my reputation must chiefly be sustained by traveling." Only when she realized that these "works of imagination, written in the retirement of [her] quiet home," in the intervals between her travels, would bring more profit and fame than her "costly ramblings," did she turn her remarkable energy and intelligent self-appraisal to these judgments to find, at the age of fifty-six, her true identity as a writer.[37]

7

Mrs. Trollope as Traveler

To keep my place before the public . . . . my
reputation must chiefly be sustained by traveling

OVER THE next ten years, Mrs. Trollope sought to repeat the success of
Domestic Manners in four European travelogues. Twenty-five years of
Napoleonic war had whetted the public appetite for information and
sketches of places so recently famous: campaigns in the Peninsula and
Egypt, such battles as Borodino, Leipzig, and of course, Waterloo, had
all made the map of Europe freshly interesting, not forgetting Elba. In
an age not mechanized, foreign travel remained high adventure, still
relatively exclusive in nature. Of course, the aristocratic Grand Tour had
ended with the French Revolution, and new modes of travel were
sounding the death knell of older ones. Soon, Murray's and Baedeker's
guide books and the international railway timetables would make it
possible, in the words of Thomas Cook, for every tourist to see "the
quaint Belgian cities, the castl'd Rhine crags, the glaciers, mountains and
waterfalls of Switzerland, and perhaps the blue plains of Italy, for
comparatively a trifling sum."[1]

In the meantime, to the increasingly literate and inquisitive reading
public, travel books had particular appeal. They were not frivolous,
light, and possibly sinful like novels. More entertaining than sermons or
books of improving lectures, they were considered appropriate instru-
ments of learning in an age very serious about the effects of reading. The
presses poured forth literature covering almost every area of the globe,
from America to the esoteric "Koonawur in the Himalaya," and "Kam-
tchatka and Siberia." By the 1830s, travel books formed a staple in the
literary market, and in the next decade so many appeared that review
magazines treated them in groups, according to subject and place.[2]

By the time Mrs. Trollope began to make her tours, the travelbook
genre was well established. One reviewer, no doubt in weary response
to the floods of voyages, visits, journals, and letters, testily asked the
writer of *A Summer Ramble in Syria,*

> If a man in making a tour, no matter where, writes a journal and publishes
> it, the public naturally ask, and they have a right to do so, why is it
> published? The author ought to be able to answer that it is for instruction
> or for amusement, or for both.

Coming under the general heading of amusement were those volumes
which professed to be written for fireside travelers. These announced a
mental lightness in their titles; they were "visits and sketches," "slight
reminiscences," "rambles," "rough notes," or even "bubbles."[3] As the
more traveled areas of the globe wore thin in reader interest, many
volumes made their way because they recounted exciting experiences of
an unusual sort in exotic areas of the world. Daring exploits and
adventures like those of Sir Francis Head, galloping across the Pampas
between Mendoza and Buenos Aires, or the Reverend Munro's Tartar
trip from Aleppo to Stamboul, he riding like a fiery Arab, keeping pace
with Ali Aga, "the *ne plus ultra* of his race, who could sit seven days and
nights on horseback without sleeping, and who ate nothing but air,"[4]
attracted readers for whom the trip from Dover to Calais was still an
expedition into the unknown.

Some travel literature served specifically as guidebooks. A few years
after Mrs. Trollope's first European tour, John Murray published his
Handbook to Holland, thus beginning a trend toward more systematic
and standardized guide books which, in 1839, Karl Baedeker, with
Germanic thoroughness, brought to completion.[5]

Some books tried to strike a more profound note, giving opinions on
subjects as serious as national character, religion, or political institutions.
Often, comments on French or German society served as thinly veiled
attempts to correct, reprove, or praise the English public. These were
not usually the products of women, who were clearly warned by one
reviewer: "Whatever you do, keep clear of politics; the moment you
trench upon Whig and Tory, you make, unavoidably, a certain number
of enemies; and that is what is to be supposed every woman with
common delicacy of feeling shrinks from."[6] Writers like Mrs. Jameson,
often praised for her works of travel, agreed and complied. Mrs.
Trollope scorned such a limited role: "when politics are thus lightly
mixed up with all things, how can the subject be wholly avoided without
destroying the power of describing any thing as we find it?"[7]

As the volume and scope of travel books increased, one reviewer in
1835 advised the discriminating reader to seek, as the true interest of a
book of travels, the personality of its author. Mrs. Trollope's travel
books stood out from the multitudes precisely because they were the
products of a unique observer. All her books have a distinctive voice. No
mere reporter of scenery and events, she is a writer who traveled with

her own set of values, strong opinions, and beliefs. This element in her travel books one reviewer called "opinionizing," while overlooking its function, akin to that of the intrusive narrator of fiction. This voice, always controversial and strongly biased, advanced ideas on many subjects, from the position of women to current politics, even while recounting entertaining tales of daring adventures.[8]

Other travelers with equally strong personalities had even more exciting adventures. But Mrs. Trollope, with her novelist's instinct, made people prominent in a genre where landscape, place, and exposition usually dominated. As she recorded outward demeanor and gesture, she speculated on the interior person. More often, she let the people talk for themselves in skillfully managed dialogues that made her books exceptional among other travel accounts of the period. But Mrs. Trollope did not merely record speech. Her American book had taught her how to shape her dramatic stories to reveal general truths about a society. In her subsequent books of travel, although she never again enjoyed the full familiarity with her subject that she had in America, she always made even the smallest facts suggestive of a larger whole. Her books were popular because they were a new type of fiction.

She had not intended to create a new type of travel book but tried hard to give the public what she thought it wanted; her plans called for the conventional rhapsodies over landscape and descriptions of the usual tourist attractions. Just as in the United States she had dutifully traveled to Niagara, in Germany she planned the pilgrimage to the tomb of the three kings in Cologne; in Paris she traveled to Versailles and proposed a special trip to witness the effect produced by the erection of Napoleon's statue on the column at the Place Vendôme.[9] In Vienna she heard the Opera, and in Italy she visited the art galleries. But her eye consistently wandered from places to people. Because she was traveling quickly and sometimes lacked fluency in the language, her encounters with people remained superficial and were limited to innkeepers, fellow travelers, border officials, and those who could be readily observed at work, play, or worship. Thus, while she often managed to provide penetrating observations on the society she found, they proved to be more often on that of the polished European traveler than on the resident of Belgium, Germany, Austria, or Italy.

Despite the altered circumstances, she proceeded to compose in her accustomed method, taking notes on the spot of all she did, saw, or heard. The first of these travel books was *Belgium and Western Germany*, a chronologically arranged description of her continental tour during four months of the summer 1833. Returning home with "notes taken at the time," she faced only the task of "threading them into a consecutive form." John Murray, her publisher, was pleased, for he too believed "that was the real way to write a book of travels, giving the genuine first impressions."[10]

To this limited raw material Mrs. Trollope brought the novelist's eye for form and scene. Again the anecdote dominated. She brought to life the gaming tables of Baden with the same skill she had used to describe religion in western America. She depicted characters with so sharp and exaggerated an outline that they were remembered long after the scenery had vanished.

She included large chunks of dialogue which, because of her language barrier, was the speech of her fellow travelers. The result was a lively and vivid account of picaresque incidents which might more correctly have been called "the travels of an Englishwoman in Belgium and Western Germany."

These methods are most successful in the Baden-Baden sections where she created out of a familiar environment a memorable pageant illuminating the devastating effects of the contemporary mania for gambling. In four different sections she depicted the casinos, each time stressing the human tragedy. Describing her first visit to the tables, her words point to the intrinsic concerns of the novelist, not the author of travel books.

> The scene was to me one of such deep and novel interest, that, spite of the sweet air and innocent gaiety without, I had no power to leave it. It was the first time that I had ever seen the human countenance under circumstances so calculated to display all the variety of expression of which it is capable. I knew not how tremendous a study a human face might be; nor can I at all understand why I found so much interest, I could almost call it fascination, in watching the working muscles of beings that I so heartily despised. [2:20–21]

As she began her next rendition of the "frightful scene of madness," she narrowed the focus to her favorite subject.

> I saw women distinguished by rank, elegant in person, modest, and even reserved in manner, sitting at the rouge et noir table with their rateaux and marking cards in their hands; the former to push forth their bets, and draw in their winnings; the latter to prick down the events of the game.

She described one in particular, "whom I watched day after day during the whole period of our stay." Concentrating on the human drama rather than the physical setting, Mrs. Trollope quickly passed from the elegant dress, white silk bonnet, gauze veil, and delicate beringed hands, with

jewelled watch of peculiar splendor, to the emotions that infused the
lady's face.

> There she sat constantly throwing down handfuls of five-franc pieces; and
> sometimes drawing them back again, till her young face grew rigid from
> weariness, and all the lustre of her eye faded into a glare of vexed inanity.

Nearby, an older woman "seemed no longer to have strength to conceal
her eager agitation under the air of callous indifference which all prac-
tised players endeavour to assume." The woman's hand trembled and
shook, "the dew of agony" lay upon her wrinkled brow (2:45–47).

From such observations, Mrs. Trollope explored the motivations
behind gambling. It could hardly be avarice, she concluded, "for a child
can tell, that to lose, and not to gain, is the certain result of playing at a
public table" (2:68). That she even raised such questions set her apart
from the conventional traveler of her day, like Sir Arthur Faulkner,
whose visit to the gaming tables at Baden prompted him to discuss the
system by which gambling earnings returned to the state, which applied
them to keeping the grounds and walks in the best repair. When Sir
Francis Head described similar scenes at Wiesbaden, he was over-
whelmed by the crowds and did not pause over individuals, preferring
instead to discuss the service and the food. Mrs. Trollope is one of the
first who sought to fulfill the reader's desire for an explanation of human
action rather than for statistics.[11]

Her speculations concluded with two long dramatic scenes which
arose out of her "strange and tragic pleasure in watching the workings of
the human soul."

> I have watched the working muscles, and read the agony they expressed;
> even where the lips have been firmly set, and the eyes fixed, almost with-
> out winking, to conceal it.
>   I have watched men . . . shrink into littleness, as the gold they had
> madly thrown upon the table, was carelessly raked up by the callous
> bankers.

She depicted the faces of "brave officers" who never feared the enemy
now "turn lividly pale," and "the quiet smile, which these reptiles [the
bankers] exchange with each other, when some indication of feeling
escapes. . . . " She was aware that such visions were not the usual
travel book fare but knew no other way to render what she had found.

> I am pretty sure, that hitherto nothing has been written, nothing painted,

that can convey to those, who have never witnessed it, the fearful miseries
of a gaming table. [2:69–71]

Returning to this theme a last time, Mrs. Trollope confessed: "I felt as if
living amidst the pages of a new novel." By relying upon imagination
rather than reporting skill, she produced a more truthful evocation of
this society than had any of her contemporary fellow travelers.

She sketched the characteristic types at the tables.

> Occasionally a party with coal-black eyes, and highly-arched noses,
> would place themselves round a table; and there one should see no
> pork. . . . Here might be seen a portly gentleman, with a fair-browed
> wife or daughter, who looked about him with less curiosity, ate his dinner
> with more tranquillity, and seemed more at home than the rest; this must
> be a high-born Baron of the empire.

Along with such respectable figures, Mrs. Trollope noticed those who
preyed upon their betters.

> There sat a pair of companions, whose roving eyes had a look of business
> in them; they spoke in whispers, ate little, and drank less; yet lingered long
> over their solitary bottle, and looked with no idle glance upon the varying
> scale of profusion with which the guests were furnished: these probably
> had deeper recesses for their play than the table of rouge et noir. [2:84]

Finally, after describing a young man being artfully robbed while
playing and her own longings to expose the thief, which she dared not
do, she closed the scene with the story of an attempted suicide who,
despairing over his gambling debts, had fired a pistol into his mouth.
Badly mutilated but still alive, he was carried past Mrs. Trollope into the
hotel. With her writer's eye for emphasis, her last words on gambling
were a terse question for the reader.

> Did the fearful business of the gaming-table go on that night? The players
> must surely be something more or less than men, if it did. [2:131]

How different such passages were from the dry informative ones of her
rival travelers. When the spirit of a place could be captured by an
imaginative recreation of people, she was unsurpassed. Unfortunately,
not all of Belgium and western Germany could be so evoked. The
gamblers at Baden and perhaps the radical students at Bonn, with their
"exquisitely dishevelled hair," are the only groups which she succeeded
in capturing in this fashion.[12]

Once on the Rhine (conventional territory for the traveler in 1833),

Mrs. Trollope rendered the expected "sublime" description of rocks and castles. More interesting were her confrontations with a new breed of tourist of whom she sketched many examples. The first, a young man, guidebook in hand, was determined to get his money's worth, despite the rapid rate of the steamboat. Frantically, he observed the scenery from

> the deck of a vessel, with a panoramic view of the Rhine in his hand, turning his head this side to see one ruin, and that side to see another;—his finger placed with nervous eagerness upon some famous promontory, and his thumb on a first-rate castle,—while kept in a state of feverish agitation, lest the panting engine should bear him out of reach before he can get a peep at either. [1:198–99]

Mrs. Trollope noted many such hapless travelers, doomed to have only superficial acquaintance with the scenes they visited. The innkeeper on a Rhine island nostalgically recalled a time when the English used to come in droves to his hotel for weeks at a time.

> "But now," he added piteously, "they drive past, as fast as they can go, and never set foot on shore, except at night, from Amsterdam to Mayence." [1:197]

Elsewhere on her tour, two ladies quickly made sketches of a passing scene in "a match against time, as well as against each other; and the odds were an hundred to one against their finishing the first turret of their castle, before it was half a mile behind them" (1:214). Many of her stories illustrate the foolishness of travelers who rushed past the daily life of the country they had come to see. In addition, she caught the vulgar and ostentatious. There were the "great linguists," who addressed the boatman confidently: "Woolen sie put cela avec the baggages?" There was the handsome woman "not quite young" and magnificent militaire "not quite old," carrying on "one of those vehement flirtations," and the old lady whose expressed intention in traveling was "to go as far as possible within the time [she] can spare," and who insisted:

> seeing sights would tire me to death—it always does in London; but driving along in this way is quite pleasant. No, no; nothing will ever induce me to tire myself by running after curiosities in every town I pass through: I make the greatest point of never seeing sights. [1:134]

So often had people boldly replaced landscape in her book that she once apologized: "It must not be thought. . . that because I sometimes withdrew my eyes from the landscape to look at my neighbours I was insensible to the great beauty, nay sublimity, of the scenery" (1:218). But in these characters, Mrs. Trollope provided amusing reading for an English public that would never set foot on German soil. The reviewers, while criticizing her descriptions "in issimo," liked the originality of these sketches "of English female vulgarity and presumption, exemplified in certain steamboat and Eilwagen travellers." "In doing these things," wrote the reviewer in the *Westminster Review*, "Mrs. Trollope is in technical phrase 'at home.' "[13]

In contrast to such tourists, Mrs. Trollope cast herself as the ideal traveler who took risks and attempted the unusual or even the dangerous. Be it the lofty steeple of a church in Antwerp where she fought a tremendous wind "stoutly for half an hour" or some picturesque but precarious cliff atop the Rhine, from which it was necessary that she be rescued with a rope hastily fetched by Henry and Hervieu, she would see and record everything from the best vantage point. To experience fully the dungeons, torture chambers, and pits of the alt Schloss at Baden-Baden, she climbed to the innermost recesses and asked to be locked in for a half hour, while Hervieu sketched the scene.[14]

The most exciting and extensive scene in which Mrs. Trollope was heroine of her own travels was her visit to the Brocken in the Harz mountains, famous in German legend as the haunt of witches and devils. With zest she described the ascent, her own insistence on continuing in a driving rain, and the hazardous descent in the middle of a storm, which required that she and her party be strapped and pinned to the donkeys. Despite her admission that "though I could hardly draw breath," she still experienced "a feeling very much like enjoyment." She wryly added: "I doubt whether I can recommend the ascent of the Brocken to the generality of female travelers." For Mrs. Trollope, the experience of travel had become symbolic, standing, in its bustle, struggle, and variety, for life itself (2:239–72).

The *Spectator* especially liked this aspect of her book, calling her "an old stager [who] learnt enterprise in her adventures in the back settlements of the West." The reviewer had caught the book's essential quality.

> She was not satisfied to tread in the footsteps of the common tourist and to yield herself implicitly up to the guidance of an innkeeper, a *valet de place*, or a coachman. She sought out objects for herself, pursued the picturesque where it was likely to be found.[15]

Truly, she had been the compleat traveler.

The book pleased the reading public, too, and went quickly into a second edition.[16] When Mrs. Trollope wrote Murray her thanks for his early payments for *Belgium*, she mentioned plans for yet another travel book:

> It is not exactly *here* [in Bruges] that I should wish to attempt another volume either of observation or description—but, did circumstances permit, I should greatly like to scribble a little gossip on the present queer state of society in Paris, where the *liberal absolutism* of the long headed monarch [Louis Phillipe] disdains not to work its will by the *very smallest maneuvering* in the world.

Apparently they had discussed such a work, and it was perhaps Murray who suggested that she cast her next book into the form of familiar letters to a friend, so as to create a sense of freshness and immediacy.[17] But nothing came of her attempts to interest him in the Paris trip and book.

She had placed *Tremordyn Cliff* with Richard Bentley, thus beginning a long, profitable association with that publishing firm. On 24 March, she negotiated an agreement with Bentley for a "work on the subject of Paris and the Parisians to be treated in a similar manner to her work on the *Domestic Manners of the Americans*." Agreeing to accept £500 for the first 2,000 copies, Mrs. Trollope set out on new travels.[18] Once again, death drove her away from memories of painful scenes. Henry was buried as the new year 1835 opened. By April, she was settled in her Parisian quarters where her old friend Mrs. Mary Garnett found her "improved in manner, more simple" and immersed in that social activity and hard work with which she sought to dispel the demons of the tragic winter in Bruges. "She goes out from morning to night to give her account in her book. She is in good spirits and with her name she can make as much as she wants. She remains here till June. We see her but little and that of an evening only."[19]

Her trip to Paris also arose from the hope of consulting French physicians about Mr. Trollope's health, which was steadily deteriorating. Indeed, Thomas Adolphus later recorded that although his father was just sixty years old, he looked at least eighty. And while Mrs. Trollope seemed financially successful and secure, ominous signs were also obvious. Mrs. Garnett noted: "She looks fatigued and it seems to me anxious."[20] Besides worries about her husband's health, she was concerned about Anthony and still hoped to find him a place somewhere in the literary world. Recent biographers have accused Mrs. Trollope of neglecting and underestimating her youngest son. But her appeals to Murray for some after-hours employment for Anthony in that summer of 1835 tell another story.

He is a good scholar and, as I believe your friend Henry Drury will allow, has very good abilities. It has been suggested to him that he might possibly find employment either by correcting the press, or in some other occupation of the kind, and I should be very grateful if you could help him in obtaining such.

Tom, too, had yet to be settled. He had received his Oxford degree in April and although promised a teaching position in Birmingham, was still idle, waiting for the appointment to be ratified (it did not come until 1837). Impatient and footloose, he joined his mother in Paris that May.[21]

These family concerns delayed the completion of her new manuscript. By October, she confessed to Bentley that she would be "behind the time at which I told you that I should hope to have finished my book on Paris. . . . This delay has been occasioned by the long and very alarming illness of Mr. Trollope. He is still confined to his bed, but his danger is past, and I am again at work." She begged permission to "retrench a hundred pages of the stipulated quantity," trying to resist the seemingly inflexible system which demanded from authors a set number of pages and volumes:

> I have never accustomed myself in writing of what I have seen to draw anything out into great length, and I cannot but believe that my success has arisen greatly from the fact that I have not been considered *tedious*.[22]

Then, when Bentley fell behind and delayed publication of *Tremordyn Cliff*, she was further disappointed and distressed. In a letter unusual in its personal references and significant for its revelation of her own image as a writer, she remonstrated with her publisher:

> Circumstances have rendered what I gain by my pen an object of importance to my family; I therefore may not indulge, as persons differently situated might do, in writing books only to beguile their idle hours, while enjoying the blessing of indifference as to the time and manner of their publication.—I do not compose rapidly—but since I have felt it my duty to write, I have devoted such a portion of each day to the occupation, as would enable me to keep my place before the public.

But the season had passed and not even an advertisement for *Tremordyn Cliff* had appeared.

> That I was employed in writing this novel was well known, and the applications and enquiries addressed to me respecting it, are, and have been very embarrassing.
> I am aware that though my novels are read, my reputation must chiefly be

sustained by traveling, and I love the occupation well enough to look forward with hope and pleasure to future excursions.—I have been often told that I ought to visit Italy (Venice particularly) and Sicily—and I hope to be able to do so—but the truth is, that however well the public may like my traveling memoranda, the expenses incurred in collecting them are much too heavy to render the employment profitable, or even prudent.— The publishing some work of imagination, written in the retirement of my quiet home, in the interval between my costly ramblings, is the only method by which I can enable myself to undertake them. The delay that has already attended the appearance of *Tremordyn Cliff* will render this arrangement much more difficult for the coming year. I would wish to start for Italy early next spring, but this will not be in my power unless I receive the whole price of another novel before I set out.[23]

The novels that Mrs. Trollope constantly turned out as she was casting her traveling notes into final form did much to influence even these travel books. As she read over her Paris notes, she was already thinking through *The Vicar of Wrexhill*, writing an antislavery novel, and contemplating one based "on the facts and traits of character collected at Paris." Thus fictional techniques became inextricably part of her third book of travel, *Paris and the Parisians in 1835.*[24]

These ingredients lie readily at hand. The travel accounts are interspersed with modes whose analogues are strictly fictional. These are dialogues, in some of which characters debate the relative merits of French and English mores, modern French literature, or the present government; catalogues of facts, set scenes, and familiar essays on light subjects (dinner parties in Paris compared to those in England). Most original are Mrs. Trollope's dark narratives, akin to those with which Dickens later spotted the bright surface of *Pickwick Papers*. Mrs. Trollope herself is the picaresque heroine of the piece, narrating the plots of violent French dramas, visiting insane patients at Vanves, and telling the pathetic story of an orphan at the *Hôpital des Enfants Trouvés*. One chapter is devoted to the story of a horrible murder, a visit to the morgue, and a lengthy tale of a double suicide. Two others recount violent and bloody stories currently on the boards: one, that of an executioner sadistically obsessed by his task, the other a Hugo drama of sexual jealousy and murder. By means of this steady stream of narratives, Mrs. Trollope imaginatively suggested the dark underside of Parisian life.[25]

Her handling of characterization also pointed to fiction. Drawn along "humor lines," her people appeared in terms of their occupational, intellectual, or political approach to life, mostly the latter, for in Paris, "the very air they breathe is impregnated with politics." The broadly stylized, highly externalized mode of characterization was appropriate to the Paris of 1835, for in that time and place political loyalties and passions gave an exceptional character to outward appearances. Satirically, she sketched the revolutionaries in their conical crowned hats and with

> the long and matted locks, that hang in heavy, ominous dirtiness beneath it. The throat is bare, at least from linen; but a plentiful and very disgusting profusion of hair supplies its place. The waistcoat, like that hat, bears an immortal name—'Gilet a la Robespierre' being its awful designation; and the extent of its wide-spreading lapels is held to be a criterion of the expansive principles of the wearer. *Au reste*, a general air of grim and savage blackguardism is all that is necessary to make up the outward mein of a republican of Paris in 1835. [Letter 24]

Whenever she was most contemptuous, the people snapped into brief vivid life: the street orator haranguing some children about the "cruel treatment of the amiable, patriotic, and noble-minded prisoners at the Luxembourg"; the young Napoleons of the École Polytechnique, the "very particularly greasy citizens and citizenesses" with their "dingy jackets, uncomely casquettes, ragged blouses, and ill-favoured round-eared caps, that look as if they did duty night and day"; the ragamuffin rioters and a "parvenue" duchess of these latter days.[26] Such types invited caricature, where Mrs. Trollope was at her best.

She used dialogue to enliven her subject matter, as well as to present contrasting ideas and practices. The *Literary Gazette* noted that the reader's main source of pleasure stemmed from Mrs. Trollope's skillful employment of this fictional device.[27] Dialogues came readily to hand because "in no place in the world is it so easy . . . to enter into conversation with strangers as in Paris." Usually she was a participant in these debates, many serving to reveal dispassionately the two sides of an issue, but more often providing her with a springboard for airing her own views.

Into this latter category fall Mrs. Trollope's by now anticipated discussions of the position and treatment of women. A Frenchman talks of "old maids" and the "miserable fate" of single women in England, claiming that "were any Frenchwoman to find herself so circumstanced, depend upon it she would drown herself." Following this conversation and a related incident, Mrs. Trollope, annoyed by the "contempt" with which spinsters were regarded, argued that no woman "has not at some time or in some manner had the power of marrying if she chose it." Those who refused were "high-minded" and showed "considerable dignity of character." Marriage, continued Mrs. Trollope, served generally to stifle the talents and abilities of women. The single "violate no duty by giving their time and their talents to society" and do not have to stop "to suckle fools and chronicle small beer." She who so seldom spoke of her own struggles came closest here to discussing the difficulties inherent in blending marriage with a career.[28] On the subject of women, Mrs. Trollope never shrank from championing even the most unpopular causes.

Except for such topics (which did not attract much attention) her material in *Paris*, as the *Spectator* perceptively noted, was rather commonplace: "In all this there is nothing much more novel than may be found in a guide-book, or at least than what has been seen by every visitor of Paris during the past year." But Mrs. Trollope was saved by her fictional techniques, and although the *Spectator's* reviewer was generally patronizing toward the book, he noted that her *method* and her *voice* distinguished the work from many others of the same sort. Indeed, he advised those who wished to learn the trade of bookmaking and the laws of the craft "so far as they are connected with tours and travels" to read *Paris*. To work up the materials "is not quite so easy as to collect them."[29]

Her accomplishments here surprised even her good friends who stood somewhat in awe of her capacity to sustain her fame and continue an active literary career. Mrs. Garnett wrote:

> Mrs. Trollope is coining money literally, but not over prudent I fear. She received five hundred pounds for her little tour in Paris which she will take to her bookseller Bentley in September, and a new novel sold as well, to appear at the same time. She is going to Italy for the winter, to write another book.[30]

Her achievements, however, were not transitory. As late as 1845, the *Quarterly Review*, examining the productions of twelve traveling ladies, paid homage to Mrs. Trollope as the first of "that more systematic set of travelers who regularly made a tour in order to make a book." Energetic, able, and every inch an authoress, Mrs. Trollope was one of the most successful practitioners of the art of travel in a century full of peripatetic and articulate travelers.[31]

Upon her return to Bruges, Mrs. Trollope sent Bentley the first volume of her *Paris*, with six plates by Hervieu. Finding herself unable to make the allotted number of pages, she included several vignettes by Hervieu, which, however, Bentley did not use. She was writing quickly and once apologized for the poor quality of the manuscript, which her "scrawl" made almost unreadable.[32] Her crabbed and torturous hand signaled the stresses under which she had been working. Her husband's wracking headaches and general physical decline had continued to make family life difficult. But she had watched him suffer so long that

when the end finally was close, she was unprepared. For Frances, her
husband's death came with a dull shock. As she told Bentley: "This
melancholy and unsuspected event—for I believed all dangers over—
has rendered me very uncapable of working." In one short week the
crisis had come and gone, and Thomas Anthony Trollope was dead.
With *Tremordyn Cliff* only recently released, and her *Paris* not yet out,
she again approached John Murray for help, to whom she recapitulated
her stunned sense of "unexpected loss."

> For so I must call my poor husband's death, as although he had been long
> ill, we had no idea whatever that his life was in danger. . . . Did I not
> know your kind feelings towards me, I should be still more reluctant than I
> am to ask if you can assist me at this very pressing moment by the advance
> of a little money on the sale of the second edition of the Belgian book. I am
> really in distress for the means of paying some very urgent claims, or I
> would not be this troublesome.[33]

In November, after her husband's burial, she returned to London,
making final arrangements for her Paris book, and with an energy born
of despair, planned another trip, this time to Italy.

But her troubles had not ended. While her friends concluded that "Mr.
Trollope's death will be a great relief to all his family," she can have had
little time for either mourning or rest. Her youngest daughter Emily now
bore alarming signs of consumption. Still, Mrs. Trollope pressed ahead
with her planned Italian trip, even while the Garnetts feared "that this
journey may not reestablish [Emily's] health."[34] Soon the girl was too ill
to travel, and the trip was postponed, as Mrs. Trollope prepared herself
for yet another interlude of hopeless nursing. By December Harriet told
Julia that "Emily looked wretchedly ill, and even her mother has no hope
for her recovery." In January, Mrs. Trollope rented a house at Hadley
near London to remove Emily from the damp climate of Bruges. With
Mr. Trollope dead and her money safe from her husband's creditors, she
could now fulfill her long-standing desire "to live in a cottage in England."[35]

That December her Paris travel book appeared in both French and
English. Harriet reported its reception in Paris. "It is abused here of
course by the liberal papers and praised by the Carlists, but I hear that
the English press speaks favourably of it." Soon the volumes reached a
second edition. Proud of his mother's success, Anthony told Tom:

> Mamma will, I feel confident, have a second thousand of the *Paris*. No
> work of hers was ever abused so much—or sold so fast—or praised in the
> periodicals so little—especially by her own party.[36]

Mrs. Trollope noticed the many powerful journals that were, as she bluntly phrased it, "very abusive," and she wrote a "spirited defense" for the second edition. But better judgment prevailed and she eventually withdrew it, satisfied that "more to the purpose than this, the book sells well."[37]

Miss Mitford congratulated her and looked forward to "two volumes on Italy," which would be "equally delightful" to her readers. Another trip would serve several purposes: "It will be the best possible remedy for all that you have suffered in spirits and in health." And indeed, her sufferings had once again been terrible. On 12 February, at the age of eighteen, Emily died. Anthony wrote his brother:

> It is all over ! Poor Emily breathed her last this morning. She died without any pain, and without a struggle. Her little strength had been gradually declining, and her breath left her without the slightest convulsion, or making any change in her features or face. Were it not for the ashy colour, I should think she was sleeping. I never saw anything more beautifully placid and composed. . . . It is much better that it is now, than that her life should have been prolonged only to undergo the agonies which Henry suffered.[38]

Once again, his mother summoned the rest of the family to her side. As a precautionary measure, Cecilia had been sent away to the same place she had stayed during Henry's final illness. Thirteen years would elapse before she, a happy young mother of thirty-three, succumbed to the same disease.

But grief was soon dispersed by the requirements of the living. On 28 March 1836, Mrs. Trollope began negotiations with Bentley for the sale of the copyrights on all her previous books. Hitherto, she had maintained these rights, but now, as she admitted, "private embarrassments . . . press . . . to reconcile me to abandoning for present convenience the prospect of ulterior advantage." There were difficulties in obtaining rights to subsequent editions of *Domestic Manners* from Whittaker. Also, she had to make financial arrangements with Bentley concerning her long-planned trip. It was not necessary to remind the publisher "that it will be needful for me before packing my trunks, to know what terms you will offer me for the tour in Italy which I meditate." She also suggested the possibility of offering her previous works in "a cheaper and more popular form."

> In the case of *Paris and the Parisians* it can hardly be doubted that a large issue in a cheaper form would go off very quickly, and in the two books now in hand (The Lynch Law, and the Unco'-Good) the steel illustrations

as well as the subjects are certainly likely to make them available in more
forms than one.[39]

To encourage Bentley in such ventures, she now offered him her
previous copyrights.

On 27 April these discussions culminated in a large, comprehensive
agreement which stipulated the writing of four more books:

> first: A novel founded on American Manners to be entitled "Jona-
> than Jefferson Whitlaw," and to form 3 volumes post 8 vo. of simi-
> lar extent to "Tremordyn Cliff."
> secondly: another work of fiction, under the title of "The Unco'
> Good" (Or by whatever name it may be hereafter called) and to
> form three volumes post 8 vo. of like extent.
> thirdly: a work describing Mrs. Trollope's Travels in Austria, and
> more particularly her Residence in Vienna, to be treated in a
> similar manner to her recent book called "Paris and the Paris-
> ians" and to form two volumes . . . 8 vo. equal in extent to that
> work.
> fourthly: A similar account of her Travels and Residence in various
> parts of Italy, to form also two volumes—8 vo. of like extent.

She sold these works and their copyright for the following
considerations: *Jonathan Jefferson Whitlaw*, £350; *The Unco' Good*,
£400; *The Travels in Austria* and *Residence in Vienna*, £500; and *The
Travels and Residence in Italy*, £550. In addition, she disposed of all
rights to *Paris*, beyond the sale of 2,000 copies.[40] This unusual agreement
reveals Mrs. Trollope's growing reputation as an established writer.

By July she and her party left for Italy, by way of Vienna. They
stopped at Paris to pick up Cecilia, who was paying a long visit to the
Garnetts.[41] Because Harriet was staying at La Grange, Mrs. Trollope did
not see her young friend, who had herself recently completed a short
novel on American life for which she had sought Mrs. Trollope's help in
placing it with a publisher. The older woman sent some professional
advice to the aspiring young author by way of her sister Julia.

> I came *full* of reasoning which I had hoped might influence her future
> literary labours—To write fully on the subject is impossible—and it was
> worse than useless to leave such reasonings in charge to your dear mother
> or Fanny [Harriet's sister], because it seems that they rather wish her to
> abandon every attempt, than that she should be subject to future
> disappointment. This is a doctrine which I greatly disapprove.

Aware of the difficulties of Harriet's life, with an aging mother and a valetudinarian sister, reduced to an endless routine of morning calls and preoccupations with health, Mrs. Trollope urged her friend to persevere.

> Success itself would in my judgment be of less importance than the blessing of *occupation*. It is the want of this, dearest Julia, which produces the *tristesse* of which they all complain, without being conscious of its cause, or aware how completely the remedy is in their own power.

Furthermore, Mrs. Trollope believed in Harriet's talents, which remained unrecognized because of her refusal to write anything except short tales and translations.

> She has *genius*—but wants firmness of character—and such a degree of condescension to the popular taste, as would enable her without pain to write in conformity to its demands.

Bentley himself had advised that translations, "be they ever so excellent, from an *unknown* hand, cannot be published with any hope of success." Mrs. Trollope urged her friend to do an original work "*of the usual size*" and consent to a half profits arrangement. But despite this opinion that "few *beginning* authors have so much encouragement even as this," Harriet had refused to listen. In words anticipating her son Anthony's later no-nonsense approach to writing, Mrs. Trollope now called for Harriet to

> rouse her courage anew, . . . the success she deserves is still before her—the best feature in the business is that this first struggle once past, the rest is easy—nothing more being required than just so much application to your pen as may suffice to produce the *quantity* you desire to *sell*. This is not very sublime but it is very true.[42]

As the party left Paris, on 14 August, Mrs. Mary Garnett recorded a glimpse of the author at the outset of her most successful decade.

> Mrs. Trollope is grown very fat. She staid but one night here and is gone with her dear Tom, his friend Mr. Banberry, Cecilia, Hervieu, and her maid for one year. She is in slight mourning and I should say much pleased with her prosperity and year's absence.[43]

On the proceeds of her pen, she was off and doing once again, surrounded as she ever wished to be, by her children and friends.

In Vienna, the Trollopes began a frantic round of social life, and by December, their funds were running short. Also, Mrs. Trollope had been obliged to part with Tom, which just at this time is vexatious, though the cause is certainly satisfactory. He has been at length summoned to take possession of the appointment at Birmingham that he has been so long wishing for. It was rather a hard struggle poor fellow between interest and inclination, for he was enjoying himself here very much, and looking forward to the excursion into Italy with great delight. Nevertheless we could but rejoice that he is thus comfortably provided for.[44]

Without his support and company she told Julia, "I am often half inclined to turn home again and leave Italy unvisited, but interest opposes this inclination, and I suppose we shall proceed thither in the spring." Short of cash, she again inquired of Murray if anything were left from the sale of the second edition of her Belgian book, even while she sent him her impressions of Vienna, "this beautiful and most interesting little city." She was introduced to Metternich, and he became her hero: she called him "one of the most admirable characters that I have ever known," claiming that his name "is never uttered by people of any rank or condition without praise, admiration, and esteem. . . . Perhaps he is the only statesman left deserving the name, who feels more pity than mirth at our present condition. In short, coming to Vienna and admiring Prince Metternich is one and the same thing—if you do the first, the last must follow."[45] While Hervieu painted her portrait, Princess Metternich chatted with Mrs. Trollope, who found the praise of her "small library labours" more gratifying than any she had so far received.[46]

A month later, Mrs. Trollope proposed to her publisher that she return to England before visiting Italy, for she had already accumulated enough material for the customary two volumes.

> I would much rather that my book on Austria be published before my journey to Italy began. They must be quite distinct, and if possible unconnected even in feeling. I shall hope moreover to gain by this delay the coronation at Milan, which will *certainly* not take place before the spring of 1838—and as I should meet there many Austrian friends, it would be equally useful and agreeable. Another advantage of the change is the power it will give me of correcting the press myself.

She proposed staying in Vienna until May, making a short excursion into Hungary and attending the May Day fêtes in the Prater, which would give her sufficient material to complete her manuscript. For this, she needed another £100 in advance. She explained: "My residence here has proved greatly more expensive than I anticipated, so that in truth I cannot start upon my return till my funds are replenished."[47]

But more personal reasons prompted her return to England: she missed Tom. Even more important, the rigors of the trip had proven too much for the frail Cecilia. She wrote Julia:

> The balls are incessant, the dinner parties hardly less so, and a visit or two in the interval between them, is very necessary to guard against accumulating arrears of incivility. Yet with all this fatigue, the gaiety and elegance of the scene is very exciting, and though I should certainly not choose that all my life should pass in Vienna Carnival, I am greatly amused by it. . . . I do assure you that la belle France herself is tame in her gaiety when compared to Austria.

Their animated winter had been followed, however, by a spring of grippe, and even Mrs. Trollope found the gaiety "rather more than desirable" for herself and her daughter. The Garnetts were dismayed at reports they had received that Cecilia was indeed very ill, and Harriet wrote: "I hope from my heart that this may be an exaggerated account, but I cannot write to express my anxiety to Mrs. Trollope. How imprudent a gay winter at Vienna was for poor Cecilia: she appeared very well when with us."[48]

By 4 July 1837, with her characteristically incredible energy, Mrs. Trollope had the work on Austria ready for the press. While this book (and later her volumes on Italy) employed many of the fictional techniques which had made her first three travel books so unique, they were largely inferior, and the reason is not far to seek. Enraptured by Vienna's scenery and Italy's art treasures and flattered by the attentions accorded her by Vienna's most prominent family, Mrs. Trollope lost control of the satiric touch and penchant for caricature that distinguished her best works.[49] Her effusive admiration for Metternich and for the Princess Melanie, as well as dazzled renditions of the "creme" of Austrian society, made for lifeless volumes. As the *Spectator* perceptively noted: "The tourist was satisfied with the city, and all that it inhabit; and honey is less pungent than gall, especially when produced from the *apis Trollopiana*."[50]

Mrs. Trollope worked hard to make the book measure up to her previous successes. She energetically made "toilsome ascents" to craggy castles, "noble landscapes," waterfalls, "majestic mountains," and "stormy torrents." Aware that her writing was at times tedious, she undertook a dangerous visit to an underground salt mine, where once again she became the super-tourist, certain that such activities "to the majority of my female acquaintance . . . would bring more pain than pleasure." The highlight of her trip was another encounter with a rapacious landlord who demanded money and almost killed Tom and

Hervieu. Such exciting scenes hearken back to the adventures of *Belgium and Western Germany*.[51]

In the second volume, Mrs. Trollope introduced Metternich and the high society of Vienna. Here she rendered the parties, dinners, and balls of carnival time, giving the reader the names of all the elite society she met: the counts, princes, barons, grand-duchesses, and arch-duchesses *ad infinitum*. She saw an installation of knights of the Golden Fleece in a real imperial palace and went to a fête and a ball at the Turkish Embassy. She recounted Princess Metternich's anecdotes of the Emperor Francis but, despite much praise of Metternich, did not presume to reproduce his conversations. One reviewer accustomed to Mrs. Trollope's usual liveliness and broad characterizations found "her portrait of Metternich . . . deficient in breadth and character. . . ." Except for her unimaginative scenes from high society, she described only the usual tourist attractions: the asylums, prisons, schools for the deaf and dumb, opera, Holy Week services, art galleries. In a lengthy passage (with which Metternich himself helped) she outlined the nature of Austrian absolutism and how it worked. Such subjects, never Mrs. Trollope's forte, revealed a distinct lapse into the conventional travel-book approach. The inevitable result was a dull book.[52]

Upon her return to England, she settled down to the care of her daughter and the completion of two more novels. At year's end, however, a problem arose. That autumn, to Mrs. Trollope's shock and dismay, Tom proposed throwing up his Birmingham appointment, which had proved less exciting than life with his traveling mother. In September she wrote him a letter which began by praising his manuscript of a tour in Brittany but which settled quietly into her real business: her amazement at his imprudent wish to "throw to the dogs an independence of £200 per annum." Had the railroad between them been completed, she wrote, she should have "left the *Romance of Vienna* [a new novel upon which she was already engaged] to its fate for a day . . ." to remonstrate with him in person. Indeed, as it was, she was almost too distracted to go on with the business of writing books. She reproached herself for the "vainglorious hint" she had thrown out "in the very spirit of family gossip," that she might use her influence to get him some more appealing work:

This idle word seems to have raised a hornets' nest of wild *stinging speculations* within you, leaving your present blessings (after which you so long vainly sighed) to gell, by setting you longing for honey that you may never get. . . .

I have sometimes thought as I have sat pen in hand meditating upon the state of mind which must have dictated such a project, instead of giving my attention to my heroes and heroines, that I must have misunderstood you. . . .

Severe admonitions followed. She forbade Cecilia and Anthony even to mention Tom's idea to the Milton family. "I trust they will never know that such a thought has entered your head." She ended with solicitous advice about his health and state of mind: "Take regular exercise . . . above all things use cold water abundantly in the morning . . . its effect upon the nervous system is perfectly astonishing." Cushioning the harsh reality of her words with the comfortings of a concerned mother, she made her message nonetheless clear: stay at your job; beware of enthusiastic and ambitious projects. Work hard and endure, for only by the sweat of the brow will success be earned. She blessed her dearest Tom and promised he would hear from her often:

> Do not think that your solitude brings no suffering to me. You know not how constantly it is recurring to me—but the remembrance of all you suffered when you were pennyless is still heavy at my heart. Let this give you strength to bear it for a while longer.[53]

It was a message that only such a mother had the right to give—and it is not surprising that the twenty-seven-year-old Tom remained, for the time being, obediently at his post.

Apparently the project which had caught Tom's fancy was his mother's bright idea of capitalizing on her growing reputation by serving as editor of a new journal. She resurrected an older plan, which she now submitted again to Bentley. Sensible and innovative, her conception would also provide her sons with steady literary work and thus bring Tom back from Birmingham. Hervieu too would have a role, with his biting social cartoons. Her name as editor would help the sales, and "without having the least intention or inclination to embark on some political discussion," she envisioned a "strongly conservative" magazine. Some two years before, she had explained what the contents might include:

> A travestie in verse of the most available radical speeches . . . I could undertake to do myself. These, with historiettes and anecdotes touching on the political interests of the hour whether at home or abroad, and embellished into a Hogarth style of caricature (all on the right side remember) would I think furnish the suitable material.

Her project, requiring "zeal and courage," and her own "*daring* ideas," would be "a decidedly strong saucy conservative publication by no means devoted to politics, but indulging as freely as the 'Anti-Jacobin' of yore in showing up to ridicule and contempt what is worthy of it." Doing this, she assured Bentley, "and doing it with some spirit *would* draw attention, and so far from shrinking from the subject, I should have no objection to take as my title 'the Literary Museum and New Political Register.' "[54] But these plans never materialized.

Moreover, she faced new troubles concerning her present career as traveler. Her literary reputation, she believed, depended upon the insights gained from her continuing trips. America, after *Domestic Manners*, had returned in *The Refugee* and in *Whitlaw*. Vienna had produced a *Romance*. A visit to Italy, she anticipated, might serve the same double function. But traveling was proving too expensive. As she later wrote: "I produced a work [*Vienna and the Austrians*] for which I received £500, giving an account of an expedition which cost me £700. This year my proposal is to remain in England and, as I hope, to put my time to better profit."[55]

In her writings heretofore, she had discovered her satiric voice. Now, when her plans for editing a journal remained stillborn and future travel seemed infeasible, she diverted her talents, strong views, and caustic spirit to her regularly appearing fiction. Out of these ingredients, she formed her best characters—Jonathan Jefferson Whitlaw, the vicar of Wrexhill, the widow Barnaby, and many others. The remarks of the influential critic of the *Westminster Review*, Charles Buller, Jr., were most encouraging. In September he sent to the publisher his advance comments on her most recent fictional effort:

> I have read Mrs. Trollope's novel and think it right to apprize you that I feel inclined to review it in a spirit of almost unqualified approbation. It seems to me to have some of the "old woman's" vulgarity, and all her shrewd and pungent power of ridicule.[56]

Bolstered by such favorable reviews and the financial success they promised, she turned, belatedly, to building a career as novelist.

8

Social Consciousness and the
Repulsive Subject

*Thorough-going gusto for what is repulsive and
horrible, as if the authoress had drunk of the witch
broth.*

ONCE MRS. Trollope had set her sights on fiction as more than a time-filling
device between journeys, she at once began to turn out novels that were
somewhat at odds with the more dominant trends of the times. Indeed,
as one critic soon noted: "Mrs. Trollope had the nature of a pioneer." Her
long-standing interest in social problems led her to write on subjects not
usually treated in fictional form, and her satiric eye soon focused on a
series of characters for which her contemporaries could find no
appellation except "repulsive."[1]

Jonathan Jefferson Whitlaw, dedicated by its author to "those states
of the American Union in which slavery has been abolished, or never
permitted," was the first novel in England or America to call attention to
the evils of slavery in the United States. It appeared more than six
months before *The White Slave: or Memoirs of Archy Moore* (1836) by
Richard Hildreth, who subsequently claimed for himself "the first
successful application of fictitious narrative to anti-slavery purposes," as
well as "the respect and honor due to the father" of the whole family of
such books, and fifteen years before Harriet Beecher Stowe's more
famous *Uncle Tom's Cabin*. Mrs. Trollope's sympathy for the condition
of the black man in America had not ended with her swift departure
from the Nashoba community. She had included several moving
anecdotes of slavery in her American travel book; now given the ample
scope of three volumes, she expanded her treatment.[2]

By bringing the slavery issue into the province of fiction, Mrs.
Trollope introduced to the popular novel that subject matter of protest
and criticism which had characterized her travel books. Over the next
few years, her writings treated controversial social issues, and she
played a part in turning fiction away from its dominant interest in
romantic subjects, the frivolities and pursuits of fashionable circles, and
gothic horror-mongering. In using fiction to arouse public consciousness

about social abuses, Mrs. Trollope contributed an impressive list of "firsts": the first antislavery novel, the first full-length exposure of evangelical excesses, the first novel on child labor in industrial areas, the first attack on the bastardy clauses of the New Poor Law. Certainly, she was in the vanguard of the movement away from the "popular pap of the 1830's."[3]

Reviewers tended to condemn her for introducing low and vulgar subjects into her books. The *Athenaeum*, for one, doubted

> the expediency of making the abominations of slavery, and their consequences, the theme of a novel. If we are to read of cruel overseers, and licentious clerks, and a brutalized race of human creatures degraded into property, let it be in the grave and calm pages of the advocate or the historian; but do not let them disfigure the fairyland of fiction.[4]

Even Thackeray, as late as 1845, asked why books written "in a light and unpretending form" should take on subjects "both heavy and pretentious" and chided Mrs. Trollope by name.

> If we want instruction, we prefer to take it from fact rather than from fiction. We like to hear sermons from his reverence at church; to get our notions of trade, crime, politics, and other national statistics, from the proper pages and figures; but when suddenly, out of the gilt pages of a pretty picture book, a comic moralist rushes forward, and takes occasion to tell us that society is diseased, the laws unjust, the rich ruthless, the poor martyrs, the world lopsided, and *vice-versa*, persons who wish to lead an easy life are inclined to remonstrate against this literary ambuscade.[5]

But by the time the 1840's were underway, a burgeoning of social-protest novels vindicated Mrs. Trollope's instincts in challenging the complacency of the English reading public.

Mrs. Trollope's *Whitlaw* established certain themes, plot devices, and character types that eventually became dominant in the antislavery novel, and *Uncle Tom's Cabin* bears striking resemblances to its predecessor. Whitlaw himself is the prototype of the sadistic overseer whom Mrs. Stowe later immortalized as Simon Legree. The loving slave couple who, after many trials, flee to a free country—Caesar and Phebe in *Whitlaw*—are George and the valiant Eliza. Mrs. Trollope's couple are aided by benevolent Europeans who take them back to Germany; Mrs. Stowe's pair effect their own dramatic escape to a more reasonable destination, Canada. Cassy is a more realistic version of Mrs. Trollope's Juno—the old slave as bereft mother. And the logic of the plot—with a woman preying upon the ignorant fears of the master and eventually conquering him—is perhaps the most significant resemblance between these two antislavery books by women.

Beyond such historical or artistic influence, *Whitlaw* has its own merits and reveals Mrs. Trollope using her characters, plot, and setting with authority to illustrate her central theme: slavery corrupts all who touch it. Her first three novels had artificially strung together the adventures of unbelievable people in synthetic surroundings. Wooden English aristocrats dragged unmercifully by Mrs. Trollope over the path of her own American itinerary, the unprincipled villainess who is Countess of Tremordyn, the Protestant abbess of the convent San Marco were contrived and lifeless, as were the settings in which they moved. But in *Whitlaw*, first-hand knowledge of people and places, deep indignation, and a central unifying focus produced an original novel which, despite its florid style, even the modern reader can find satisfying.

Perhaps *Whitlaw's* most notable feature is Mrs. Trollope's use of setting, which provides a backdrop for the many varieties of slavery and advances her thematic point, the all-pervasive influence of this institution. The early sections of the book, set at Mohanna Creek on the Mississippi, are heavily dependent on *Domestic Manners* and set an authentic tone that gives credibility to the whole book. The fearful loneliness, the presence of alligators and crocodiles, the need for constant vigilance—all these appeared in her earlier descriptions of squalid woodcutters' huts. There the Whitlaws own a few house slaves upon whom they work their petty cruelties.

Entirely different are the rice fields of Colonel Dart, who owns some five hundred slaves at Paradise Plantation, in whose grim environs the major action of the book takes place. A third setting is the nearby Reichland, property of the German Baron Steinmark and family, worked by its nonslave-owning proprietors. There family members share labor, and the resulting scene—prosperous, green, and flourishing—is the book's real paradise. To these rural settings, Mrs. Trollope adds Natchez, where the brutal cattle-market trade in slavery transforms the city into a living advertisement. Everywhere posters for upcoming sales and notices of rewards for runaway slaves dominate the scene. Most degenerate is New Orleans, with its gambling halls, billiard rooms, quadroon balls, and low characters. There Mrs. Trollope introduced the idle wives of the great southern planters, made immature, frivolous, and cruel by the degrading luxury of their lives. By casting these events in such diverse settings (unlike Mrs. Stowe, whose scenes are the plantations), Mrs. Trollope establishes her theme: slavery harms, degrades, soils, corrupts, and destroys all who touch it, even those who think themselves most free from its stain and pollution.

Mrs. Trollope's most suggestive use of setting is her symbolic treatment of the forest, in which much of the book's important action takes place. Outside New Orleans, beyond the suburbs of Natchez, the cultivated farm land of the Whitlaws and Steinmarks, and the plantations of Colonel Dart, lies the primeval forest, still unsullied by man, clear and bright in the white moonlight. There occur the book's redemptive activities. "In the thickest part of the forest," a young preacher brings the saving message of Christianity to "dusky groups, sometimes but dimly visible, still as the solid earth on which they reposed, and silent as the stars that gleamed above them. . . ." (2:255–56). Also in the forest, he and his sister minister to a runaway slave, hiding him by day in the deep bushes. Later, when the girl flees Natchez to warn her brother of an impending lynch mob, she is almost apprehended by the pursuing Whitlaw. Suddenly, in one of the most spectacular and symbolic scenes of the book, she encounters a group of wandering Choctaws, whom Mrs. Trollope uses not only for plot and colorful interest but also to represent a more simple if savage way of life that has been destroyed by the white man. The girl trusts herself to the Indians, for she finds "something . . . in the general appearance of the *civilized* man which terrified her even more than the painted and scarred features of the Indians" (3:132). They treat her with kindness, courtesy, and true goodness, strongly suggesting that in a slave state, the only truly civilized people are those who move helplessly and hopelessly on the outskirts of the white man's culture.[6]

In Mrs. Trollope's cast of characters, Whitlaw and Juno, the old black witch, are the most carefully drawn, while the slaves have little individuality. The Steinmarks are another of her uninteresting attempts to depict aristocrats. More deeply and feelingly drawn is the self-styled missionary, Edward Bligh; he resembles Frances Wright, who though no advocate of Christianity, was a fervent reformer and emancipator, and who too was

> self-elected and self-devoted, to raise the poor crushed victims of an infernal tyranny from the state of grovelling ignorance to which they were chained by their well-calculating masters. [1:181]

While Edward Bligh is on the whole a sympathetic character, Mrs. Trollope suggests that his nonviolent Christianity is powerless to fight the evil of slavery. Indeed, his encounters with the system leave his mental faculties increasingly shaken and weakened, and it is no surprise that he falls victim to Whitlaw's lynch mob. His idealism, clearly "not for this world," reveals her impatience with a religion that had failed to deal directly with the slavery issue. Frances Trollope would have had no use for Mrs. Stowe's Uncle Tom who dies forgiving his tormentor, with the author's obvious approbation. Mrs. Trollope's principal slave fights back, and with four strong helpers she recruited from among those not persuaded by Christian teachings, ambushes Whitlaw and brutally assassinates him. The reader believes that Whitlaw has been disposed of in the only possible way. Nowhere in Mrs. Trollope's cast of black characters does anyone suggest an ethic of patient submissiveness.

The ignorant and debased Whitlaw has been corrupted absolutely, made sadistic by his power over human beings. He asks:

> What's freedom for, if we can't do what we like with our own born slaves? There's nothing so dispicable in my mind as a man what's afraid to kick the life out of his own nigger if he sees good. . . . 'Tis that gives us the right to call ourselves free. . . . [1:122-23]

He gambles, rapes female slaves, and leads lynch mobs. But while seemingly omnipotent when he becomes sole owner of Paradise Plantation, he falls at the hand of a woman—the seventy-year-old black believed by Colonel Dart and Whitlaw to possess supernatural powers. Mrs. Trollope works hard to make this part of her plot credible, stressing that those who trafficked in slavery were a prey to fears and superstitions and devoting a lengthy chapter to a recapitulation of Juno's past, rooted firmly in slavehood and sex. No sorceress, she is a black matriarch bereft of her family. As a young beautiful woman, she had become the mistress of an English settler who, after giving her "a glimpse of happiness," departed for Europe with their baby girl "on whom he determined to bestow an education which should atone by its expense for the cruelty he considered himself *obliged* to practice by abandoning her mother" (2:5). "Given" to one of his friends, she passed from man to man, bearing many children toward whom she trained herself to be apathetic, performing the task of child-bearing, "as she did all others . . . more like a well-regulated machine than a human being" (2:6). Sufficiently well-educated to capitalize on the ignorance of her owners, she utilized her unique position to help slaves in need. In her old age, when sold to Colonel Dart, she enjoyed a reputation for possessing mysterious powers and associating with spirits. Her one hope was to see her English granddaughter, who she had heard "was beautiful, beyond even the far-famed beauty of the fair race among whom she dwelt." Surrounded by the sordid reality of slavery, she dreamed of being "ancestress of a very beautiful and glorious race" (2:12).

In one of the plot's more incredible turns, Mrs. Trollope brings this girl to New Orleans, where her father, portrayed as a decent, well-meaning man, has determined to sever all connection with slavery by selling his inherited plantations. But when young Selina learns the truth about her ancestry, she commits a dramatic suicide. Stripped of her dreams, Juno now resolves to destroy Whitlaw, who has spitefully told the girl of her racial background. Mrs. Trollope emphasizes the physical degradation of women, as Juno recollects her own painful history:

> She recalled with maddening truth the first warm touch of her dear infant's lips upon her bosom,—the last agonising kiss that she was permitted to press upon them as she was torn away from her; the savage transfer of her loathing person to another—the brutal force that kept her soul and body in a subjection that seemed to make every breath she drew a poison to her nature. . . . [3:38–39]

After successfully concealing Whitlaw's murder, Juno buries him in a hand-dug grave with symbolic significance: "It was my child he killed, and it was my hands that hollowed out his grave." After Whitlaw's unexplained assassination, his unselfish Aunt Clio inherits Paradise Plantation. In this woman's book, a black woman avenges a terrible injustice, and a white woman has the opportunity to set things right again. Was ever wish-fulfillment more graphically rendered?

It is appropriate that women should have been the first champions of slave emancipation, for their sex experienced slavery's worst tortures: a mother's separation from her children and sexual abuse. At one point in the book, when a young slave girl is about to be beaten and stripped, her mother grabs her two younger children and retreats to the forest "in the hope of placing herself and the little ones beyond reach of hearing the groans which she knew would soon be wrung from the innocent being she left." Mrs. Trollope interrupts the narrative with a pointed comment:

> Let not the tender European mother turn with disgust from the apparent selfishness of this retreat. Those only who have seen with their own eyes how slavery acts upon the heart, can fairly judge the conduct of slaves. They are, in truth, where the yoke is laid on heavily, hardly to be considered as responsible for any act, or for any feeling. The dogged quiescence of silent endurance which often gives to the negro an aspect of brutal insensibility, may originate from a temper whose firmness might have made a hero had the will been free; and poor Peggy, when she hurried from the scene of her child's suffering, might have carried with her an anguish the bitterness of which no mother blessed with the power of protecting her offspring can conceive. [1:214–15]

Instead of stopping with such abstract comments, Mrs. Trollope proceeded to shock her readers by including dramatized scenes of Whitlaw's erotic brutality when the girl tries to run away. He is delighted by the prospects of a chase. "She's a neat little craft for a nigger; and she'd skip handsome over them stumps younder. . . ." When she pleads instead to be beaten but not stripped, Whitlaw becomes savage: "Strip, black toad—strip, or you shall be soaked in oil and then singed. Strip her Johnson, d'ye hear?" (1:218 ff.). Many years later, in offering to the public an authentic account of a female slave's life in the South during this period, Mrs. Maria Child apologized that her story contained so much material relating to the sexual abuse of young black girls by their white masters. "This peculiar phase of slavery," she informed her readers in the 1880's, is worth relating, because it "has generally been kept veiled." Mrs. Child's narrative concluded: "Slavery is terrible for men, but it is far more terrible for women. Superadded to the burden common to all, they have wrongs, and sufferings, and mortifications peculiarly their own."[7] But Mrs. Trollope, with her woman's outrage, had called attention to this fact in her book in 1836.

Mrs. Trollope also depicts sympathetically, if only briefly, the problems of women who are associated with slavery, the quadroons, born of mixed relationships, a "race whom all men are permitted to insult" (1:268), and the southern woman, whose intellectual and emotional maturing this system hampers. From the poor tortured black to the southern lady on her pedestal, slavery has blighted all who touch it. Only the Europeans, who flee a lynch mob to return to their native Germany, and the briefly glimpsed Indians escape unsullied.

The very topicality of the controversial subject matter made it successful with the general public (who bought out three editions within the year) and aroused the ire of the critics. The *Literary Gazette* rather ingenuously protested that the subject was not "well calculated for the English reader. The abuses of the slave system scarcely come home to ourselves." This stance was less than candid, since during this period, the British were painfully extricating themselves from their own slavery problems. Although slavery had been outlawed in 1833, only in 1838 (after a slave revolt in Jamaica which had been brutally repressed by British troops) were all slaves legally freed. The reaction of the literary journals to Mrs. Trollope's slavery book showed that she had found her mark. The *Athenaeum* considered it an unpleasant and repulsive book; the *Spectator* quarrelled with her depiction of southern planters who were "the gentlemen of the States." Both the *Gazette* and the *Athenaeum* considered Whitlaw "disgusting—sunk below the vilest level of humanity." Indeed, the latter alluded to Mrs. Trollope's sex in calling Whitlaw "one of the most thorough-going scoundrels ever conceived by female imagination (it is amazing, by the way, to see what desperate specimens of *out-and-out* villainy are to be found in the works of some of our lady-novelists)." The reviewers generally accused Mrs. Trollope of exaggeration and caricature, and even her adulatory daughter-in-law, writing some fifty years later, found the story "painful" and questioned whether such unpleasant social issues properly belonged within the province of fiction.[8]

When Mrs. Trollope followed with *The Vicar of Wrexhill* a year later, reviewers were quick to note its association with her previous work, both of which struck them as a defiant (and unfeminine) continuation of a "delight in subjects which are painful and repulsive."

> She scents out moral deformities with a sort of professional eagerness, and applies herself to their exposure, regardless of the uncleanness into which her task may lead her, and the soil and foul odours she herself may contract in prosecuting the beloved work. In her last novel she plunged over head into the abominable sink of slavery; here, again, she is up to the neck in another kennel of corruption,—*The Vicar of Wrexhill* being a tale written for the express purpose of *showing up* the errors of a sect increasingly prevalent and powerful among us—the Evangelicals.[9]

From the beginning of the century, the Church of England had been "one vast arena of controversy." Never one to shy away from conflict, Mrs. Trollope attacked evangelical excesses and their unfortunate effects upon women by making them the theme of *The Vicar of Wrexhill*, which appeared in three volumes in 1837. It was a subject that had already drawn her attention in America.

The story's outline is simple. A country gentleman, possessed of £14,000 a year, dies suddenly and, having received the bulk of this immense fortune through his wife, leaves it entirely at her disposal, without providing separately for his children. The newly appointed vicar of Wrexhill intrudes himself on the family in their bereavement, supposedly to administer spiritual consolation. Eventually, he alienates two of the three children from their mother and marries the rich widow. Discovering his true character just before it is too late, she revokes her will in his favor, and after her death the hypocrite is expelled in the very moment of his supposed triumph.[10]

Mrs. Trollope's theme, however, extended beyond the excesses of evangelical fervor or the vices of a particular vicar. Her story showed what happened to weak, untrained, and dependent women in Victorian society. When the forty-five year-old Mrs. Mowbray is unexpectedly widowed, she is forced to cope with a new reality. But, Mrs. Trollope notes, she had

> passed her life in such utter ignorance of every kind of business, and such blind and helpless dependence, first on her guardians, and then on her

husband, that the idea of acting for herself was scarcely less terrible than
the notion of navigating at seventy-four would be to ladies in general.
[1:187]

Is it any wonder that such a woman would turn to the vicar "as to a
champion equally able and willing to help and defend her"? When, after
a barely suitable mourning interval, he proposes, the widow accepts,
less out of any liking for the man or evangelicalism than because
marriage will again give her someone to lean and depend upon:

> I will Mr. Cartwright, for my spirit is too weak to combat all the difficulties
> I see before me. My soul trusts itself to thee—be thou to me a strong tower,
> for I am afraid. [2:239]

This need for male support is her undoing. Here was Mrs. Trollope's first
rendering of the theme of the woman alone to which she would return
many times in her writing career.

In her depiction of the vicar himself, Mrs. Trollope returned to the
repulsive subject. The reviewer in the *Examiner* found the character
"revolting" and many of the scenes described "eminently disgusting and
repulsive," but he hastened to add, as did so many other critics, "there is
extraordinary power about them nevertheless."[11] Most offensive to the
public were Mrs. Trollope's explicit renderings of the vicar's kissing,
caressing, and praying in the garden with young girls. She frankly
described his sensual appeal to women, and even those reviewers who
criticized the book admitted the truthfulness of the vicar's portrayal:

> Handsome, silky-spoken . . . with his black eyes and caressing hands,
> which make such sad havoc among the bevy of admiring village ladies. He
> glides on his way, like a serpent—glossy, silent, and poisonous—throwing
> out hints here, innuendos there; blighting with the language of brotherly
> love, and under the mask of Scriptural sanctity, creeping steadily upwards
> towards wealth and power. His is a fearful character; and some of his later
> doings are too dark and terrible to have been written down by a woman,
> —aye, or a man either; but Mrs. Trollope loves debateable ground.[12]

Novels were a family affair in the nineteenth century, and at least two
reviewers modestly departed from the usual practice of printing ex-
cerpts from this novel fearing "the hazard of giving profitless, and,
therefore, needless offence." Thackeray, writing for *Fraser's*, censured
the blasphemy of the vicar's prayers "when he contrives, in addressing
the Deity, to make the most passionate and licentious avowals to the
young girl. These prayers we shall not make it our business to transplant
into our columns. . . ." Other scenes Thackeray called "a display of

licentiousness, overt and covert, such as no woman conceived before,"
calling Mrs. Trollope's depiction "as improbable as it is rankly indecent. . . ."[13]

Although it was permissible for women to write improving tales (like
those of Hannah More or Maria Edgeworth), they should not enter the
heated debates of the period. Thackeray found that Mrs. Trollope

> has only harmed herself and her cause, and had much better have
> remained at home, pudding-making or stocking-mending, than have
> meddled with matters which she understands so ill.

> In the first place (we speak it with due respect for the sex), she is guilty of a
> fault which is somewhat too common among them; and having very little,
> except prejudice, on which to found an opinion, she makes up for want of
> argument by a wonderful fluency of abuse. A woman's religion is chiefly
> that of the heart, and not of the head. . . . She goes through, for the most
> part, no tedious processes of reasoning, no dreadful stages of doubt, no
> changes of faith: she loves God as she loves her husband—by a kind of
> instinctive devotion. Faith is a passion with her, and not a calculation; so
> that, in the faculty of believing, though they far exceed the other sex, in the
> power of convincing they fall far short of them.

> Oh! we repeat once more, that ladies would make puddings and mend
> stockings! that they would not meddle with religion, except to pray to
> God, to live quietly among their families, and more lovingly among their
> neighbours![14]

Here, from one of the leading literary figures of the age, came once again
the stance Mrs. Trollope so often encountered: women cannot write
objective accounts and should remain within the narrow domestic
sphere.

Thackeray also revealed another common prejudice against women
who wrote realistic fiction. Raised upon pedestals of purity and perfection, female writers must not show acquaintance with the sordid,
according to him:

> With all her rage for morality, had not the fair accuser have better left the
> matter alone? That torrent of slang and oaths, O nymph! falls ill from thy
> lips, which should never open but for a soft word or a smile; that accurate
> description of vice, sweet orator (-tress or -trix)! only shews that thou
> thyself art but too well acquainted with scenes which thy pure eyes should
> never have beheld.

The *Examiner* complained of the "coarse, violent spirit which pervades
all Mrs. Trollope's writings," and the *Times* believed that she had

exceeded the accepted limits of satire. "NO moralist (and above all, no woman moralist) can use such weapons as these without injuring herself far more than her adversary."[15]

Despite these controversies, 1837 ended on a positive note. Mrs. Trollope was on the verge of receiving better reviews. She sold *A Romance of Vienna* to Bentley in December, but the success of *The Vicar*, combined with the expensiveness of her travels, confirmed her in finally concentrating on writing fiction. She made an agreement to produce yet another novel "in three volumes containing not less than 900 pages for which I shall receive £600" but stipulated her own terms to the publisher, revealing confidence and independence. After seeing a sketch for the new novel, Bentley had suggested possible developments and changes in the main character, but Mrs. Trollope stated her own concept with authority:

> I cannot, in a work of imagination, consent to write to order.—In the sketch which I have already made, I have a character that will give occasion I hope for some comic situations, from efforts and pretensions resulting from vanity, and a vulgar desire of fashionable notoriety.[16]

In the light of such steady activity, it was easy to forget that Mrs. Trollope was becoming an old woman. Her letters from this period—although usually cheerful—catch a new note of her "heavy, uphill work":

> I am fifty-eight years old, my dear Tom. And although, when I am well and in good spirits, I talk of what I may yet do, I cannot conceal from you or from myself, that my doings are nearly over.

Tom had complained of dullness after a friend had departed following a long visit. Her comment is worth quoting:

> Think you that my work is not dull? Think you that at my age, when the strength fails and the spirits flag, I can go on for ever writing with pleasure?

Yet she was soon preparing for yet another houseful of Christmas visitors and planning games and fun for all:

> I *have* finished my book (all but re-reading it), and I *am* ready to enjoy my holidays as much as you are, dear Tom! —Though I mean to *set off again* with small interval. But I shall only work an hour or two a day as long as you are here.

She added: "Don't think me wickedly extravagant for this. I have worked so hard, that I think I may try to give my children a merry Christmas with a safe conscience." She looked forward to regular walks with her son, "spite of wind and weather, as in days of yore," for, as she concluded with modest gratitude: "I do truly believe that so many pages in proof of my industry would not now be burthening bookshelves, had you not done me this good service at Harrow."[17]

She prepared, too, for subletting Hadley and moving to London lodgings, "a change," she told Julia, "which both Anthony's occupations and mine renders very desirable, albeit I love my pretty cottage here much, and we have fallen into one or two cordial village intimacies that I shall regret to lose." But she needed to be close to her son, too, and "in truth four hours out of every day is too much for Anthony to pass in, or on, a coach, which is what he now does." Moreover, her own successful career made it convenient for her to be nearer the center of literary activity. "I find the necessity of seeing London people, whether for business or pleasure, recurs too frequently for convenience or economy . . . I hope to be among clever literary people."[18] Her work went busily forward. In February she was correcting the last sheets of *Vienna and the Austrians* and arranging for presentation copies to be sent to Metternich and other dignitaries.

While her confidence that she could sustain a successful writing career was growing, she did not believe that Tom could as yet abandon his dull mastership at Birmingham. She had told her increasingly restive son to hang on until Christmas, reasoning: "Should I continue to make money by my pen, the immediate inconvenience will not be much felt, and should this resource fail me, the necessity of your having a profession becomes infinitely greater." Now, however, though still unable to rent Hadley, she took a house in York Street, Portman Square, London, and in the fall, she, Tom, and Anthony moved in.[19]

Soon she was ready with the ideas for two more novels, which she proposed to Bentley. The first "will have a special subject, which I believe I manage best, and be called 'Tempers' [later to be renamed *One Fault*]." With assurance, she stated her own terms:

> Provided the kind public continues to abuse and read me, I shall write and *publish* two novels in each year—if I wish to do so.

> Notwithstanding that much has reached me from many quarters on the subject, I most assuredly shall engage with no other publishers till I have your refusal of the terms I offer.

Bentley agreed that should she in fact produce two works of fiction each year, he would take them as specified. Her energy in contemplating this project and writing schedule is amazing.[20]

In August 1838, Cecilia married John Tilley, Anthony's good friend from the Post Office Department. Tom continued to write and involved himself in an abortive attempt to publish a book of his own on America, for which his mother promised him the use of her notebooks "as well as the benefit of her perusal and corrrections of the manuscript."[21] His sights were clearly set on following her illustrious footsteps. It was, however, to be Anthony, laboring quietly in the vineyard of the Post Office in 1838 who would achieve that strenuous honor.

Established at Portman Square, Mrs. Trollope worked hard. Miss Anna Drury, then a teen-aged girl, recalled a two-day visit with the author, the principal feature of which was "an unlimited allowance of books by day, and as I shared her room, a most delightful talk at night until one next morning!" The young Anna could sleep late, "but as she was full of work by day, it was different for her! And she said afterwards, that it must not be repeated." Miss Drury remembered Mrs. Trollope's "kind indulgence in listening to my youthful aspirations and plans for possible stories, and the good practical advice which she gave me from her own experience." Her principal recollection involved an amusing incident. Rogers the poet had come to meet Mrs. Trollope at the home of a mutual friend. At dinner,

> she sate next him at table; and presently he turned to her and observed, "They told me Mrs. Trollope was to be here. She has written a great deal of rubbish, hasn't she?" "Well," she immediately replied, "she has made it answer!"

Pleased with her successes, Mrs. Trollope repeated the story afterwards with great glee.[22]

She was indeed making the writing of fiction "answer," and it had not been easy. Trying to cheer Tom, who was depressed that his writings had not yet been published, Mrs. Trollope noted:

> For your spirits, I know no better receipt than telling you to cast your eyes back over my literary history: a MS sent to Colburn, declined; one to Murray returned at the end of six months, unopened; another to a man in the Strand, sent back with the assurance that the trade was so bad, no one could publish without loss. All this I bore, and worked up against it all— with what result you know.

But her family's fortune was not yet made, and expenses seemed always to be mounting. She would not, however, be crushed:

I work, and work, and work, and if God spares my life and health, I hope that the time will come when I may call myself out of debt, and may calculate on *spending* the money I have earned, instead of fretting that it does not cover all my liabilities.[23]

By the end of November 1838, she had completed her new novel. R. H. Barham, reviewing the manuscript for Bentley wrote: "I have looked over the first two chapters of *The Widow Barnaby* and like the opening much. . . ." On 26 December 1838, "the redoubtable widow Barnaby" appeared, "conjured up—a jovial New Year's guest—by the busy wand of Mrs. Trollope." An unusual and unexpected guest indeed to the "fairyland of fiction" in the early days of 1839.[24]

Fig. 1. Julians Hill, by J.E. Millais. From the frontispiece to *Orley Farm*, 1862, by Anthony Trollope.

Fig. 2. The farm house at Harrow Weald. From James Pope-Hennessey, *Anthony Trollope*.

Fig. 3. Portrait of Frances Wright. From a portrait in private hands.

Fig. 4. Nashoba, Auguste Hervieu's illustration for *Domestic Manners* (1832)

Fig. 5. Contemporary caricature of the Trollopes in Cincinnati. Printed in Clara Longworth deChambrun, *Cincinnati: the Queen City* (1939)

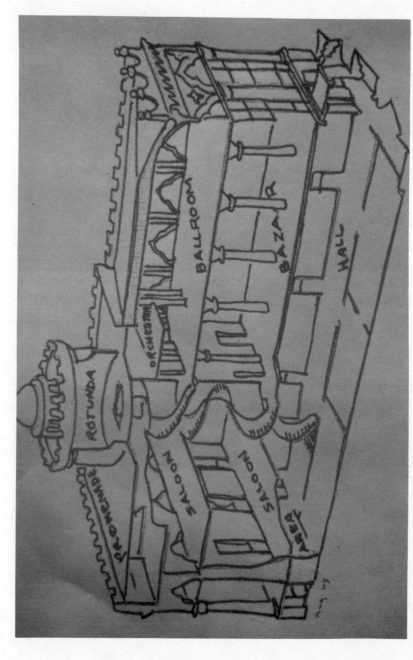

Fig. 6. Conjectural restoration of The Bazaar, by Clay Lancaster. From his article "The Egyptian Hill and Mrs. Trollope's Bazaar," *Magazine of Art*, 43 (1950)

Fig. 7. Contemporary print of The Bazaar. From H.A. and K.B. Ford, *History of Cincinnati, Ohio, with Illustrations and Biographical Sketches* (1881)

Fig. 8. Riverfront view of Cincinnati in 1840. From Chambrun, *Cincinnati in 1840* (1939)

Fig. 9. The separation of the sexes in a Cincinnati Ballroom, Auguste Hervieu's illustration for *Domestic Manners* (1832)

Fig. 10. Evening at a boarding house, Auguste Hervieu's illustration for *Domestic Manners* (1832)

Fig. 11. Portrait of Frances Trollope, from Auguste Hervieu's frontispiece for the 5th edition of *Domestic Manners* (1839)

Fig. 12. "A loose, slatternly woman," American caricature of Mrs. Trollope. From *Trollopiana: Scraps for the Year 1833*, by D. C. Johnston (Boston: 1833)

Fig. 13. "Tail Piece," American caricature of Mrs. Trollope. From *Trollopiana: Scraps for the Year 1833*, by D. C. Johnston (Boston: 1833)

Fig. 14. Frances Trollope's two sons: Thomas Adolphus and Anthony. From a photograph in the possession of Robert A. Cecil. (Used with his permission).

Fig. 15. Factory boys competing with the pigs, Auguste Hervieu's illustration for *Michael Armstrong* (1840)

Fig. 16. The Widow Barnaby in the United States, John Leech's illustration for *The Barnabys in America* (1843)

9

The Strong Woman Theme:
The Barnaby Novels

Was für eine Frau *is the Widow Barnaby*.

AFTER FOUR novels peopled by lifeless aristocrats (*The Refugee, The Abbess, Tremordyn Cliff, A Romance of Vienna,*) and two serious exposés of "repulsive" subjects (*Whitlaw, The Vicar*), in December 1838, Mrs. Trollope entered the popular field of the literature of roguery with *The Widow Barnaby*. William Makepeace Thackeray, another writer sensitive to popular tastes, had begun his career with this kind of fiction, even while complaining a year after the appearance of the first widow book that "the public will hear of nothing but rogues . . . and the only way in which poor authors, who must live, can act honestly by the public and themselves, is to paint such thieves as they are."

But in the early Victorian period, coaching, sporting, gambling, cheating, hunting, adventuring, and living by one's wits had been the material of male writers about male characters, who used their sketches to reinforce a masculine sense of unlimited freedom and dominance. Dickens used the form, as did Borrow, Hook, Marryat, Mayhew, and Thackeray. The few women picaras were always minor characters, in most cases low types and gypsies, the best of whom usually repented at the end. Contemporary standards did not permit a woman at the center of a tale of roguery. It would be an unedifying spectacle for a female to rove the world in search of her fortunes and fair game. With the widow Barnaby, Mrs. Trollope created the feminine picaresque, a lady ready to pack her trunks of a moment's notice, one who enjoyed herself immensely while exploring and exploiting life's possibilities for a middle-aged woman.[1]

In this, Mrs. Trollope diverged from the stereotyped heroines of the day, these "suffering angels," in Thackeray's telling phrase, "pale, pious, pulmonary, crossed in love, of course," and added a new dimension to the treatment of women in fiction. Far from being wilting or spiritual, the widow Barnaby was, in one reviewer's words, "showy, strong-

157

willed, supple-tongued, audacious, garrulous, affected, tawdry, lynx-eyed, indomitable in her scheming, and colossal in her selfishness—*Was für eine Frau* is the widow Barnaby."[2]

Mrs. Trollope's successful portrayal of this new kind of heroine greatly impressed her generation. Even Thackeray once confessed: "I do not care to read ladies' novels, except those of Mesdames Gore and Trollope." Some ten years after the widow's appearance, he brought out his own great version in the wily Becky Sharp. The similarities between the widow Barnaby and Becky are striking. Both are completely passionless; their hearts are really never engaged, even by the men they relentlessly pursue. When they chance to be occasionally discarded, they simply seek fresh conquests unperturbed. Neither has a conscience, and both are dedicated, from the outset, to getting on in the world as they find it. Both tap their admirers for presents, and both learn quickly and well how to lead the gullible to ruin by means of their husbands' card-playing prowess. Neither places much faith in gambling as a permanent living, but they indulge their husbands, even while plotting themselves to secure something far more grandiose and permanent. Creatures of total mendacity, absolute cheats and liars, they are remarkably appealing heroines. The widow, like Becky, leaves a comfortable home in search of greater things. Neither is forced by absolute necessity. They are not low-born prostitutes and criminals like Moll Flanders. Mrs. Trollope's widow is a woman of the middle class with a little money, who is driven by ambition and aspiration to search for more. She could easily have stayed in Silverton and lived a genteel and respectable life. Becky could have stayed with the Crawleys, but both want something more. They refuse to settle for that "lamentable insignificance" which Mrs. Trollope had found so regrettable in American women. And while Thackeray ultimately put the fascinating Becky in her place and punished her, Mrs. Trollope dispatched her widow on to ever greater triumphs, as her creator revelled in the fanciful exploration of aspiration in a woman, middle-aged, coarse, and vulgar though she was.

Mrs. Trollope found the faults, foibles, vulgarities, and vagaries of her widow both amusing and deeply congenial to her writing talents. Her earlier fiction had drawn praise for its satiric portrayals of minor low-life characters, whom reviewers had found more in her line than noble heroes and heroines. Martha Barnaby was gossipy, vain, complacent, pretentious, and vulgar, a social-climber of epic proportions, and a compendium of all the worst middle-class vices. But in addition, Mrs. Trollope clearly gave this favorite character not only a large dose of her own ebullient personality but also some obviously autobiographical touches. The widow was always able to pick herself up after losses, dropping unsuccessful ventures without undue regrets and moving on to the next scheme. A woman whose horizons seemed endlessly expanding, she cheerfully endured a whole host of transplantings and radiated, in spite of her faults, a special brand of *joie de vivre*. In the greatest of her swindles, the widow even decided to pose as an authoress with plans to make money by writing a best-selling travel book on the United States!

Mrs. Trollope enjoyed her heroine so much that she brought her back in two sequels, which allowed ample opportunity to develop situations well suited to her talents. This willingness to repeat a well-beloved character in succeeding novels was later exploited even more successfully by her son Anthony. His reluctance to "dissever" himself from one of his favorite creations (the vulgar, bullying Mrs. Proudie) resembled his mother's openly expressed weakness for her own progeny:

> I scruple not to confess that with all her faults, and she has *some*, I love her dearly: I owe her many mirthful moments, and the deeper pleasure still of believing that she has brought mirthful moments to others also. Honestly avowing this to be the case, can any one wonder, can any one blame me, for feeling an affectionate longing at my heart to follow her upon the expedition upon which I sent her when last we parted?[3]

Mrs. Trollope had originally conceived of Martha Barnaby as the stereotyped husband-hunting widow. Gradually, over the course of three novels (*The Widow Barnaby*, 1838; *The Widow Married, a Sequel to the Widow Barnaby*, 1840; and *The Barnabys in America, or Adventures of the Widow Wedded*, 1843), she evolved a more fully developed and complex character.[4] In the first book, Martha Compton eagerly attaches herself to the best prospects currently quartering in the vicinity. As the years pass (along with the regiments and her matrimonial prospects) Martha, failing to catch a young husband, settles for the older (if admirable) Mr. Barnaby, the apothecary, who soon conveniently dies, leaving her as sole executor and sole legatee in possession of a tidy £400 a year. The remaining action concerns her humorous attempts to land a rich and fashionable husband. Advancing toward middle age, she rouges her cheeks, affects dark false curls, and concocts elegant draperies to conceal an increasingly ample figure, thus completing the conventional aspects of the stock character.

Elements of Mrs. Trollope's original plot were openly derivative, a tribute to the great success of Dicken's *Pickwick Papers*, itself an important variant of the literature of roguery. While Mrs. Trollope was writing her novel, she discussed *Pickwick*, the broad humor of which did not overwhelm her, even while she was notably impressed by its sales:

I doubt . . . if I have so much fun in me as heretofore, for I do not laugh at "Boz" half so perseveringly as most others do, and as I will not put this obtusity down to my want of capacity, I must attribute it to my age. You, my dear friend, who are . . . some half score of years or more my junior, can judge of these popular pleasantries more fairly, and I really wish you would tell me, if you go on number after number sharing the ecstasy that causes thirty thousand of the "Pickwick Papers" to be sold monthly.[5]

While the Pickwickian vein is not evident in the first volume (which she had completed by August), the last two, in plot and style, bear evidence of hopes to capitalize on the current mania. Thus, in the second volume, Mrs. Barnaby sets her sights on the fashionable (if aging and fat) Lord Muckleberry. The resulting contretemps clearly owed its conception to the Bardell-Pickwick affair, and in the ensuing lawsuit, complete with letters now dubbed the "Barnaby Papers," Sergeant Buzfuz is cited by name (2:370, 3:36–37).

If the character and plot had emerged from old recipes, they soon became uniquely her own. In the return of the character as *The Widow Married*, Mrs. Trollope expanded the husband-hunting heroine to suggest that the conventional female stances, the "cult of true womanhood" that she had scorned in *Domestic Manners*, masked vicious realities in the contemporary marriage market. Although Mrs. Barnaby was not above using pretenses of delicacy and helplessness to win a husband ("Alas ! . . . there is so much weakness in the heart of a woman. . . . We are all impulse, all soul, all sentiment"), Mrs. Trollope assures the reader that her heroine made "very sure of the Major's rent-roll before she bestowed herself and her fortune upon him; for notwithstanding her flirting propensities, the tender passion had ever been secondary in her heart to a passion for wealth and finery."[6] Similarly, the tender girl who faints at the thought of meeting a man clearly does so only for effect (3:58–59). By emphasizing the insincerity of the expected polite female behavior, Mrs. Trollope makes the widow's exploitation of it not only endurable but laudable. She at least is honest with herself, if not with others.

With exquisite irony, Mrs. Trollope demolishes the myth that contemporary marriages were built on love. In one of the book's minor episodes, a man discreetly inquires of his future sister-in-law:

Alas ! before I can throw myself at her feet, the odious trammels of the world force from me another inquiry, hardly less necessary, such unhappily is the formation of society, than the first. Before I offer my hand in marriage to your sister . . . it is absolutely necessary that I should ascertain from you whether our united incomes would amount to such a

sum as I should deem sufficient for ensuring the happiness of the woman I
so fondly adore.

When the sister reveals that she alone has all the money, the gentleman
instantly switches gears:

How can I make known—how, by any language used by man, can I hope
to explain the vehement revulsion of feeling which has taken place in my
very heart of hearts since first I entered this fatal room.

Without missing a step, he now proposes marriage to "the angelic
woman" before him:

Oh! Louisa! he added, throwing himself on his knees before her, determined, as it seemed, to stake all on this bold *throw*, "Oh! Louisa! it is
yourself: Speak to me, adored Louisa! Tell me my fate in one soul-stirring
word—will you be my wife?" [3:82 ff.]

This broadly farcical scene could stand as a paradigm of the book.
Things are seldom what they seem, especially when the rhetoric is most
fulsome and heart-stirring. In a society built upon such hypocrisies, the
Barnabys of this world are bound to succeed.

The independent Mrs. Barnaby, never accepting male domination,
and "a vast deal too clever to believe a single word of all [her husband]
said" (1: 69–70), must have come as a refreshing breeze to those women
who felt cramped by the inhibiting manners and rhetoric of the time.
Her lesson was one easily mastered. While paying lip-service to the
conventions, women must always safeguard their rights and financial
independence. With each of her husbands, Mrs. Barnaby won the battle
to keep her money to herself; significantly, the Trollopes had worked out
a similar arrangement.[7]

At the end of *The Widow Married*, when her third husband, Major
Allen, is caught cheating at cards, Mrs. Barnaby leads the family in flight
from England and prosecution. As they depart for a sojourn in the
United States, the reader feels as sure that they will land on their feet
across the Atlantic as that Mrs. Trollope will bring them back again. And
indeed, three years later, the widow returned in all her full-blown glory a
third time, in what was to prove the best of the widow books, if not the
most successful of all Mrs. Trollope's thirty-four novels: *The Barnabys in
America*.

The widow's new appearance represents Mrs. Trollope's most ingenious combination of her American experience and the character of the
widow Barnaby. It was right and proper to send her favorite female

character on "an expedition . . . to a land which all the world knows I cherish in my memory with peculiar delight" (1: 2–3). What followed was a farcical vision of what, in Mrs. Trollope's most mischievous dreams, might indeed (and perhaps should) have happened to a traveler in America. The family lands in New Orleans, certain that Mrs. Barnaby's cleverness and the major's skill at cards will bring success in the new world. In the subsequent adventures, Mrs. Barnaby increasingly resembles Mrs. Trollope—well-built, highly colored, a matriarchal type, with a flair for the dramatic, who has had to leave the old world for financial reasons. Mrs. Barnaby's instant acceptance in polite American society surely burlesques Timothy Flint's published explanation for "the circumstances which caused [Mrs. Trollope] so uncourteous a reception at Cincinnati." He had singled out:

> The habit of the ladies there of estimating people according to their show and dress. Had she come with numerous letters, and been an elegant figure dressed in the most approved fashion, there is no doubt, that she would have made her way in every circle.[8]

Twelve years later, past all bitterness and enjoying her many successes, Mrs. Trollope presented Mrs. Barnaby, gradually unfolding to the delight of the New Orleans ladies eight hampers full of velvets, satins, and lace (all unpaid for). With this elegant wardrobe, Mrs. Barnaby is launched in the best circles and thereafter proceeds swiftly to swindle everyone. Mrs. Trollope's honest and innovative business venture had been a miserable failure; Mrs. Barnaby's frauds are a huge success.

Mrs. Trollope's prejudices are, as always, quite clear. The clash of English and American values is again resolved when an Englishman marries and carries back to London the only decent American girl in the book so that she can share "his heart, his hand, a noble settlement, and the alliance of an ancient English race, whose motto might very honestly have been—*Sans peur, et sans reproche*" (p. 195). There are the usual number of American types, from the "patriot lady" to the "evangelical saints," from slave-owners and Quakers to New York speculators. Mrs. Barnaby and family swindle them all, and masquerading as an itinerant preacher, the major is even able to fool the deadly serious female members of the United States Needle Steeple Congregation.

All of these adventures gradually emerge as a vicarious revenge, or as Mrs. Barnaby describes one ruse:

> As a jest played off to avenge, as it were, the numberless tricks which we hear of as practised against our countrymen it is more than justifiable; and in that light, my dearest major, it commands my warmest and most patriotic admiration. [p. 85]

At long last the sharpies have been outdone by the English, a feat that Mrs. Trollope herself was unfortunately unable to accomplish in real life. *The Barnabys in America* documents all of Mrs. Trollope's prejudices about America and satirizes all her grudges. She makes fun of everyone—the gullible Americans, the vulgarians of the old world, and even the middle-aged English lady, who several years ago crossed the Atlantic and wrote a book about the Americans.

The central swindle is Mrs. Barnaby's ingenious plan to write a book on America and thus procure access to the best society. In her proposed work, she assures the Americans, she will counteract all the perfidious lies published previously by other English travelers. Ever since the publication of Hall's volumes and *Domestic Manners*, Americans had railed against the lies of superficial English tourists. In Mrs. Trollope's satiric novel, a true "patriot lady," beseeches Mrs. Barnaby to write "an out and out good book of travels upon the United States," declaring that

> there has never yet been a single volume written upon the United States, that was not crammed with the most abominable lies from beginning to end, and . . . any body who would come forward to contradict all these wicked and most scandalous falsehoods, would be rewarded in the very noblest manner possible: first, by a great quantity of money; and next, by the admiration and respect of all the people in the country.

This lady expects only one thing from Mrs. Barnaby:

> All I want in return is that you should portrait us out to the world for just what we really are, and that is the finest nation upon the surface of God's whole earth, and as far ahead in civilization of Europe in general, and England in particular, as the summer is before winter in heat. [pp. 24, 59, 91]

Musing upon the project, Mrs. Barnaby considers the book she might write about America if she wanted to tell the truth, for the inhabitants were "curious enough, to be sure," and the work would "amuse the folks at home to know, if one did but dare to tell it." But she quickly rejects this notion, since the endeavor is primarily a question of dollars:

> It would be just as easy for me to write all truth as all lies, about this queer place, and all these monstrous odd people, but wouldn't I be a fool if I did any such thing?—and is it one bit more trouble I should like to know, writing them all in one sense instead of the other? [p. 126]

Mrs. Barnaby's project is Mrs. Trollope's answer to those who claimed she had told outrageous lies about the Americans in order to make money.

At a big evening party in her honor, Mrs. Barnaby endures the first public test of her talents, as she reads sections from her work, entitled "Justice Done at Last, or The Travels of Mrs. Major Allen Barnaby through the United States of America." One paragraph of exaggerated and meaningless praise is particularly welcomed:

Nobody properly qualified to write upon this wonderful country could behold a single town, a single street, a single house, a single individual of it, for just one single half-hour, without feeling all over to his very heart convinced, that not all the countries of the old world put together are worthy to compare, in any one respect, from the greatest to the very least, with the free-born, the free-bred, the immortal, the ten hundred thousand times more glorious country, generally called that of the "Stars and the Stripes !" The country of the Stars and the Stripes is, in fact, and beyond all reach of contradiction, the finest country in the whole world, and the simple truth is, that nobody who really knows any thing about it, can ever think of calling it any thing else. It is just the biggest and the best, and that is saying everything in two words. [pp. 132 and 140]

To cries of "admirable, admirable," Mrs. Barnaby bows gracefully, smelling of lavender water, coyly pushes back her curls, and carefully smoothes down the pages while the credulous Americans nod with pleasure. The novel's pattern is a mirror image of *Domestic Manners*, refracted into pure parody. Here, says Mrs. Trollope, is what the Americans wanted in an author; here, too, is what they deserved. Suddenly, while the audience is still ruminating on the fulsome praise of the talk, Mrs. Barnaby intrudes five "harmless" questions, which for a moment dispel the giddy and superficial mood and give a glimpse of the critical author of *Domestic Manners* and *Jonathan Jefferson Whitlaw*. She would appreciate it, she tells her listeners, if they would answer these queries:

1. In what manner does the republican form of government appear to affect the social habits of the people?
2. How far does the absence of a national form of worship produce the results anticipated from it?
3. At what degree of elevation may the education of the ladies of the union be considered to stand, when compared to that received by the females of other countries?
4. In what manner was slavery originally instituted?
5. And what are its real effects, both on the black and on the white population? [p. 128]

The questions, however, do not disturb the Americans, and Mrs.

Barnaby continues her progress. Pandering to southern prejudices, she claims to include praise of slavery as the highest institution known to man. All goes well until the major wins too heavily at cards and the family must move to Philadelphia, where Mrs. Barnaby again poses as a famous authoress, traveling incognito. This time, for her audience of abolitionist Quakers, she proposes a book that will help wipe out the menace of slavery from the face of the earth. The task of appearing demure and principled requires a complete and troublesome metamorphosis in dress only:

> From her morning gown she abstracted every bow, together with a deep trimming of very broad imitation black lace from the cape of it, which left this addition to her grave-coloured silk dress of such very moderate dimensions as entirely to change its general effect, and to give to her appearance a snug sort of succinct tidiness, such as it had probably never exhibited before.

> The cap she selected for the occasion was one which owed almost all its Barnabian grace to a very magnificent wreath of crimson roses, which ran twiningly and caressingly round the front of it, and these being removed by the simple operation of withdrawing a few pins, left as decent a cap as any one could wish to see.

> Of her half-dozen luxuriously-curling "fronts," she chose the least copious and the least curling, and having bedewed it with water from a sponge, induced its flowing meshes to repose themselves upon her forehead with a trim tranquility that might have befitted a Magdalen. [p. 238]

With a talent for impersonation rivaled only by her creator, Mrs. Barnaby manages to leave Philadelphia five hundred dollars richer. The Quakers, who have naively hoped to use the Englishwoman for their own purposes, are both poorer and wiser.

After successfully duping the Quakers, the family again departs; this pattern is repeated a third and fourth time, after which, richer by some ten thousand dollars, they return to England, well satisfied with themselves and with America. As the book rolls to its hilarious conclusion, the reader realizes that Mrs. Barnaby is actually Mrs. Trollope in disguise. This transformation had already begun in *The Widow Married*, when Mrs. Trollope had her heroine reflect upon her progress from adversity to pleasure and profit in a triumphant monologue:

> I do sometimes think . . . that great abilities, thorough real cleverness I mean, is a better fortune for a girl . . . than almost any money in the world. . . . I don't mind telling you that my father and mother . . . had

no more right to expect that I should ever be in such a place as this, ordering court-dresses for myself and my daughter, than you have to be Queen of England. Oh ! dear !—how well I remember going shopping in our little town, where my father was the rector. . . . I have managed from that time to this to get on monstrous well. [1: 193]

In the last book, Mrs. Barnaby several times soliloquizes on this important theme, marveling over her great success:

I do wonder sometimes where I got all my cleverness from. There isn't many, though I say it, that shouldn't—but that's only when nobody hears me—there isn't many that could go on as I have done, from the very first almost, that I remember any thing, always getting on, and on, and on. There's a pretty tolerable difference, thank Heaven ! between what I am now with judges and members, and I don't know who all, smirking and speechifying to me, and what I was when my name was Martha Compton, without two decent gowns perhaps, to my back, and not knowing where on earth to get another when they were gone ! [1: 127]

Mrs. Barnaby and Mrs. Trollope certainly were women who succeeded on their own efforts. Moreover, both shared a keen interest in life. As Mrs. Trollope noted fondly of her heroine:

To do her justice, [she] seldom felt any thing to be tedious; she could always find, or make opportunities for displaying both her mind and body to advantage; and who that does this can ever find any portion of existence fatiguing? [1: 127]

Besieged by her admirers, she heartily enjoys her success: "I wonder what would happen if I were to take into my head to make myself a queen? I wonder whether anybody, or anything, would be found able to stop me?" [1: 77] Falling into a deep sleep, "she became . . . the subject of her own high imaginings." In a brief dream dialogue with her husband, Martha Barnaby has a vision of her own womanly greatness:

It is not *you* who have written all these books; and if, as you all justly enough say, a title must and will be given, as in the case of Sir Walter and Sir Edward, it cannot be given to *you*. No, Donny, no. It must and will be given to ME. Yes, yes; hush, hush, hush. I know it, I know it. I know perfectly well, Major Allen, without your telling me, that no ladies ever are made baronets. I know I can't be Sir Martha, foolish man, quite as well as you do, and I know a little better, perhaps that *you* will never be Sir anything. . . . Why should I not be called Lady Martha? [2:83 ff.]

Since she cannot be Sir Martha, her husband must become Mr.

Barnaby! In the end, the major, in a burst of honest admiration, changes his name to Barnaby "as a still farther compliment" to the cleverness of "his ever-admired wife." Clearly conceding her preeminence, the major salutes her "with all the fervour of young affection. . . . I can never hope to equal you in anything" [2: 243]. In one way or another, the superiority of women had been Mrs. Trollope's theme since *Domestic Manners*. Surely, Martha Barnaby is her apotheosis of the new woman.

All the Barnaby books were immensely popular. The second and third were illustrated by two of the most prominent artists of the time, R. N. Buss and John Leech. But while enjoying the books, reviewers hardly seemed to know what to do with the heroine. The *Spectator* considered the first Barnaby novel an advance "much beyond her previous fiction" and found the widow merely supplying "the broad humour," while the love-distresses of her young niece provided "the interest of the piece as a novel." Apparently the reviewer was uncomfortable with the idea that a fat, middle-aged widow with inflated hopes, calculations, and vulgar airs could constitute the true heroine of a Victorian novel. And the *Athenaeum*, while favorable toward the chief character, reassured the reader that there was nothing to be feared from this latest of Mrs. Trollope's fictions, for "Affection and Good-Fortune, and Justice . . . bring to confusion Selfishness and vulgar Pretension."[9] Yet the widow triumphs in the end, rising above her difficulties to begin a new career. The reviewer was clearly interpreting the book according to the convention that fiction should teach and be elevating, and the widow offered no healthy example to young ladies clustering around the fireplace to hear father read aloud. Mrs. Trollope is making fun in this novel of the idea that a heroine can offer an example. No reader dared take the widow as model, but there was enjoyment to be gained in watching her exploits and adventures.

Indeed, even the *Times*, which had often felt itself "compelled . . . to cry out against the errors and literary crimes of Mrs. Trollope," once resolving "to pass over altogether her future productions," made peace with the author on the strength of *The Widow Barnaby*. "Pardon, sweet Barnaby," the reviewer wrote, "that we should have spoken ill of your brethren; henceforth your name shall be a signal of truce to us—a teaspoonful of oil to allay and spread smoothly over a whole ocean of critical anger." In this review, as in all the others of this remarkable series of books, the writer marveled at the originality of the conception, which made the reader's enjoyment somewhat paradoxical and puzzling: "The Barnaby is such a heroine as never before has figured in a romance. Her vulgarity is sublime. Imaginary personage though she be, everybody who has read her memoirs must have a real interest in her." Indicating the dilemma of those who enjoyed such a heroine, the

reviewer spoke of the "charming horror" that had carried him through
the volumes, to mark the majestic developments of this woman:

> Such a jovial, handsome, hideous, ogling, bustling monster of a woman as
> maid, wife, and widow, was never, as we can recollect, before brought
> upon the scene. Not Madame Duval, not Miss Snap (who afterwards
> married Mr. Jonathan Wild), not Mrs. Towwows, nor the immaculate Mrs.
> Slipslop, live in fiction, or appear to us in a light more amiably disagreea-
> ble, more delightfully disgusting, than the Widow Barnaby.[10]

An 1855 reviewer, surveying the field of "modern novelists—great
and small," grudgingly admitted Mrs. Trollope's proven talents as a
writer ("to have remained so long in possession of the popular ear is no
small tribute"). Although insisting that her widow character was extremely unpleasant, with "coarse tricks and coarse rouge," the writer
wished that Mrs. Trollope had made the widow mend her ways; nevertheless the reviewer admitted that "Mrs. Barnaby is a real kind of
woman," a contrast to "those mincing genteel histories of *Cecilia* and
Evelina which Johnson and Burke sat up all night to read." Still, the
critic confessed to missing "the silken rustle and ladylike pace of her contemporary, and [found] Mrs. Trollope a less agreeable companion than
Mrs. Gore." The writer recalled the good old days in fiction, when "our
ladies were beautiful" and those who loved them revered them with a
"knightly, chivalrous true-love which consecrated all womankind." The
change began with Jane Eyre, "a little fierce incendiary, doomed to turn
the world of fancy upside down." Ten years *before* Jane Eyre, however,
Mrs. Trollope had prepared the ground for the revolution. Her Barnaby
was a type of the new woman, a female on her own in a male-dominated
world who must struggle for existence, advancing herself by dint of her
own wits. That writer of 1855, bemoaning the disappearance of the
conventional heroine, used words that might well have been applied to
the widow Barnaby:

> Do you think that young lady is an angelic being, young gentleman? Do
> you compare her to roses and lilies, and stars and sunbeams, in your
> deluded imagination? . . . Unhappy youth ! She is a fair gladiator—she
> is not an angel. In her secret heart she longs to rush upon you and try a
> grapple with you, to prove her strength and her equality.[11]

Mrs. Trollope's widow books are the farcical story of such a struggle, in
which Martha Barnaby proves to be, beyond the shadow of a doubt, not
merely equal but obviously superior to men.

10

Michael Armstrong:
Fiction With a Purpose

*The most probable immediate effect of her pennings
and her pencillings will be the burning of factories
. . . [and] the plunder of property of all kinds.*

AS HER daughter-in-law Frances Eleanor reported, "the year 1839 must
have been one of exceptional activity even for that marvellously
industrious worker Frances Trollope." She wrote two novels (*The
Widow Married* and *One Fault*, both published in 1840), oversaw a fifth
and cheap edition of *Domestic Manners*, planned a trip to Italy for the
following year, and fulfilled an old promise to Anthony of an excursion
to Paris. She also researched and wrote the monthly parts of one of the
most controversial of all her books, *The Life and Adventures of Michael
Armstrong, the Factory Boy*. With this novel of the industrial poor, Mrs.
Trollope reentered the field of reform; twice before she had translated
contemporary social conditions into fiction. While most current commentators regard her factory book as merely another example of her
never-ending search for the material of best-sellers, her interest in the
novel with a purpose was neither new nor superficial.[1]

When she decided to write a novel "on the condition of factory
hands," she engaged in a method of research that bespoke a serious
dedication. She embarked on a fact-finding mission to Manchester (the
"shock city of the industrial revolution"), where dreadful conditions
were said to exist. Even with Tom as escort, the expedition to what
seemed to many the cradle of an incipient revolution was a daring one,
especially for a woman. But it was not out of character; some dozen
years before she had, after all, followed Frances Wright to Nashoba.[2]

She remained in and around the city for several weeks, and her son
later emphasized the persistence with which she had gone about her
work. Armed with a sheaf of introductory letters from Lord Shaftesbury, she approached the main radical reform leaders. Inviting them to
her dinner table, she freely encouraged them to talk. They came, a
steady stream of earnest, almost desperate men, some of them convicted
of sedition and awaiting trial, all of them no doubt rather shocking and

dangerous visitors to a lady-novelist's quarters. Tom recalled that in addition to the well known, there were others:

> nearly all of them, men a little raised above the position of the factory hands, to the righting of whose wrongs they devoted their lives. They had been at some period of their lives, in almost every case, factory workers themselves, but had by various circumstances, native talent, industry and energy, or favoring fortune—more likely by all together—managed to raise themselves out of the slough of despond in which their fellows were overwhelmed.[3]

Mr. Doherty, a trade-union leader and a small printer and publisher, had attacked the factory system in his weekly paper, *The Poor Man's Advocate*, and reprinted a memoir that Mrs. Trollope would find a valuable source. Doherty came to dine, but, as Tom recalled, "it was . . . with some difficulty that we persuaded him to do so . . . his excitement in talking was so great and continuous that he could eat next to nothing."[4]

Whenever possible, she personally visited the slums, scenes of "pitiable wretchedness and revolting squalor," an activity which required a "stout heart and . . . healthy frame." Gathering material that subsequently provided the background for her book, she went to hear the preachers, especially the leading advocate of parliamentary legislation for a ten-hour day, Richard Oastler, the "Danton of the movement," and Joseph Raynor Stephens, its most spectacular evangelizer. Tom later remembered Oastler as "the very *beau-ideal* of a mob orator . . . an advocate whom few platform orators would have cared to meet as an adversary," but he was not so impressed by Stephens. He devoted a frustratingly small amount of space to describing these men in his autobiography. Unlike his mother, whose novel shows she came to understand and respect them, the conventional Tom found them "a rather strange assortment of persons." Still, he and his mother crowded into small chapels to hear the rhetoric of reform. Jostled, probably vaguely frightened, almost suffocated by the crush of crowds, Mrs. Trollope was caught up by the energy and conviction of these men, at least one of whom she would portray favorably as an important element in her book.[5]

Warm-hearted and generous, she announced her plan "to do something towards attracting the public mind" towards the "hoped-for factory legislation." She visited the factories owned by those in favor of the pending legislation and toured Bradford incognito to see with her own eyes "the dirtiest, filthiest and worst regulated town in the Kingdom." This hard-working author, with her crusading spirit, produced as a result a powerful and authentic work, and Tom, for his part, stressed the faithfulness of the final product. "Where it would have been difficult for her" to look for facts, he went in her behalf, and thus she "neglected no means of making the facts stated in her book authentic and accurate, and the *misé en scene* of her story graphic and truthful." He stoutly defended his mother against the charge of exaggeration: "What we are there described to have seen, we saw."[6]

With the writing of *Michael Armstrong*, Mrs. Trollope boldly led the way in making fiction "the medium of interpretation" for a new age, and the novel with a purpose rapidly became a common and then a dominant type as the 1840s progressed. In 1845, Benjamin Disraeli advertised his *Sybil* as a study of the unknown, and one reviewer called him "a traveller into new regions of humanity . . . who setting out from the salons of the luxurious, penetrates into the dark and unknown regions of the populace." But, ironically, Mrs. Trollope's innovative first novel of the industrial poor in England, which had appeared five years earlier, never proved popular with reviewers. She was castigated for a "strange delight in the hideous and revolting" and for "detailing the faults of low-bred people." Critics were offended by her "low people . . . sunk deeper than the lowest depths, as if they had been bred in and in, to the last dregs." In drawing this indictment of the "new spirit of the age," R. H. Horne concluded with a devastating attack on the realistic novel: "Nothing can exceed the vulgarity of Mrs. Trollope's mob of characters . . . We have heard it urged on behalf of Mrs. Trollope, that her novels are, at all events, drawn from life. So are sign paintings."[7]

She herself was cognizant of the crucial differences between this work and that favorite creation of her heart, the widow Barnaby, and later wrote Tom: "The *Widow* continues to be in great favour. But between ourselves, I don't think any one cares much for *Michael Armstrong*—except the Chartists. A new kind of patrons for me!" Mrs. Trollope, however, played an important part in extending the social and geographical range of Victorian fiction and moving it away from making "love and marriage seem the main business of life."[8] In this she joined her more distinguished contemporary Charles Dickens. Mary Russell Mitford bemoaned the effect of such novels: "What things these are—the Jack Sheppards, and Squeers, and Oliver Twists, and Michael Armstrongs—All the worse because of their power to move men's souls."[9]

But in her treatment of the industrial poor, Mrs. Trollope pursued a theme entirely different from those of her contemporaries who subsequently turned to this subject. Harriet Martineau's contribution ("A Manchester Strike," 1834), the seventh of her *Illustrations of Political*

Economy, was a short tale which, although compassionate, demonstrated that the poor must help themselves. Indeed, the twenty-three principles of political economy that her tale attempted to illustrate reinforced those liberal, laissez-faire ideals which had created and prolonged the intolerable conditions of the factory workers. Charlotte Elizabeth Tonna's *Helen Fleetwood* (1839–1840) emphasized the wickedness of workers, who were more morally than physically debased by the factory system. Her solution for the poor was an inward turning to Christ; conditions in the factory seemed inevitable and permanent.[10]

Mrs. Trollope's purpose, on the other hand, was to awaken the national conscience on behalf of the factory children. It is today difficult to imagine the "dead-weight of indifference" prevailing when Oastler and the other reformers first embarked on their mission. Mrs. Trollope sought to bring their message to a middle-class public who had often accused them of exaggeration. To allay such charges, and to emphasize her main point, she spoke directly to her readers:

> Woe to those who supinely sit in contented ignorance of the facts, soothing their spirits and their easy consciences with the cuckoo note *"Exaggeration!"* while thousands of helpless children pine away their unnoted, miserable lives, in labour and destitution *incomparably more severe* than any ever produced by negro slavery.[11]

Mrs. Trollope's innovativeness, dedication, hard work, and imagination helped change such indifference into concern.

Several early critics regarded Mrs. Trollope's book as merely imitative of Dickens's *Oliver Twist*, which had been appearing in shilling numbers from March 1837 to March 1839.

> Boz, like Byron, has his imitators: since the increasing demand for the Nickleby article, Boz, not being protected by patent like Mackintosh, has been pirated; cuckoos lay their eggs in his nest; countless are the Factory-Boys which Mrs. Trollope has turned loose.

Both novels hoped to alleviate abuses in lower-class lives and to exhibit such evils in the strongest possible light. Both centered on a young child, and both were attacked for coarseness and vulgarity, for having brought "the novel out of the drawing-room into the streets." To complete the comparison, both appeared in the form of a monthly illustrated publication ("so much in vogue at present," one commentator noted) and were aimed at a broad reading public. In her time, Mrs. Trollope was the only woman author to issue her novels in monthly parts. The practice was a difficult one, which made great demands on the novelist, who had to work against time and provide the suitable number of crises, even while sustaining overall unity. Like Dickens, Mrs. Trollope used the form to establish a feeling of immediacy and a close relationship with her readers. Her technique was successful; the *New Monthly Magazine* praised the form as admirably well chosen:

> This striking and forcible tale improves on the reader at every step. Nothing can be more fearfully, yet touchingly true, than some of the descriptions; and the interest and excitement of the plot have now reached their height, yet without affording any glimpse of the *denouement*.[12]

But *Michael Armstrong* was not an imitation of *Oliver Twist*. At no time did Dickens describe actual factory conditions or the plight of factory children. His world of the village workshop and London street urchin was entirely different from her scenes of the industrial hell of Manchester and its environs. More important, Mrs. Trollope openly rejected Dickens's retreat to an eighteenth-century moral atmosphere, with its hopes that individual benevolence could solve the problems of modern society. Mrs. Trollope had seen private philanthropy fail at Nashoba; her new novel advocated the passage of public legislation, such as the Factory Act and the Ten-Hours Bill. Indeed, her decision to publish in shilling numbers was motivated not purely from the financial advantage that a large sale would bring but by a determination to be sure that her message would receive "the most eager attention from many thousand of her countrymen."[13] To this end, she made masterful use of Hervieu's powerful illustrations. In this practice, she had been a pioneer since the first appearance of his brilliantly interpretive drawings in *Domestic Manners*. In *Michael Armstrong*, Hervieu caught the urgency of her theme, and at least one reviewer bitterly protested the result:

> But if the text be bad, still worse are the plates which illustrate it. What, for instance, must be the effect of the first in No. VI [mill children competing with pigs for food], on the heated imaginations of our great manufacturing towns, figuring as they do in every book-seller's window?

Another reviewer, noting the appropriateness of the form, also saw the seriousness of her purpose:

> Those will grievously mistake the design of this work who look to it for nothing beyond the mere amusement of an idle hour. It seeks at once to impress a deep moral lesson, and to work a great social change, and we are greatly mistaken if it do not ultimately effect its purpose.[14]

In *Michael Armstrong* the manufacturer Sir Matthew Dowling publicly adopts a factory child in a moment of sentimental extravagence to impress a lady and to divert attention from a recent death in one of his factories and takes the boy into his own home, to feed, clothe, and educate him, much as Mr. Brownlow befriended Oliver. He trumpets his action through the community as a sign of his charity and benevolence. Soon, however, he tires of the boy, whose presence gradually brings out his incipient sadism. Sir Matthew finally gets rid of "the brat" by apprenticing him to a sinister establishment for unwanted pauper children. After many trials and a nearly fatal attack of typhus fever, Michael escapes and becomes a farm laborer. In the end, he is reunited with the girl he has come to love, his crippled brother is now grown to handsome manhood, and his heiress-protector, in a fairy-tale ending, whisks them all away to the Continent, where they improve their minds with education and marry the choices of their hearts. These latter sections weaken Mrs. Trollope's novel but do not detract from its powerful message; all the characters eventually discover that individual philanthropy is an inadequate solution to the problems of industrialization.

Besides illustrating this theme, her book provided an effective description of the world of the industrial poor in England's factory districts. Even as Dickens had moved from Pickwick's sunny world to the thieves' den of *Oliver Twist*, Mrs. Trollope left behind the comical Barnaby to plunge into regions as yet unfathomed and undescribed by novelists. After Dicken's visit to Manchester in 1838–1839, he had vowed to "strike the heaviest blow in my power for these unfortunate creatures," but as one of his biographers notes, the "dust-laden mills and their thunderous machines" were too strange to his imagination. And he waited a decade and a half (*Hard Times* appeared in 1852) until he took up the fight against the utilitarian philosophy which, in his opinion, was the cause of the troubles. Hard on the heels of her own Manchester visit, however, Mrs. Trollope produced *Michael Armstrong*, directly setting forth her impressions, dark and scalding pictures of the squalor, unhealthiness, and brutality of town life in the manufacturing districts and in the factories themselves. While such details were known and had been described in the dry language of contemporary parliamentary reportage, Mrs. Trollope transformed them into palpable reality in her fiction.[15]

Relentlessly, factually, dramatically, Mrs. Trollope wove into her story the horrible details of everyday life in the factory districts. Her rendering of an industrial slum was the first such scene in English fiction. Ashleigh was "the most deplorable hole in the parish," with its narrow, deep-rutted road serving in part as conduit for the town's refuse, into which "every summer storm and winter torrent deposited their fatherings, there to remain and be absorbed as they might." There stood the "long, closely-packed double row of miserable dwellings, crowded to excess by the population drawn together by the neighbouring factories." Their "squalid, untrimmed look" seemed "the moral delinquencies of a corporate body, of which no man is ashamed, because no man can be pointed at as the guilty ONE." Vividly, she stressed the hopeless, circular dilemma of such abject poverty, depicting gateless dwellings covered with filth "and the dogs and the pigs who made good their entry there. . . ."

Further narrowing her focus, she included "the very vilest rags" hanging before most of the doors, the "crawling infants, half-starved cats, mangy curs, and fowls that looked as if each particular feather had been used as a scavenger's broom." Over all was an indescribable stench, "an odour, which seemed compounded of a multitude of villainous smells, all reeking together into one" (1:87–88). Above this urban wasteland loomed the loathsome factory itself, tinting with black every conceivable object:

> The walls are black, the fences are black, the windowpanes (when there are any) are all veiled in black. No domestic animal that pertinaciously exists within their tainted purlieus, but wears the same dark hue; and perhaps there is no condition of human life so significantly surrounded by types of its own wretchedness as this. [2:55]

Boldly she described factory conditions and the processes of child labor among the machines, using her story to familiarize middle-class readers with the settings, procedures, and terminology of industrialization. She brought her sheltered and comfortable public inside Sir Matthew's extensive factory, behind walls customarily locked and silent, to that place from which the delights of childhood have been banished for ever:

> The ceaseless whirring of a million hissing wheels seizes on the tortured ear. . . . The scents that reek around, from oil, tainted water, and human filth, with that last worst nausea, arising from the hot refuse of atmospheric air, left by some hundred pairs of laboring lungs, render the act of breathing a process of difficulty, disgust, and pain. All this is terrible.

But as the eye circled that "horrid earthly hell," all "villainous smells" and "ear-racking sounds" vanished at the sight of the helpless, suffering infants at their relentless labor:

Lean and distorted limbs—sallow and sunken cheeks—dim hollow eyes, that speak unrest and most unnatural carefulness, give to each tiny, trembling, unelastic form a look of hideous premature old age. . . . In the room they entered, the dirty, ragged, miserable crew were all in active performance of their various tasks; the overlookers, strap in hand, on the alert; the whirling spindles urging the little slaves who waited on them to movements as unceasing as their own. [1:199]

Next, Mrs. Trollope's eye went to a child engaged as a piecer, whose duties were explained in a footnote: "to walk backwards and forwards before the reels on which the cotton, silk, or worsted is wound, for the purpose of joining the threads when they break" (1:183). Another miserable waif, a girl of about seven, is described as a "scavenger," whose job

was to collect incessantly, from the machinery and from the floor, the flying fragments of cotton that might impede the work. In the performance of this duty, the child was obliged, from time to time, to stretch itself with sudden quickness on the ground, while the hissing machinery passed over her; and when this is skillfully done, and the head, body, and out-stretched limbs carefully glued to the floor, the steady-moving, but threatening mass, may pass and repass over the dizzy head and trembling body without touching it. But accidents frequently occur; and many are the flaxen locks rudely torn from infant heads in the process. [1:201]

Later, the infamous "billy roller" is defined by a young drudge as "a long stout stick . . . that's used often and often to beat the little ones employed in the mills when their strength fails—when they fall asleep, or stand still for a minute" [2:78-79]. While the "stern and steady machinery" moves relentlessly onward amid pathetic and sometimes sadistic scenes of beatings, the visitors philosophize:

Nothing in God's world but sheer wilful laziness makes those obstinate little brutes . . . pretend to totter, and stumble, and faint, and the devil knows what; when all their work is to walk backwards and forwards as leisurely as if they were parading for pleasure. [1:184]

But the visitors soon tire even of this edifying spectacle and depart for Sir Matthew's "cool and lofty library," where they order iced water and claret "to wash away the effect of their half hour's visit to the factory" (1:208). It is unlikely that Mrs. Trollope's readers were able so easily to forget the powerful scenes of this inferno. Indeed, one touching plate by Hervieu, showing Michael greeting his younger brother amidst the humming machinery, has become the standard illustration of the evils of child labor.[16]

To assist her in dramatizing the evils of the factory system as they affected children, Mrs. Trollope used as a source for several lengthy sections of her book a pamphlet which she had been given by its printer, entitled "A Memoir of Robert Blincoe, An Orphan Boy; Sent from the Workhouse of St. Pancras, London, at Seven Years of Age, to endure the Horrors of a Cotton-mill, through his infancy and youth, with a minute detail of his sufferings, being the First Memoir of the Kind Published." The Blincoe story centered on the sham apprenticeship system, wherein unwanted parish pauper children were sent in large numbers to work long hours, often under extremely unhealthy conditions, in textile mills which, partly because of water-power requirements, were commonly located in remote riverside areas, where it was difficult to recruit labor.[17] Although the conditions described by Blincoe existed primarily in the early years of the century, the industrial picture still contained much to disgust and appall. Even as Stephens and Oastler had utilized stirring and spectacular rhetoric in their public speeches, Mrs. Trollope chose to use the heart-rending pamphlet to arouse her readers' moral indignation and compassion.

She took from the Blincoe pamphlet details of atmosphere and setting to which she believed most factory children had been at some time or other exposed but eliminated uniformly its strong sadistic side. Blincoe had described kicks, cuffs, murderous threats, tortures, handcuffings, and mortifications. Once his master had abstained from a promised "flanking" because "the poor boy's body was so dreadfully discoloured and inflamed by contusions" as to terrify even his despotic master. "There was not, at the time, a free spot on which to inflict a blow! His ears were swollen and excoriated; his head, in the most deplorable state imaginable; many of the bruises on his body had suppurated! and so excessive was his soreness, he was forced to sleep on his face. . . ."[18] Stories of scalded heads and "the terrible scalping remedy," infestation by lice, incurable lameness, stretchings—all these Mrs. Trollope omitted. She was not interested in telling a sensational tale of the physical brutalities suffered by some who fell prey to sadistic masters. She would not use the worst elements of a system having enormous ranges because she hoped to indict the whole society which permitted the exploitation of the young.

Mrs. Trollope used the pamphlet instead to cull particulars, some trifling, some suggestively significant, which gave her story specificity and an air of authority. Thus she was obviously impressed by Blincoe's account of the filthy and unappetizing food:

The store pigs and the apprentices used to fare pretty much alike; but when the swine were hungry, they used to speak and grunt so loud, they

obtained the wash first, to quiet them. . . . The fatting pigs fared
luxuriously, compared with the apprentices! They were often regaled
with mealballs made into dough, and given in the shape of dumplings!
Blincoe and others . . . used to say to one another, "*The pigs are served;
it will be our turn next.*" Blincoe . . . used to keep a sharp eye upon the
fatting pigs, and their mealballs and, as soon as he saw the swineherd
withdraw, he used to slip down stairs and, stealing slyly towards the
trough, plunge his hand in at the loop holes, and steal as many dumplings
as he could grasp! The food thus obtained from a pigs trough, and,
perhaps defiled by their filthy chops, was exultingly conveyed to the
privy . . . and there devoured with a much keener appetite, than it
would have been by the pigs.[19]

In her own book, this scene became a "loathsome and fearful spectacle"
as a group of boys steal "from a filthy trough just replenished for the
morning meal of two stout hogs, a variety of morsels" that represented
"dainty eating for the starving prentices of Deep Valley mill." One boy
good-naturedly calls to the faint, sick, and broken-hearted Michael:

"Make haste, young'un . . . or they won't leave a turnip-paring for us."
And on he rushed to the scuffle, leaving Michael gazing with disgust and
horror at the contest between the fierce snouts of the angry pigs, and the
active fingers of the wretched crew who contested with them for the offal
thus cast forth. [2:159]

Mrs. Trollope also took from the Blincoe memoir characters who
represented an authority determined to do nothing to ameliorate
conditions. Blincoe's meal-time supervisor, "a huge raw-boned man,
who had served in the army, and had been a drill serjeant," and who
carried "a large horse-whip," she transformed into the "master of
ceremonies" at a "feast of misery," bearing his "huge horsewhip in his
hand, without which indeed, it is said, he seldom appeared on the
premises," his eye quelling "the will of every little wretch it looked
upon" (2:152, 156–57). Blincoe's "medical gentleman" who prescribes
"kitchen physic" for the children desperately ill during a typhus epidem-
ic, appears in *Michael Armstrong* to declare "that nothing would be so
likely to stop the contagion as nourishing food; upon which the terrified
manufacturer astonished all the butchers within his reach, by commanding a large supply of beef and mutton *good enough to make wholesome
soup* (2:236–37). When deaths multiply because of the lack of medical
treatment, Blincoe's master has "pitch, tobacco, etc. . . . burnt in the
chamber, and vinegar sprinkled on their beds and on the floor" to
disguise the stench. Mrs. Trollope's master of apprentices also orders "a
cask of vinegar to sprinkle the chambers," adding, "Trust me that this

will do more good than all the doctors that ever were hatched. Besides the vinegar cask will never sing out . . . and the doctor might (2:237). Blincoe's master hides the extent of the mortality by dividing the burials, even though "the burial fees [for the other church yards] were double the charge of those at Tideswell."[20] In *Michael Armstrong*, officials have "all that died by day buried at night, without making . . . any fuss or fidget about it whatever," and arrange to have fifteen of the group "noiselessly buried in Tugswell churchyard" (2:243). The events and details Mrs. Trollope selected from Blincoe's account indicate the theme she wanted to emphasize: the conspiracy of silence engaged in by the officials who were in charge of the working children of England.

Mrs. Trollope was always alert for the concrete detail that captured some symbolic truth, and for this too she used the Blincoe pamphlet. The matter-of-fact Blincoe related how sick children were simply worked until they fell, "and when it was no longer possible . . . they were put into a wheel-barrow, and wheeled to the 'prentice-house.' "[21] Struck by this brief scene, Mrs. Trollope transformed it and included it in her novel: "It was not an uncommon thing to see two or three wheelbarrows at a time, towards the evening of every day, conveying children from the factory to the apprenticehouse who have fallen while following the machinery" (2:246). This poignant detail showed simply and starkly how the factory children were reduced to industrial fodder.

But Mrs. Trollope was not satisfied merely to recreate and heighten the dreadful settings of slum and factory to arouse the consciences of her readers. Her book showed the way in which public legislation, not private beneficence, could solve the problems of an industrial society. This important focus Mrs. Trollope worked out in the person of her independent, thoughtful heroine, Mary Brotherton, who inquires into the causes of such conditions. Determined to learn the truth about the factory system, Miss Brotherton seeks to find "whether, by the nature of things, it is impossible to manufacture worsted and cotton wool into articles useful to man, without rendering those employed upon it unfit to associate with the rest of their fellow creatures" (1:282). Systematically, she visits the factory districts, hoping to improve the conditions under which one family lives. Her questions show her at first possessed by the prevalent middle-class notions of poverty.

Perhaps the children's father has wasted away his wages in drink, she suggests. But the answers reveal a more complex picture:

Mother said he took to it, as most of the others do in all the mills, on account of hating to come home so, when we young ones comes in from work. I have heard mother say that father cried when I, that was the biggest, com'd hom first beaten and bruised with the strap and the billy-roller. [2:78–79]

Even when employed by a benevolent master who maintained a Sunday school in the factory, the children fail to benefit. To Miss Brotherton's amazement, they cannot even read.

> We was often and often kep going till twelve o'clock on Saturday night, and when the Sunday comed we couldn't sit down upon the bench, neither Grace, nor Dick, nor I, without falling dead asleep. [2:80–81]

Gradually, Miss Brotherton's comfortable notions of thrift, hard work, and self-help prove inadequate.

Her search for a practical solution brings her to the drawing-room of the Reverend Bell of Fairley, whose impassioned plea for legislative interference forms the thematic center of the book. This character was a thinly disguised version of the real Parson Bull of Brierly, whom Tom Trollope remembered as "an ardent advocate of the ten-hours' bill" but who had lately come to have "very little hope of legislative interference." The gloomy Bull told Tom "that he looked forward to some tremendous popular outbreak, and should not be surprised any night to hear that every mill in Bradford was in flames."[22]

Reverend Bell made it clear that the fault lay in the system itself, not in individuals. From the time of his birth, a factory child in Great Britain was little better than a slave, for—"he too is a property." Dramatically describing a typical day of labor for such a child, Bell curses the "*lawless and irresistible*" power of the manufacturing wealth of England. While Mary Brotherton marvels that such things exist "and the rulers of the land sit idly by to witness it," Bell tells her that the oppression of the "degraded class" can only be changed should Parliament make it "illegal for men, women, and children to be kept to the wearying, unhealthy labour of the mills for more than ten hours out of every day, leaving their daily wages at the same rate as now" (2:215). Bell is sure that "individual benevolence" will be inadequate to "heal the misery of those who suffer: The oppression under which they groan is too overwhelming to be removed or even lightened, by an agency less powerful than that of the law" (2:221). When the heiress-heroine proposes giving aid herself, Rev. Bell is skeptical:

> That you may save your own excellent heart from the palsy of hopeless and helpless pity, by the indulgence of your benevolence in individual cases of distress, I need not point out to you; but that any of the ordinary modes of being useful on a larger scale, such as organising schools, founding benefit societies, or the like, could be of any use to beings so crushed, so toil-worn, and so degraded, it would be idle to hope. [2:222–23]

The effort of some few enlightened factory owners who have tried to do business "with comfort and advantage to every individual concerned" have been futile; no individual can break the back of the entire capitalistic system:

> You can hardly guess what up-hill work it is, when one good man has got to stand alone, and breast the competition of a whole host of bad ones in his commercial enterprises. The high-minded owners of yonder factory are losing thousands every year by their efforts to purify this traffic of its enormities—and some thousand small still voices call down blessings on them for it. But while it costs them ten shillings to produce what their neighbours can bring into the market for nine, they will only be pointed at as pitiably unwise in their generation by all the great family of Mammon which surround them. Few, alas! will think of following the example. All they can do therefore is in fact but to carry on a system of private charity on an enormous scale—but till they are supported by law, even their vast efforts and most noble sacrifices can do nothing towards the general redemption of our poor northern people from the state of slavery into which they have fallen. [2:227]

The most important turn of the plot clearly reinforces Mrs. Trollope's main point. Years after his successful escape from Deep Valley, Michael Armstrong, now eighteen, hears of the great Yorkshire meeting where a vote will be taken on the ten-hours bill. Reading some handbills calling the interested people to this gathering, his heart instantly kindles: "Such terribly true representations were found among them of the well-remembered agonies of his boyhood, that Michael was fain to put his spread hand before his face to conceal the emotions they produced." A passing stranger asks that he sign the petition and attend the meeting, predicting that the assembly

> will offer a spectacle such as never was witnessed before, and most likely never will, or can be seen again. A multitude, probably amounting to above a hundred thousand over-worked operatives, will meet in peace and good order, to petition for legal relief from the oppression of a system which has brought them to a lower state of degradation and misery than any to which human beings have ever been brought before. [3:145–46]

His praise for the movement's leadership was Mrs. Trollope's own for the men she had learned to trust, admire, and respect.

And so Michael Armstrong, a factory worker who has, through his own wits and good luck, been able to escape, determines "to attend the great Yorkshire meeting, and hold up his hand for the ten hours' bill" (3:149). In this single, significant act, the central meaning of the novel emerges. Only after fulfilling this obligation to the hopes for reform does Michael find his brother and the benevolent heiress, whence follows the book's facile ending.

In addition to being a plea for legislation and an exposé of actual conditions, Mrs. Trollope's book recorded the rhetoric of middle-class self-justification which, in her view, sustained the system. Adept as she always was in convincingly rendering the language of the hypocrite seeking to conceal base motives behind the pious phraseology of larger ideals, she portrayed the manufacturers, the factory owners, and their accomplices. Their rhetoric resisted reform in the name of "national wealth and prosperity":

England will become the paradise of manufacturers!—the great work-shop of the world! When strangers climb our chalk cliffs to get a peep at us, they shall see, land at what point they will, the glowing fires that keep our engines going, illuminating the land from one extremity of the island to the other! Then think how we shall suck in . . . gold, gold, gold from all sides. The idea is perfectly magnificent. [1:296-97]

For, even as God had providentially sent steam, children had been made to labor.

To sustain this image of national welfare, Mrs. Trollope saw that those in power created another myth, namely that the poverty of the factory people was their own fault. They were shiftless, idle gin drinkers; why should the solid middle classes worry about them? Many of her characters believe that factory people are "the worst set of creatures that burden God's earth."

The men are vicious, and the women dissolute, taking drams often, and often when they ought to buy food; and so horridly dirty and unthrifty, that it is a common saying, you may know a factory-girl as far as you can see her. [1:239]

Given the ineluctable nature of the poor, the great reformers were simply trouble-makers. As one character sees it:

I don't know what poor people will come to! It's quite out of the question to attempt pleasing 'em. If they've got no work they are perfectly outrageous about that, and ready to tear people to pieces just to get it; and no sooner is there enough to do, than away they go bawling again, swearing that the children are overworked. [2:192-93]

One by one, Mrs. Trollope marshaled the arguments and justifications for the status quo, exposing each in turn as ignorant, self-seeking, or complacent.

Mrs. Trollope's heroine, Mary Brotherton, is another of her strong, independent women who makes her way alone. A wealthy young girl, she had often been lectured on the comfortable notion that "where ignorance is bliss, 'tis folly to be wise," a notion that had kept the repulsive subject out of much polite fiction. But she determines to be guided not by the common misconceptions of her class but by her own inner instincts. She sets off to find and help the factory boy, in spite of the disapproval of friends and relatives, presenting the logic of her case in revolutionary language for a young lady of 1839:

> Did I belong to any one, I think I should willingly yield to their guidance. But I am alone in the world; I have no responsibilities but to God and my own conscience; and the only way I know of, by which I can make this desolate sort of freedom endurable, is by fearlessly, and without respect to any prejudices or opinions whatever, employing my preposterous wealth in assisting the miserable race from whose labours it has been extracted. [2:270]

Even the Reverend Bell finds her mission somewhat improper, but she vigorously rejects "the etiquettes by which the movements of other young ladies are regulated" (2:283). In this character, Mrs. Trollope continued to sound a new voice for women. Years before Jane Eyre announced to Mr. Rochester "I care for myself," Mary Brotherton defined the only duty, that which "you owe to your own soul." She moves not from poverty to riches but from ignorance and complacency to social awareness and responsibility, to the demands of the inner conscience over the conventions of the polite world.

In the field of fiction, Mrs. Trollope, like her heroine, had refused the heavy harness of gentility. In the year of the book's publication, Miss M. A. Stodart, in her hints on readings for young ladies, made specific and disapproving reference to *Michael Armstrong*. She found it a particularly unfit subject for a woman writer. Dreading "specious emotional excitement," she condemned the social-problem novel in general, advising women against reading something like "Mrs. Trollope's Factory Boy" because its unhealthy effect on the mind was an evil outweighing any possible good done by the social message.[23] Letitia Landon, who wrote principally of love, was characterized by *Fraser's* as knowing the proper subject matter for a female writer:

> Is she to write of politics, or political economy, or pugilism, or punch? Certainly not. We feel a determined dislike of women who wander into

these unfeminine paths; they should immediately hoist a mustache—and, to do them justice, they in general do exhibit no inconsiderable specimen of the hair lip. We think Miss L. E. L. has chosen the better part . . . she does right in thinking that Sappho knew what she was about when she chose the tender passion as the theme for woman.[24]

Similarly, Miss Mitford's graceful rustic pictures were immensely popular, and in presenting them to the public, one reviewer noted, "she dares do all that may become a woman." Lady Blessington's novels of aristocratic life also drew praise because their attributes and qualities were peculiarly "feminine." One reviewer insisted, "Women are more at home in the flower garden and by the domestic hearth. Their portraitures of familiar scenes, of every-day incidents, are matchless for truth and grace."[25]

Mrs. Trollope, on the other hand, provoked the reviewers, one of whom was relieved to find "the class to which she belongs . . . fortunately very small":

> She owes everything to that audacious contempt of public opinion, which is the distinguishing mark of persons who are said to *stick at nothing*. Nothing but this . . . could have produced some of the books she has written. . . . She serves up everything with the same sauce; the predominant flavour is Trollope still.[26]

Her defiant and unladylike message came clearly through to her contemporaries. And even as Oastler and Stephens had frightened the powerful with their menacing rhetoric ("England stands on a mine; a volcano is beneath her!"), language characterized by both their critics and supporters as intimidating, violent, and revolutionary, Mrs. Trollope seemed an even more serious (if unlikely) agitator. They had gone to jail for their seditious talk, and at least one reviewer thought "the author of *Michael Armstrong* deserves as richly to have eighteen months in Chester Gaol as any that are there now for using violent language against the 'monster cotton mills.' "[27]

The *Athenaeum*, breaking with customary practice to review the first six parts of *Michael Armstrong*, gave those pages the longest and most scorching notice Mrs. Trollope ever received from that prestigious journal. Accusing her of "scattering firebrands among the people," of "setting fire to the four quarters of the kingdom," the reviewer implored her to remember "that the most probable immediate effect of her pennings and her pencillings will be the burning of factories . . . [and] the plunder of property of all kinds." Astonished "to behold a lady, a professed admirer of aristocracy in all its excesses, setting about the work of charity, on principles and by means peculiar to the wildest sectarians of fanatical licentiousness," the reviewer, with the typical bias of the period, "in honour of her sex," gave her credit "for an honest belief in the creed she preaches" and even conceded the possible existence of Deep Valley. "If such a hell there be," however, it was surely "an individual solitary instance of the intensity of ill she has delineated." Accusing her of neither deceit nor inaccuracy, the reviewer pleaded that she remain quiet for the good of all. Pointing to "the mischief she is doing," and "the dangers she is provoking," the writer feared the consequence her book "must produce, when disseminated among an ignorant and excited population to which her shilling numbers are but too accessible." Conceding that "the apprentice system is chargeable with evils enough," the reviewer consoled himself that "so too is every other form and consequence of poverty." To her credit, Mrs. Trollope was never comfortably complacent in the presence of human suffering.[28] Her month in Manchester had made of her, even as events had done for Oastler, Stephens, and Bull, that strange anomaly, a Tory radical. Undaunted by critical attacks, Mrs. Trollope persisted in her interest in the lives of the unfortunate. Three years later, she returned to a closely related subject with *Jessie Phillips, a Tale of the Present Day*. The subtitle stressed her determination to use relevant contemporary material for her fiction.[29]

11

Productive Years

A blue-stocking who travels in seven-leagued boots

ON HER return from Manchester, Mrs. Trollope immediately settled with Colburn profitable terms for the two novels she had agreed to publish with him, both in parts. *Michael Armstrong* appeared in shilling monthly numbers between 1 March 1839 and 1 February 1840, and *The Widow Married* was serialized in Colburn's *New Monthly Magazine*, beginning in May 1839 running concurrently until June 1840. She received eight hundred guineas for each, her highest earnings so far, including travel books.[1] Remarkably, she sustained these two very different parallel productions during a busy year, crowded with family happenings, illness, travel, and the writing of yet another novel (*One Fault*). "*Time* was so very precious a commodity," that she put off visiting her brother, while proudly announcing her recent earnings and her determination "to work, to work, to work." Tom had arranged the money settlements, a task and responsibility which she did not like and which he increasingly made his own, functioning as her literary agent. Anthony, conveniently employed in central London at the General Post Office, usually collected his mother's earnings. Ever solicitous for her son, she once reminded Colburn to have the payment checks ready sufficiently early in the day "in order to permit [Anthony] getting to his office at the usual time."

Her business arrangements settled, she took a flying tour of the Lake District with Tom, visiting the venerable Wordsworth whose talk ("about himself and his works") and poetic recitals the gregarious Mrs. Trollope enjoyed, while her more sensitive and self-centered son found them perfunctory, suggesting "the idea of the performance of a part got up to order, and repeated without much modification as often as lion-hunters, duly authorized for the sport in those localities, might call him up for it."[2]

Afterwards, Tom left for Brittany to write his own first travel book, while his mother, exhausted by the pace of the last few months, returned to her York Street house, where she immediately fell seriously ill with an acute inflammation of the trachea. During this illness, she was attended by Dr. Elliotson, who, earlier that year, had to resign his position as lecturer in medicine at University College and senior physician in the North London Hospital because of his experiments in "animal magnetism." While her recovery was probably a matter of her strong constitution, she gave most of the credit to Eliotson; from her association with him dates her later fascination with mesmerism. But for the present, at least, she was fully occupied with the things of this world.[3]

When she recovered, she made her first visit to Cecilia's new home in Penrith, where her husband, John Tilley, had become post office surveyor of the northern district. She quickly fell in love with everything, and especially with Cecilia's husband who, as she told Julia, was "a very admirable person" and provided "all the minor matters of income, house, and so forth . . . quite as I could wish." She expressed some relief to see that "*that* part of my business on earth has been very well accomplished." She was also charmed by the physical surroundings.

> Nothing can be prettier than her residence. Her windows look out upon the pretty lake mountains, which though on no very large scale, are beautiful in no ordinary degree from the boldness of outline, and the great variety of picturesque combination which they display.

She liked the area so well that she bought some land "in a very beautiful situation, overlooking the ruins of Brougham Castle and the confluence of the Eden with the Lowther," and planned to build a house on the highest elevation of it.[4]

The new property was named Carlton Hill, and it seems Mrs. Trollope had set out to recreate her beloved Julian Hill. Like her old Harrow home, the new structure would be set on a high hill that dropped off sharply from the beaten road and would enjoy similar architectural and landscaping features. She threw herself into designing the house and its furnishings with her usual enthusiasm. Tom was in charge of beautifying its surroundings:

> I put in some hundreds of trees and shrubs with my own hands, which prospered marvellously. . . . I was bent on building a cloistered walk along the entire top of the field, which would have afforded a charming ambulatory sheltered from the north winds and from the rain, and would have commanded the most lovely views, while the pillars supporting the roof would have presented admirable places for a world of flowering climbing plants.[5]

Mrs. Trollope's London life had been expensive. She enjoyed entertaining, and the tradesmen's bills regularly came in larger than expected. Tom recalled that "she had spent a good deal more than she had supposed." One morning she had playfully, if somewhat shame-facedly, announced, "The fact is . . . that potatoes have been quite exceptionally dear." In reviewing their subsequent decision to give up the York Street house, Tom never let his mother forget "those exceptional potatoes," even while placing primary emphasis on Mrs. Trollope's desire to live closer to Cecilia, as well as on a more indefinable feeling which they shared in common "that we had eaten up London, and should enjoy a move to new pastures."

While she visited her daughter at Penrith, Mrs. Trollope was working on a novel whose characters and situation had been conceived in the preceding year but in which the surroundings of this visit had rekindled an interest. She wrote *One Fault* hurriedly and under distracting conditions; she herself expressed "unspeakable astonishment" that "the leaden production called 'One Fault' has been eminently successful— who would have thought it?"[6]

Still, the novel has a certain uniqueness. Most popular fiction in Mrs. Trollope's day concerned the relationships between men and women in courtship, not marriage. Very few writers used the lives of married people as a theme, and only seldom did they show "the less attractive side of matrimony from the inside." Even more rarely was the failure of a marriage implicit in the characters, and it was never readily recognized that marital difficulties could be encountered by "people of ordinary good will." Mrs. Trollope's *One Fault*, a study of a progressively deteriorating marriage, contains a cast of characters who are, in her own words, "ordinary every day human beings"; indeed ordinary, everyday events "were her avowed theme" (1:1-2). Even had she not stipulated "that they shall be such men and women as I have seen and known," it would be inevitable for us to see many of them in relationship to her own life.[7]

The book's primary interest lies in Mrs. Trollope's exposition and analysis of a collapsing marriage, the one which takes place at the book's beginning when the rich Mr. Wentworth sweeps the beautiful Isabella Clarke off her feet, proposing to her poor clergyman father an extraordinarily liberal settlement, while appearing to the girl as the very model of "fond gallantry." Seeds of discord emerge on their Paris honeymoon, when Wentworth imagines a minor affront from his wife. Mrs. Trollope stops to note "one peculiarity of character, which Mr. Wentworth shared with many other very estimable indivi-duals. . . . He detested every approach, however distant or delicate, to a joke" (1:166). Increasingly difficult and jealous, he soon requires his wife's absolute submission on all matters. He outlines the rules of behavior he expects her to follow in a series of lectures, the worst of which brings on the premature delivery of a son. The boy's delicate health becomes Wentworth's next obsession, and after a brief interval of somewhat improved relations, the marriage collapses when the boy dies and Wentworth's temper worsens. Suspecting his wife of unfaithfulness, he challenges her supposed lover to a duel in which he is conveniently killed, leaving Isabella, after an appropriate period of recovery and mourning, to take the initiative and marry the story's romantic young hero. Following this improbable resolution, Mrs. Trollope commits her tale "to those for whose especial use it has been written," with an Envoy:

> To all mothers and all daughters, with most kind wishes for success in all their projects; together with a friendly request that they will bear in mind one important fact; namely, that all ill-tempered men who may make large settlements, do not die at the age of twenty-six years. [3:312]

Throughout, Mrs. Trollope's main preoccupation is Wentworth's sour temper. The inspiration for her analysis of this character trait was undoubtedly Thomas Anthony Trollope. In all her correspondence, there is only one brief and guarded allusion to her husband's similarly difficult disposition, but it is telling. In an early letter to Harriet Garnett, she explained her American trip as promising "frequent intervals of tranquility in the absence of Mr. Trollope," whose temper, she explained, was increasingly "dreadful."[8] Certainly his disposition had gradually worsened, and his family had found his presence intolerable. The less reticent Tom later recalled:

> The terrible irritability of his temper, which sometimes in his later years reached a pitch that made one fear his reason was, or would become, unhinged . . . made the misery of all who were called upon habitually to come into contact with it. I do not think that it would be an exaggeration to say that for many years no person came into my father's presence who did not forthwith desire to escape from it. . . . Happiness, mirth, contentment, pleasant conversation, seemed to fly before him as if a malevolent spirit emanated from him. And all the time no human being was more innocent of all malevolence towards his fellow-creatures; and he was a man who would fain have been loved, and who knew that he was not loved, but knew neither how to manifest his desire for affection nor how to conciliate it.[9]

Significantly, on the subject of Mr. Wentworth's temper, Mrs. Trollope repeatedly intruded into the narrative. "And why was this marriage so fatally unhappy? . . . Why was all joy for ever a stranger to her heart? . . . Why was peace unknown to her? . . . Solely because her husband was an ill-tempered man" (2:249). With a hard-earned wisdom, Mrs. Trollope insisted that "as a material of human happiness or misery, TEMPER is infinitely more important, because so much oftener brought into us, than high-mindedness. Opportunity for a generous action may occur perhaps once in a year; while temper is actively at work for good or for evil, during every hour of our existence" (2:141). In her emphasis on Wentworth's fundamentally upright nature, she surely recalled her husband's excellent high-minded character but affirmed that the final quality of any life is produced by minute phenomena whose importance the world of fiction has generally ignored:

> Probity, liberality, temperance, observant piety, may all exist with a sour temper; yet many a human being has been hung in chains whose justly punished deeds have not caused one hundredth part the pain to his fellow men which a cross temperament is sure to give. [1:283]

One Fault also questions the popularly held idea that female submissiveness is essential to marital success. Mrs. Trollope's heroine, gradually realizing that she was to "live, move, and have her being, wholly and solely, in great things and in small, for weal or for woe, according to, and dependent on, the will and pleasure of Mr. Wentworth" (1:233), tried hard to obey him in all things. Another popular novel's heroine (in Lady Scott's *The Hen-Pecked Husband*, 1853) clearly enunciated the contemporary ideal: "More than half of the happiness of married life depends upon us! Whatever faults your husband has, shut your eyes."[10] Mrs. Trollope's plot illustrates how submission and silence not only are ineffectual but exacerbate bad situations. The author poses the problem:

> It would be well if some philosophical moralist would tell us how a woman ought to behave when yoked to a temper in any degree resembling that of Mr. Wentworth: for it is an unfortunate fact, and in puzzling contradiction to that wholesome axiom, "Virtue is its own reward," that the sweetest, kindest, and gentlest spirits invariably fare the worse under such circumstances. Had Isabella been what is called a high-spirited violent woman, it is probable that her liberal, gentlemanlike, and honourable husband might have been cured, after a few years struggling, of those pampered vices of temper which now neutralised or smothered all his good qualities. . . . and she might have remained, perhaps, a much happier woman. [2:153]

Writing in clear contradiction to the models suggested by Mrs. Ellis,

Mrs. Sandford, and Miss Stodart, Mrs. Trollope suggested a new kind of behavior, recently embodied in her own "high-spirited violent woman," the widow Barnaby.

Finally, in her novel Mrs. Trollope touched upon a subject which was almost never raised even by implication in popular fiction of the time: the quality of conjugal relations in an unhappy marriage. Following one of Isabella's first quarrels with her dominating husband, he orders his wife to kiss him. Mrs. Trollope comments:

> Poor Isabella. . . . She hardly knew herself why this obliging command seemed more difficult to obey than any other he could have laid upon her. . . . She had no time to reason then upon the monstrous weight of conjugal chains when the cotton and velvet of affection cease to envelope them . . . but she held up her sweet innocent face, and he kissed her. [1:230]

In this troubling scene, Isabella seems more than faintly sacrificial. Quarrels multiply, but after each Mr. Wentworth is sure that "his caresses could heal the wound he had given." But Mrs. Trollope's heroine "would far rather that he had not kissed her" (1:297). Ultimately the author hints that Wentworth's physical attentions have grown repulsive to his wife, who in one angry scene refers to "the fiddle-faddle demonstrations of connubial love." Thus the novel provides an analysis of an unhappy marriage from the feminine viewpoint. Isabella, who courageously endures insults, jealousy, bad temper, and unwanted caresses, is rewarded at last with an admirable second husband, whose instinctively gentle and tender love for his own mother promise better things at last for the beleaguered heroine.

The novel also presents an early study of an obsessive temperament in the character of Mr. Wentworth, a man apparently incapable of controlling the fatal flaw that gradually blights his life. Contemporary reviewers found the character incomprehensible. The *Spectator* called his incorrigible ill-temper "a perfect bore" and professed to be "as well pleased as his persecuted wife . . . to get rid of him," while the *Literary Gazette* asked: "How could any body in their senses behave in such a way?" This reviewer concluded:

> To have three long volumes devoted to the development of one ingredient, and confined to the effects of the conduct of a husband upon a wife . . . is too much. The perpetual repetition of the same causes, with the same results, grows tiresome; and we feel that a tithe-part of them would have wrought out the design more impressively than the whole.

While praising parts of the novel as "worthy of the writer's reputation," this 1839 reviewer found the tale generally unrealistic and himself "ill-taught by singular beings and rare events."[11]

One cannot blame them; it would be thirty years before another such depiction of so obsessive a personality appeared, in Anthony Trollope's greater novel, *He Knew He Was Right* (1869), often hailed as the first such study. Of all Mrs. Trollope's children, Anthony had come to know his father's darker moods most intimately, living alone with him in the gloomy Harrow Weald farm during the three years the rest of the family was in America and Tom away at school. Both Frances and Anthony, sunny and supremely stable temperaments, were drawn to render a personality foreign to their own deepest natures but with which they had suffered so many painful encounters. Both Mr. Wentworth and Louis Trevelyan had their origins in the character of Thomas Anthony Trollope, that proud, upright, humorless, and unbending man who had loved his family well and who, before illness totally ravaged him, had been forever fascinated by the playful, high-spirited, mirth-loving Frances Milton. Here at Penrith, watching the buoyant spirits of the young Tilleys who, it seemed to her, had all the world before them, Frances Trollope hurried to complete her latest novel amidst an old woman's feelings of regret at the tragic fate of her own husband whom she had loved faithfully to the end.

Mrs. Trollope left Penrith not only with such memories but with a nearly completed manuscript. In London she resumed work on her serialized novels (*Michael Armstrong, The Widow Married*). Tom was preparing his Brittany manuscript, for which, his mother proudly announced, "he is to have 300 guineas, a very good rate for a first attempt." And even though building had started at their north country site, she and Tom went ahead with plans for a trip to Italy for the following year. But first, to fulfill a "promise of long-standing" to Anthony, whose official duties had thus far prevented "his sharing the travelling delights of his errant family," she prepared for an excursion to Paris. She had sensed Anthony's unhappiness with his humdrum clerkship and hoped that a trip to Paris would buoy his spirits. She planned an extended stay, adding that Anthony "will be permitted to be with us for a few weeks—a couple of months we hope—which will give him, perhaps the only opportunity he may have of seeing *la belle ville.*"[12] Hurriedly, she put the finishing touches on *One Fault* and completed the final installments for *Michael Armstrong*, which appeared in three volumes in December, while the parts ran until the following February. With all her work completed, Mrs. Trollope and Anthony set out together, arriving on 4 December at Boulogne, where they walked in from the Dover packet to dine and drink tea with the Garnetts. Harriet described Mrs. Trollope at the highest peak of her powers and reputation: "I never saw her looking better, thinner, and I think with less colour—her manners gentler & better, and as kind as possible." Flattered by her old and famous friend's visit, Harriet regarded her attentions as proof of great "kindness and friendship."[13]

In Paris, Mrs. Trollope was "much sought after and *fêted*," and Mrs. Garnett wrote Julia:

> Mrs. Trollope is more than ever the fashion in Paris. Not a fine ball or a soiree at any Ambassador's that her name is not mentioned in the papers. She remains til June in Paris, goes for a month to see Cecilia, and then to Italy for one year. She is the most indefatigible person at 66 [*sic*, 61] I ever heard of. She brings out novels in succession and makes doubtless a fine income.[14]

She visited Miss Clarke's resplendent soirees, saw Madame Recamier and General Pepe from Harrow days, met Rosina, Lady Bulwer, and was presented to the king. Even for such a strong constitution as was hers, the "incessant dissipation" was gruelling. She told Julia:

> Once entered into it, I found it perfectly impossible to stop. . . . I might truly say that I have never had a single hour disengaged after my first week here. I look back upon it all as if I had been in a mill whirling round and round with unceasing velocity—and truly sometimes I have felt somewhat giddy.

But while she enjoyed her obvious celebrity and boasted to Julia that "at the Tuilleries I was received in a style that made many folks stare, and a few, I suspect, angry," the professional writer began to chafe at the way in which the social whirl restricted her writing schedule. She wrote Cecilia:

> I am looking forward to the end of the *party* season with the greatest delight. Three parties of a night, sometimes too beginning with a dinner, is too much to bear—I go to bed almost when it is time to get up—and of *work*, I do very little indeed. But all this will I trust be amended speedily.[15]

Still, her pen was not utterly idle. She had brought along an outline for a novel of which she had "sketched the plan, intending to complete it in three months" but to which by May she had "not added a single line." She began work on yet another "for which I had engaged myself by a certain time" and which she was annoyed at being forced "to scramble through"; she felt it was marred accordingly. "So much for the *profitable* result of being fêted!" She was sorry that she had not had more time for writing, for her reputation was at its peak. Tom's reports from Colburn, "by no means disagreeable," had been that "he could have sold half a dozen more books for me, if I had been ready with them—Would that I were!"[16]

By August, she would be ready with *The Ward of Thorpe Combe*, or as she preferred calling it, "the Cousins." She received £650 for it, and the novel appeared in 1841 to favorable reviews and good sales. The following year, it was reprinted as one of Baudry's European library in an inexpensive single-volume edition.[17] It is a clever inversion of the usual rags-to-riches story of an orphan girl, an unlovely and sycophantish waif who succeeds in wheedling her trusting relative out of his estate. In the absence of a long-lost son, she is made the heiress; falling one year short of adulthood, she moves into her property as ward. The reader swiftly realizes that the girl, instead of being virtuous, deserving, and grateful, is in fact what one reviewer called a "cold, subtle, selfish creature of 20, without one single counteracting virtue, one green spot in the desert of her feelings"; she represents another of Mrs. Trollope's repulsive subjects. The self-centered young lady isolates herself in a gorgeous boudoir of the estate, bedecking herself in the family diamonds and indulging herself in rich foods, while imposing on her servants and dependents a parsimonious regime. Increasingly parasitical, almost physically loathsome, her cold and subtle malevolence is strangely appealing. *John Bull* believed that Mrs. Trollope had added "a new creation to the stock of the novelist, and a new study to the student of human nature." Even the *Athenaeum*, objecting to the novel's vivid portrayal of "greediness, vanity, flattery, falsehood, and the crimes to which those appetites and attributes lead," nevertheless admired the unusual story and marveled at "the misdemeanors of Sophy Martin."[18]

Once again, Mrs. Trollope had made her repulsive subject credible by surrounding her with the paraphernalia of everyday life that she always handled so well: solid India cabinets, wills, bequests, housekeeping finances, "nice coffee . . . well-served desserts . . . scrubbing, saving, and spending," and the broad acres of a country estate. Mrs. Trollope had left behind forever the precipitous cliffs, castles, and dark, forbidding convents that had earlier provided the backdrop for her villains. Although some reviewers railed against her now prevailing realism ("life belowstairs") and deplored her tendency "to peep into the pantry, to gossip with a comfortable old housekeeper, or intrigue with an astute lady's maid," she persisted in becoming a chronicler of the actual while continuing to explore the endless varieties and eccentricities of the human character.[19]

On her return to England, Mrs. Trollope stopped again at Boulogne to see the Garnetts, who found her "fagged" but pleased with the attention she had received in Paris. Faintly envious, the stay-at-home Harriet breathlessly recounted Mrs. Trollope's plans for the months ahead: "She is now going to [her granddaughter's] christening, passes six weeks with Cecilia, and then sets out for Italy, full of spirits and enjoyment. What an extraordinary woman she is!"[20] Harriet was not the only astonished one. *John Bull* had more than once noticed Mrs. Trollope's "power and indefatigability," characterizing her as "certainly the most fertile of all writers, having during the year published—how many novels it is scarcely possible to say." Years later the *New Monthly Magazine*, reviewing her achievements for one of their "Female Novelists" series, drew a witty picture of her industry and exuberance of invention, both of which entitled her "to the proverbial name she enjoys, or endures, for prolific authorship."

In vain have reviewers tried to keep up with her. A blue-stocking who travels in seven-leagued boots may well run critics and criticasters out of breath—*she* triumphantly ascending the hill Difficulty, as fresh as a daisy, while *they* wallow, and struggle, and give up the race (and almost the ghost) in the Slough of Despond. Pant and puff as they will to run her home, she is in a trice miles out of sight, over the hills and far away, and wondering what those sluggard lameters are doing in the rear.[21]

12

Frances and Anthony

I have written many novels under many circumstances;
but I doubt much whether I could write one when my
whole heart was by the bedside of a dying son.

MRS. TROLLOPE left Paris in high good spirits, heading for Penrith to attend the christening of her first grandchild and namesake, Frances Trollope Tilley. But it was not to be, for yet another trial lay in store. Her son Anthony, following his own return from Paris, had fallen desperately ill. She abandoned her plans to attend the christening and again put off her trip to Italy. Although she had already given up her London house in anticipation of this journey, her concern about Anthony kept her in his lodgings until the autumn of 1840, when he was finally out of danger.

For many years, Anthony had not lived near his mother. In 1827, she had gone to America, leaving him behind for some three years with his father. In 1831 the family was reunited for a time, but the increasingly serious illnesses of Henry, Emily, and finally Mr. Trollope had prompted his mother to find him a position at the London Post Office in 1834. That October, he bade farewell for the last time to his father and Henry and took up the London life, sharing Tom's lodgings in Northumberland Street, near the Marylebone Workhouse. His mother had visited him whenever possible, but her stays were brief and irregular until 1838, when she took a house in nearby York Street.

Anthony later recalled this separation with regret, obliquely referring to his mother in his account of the failure of his first seven years in London.

> There was no house in which I could habitually see a lady's face and hear a lady's voice. No allurements to decent respectability came in my way. It seems to me that in such circumstances the temptations of loose life will almost certainly prevail with a young man.[1]

His reputation in the Post Office steadily deteriorated. Indeed, Mrs. Clayton Freeling, Mrs. Trollope's old friend who had found Anthony this position, once brought him a rumor that he was in danger of being dismissed for unseemly conduct and, "with tears in her eyes, besought me to think of my mother." His life was lonely and dissipated, an irregular existence of which he knew his mother had not been proud. He had mired himself in hopeless debts, of which he was free during only two intervals "amounting together to nearly two years, in which I lived with my mother, and therefore lived in comfort." Anthony recalled that "she paid much for me—paid all that I asked her to pay, and all that she could find out that I owed." But he knew how hard her life had been and how desperately she needed money herself, and often a sense of shame led him to concealment. As he remarked, "but who in such a condition ever tells all and makes a clean breast of it?" Things were twice so bad that he was imprisoned for debt until he was anonymously bailed out. Anthony did not know his benefactor's identity, nor did he wish to know the truth. It had been, of course, his mother. At twenty-five years of age, he seemed to be going nowhere, and cast about him for some escape.[2]

From 1830 to 1840, he had kept a private journal of his own hopes for a literary career, and while he probably never showed it to his mother, she no doubt knew that he, like every other family member, had been afflicted with the "literary disease." Mr. Trollope had begun an ecclesiastical encyclopedia and had published a law book in 1823. Tom was following in his mother's footsteps as a writer of travel books. Henry had hoped to write geological studies, and even Cecilia had tried her hand at a clerical romance (then in manuscript, it was subsequently published as *Chollerton*). By 1840, the contagion had spread to Mrs. Trollope's brother, who had tried to compete with a novel appropriately entitled *Rivalry*. It was only natural for Anthony to entertain similar aspirations, amounting so far to what he described as "castle-building." He had promised himself to venture a novel, and "no day was passed without thoughts of attempting, and a mental acknowledgment of the disgrace of postponing it." His mother had taken him to Paris hoping he would throw off the depression under which she knew he was laboring, but the trip had apparently worsened the situation, precipitating his desperate illness. As he watched his mother's industry, success, and good fortune, he could think only of his own deplorable state. "I hated the office, I hated my work. More than all I hated my idleness."[3]

After his return from Paris, Anthony had collapsed, and his mother found him in his lodgings "in a state that defies the views of his physicians as effectually as it puzzles my ignorance." While the doctors characterized his symptoms as asthmatic, they could not define the disease or find the cure. Mrs. Trollope was anxious and frantic. She told a friend, who had recently met Anthony in Paris:

He is frightfully reduced in size and strength; sure am I that could you see
him, you would not find even a distant resemblance to the being who,
exactly three months ago, left us in all the pride of youth, health, and
strength. Day by day I lose hope, and so, I am quite sure, do his
physicians; we have had three consultations, but nothing prescribed re-
lieves him, nor has any light been thrown on the nature of his complaint.
. . . Alas! the sad change from the gay hopes with which I left you.[4]

In her despair, Mrs. Trollope even engaged Dr. Elliotson, her own
physician of former years, who was an advocate of cures by hypnosis
and posthypnotic suggestions (then called mesmerism or "animal magnetism"). When he too could not effect a cure, he brought to Anthony's
bedside the Okey sisters, cataleptic patients of his who were in the habit
of seeing an apparition named Jack in the presence of people who all
subsequently died. Brought to Anthony during the period of his greatest
danger, they claimed that they "saw Jack by his side, but only up to his
knee." This partial manifestation seemed to Dr. Elliotson evidence that
Anthony would recover. This strange episode, called by some of Mrs.
Trollope's biographers "unjudicious" and "absolute folly," revealed
rather her perceptive awareness that Anthony's illness was primarily
psychological, a "sickness unto death" whose solution was beyond
physical medicine. That she relied for help upon those who claimed to
have some psychic power shows how clearly she sensed the real source
of Anthony's troubles.[5]

Participating once again in the sadly familiar task of nursing one of
her family throughout most of the summer and early autumn of 1840,
Mrs. Trollope took up a theme that she had earlier determined could
make a new novel—the pitfalls of literary London life. Her original
concept was to write a tale of a young man thirsting for literary
advancement, but because her imagination was always fertile and her
energies Herculean, she decided that the material she had in mind could
supply two novels. One concentrated on those who tried to write for a
living, and the other exposed the lionizing coteries of intellectual
London. Taken together, *Charles Chesterfield: or the Adventures of a
Youth of Genius*, and *The Blue Belles of England*, appearing simultaneously in monthly parts between July 1840 and December 1841 in the
New Monthly Magazine and the *Metropolitan Magazine*, anatomized
the society which Mrs. Trollope had come to regard as a vanity fair in
which literary talent was devoured. The impetus for working this theme
was all too painfully present, for it saddened her to see how Anthony had
made himself sick with longings for such success; these feelings contributed to make both books some of the bitterest satire she was ever to
write.[6]

In *Chesterfield*, Mrs. Trollope ridiculed the prevailing fads: the literature of nothingness, the antihero (one of her characters writes a novel called *The Convict Footman*), and the rejection of traditions ("Pitiable reverence for antiquity," one of her literati remarks, "is now, happily, passing from the earth for ever."). In *Blue Belles*, her satire concentrated upon the destructive phenomenon of literary celebrity. Her hero-poet, after the publication of his first volume, receives in one month 376 invitations to dinner, 120 requests for personal inscriptions, 70 for autographs, and 103 appeals for a lock of his hair. Included in her indictment were thinly disguised characterizations of real personalities, such as Lockhart, Dickens, and Wordsworth. Contemporary readers found them intriguing, and in her own copy, Mrs. Trollope penciled in the names of the originals, obviously relishing the fun.[7]

In *Chesterfield*, Mrs. Trollope's real subject is the tribe of book reviewers before whom she had now appeared sixteen times in eight years. They are epitomized by Marchmont, editor of, contributor to, and reviewer for an influential periodical magazine named *The Regenerator*. This outrageous character demolishes literary reputations, for "nobody can have any hope of getting on if Marchmont is against him" (2:37). Freed by anonymity, he revels in "that cut-and-thrust manoeuvring from behind a golden screen, lined with a mirror that reflects to our own pleased eyes each daring stroke . . . sure the while to be cheered by the plaudits of the laughing crowd" (1:181). Through him, Mrs. Trollope implies that reviewers are influenced by the name, reputation, or principles of authors and find it unnecessary even to read the books. Proudly, Marchmont describes his methods:

> All we require to know is the name of the author in all cases where the name is known, or the principles in which he writes where it is not. This is sailing by a compass that cannot fail us, my dear Chesterfield, and is an occupation superior to the pitiful employment of dissecting, analysing, and pretending to understand and judge the magnificent mass of literature poured forth by our groaning press. [3:14–15]

Arrogant, opinionated, and disreputable, Marchmont is Mrs. Trollope's revenge upon the reviewers of her day.[8]

Herself a far-ranging pioneer in the subject matter of fiction, she had received little serious critical recognition. Her better novels evoked hostile notices, almost as if reviewers, unable to categorize such works, castigated what they did not understand. Reviewers had settled early on a uniform approach to Mrs. Trollope's style and subjects, calling them coarse, racy, vulgar, bold, repulsive, unpleasant, disagreeable, destructive, and, often, unfeminine. Paradoxically, her popular success had been aided by just such reviews. At first hurt, she eventually shrugged off vituperative notices, for she discovered, as with her hotly debated American and Parisian volumes, that ultimately such attacks helped sales. As Marchmont notes, sometimes the greatest boost a reviewer can give is to "sing out that such a work is too improper to read" (2:276). Of such attention, Mrs. Trollope had received more than her share.

She also used the character to expose some of the pretentious and romantic nonsense surrounding the inspiration for artistic creation. Marchmont's rhetoric is uproariously sublime: "My grammer is man-kind, my friend; my dictionary is in the clouds. The winds are my syntax, and rushing cataracts my prosody" (1:176). His inspiration is mysterious and religious: "Mark me . . . at this moment the divine essence is at work within me! Like the immortal oracles of old, I feel the sacred voice within, and give it utterance, almost without volition" (1:296). In reality, his muse is merely alcohol, his "golden elixir." For the hard-working woman who rose early to write her appointed number of lines before the day began, exalted ideas about art were ridiculous. This attitude she communicated to her son Anthony, who a half-century later shocked the literary aesthetes with accounts of his own composing habits, which he clearly inherited from his mother. For Anthony, "the surest aid to the writing of a book was a piece of cobbler's wax" on the chair. His mother's son, he defiantly announced: "I certainly believe in the cobbler's wax much more than the inspiration."[9]

Both books show Mrs. Trollope's skillful handling of London society and manners and depict the hollowness and hypocrisy of the inhabitants of the literary world. In her career, she had moved easily and freely in that society and she used her shrewd observations and insights to good advantage in these novels. But their real interest is biographical. Both follow the fortunes of a country person who comes to the city, is dazzled by literary success, then is disillusioned and returns to provincial honest life. Mrs. Trollope's own pilgrimage from Bristol, Heckfield, and Harrow to London and her life among "clever, literary people" had produced in her a similar disenchantment: three years after these novels appeared, she would leave England forever.

Even more important, these books are a fictional transformation of her fears about Anthony. Young Charles Chesterfield, pitifully beguiled "by the heartless puppet-show of London!" (2:58) and dreaming "wildly ambitious hopes" for literary fame and fortune is clearly modeled on her son. "It was the world, it was London, for which he panted," she writes of Charles Chesterfield. "Fame, renown, applause—applause, renown, and fame, such as he had heard tell of . . . as having been achieved by an individual called Sir Walter Scott, and by another named Lord Byron. . . . These were the sort of people . . . whose fame in his heart of hearts he hoped to equal" (1:40–41). She knew that her son too dreamed of being "a writer of novels" and felt himself "destined to immortalize himself by his pen" (1:88). These two books are as much a sign of her maternal concern for her youngest son as were the hours spent at his bedside during their months of composition.

And Anthony, as he lay recuperating, cannot have failed to follow with interest the installments of his mother's accounts of London life. Attempts to trace literary influence are at best speculative, but many indirect pieces of evidence from these years (especially July 1840 to August 1841) suggest the impact of Frances Trollope upon the writing career of her youngest son. Beyond her heroic breadwinning, Anthony owed his mother a three-fold debt: his rigorous and disciplined writing habits, his prevalent realism, and his understanding of the multifaceted female character. When, two years later, he began his own literary productions, he unconsciously followed her example. The seeds of his greatness were sown in the London of 1840–1841, as Anthony observed Frances working steadily amid distractions, transforming her experiences into the stuff of fiction and embodying herself that sense of the "triumphant feminine" that she brought to so many of her works.

Gradually, Anthony extricated himself from his hateful idleness. He discovered the art of compartmentalizing, mastering his mother's "power of dividing herself into two parts, and keeping her intellect by itself, clear from the troubles of the world, and fit for the duty it had to do." He also learned to look about him, even as his mother was doing, and never lost a firm appreciation of the everyday; in one way or another, all his greatest books are chronicles of the actual. Subsequently, he confessed the influence of his mother in this regard, acknowledging that his grasp of the human character had been enlarged by his special "sonship," without which "I should have had to wait much longer than I did for my initiation into life and society upon all those levels which it is part of a novelist's stock-in-trade to know."[10]

Finally, he learned from his mother and from her sturdy heroines the complexity and toughness of the female character. Specifically, Mrs. Trollope's two novels of London life included conceptions that Anthony later used for three of his own fine female characters. Among her gallery of London literati, Mrs. Trollope included the hard-working professional authoress, Mrs. Sherbourne. Like her creator, she "almost entirely depended for her existence" on the success of her writing, and ground out a series of best sellers:

No circulating library from the Orkneys to the Land's End, dared to confess that they had not got Mrs. Sherbourne's last work; and 'The Condemned One'—'The Entranced One'—'The Corrupted One'—'The

Infernal One'—'The Empyrean One'—and 'The Disgusting One,' and all in succession conveyed her intensity into every village of the empire, and brought in return wherewithal to 'live and love, to dress and dream' (which in one of 'Occasional Poems' she had declared ought to be the whole of woman's existence), very much to her satisfaction. [2:102]

Yet her real success arose less from the quality of the novels than from her determined efforts at pushing them onto the public and the critics.

Her professional existence depended upon her welcoming without reserve all those who could assist her in her pursuits, either by criticism or patronage. . . . Her existence glided on through a series of small literary labours, cheered by a series, equally unbroken, of small literary flirtations, each helping forward the other by a reciprocity of influence, by no means unskillfully managed. [2:104]

Mrs. Trollope's sympathetic renderings of the lady's manipulations provided Anthony with a model for his Lady Carbury (*The Way We Live Now*, 1875) and her dealings with Mr. Broune, editor of the *Morning Breakfast Table* and reviewer of her *Criminal Queens*. But while Anthony's heroine eventually settled down to accept a comfortable marriage proposal, thus releasing herself from the exertions of a writing career, Mrs. Trollope's authoress successfully duped her editor with a profitable sale of her fraudulent memoirs, continuing to survive without male support, forever to rule triumphantly over the circulating libraries.[11]

In *Blue Belles*, Mrs. Trollope also explored another facet of the female mystique in the portrait of Mrs. Gardiner-Stewart, a charming *invalide* who drapes herself decoratively "amidst hyacinths and jonquils upon her soft silken sofa" and is picturesquely exotic and dangerous. She can stand only with effort, preferring to repose surrounded by "masses of refreshing green," backed by venetian blinds and "hangings of lemon-coloured satin, gilt ornaments, and a multitude of mirrors." Amidst a forest of bloom, sipping her perfect coffee "as black and as clear as the Eastern eyes," Mrs. Gardiner-Stewart closes her eyes, stretches out her pretty little feet "upon their embroidered *tabouret*," and enjoys a "perfect absence from all exertion." Her character suggests exotic knowledge, satiety, and sensuality; she clearly differs from the modest, sensible girls whom most novelists created to delight, amuse, obey, and become the average country gentleman's wife. Mrs. Stewart's strangely languid and recumbent attitudes surely influenced Anthony in the creation of Signora Neroni (*Barchester Towers*, 1857), a lady mysteriously crippled by her worthless Italian husband, thus enhancing her enigmatic charms.[12]

Finally, Mrs. Trollope's desperate fortune hunters also influenced Anthony's imagination. In *Blue Belles*, she drew the first in a series of such ladies for whom the reader learned to feel not only compassion but even respect. Margaretta Hartley captures the slightly stupid Sir James Ridley by appealing to his vanity. Playing a feminine part, she raises her timid eyes, averts her blushing cheek, and gives "a trembling hand" to a man she clearly regards as a fool. Then, tired from the rigors of "the job," she settles down in her chosen life "with nothing but steadfastness of purpose to sustain her under what she felt to be a most prodigious bore." Her only diversion is to rule Sir James, who meekly learns to obey "the tyranny of an artful and imperious wife." Miss Ridley and her numerous successors influenced Anthony's fine and sympathetically drawn fortune hunters, especially Arabella Trefoil (*The American Senator*, 1877). Alone among the great male writers of his century, Anthony produced vibrant, robust, and complex female characters—one has only to recall Lady Carbury, Madame Max Goessler, Mrs. Winifred Hurtle, Arabella Trefoil, Violet Effingham, and of course, the great Lady Glencora. What has escaped attention is the degree to which he drew his inspiration for these ladies from his own indomitable mother and the triumphant females with whom she populated her many novels.[13]

The year 1840 closed amid the cares of the sickroom, the relentless duties of monthly composition, and family visits. Mrs. Trollope's first grandchild she found "of all my honours and glories, the one I like best." Cecilia had invited her mother to come for the christening instead of the birth, an arrangement which had faintly scandalized the Garnetts, who saw in Mrs. Trollope's acquiescence a reluctance "to exchange the gaieties of Paris for a sick room." Instead, Mrs. Trollope sent her convalescing daughter "such a batch of maternal literature as will satisfy you for some time to come."[14] Prevented by Anthony's illness from attending the christening, by the time Mrs. Trollope visited Penrith in the autumn, Cecilia was already preparing for a second confinement. Always protective of her frail daughter, Mrs. Trollope was not happy to learn of this new pregnancy. She told Julia: "Helas! another is coming upon her heels already!" Before long, her fears for Cecilia would materialize. Despite her apparent good health, the bearing of five children in as many years took its toll, and signs of a latent consumption began to intensify. In nine years, Cecilia would be dead, and of her five children only one would grow to adulthood. Little Frances Trollope Tilley was not fated to inherit her grandmother's longevity nor bring her name to posterity.[15]

Also at year's end, Mrs. Trollope's warm-heartedness involved her for a time in the marital difficulties of Rosina Bulwer whom, in a compassionate moment, she had befriended during her recent Paris trip.

Separated from her husband (the novelist and critic Bulwer-Lytton) after nine years of marriage and two children, the tempestuous Rosina had a history of "passion, disillusionment, quarrelling, hatred, ostentation, toil, and achievement." Long after their separation, Rosina continued to involve herself in public brawls and denunciations of her husband. Lately, she had taken up writing, and in a burst of gratitude for Mrs. Trollope's bravely offered friendship and encouragement, she dedicated her novel (*The Budget of the Bubble Family*,1840) to her new friend but included in the preface references to her own numerous personal problems. Although she was pleased to see Rosina busy with the therapeutic activity of writing, Mrs. Trollope disapproved of "dipping your brilliant wing in the dirty troubled waters of personal affairs." Instead, she encouraged Rosina to persist in actively following a writing career:

> That you have been *sorely tried* is true; but you have that within you that *ought* to enable you to rise unscathed from it all. Now do not shake your head and say, 'Foolish old woman!' but be good, and mind what I say to you, and I shall live yet to see all the world admire you as much as I do, and I shall be proud of my friend.[16]

But her attempts to teach the younger woman the lessons of patience, quiet endurance, and hard work—which had shaped her own success and had so deeply impressed her son Anthony—went unheeded by Rosina, who continued to expend her energies on savage resentments against her husband.

Mrs. Trollope's championship of those in need also entangled her again in the affairs of the Okey girls, who had fallen ever deeper under the control of Dr. Elliotson. At first fascinated by their trances and seizures, Mrs. Trollope now sought to free them from economic dependence upon the doctor. Not surprisingly she suggested that one of the girls "throw together the singular history of her own sensations, together with the vast mass of mesmeric facts which have come to her knowledge." The resulting book, thought Mrs. Trollope, "published (perhaps by subscription) could hardly fail to bring a considerable sum."[17]

It was entirely characteristic that this "blue-stocking in seven-league boots," who had herself found salvation through writing, would make such a suggestion. Rosina Bulwer, the Okey girls, Anthony—all of them could conquer private psychological difficulties or turn their experiences to good account in the great marketplace of nineteenth-century literature.

That autumn, she and Tom revived plans for their trip to Italy. She tactfully reminded Bentley, from whom she was awaiting the payment for *The Ward of Thorpe-Combe* that would finance their expedition, that she had engaged to meet Madame Recamier, Madame de Chateaubriand, and Lady Bulwer at Vienna in October, "a brilliant knot, that it would grieve me to fail in promise to, even for a day."[18] Brief visits to Manchester and the Lake District, building a large and lavish country home near Penrith, two serialized novels appearing concurrently, a brilliant visit to Paris, the care of a sick son, the completion of two more novels and plans for another, and now a prospective trip to Italy—is there any wonder that her contemporaries marveled at her energy and activity? Frances Trollope was now sixty-one years of age.

13

Emergence of the Feminine
Consciousness

*Her own sex she seems
to have studied with
profound attention.*

IN THE spring of 1841, serious differences erupted between Mrs.
Trollope and Charles Colburn; while he had been publishing *Charles
Chesterfield*, she had simultaneously brought out *Blue Belles* with
Saunders and Otley, a rival firm. Since the novels treated similar
subjects, Colburn believed he was properly aggrieved and that the sales
had suffered. Abruptly, he refused to pay the agreed-upon commission
for her new three-volume novel (*Hargrave, A Man of Fashion*), threatening to fight the case in open court and publish all the particulars. Mrs.
Trollope shrank from the prospect of being held up publicly as a
"greedy, grasping, conscienceless woman." Uncharacteristically discouraged and for a time even incapable of writing regularly, she had
almost taken her brother's advice to "lay [*Hargrave*] aside and write
another." But she hated the thought of wasted effort and held tenaciously
to the legality of her claim, and in the end Colburn relented, publishing
Hargrave in 1843. He paid £625 for the novel, and contrary to his fears, it
sold well, even reaching a second edition.[1]

The story concerns a vain Englishman who maintains an expensive
Parisian home in that extravagant style of which Mrs. Trollope had
herself complained only a year ago. The plot revolves around Hargrave's efforts to extricate himself from increasing debts. He stoops to
gambling, theft, and finally kidnapping, providing the most interesting
event of the story. For at least one volume, the reader remains in
suspense about the victim's fate. When the bloody settings of jewels are
found buried in Hargrave's garden, it seems like murder, and Mrs.
Trollope brings in the Parisian Correctional Police in eager pursuit. For
awhile, *Hargrave* moves like an exciting mystery story, briefly anticipating another as yet undeveloped genre, but the novel declines into
melodrama, and Hargrave himself becomes a monstrosity. The last
volume grinds to a conclusion amid Roman Catholic intrigues, sudden

conversions, submerged castles, missing letters, and hastily contracted marriages. Still, even the *Athenaeum,* which found the book highly improbable, the man of fashion's deeds outrageous, and "the miracle by which he escapes punishment . . . little less startling," admitted "in defiance of our testimony against the probabilities of the book," that readers "will find it difficult to lay it aside, when once they have taken it in hand."[2]

Her business matters set in order, she and Tom were on their way to Italy. As usual, they stopped to see the Garnetts, and Harriet described Mrs. Trollope's plans and appearance.

> She is building a house close to Cecilia near the lakes, which will be her permanent home. She is well, active, and affectionate as ever, and full of enjoyment of her Italian tour; she intends being absent about one year.

She was pleased by the satisfactory arrangements of Cecilia and Tom, both of whom seemed well settled in the world:

> Cecilia is perfectly happy . . . and Mrs. Trollope likes her husband very much and is much attached to Fanny the eldest child. Tom is very like his father in manner, cross and contradictory, but his mother seems very fond of him, and bears with all his irrationality with great sweetness of temper. He has published an account of Brittany which is much admired.[3]

Once arrived in Italy, they made "several pleasant acquaintances and some fast friends, principally at Florence," thus paving the way for what neither of them foresaw at the time: a permanent home in that city. Because Cecilia was expecting her third child, they shortened their visit, leaving Rome in February 1842, crossing Mont Cenis on sledges in bitter snow, sleet, and "very severe weather." Mrs. Trollope dutifully recorded the scene for inclusion in what she told Bentley "will make two interesting volumes" on Italy. *A Visit to Italy* was written with her usual speed, but this last of her travel books was a departure from her usual form. She avoided broad, stylized caricature and even eschewed her customary depictions of country and people. "Often as the ground has been trod," she explained to her publisher, "there was no necessity of making even a *twice* told tale of it." No attempt was made to shape her material into scenes and dialogues. Instead, she concentrated primarily on Italy's art treasures, and the result is a flat, rather generalized series of rhapsodies over the great works of Michaelangelo, the dome of St. Peter's, and the architecture of Palladio.

The reviewers did not like the book. They complained about the absence of her customary "opinionizing" and her "original and amusing views." "The last thing one should have expected from Mrs. Trollope," one wrote, "is a work whose pages are characterless."

> The caustic spirit that ran riot amongst republicans, and wore its cockney-isms unabashed, in the presence of a nation which appeared to it half savage, wanting the feathers and conventionalisms of the past, seems fettered by the presence of antiquity, and restrained by the weight of authority.

She seemed herself dissatisfied with the book and wrote Bentley: "I cannot help wishing that the work might have the advantage of such illustrations as the Paris and Vienna." She hoped that Hervieu might find time to give some life to the project, but it was not to be, for he was busily engaged elsewhere.[4] Most reviewers were bored with *A Visit to Italy*, wearied by the "host of familiar objects exhibited, and none of them in new lights." The very dullness "almost reconciled" one to "Mrs. Trollope's more caustic manner," and he commented:

> Assuredly, Mrs. Trollope cannot produce effective etchings without *acids*; her subjects, to convey any notion of her artistic ability, must be *bitten* in. . . . The language of panegyric fits her pen badly. . . .

> We earnestly desire to see her temper rouse itself against some offence, and her Muse put on, were it but for a page or so, its more striking and characteristic expression of disgust.[5]

By March 1842, she was with Cecilia, where she stayed until Carlton Hill was "sufficiently dry to receive her." She had returned in time to greet the arrival of a third grandchild, another girl. For the time, Mrs. Trollope seemed to enjoy her life at the Lakes and was "very fond of her grandchildren." Her new house stood within half a mile of her daughter, who also was "perfectly happy." She had enjoyed her Italian tour very much and was pleased with her reception there, for she had been much sought after and admired. Since Julia Pertz had no daughters and Mrs. Trollope no grandsons, Harriet joked that "a union must be formed between the three young Pertz and her three little granddaughters." Mrs. Trollope, once again the hostess, sent a warm invitation for the Garnetts to visit her as soon as the house would be ready.[6]

That summer Anthony visited his mother in the new house and afterwards accompanied Tom for several weeks in Ireland. Tom found his brother "already a very different man from what he had been in London," and the two unexpectedly became friends. They hunted together, took an unforgettably "grand walk over the mountains above the Killeries," and rescued (with considerable dash) a priest and others injured or trapped at an election meeting at which the hustings had collapsed.[7]

While the brothers renewed old ties, their mother worked on at Penrith. By November, *Italy* was out, and she presented a copy to her neighbor Lady Musgrave, who had a long acquaintance with that country. In December Mary Russell Mitford's father died, and Mrs. Trollope sent condolences to her old friend, entreating her to believe that "though my poor, worn-out stump of a pen has well-nigh lost the power of writing letters," her "heart and affections are by no means in the same dilapidated condition." To Miss Mitford, she emphasized her perfect contentment, inviting her friend to share "some bright future summer" with "me, my lakes, and my grandchildren, and my son Tom, and my pretty cottage."[8]

Toward the end of 1842, Dickens's *American Notes* appeared, to the shock of the Garnetts and the amused delight of Mrs. Trollope. Anna Maria Stone, Mrs. Trollope's old friend in America, deplored to her sister Julia the publication of this work which, she feared, "will drive all travelers from hence." She was sure the whole thing was a pack of lies.

> No one who knows our country will believe his account. You remember the conversation repeated as having passed between himself and a driver to the south. When the man saw it he published in all the Newspapers that the dress and every particular he related was totally false—that he thought he had been driving a gentleman—and such exaggerated accounts of spitting—You must fight for your old country.

Harriet, who "never read a more disagreeable account of people," was nevertheless disposed to regard Dickens's account "a true one." She would not let it interfere, however, with her own golden memories of America: "What disgusting people they must be! and they must have changed since we were there—but indeed we never traveled or saw much of the people. Dickens does not make me wish to return."[9]

On the other hand, Mrs. Trollope was delighted to see herself vindicated. While many had accused her of injustice and exaggeration, the great Boz himself had confirmed the rightness of her judgments. She wrote to praise him, and his reply was a compliment to her own talents.

> As I never scrupled to say in America, so I can have no delicacy in saying to you, that allowing for the change you worked in many social practices of American Society, and for the time that has passed since you wrote of the country, I am convinced that there is no writer who has so well and accurately (I need not add, so entertainingly) described it, in many of its

aspects, as you have done; and this renders your praise the more valuable
to me.

I do not recollect ever to have heard or seen the charge of exaggeration
made against a feeble performance, though, in its feebleness it may have
been most untrue. It seems to me essentially natural and quite inevitable,
that common abusers should accuse an uncommon one of this fault. And I
have no doubt that you were long ago of this opinion; very much to your
comfort.[10]

She had herself just completed the monthly installments of *The Barnabys in America*, the success of which perhaps set Dickens to thinking
when his *Chuzzlewit* sales began to drop. Hoping to spark interest and
increase sales, he, like Mrs. Trollope before him, sent the hero on his
travels to America.

Then, ever so gradually, Mrs. Trollope's old restlessness returned.
After stressing to everyone her complete contentment in Carlton Hill,
she soon began making plans to leave the house, after occupying it for
not even a complete year. When she had first chosen the placement of
the buildings, it had been necessary to change the course of a tiny spring
that rose near the roadside, a matter that seemed to Tom and his mother
a trivial detail. But one of their neighbors was dismayed and predicted
"that we should never succeed in establishing ourselves in that spot."
When Mrs. Trollope now abruptly sold the house to the Tilleys, Sir
George Musgrave referred to his original statement, for he "knew
perfectly well that it must be so, ever since the time that Trollope had so
recklessly meddled with the holy well."[11]

Several factors prompted Mrs. Trollope to leave the quiet life of the
Lake District. The severe winter climate had proven hard on her health.
She had found the house very expensive to maintain. She felt keenly, for
the first time, the pressures of her busy schedule, and her writing could
not cease if the bills were to be paid. She spoke to Tom of the need for
strict economy. "If you were 62 years old, and had to get up at 4 o'clock
every morning to work for it, you would not wonder at my saying this!"
Tom later told his nephew another reason behind the move:

> The assignment of the severity of the climate as the cause is an admirable
> euphemism. The truth is that we found our neighbours too dull and stupid.
> You need not mention this to Tilley—not that we found him or my dear
> sister or his house dull;—but the neighbours were all his friends![12]

The real truth is probably her innate restlessness. Both she and Tom
had compelling memories of Florence, and during the spring they
contemplated returning for an extended visit. After quick trips to see old

friends in Clifton and Devonshire, and after a lengthy conversation with
Tom on 7 June 1843, they decided to try living at Florence "at least for a
year," returning regularly to visit Cecilia and Anthony. Harriet Garnett
was skeptical about the success of the plan.

> I doubt her being able to accomplish this, and I fear she will find the
> climate and mode of life in Florence fatiguing for a continuance. She says
> she has found it the cheapest capital in Europe—but what a distance from
> her friends and from Cecilia and Anthony![13]

All that summer and early fall, she worked away at her new novel,
Jessie Phillips: A Tale of the Present Day, which was to be the first of a
series of her novels to focus upon the particular problems of women in
English society. Since its purpose was to arouse readers to the need for
reform, Mrs. Trollope again chose serial publication, and it appeared in
eleven monthly parts beginning on 31 December 1842, with illustrations
by John Leech. Not surprisingly, Colburn's advertisement for this new
novel appeared the same day in that beacon of radicalism, the *Northern
Star*:

> JESSIE PHILLIPS, OR THE PARISH GIRL,
>   By Mrs. Trollope, Authoress of "Michael Armstrong, the Factory
>   Boy," etc.
> The object the authoress has had in view in the composition of this work
> has been to call the attention of her readers to the absolute necessity of
> some alteration in the law which at present regulates the maintainance and
> management of the poor. Her conviction of its tyranny and injustice, of the
> impracticability of enforcing its provisions with uniformity, and of the
> cruel hardships which are inflicted on the poor by the attempt to enforce
> them is strong, and she conscientiously believes well founded.[14]

The novel was Mrs. Trollope's second excursion into specific issues of
social reform, this time the abuses consequent to the new Poor Law of
1834, closely connected with the problems of factory legislation with
which she had dealt in *Michael Armstrong*. In the early decades of the
century, intellectual and upper-class circles were convinced that the
intolerable burden of poor-relief that went back to the days of Queen
Elizabeth ought to be entirely abolished. New ideas of political
economy supported laissez-faire principles; since natural laws regulated
life, factory legislation and poor relief were widely regarded as
unfortunate and quixotic schemes of interference. Parish relief, in
particular, came under attack as a drain on wages, a destruction of the
incentive to work, and an encouragement to a reckless increase of
population among the poor. After two years of investigation, a

parliamentary commission presented its report in February 1834, condemning on principle all doles given outside the poor house— "outdoor relief." The central principle of the report was a rigorous workhouse test: either the poor came into the public workhouse or they got no relief. To make this test effective, the new workhouses must be made more unpleasant than the condition of the worst-paid laborer on the open market outside, and new administrative units replaced the parishes, each with a board of guardians who were to enforce the new law and be responsible to a central regulatory group. The act, quickly passed in 1834, was a momentous change in English traditions and history, and the debate over its effectiveness and morality raged into the spring of 1841, when the government was forced to abandon its plan to extend the New Poor Law for another ten years. Instead, the bill proceeded by one-year extensions until 1847, when it was renewed for five years, and in 1867 made permanent. Thus 1843, the year of the appearance of *Jessie Phillips*, was a time of intense interest and debate about the New Poor Law.[15]

Mrs. Trollope opposed the change in the poor laws partly because of her Tory sympathy with the workings of the traditional paternalist society of the English countryside and partly because she believed that the new law opposed fundamental Christian principles. The roots of her thinking lay in her visit to Manchester and her brief but important association with Oastler, Bull, and Stephens, who were strongly involved in anti-Poor Law agitation. In addition, Mrs. Trollope's concern for the outcasts of humanity was not new. The characters of her novels had often been those called "repulsive" by society. They were slaves, the poor, factory children, and now in *Jessie Phillips* that lowest member of early nineteenth-century society, the fallen woman. *Michael Armstrong* had come heralded as support for "the cause of the helpless, the hopeless, the oppressed"; *Jessie Phillips* was an inevitable progression in the advocacy of that cause, which Mrs. Trollope now took up, inspired by Tory ideals, Christian principles, compassion for the downtrodden, and an unquenchable hope for social reform.[16]

Her novel delineated and attacked the major elements of the New Poor Law of 1834, especially the explicit premise that "workhouses looked like prisons and were administered like them." She hoped to demonstrate the evils and injustices resulting from the rigid application of these principles to frail and suffering humanity. Through a host of minor characters, she illustrated the inadequacy of impersonal centralization and the intentionally harsh conditions of workhouse life.[17] Other brief vignettes illustrated perhaps the most serious evil of the new law, the separation of families within the workhouses. One nameless old inmate scolds a newcomer for "sobbing and howling" at her forced separation from her husband and son. While the woman means to be harsh, the poignancy of her own case is clear.

> I haven't set eyes upon my husband for almost a year, and yet there he is, I suppose, somewhere or other, within a few yards of me. And I don't expect ever to get sight of um again. . . . So here we be for life, old Thomas on one side of the house, and I on t'other; and yet we have stood side by side together, loving and kind enough, for above 40 years, since Parson Buckhurst told us that we were man and wife, and that no man was to put us asunder. But that's all changed now, and they tell us it's just their bounden duty to do it, which seems odd too, considering the book that the parson read it out of. [p. 215]

Inspired by Malthusian logic, the commissioners made poverty and hardship a crime, punishable by confinement and degradation. The poor can live, but not well. Many of these brief scenes, while undoubtedly somewhat melodramatic, were worth more than pamphlets, broadsides, or open-air sermons. None were pure invention, and all can be documented from the contemporary literature and subsequent accounts. They brought home to the middle-class reader the injustices, brutalities, and insensitivities of the prosperous toward "the other England."[18]

Well aware of the complexities involved and of how difficult it would be to correct the problems, she never wavered in believing that the new Poor Law was wrong. In the conclusion of the book, she repeated her conviction that:

> A new poor-law, differing essentially from the old one, was absolutely necessary to save the country from the rapidly corroding process, which was eating like a canker into her strength, but that the remedy which has been applied lacks practical wisdom, and is deficient in legislative morality, inasmuch as expediency has on many points been very obviously preferred to what the Christian law teaches us to believe right. [p. 352]

To one correspondent who had sent her material arguing the other side, she replied in a courteous and friendly note that reiterated her determination to continue to expose the evils of the system which she had seen in operation.

> Your clever pamphlets have much in them that no reasonable and honest reader can gainsay, yet they do not remove the impression which I have received from watching the effects of the new poor law in several unions that the improvement ought to be still farther improved. I am well aware how much easier it is to perceive this, than to perceive how the desired

improvement can be affected, nevertheless, I earnestly and confidently hope that the wisdom and morality of Englishmen will not abandon the subject, till some means have been discovered by which relief from labour shall be made unpalatable to the idle and profligate, without making parochial relief come in the shape of isolation and imprisonment to the aged and infirm.[19]

In addition to her concern with the general injustice of the New Poor Law, Mrs. Trollope pointed to its particular and devastating effects upon women. Her main plot concentrates upon the village beauty Jessie Phillips, a proud and talented seamstress who, believing the false promises of an unprincipled young squire, is seduced, made pregnant, and finally abandoned. Scorned by the polite young ladies of the parish, Jessie can find no work and is forced to take shelter in the union workhouse. Despite attempts to adopt a Christian attitude towards her fate, Jessie fails:

> It was in vain that she repeated to herself, "I have deserved it all." The magdalen humility by which she strove to reconcile herself to offended Heaven was no longer genuine and sincere. She did not deserve the degradation to which she was now exposed, and she knew it. [p. 209]

In her desperation, she manages to slip out of the workhouse to ask her seducer for maintenance of the unborn child. When he viciously refuses, she runs away, and her exertions bring on the birth of the baby. While she is still unconscious, the baby is taken by a passer-by and eventually is found by her seducer, who murders it. Herself unjustly accused of the child's death, Jessie dies before learning of her acquittal.

The plot rather melodramatically turns on the young squire's arrogant refusal to help Jessie precisely because of the changes in the new Poor Law, the bastardy clauses of which had made the mother of the child liable for its support. These clauses had been added to the bill's original provisions. Under the old law of Elizabethan days, if a single woman declared herself pregnant and charged a man with being the father of the child-to-be, a warrant could be issued for his arrest, unless he could give security to indemnify the parish for its support. Under threat of longer imprisonment, the woman could force the man to marry her, or, alternatively, to pay her a weekly allowance for seven years. The Royal Commissioners who drafted the new clauses considered these older provisions as encouragement to women of immoral habits, incitement to perjury, inducement to extramarital intercourse, undermining of female modesty and self-reliance, and encouragement for early and improvident marriages. Pointing to social demoralization as well as crippling expense, they proposed, "as a step towards the natural state of things," to exempt the putative father from all legal responsibility for the maintenance of the child; they insisted that "if a mother really could not support her illegitimate child, the place for both was in a new Union workhouse." The commissioners wrote that bastardy would never decline until a bastard was "what Providence appears to have ordained that it should be, a burthen on its mother, and, where she cannot maintain it, on her parents." Thus, in April 1834, "all laws enabling a woman or a Local Authority to charge a man with being the father of an illegitimate child, and enabling a magistrate to levy maintenance upon him, arrest him, or attach his goods and chattels, were repealed."[20]

The story of Jessie illustrates the injustices of these new arrangements. Occasionally Mrs. Trollope's treatment is somewhat overdramatized and improbable—as for example when the young squire deliberately contemplates seducing Jessie *because* he knows about the new bastardy clauses:

> The terror that formerly kept so many libertines of all classes in check was no longer before him, the legislature having, in its collective wisdom, deemed it "discreetest, best," that the male part of the population should be guarded, protected, sheltered, and insured from all the pains and penalties arising from the crime he contemplated. "No, No," thought Mr. Frederick Dalton, "thanks to our noble lawgivers, there is no more wearing away a gentleman's incognito now. It is just one of my little bits of good luck that this blessed law should be passed." [pp. 252-53]

More realistic are the scenes Jessie and the young squire have with the parish lawyer, to whom both go for assistance. The learned solicitor soothes Frederick's worry that Jessie has threatened "to swear a child" to him and ruin his reputation: "Whether the girl's charge be true or false, it makes no sort of difference to you. Is it possible . . . that you are ignorant of this most important clause in the new act?" (p. 255). When Jessie tries to plead her case and make the wealthy young squire give financial support, the lawyer's cruel reply underlines the helpless position of the woman: "I . . . tell you, my girl, that you may stand all day swearing that one man or another man is the father of your child, and no more notice will be taken of it than if you whistled" (p. 255). Jessie becomes aware of the double standard built into the New Poor Law and the following passage details her sexual politicization:

> Jessie knew well enough, as every body else did, that the new law had ordained many severe enactments against women in her unhappy situation, but so far from complaining of this, she had often, in the silence of the

night, prayed with penitent humility that the knowledge of all the anguish
which would follow the fault, might save others from committing it, and
never had she murmured at the portion of retribution allotted to her. But
Mr. Lewis's exposition had opened to her a perfectly new view of the case.
It was not only then to punish the offending woman, but to spare the
pocket of the fondly protected man, that this new regulation was established. She heard it declared, that all men so circumstanced, whether, as
Mr. Lewis comprehensively expressed it, they were kings or cobblers,
were proclaimed by the law of the land to be henceforward, and for ever,
clear from all blame and all shame. Any atonement to the "gentle fool"
who had condemned herself to pretty nearly every imaginable species of
suffering, for believing that the man she loved might smile, and not be a
villain, having been rendered as nearly impossible as very careful
legislation could make it. [p. 256]

But as Mrs. Trollope dropped the curtain for the last time "over the
name of Jessie Phillips," she reiterated her indignant claim that women
had been made scapegoats and victims by these clauses:

Too weak, too erring, to be remembered with respect, yet not so bad but
that some may feel it a thing to wonder at that she, and the terribly
tempted class of which she is the type, should seem so very decidedly to be
selected by the Solons of our day as a sacrifice for all the sins of all their sex.
Why one class of human beings should be sedulously protected by a
special law from the consequences of their own voluntary indiscretions, it
is not very easy to comprehend; but it is more difficult still to assign any
satisfactory reason why another class should be in like manner selected as
the subject of special law, for the express purpose of making them subject
to all the pain and penalties, naturally consequent upon the faults committed by the protected class above mentioned. [p. 351]

Mrs. Trollope ended with a wish that "the unhappy class, thus selected
for victims, were not so very decidedly, and so very inevitably, the
weakest, and in all ways the least protected portion of society. There is
no chivalry in the selection, and, to the eyes of ignorance like mine, there
is no justice" (p. 349).

The bastardy clauses had been among the most unpopular parts of
the New Poor Law. But while a steady stream of petitions flowed into
the House of Commons demanding their repeal, not a single novel, with
the exception of Jessie Phillips, dramatized the problem, even though by
1843 it had become relatively common for novelists to deal with specific
contemporary problems. In turning to this issue, Mrs. Trollope again
took up a controversial subject, one considered inappropriate for a
woman to discuss. For her daring, she was vilified by the reviewers.

John Bull, a lightweight publication that had been traditionally friendly to Mrs. Trollope, often indulging in hyperbole in describing her many works, took a decidedly hostile view of the completed *Jessie Phillips*.

> Mrs. Trollope has sinned grievously against good taste and decorum. The particular clause of the Act which she has selected for reprobation is the *bastardy clause*—not perhaps the very best subject for a female pen.

The *Spectator*, reviewing only the first part of the novel, compared it unfavorably to Dickens's current production (*Martin Chuzzlewit*). The authors were treated together, said the reviewer, because they more systematically pursued publication in serial parts than any other writer. But while excusing Boz his use of this "fashionable" mode on the ground of superior literary talents, the writer accused Mrs. Trollope of using this method for purposes of rank sensationalism, sacrificing

> future fame to present popularity, by taking advantage of attractive temporary circumstances, and so working them as to produce their greatest effect at the time of production. Mrs. Trollope does this openly and palpably: the titles of her lucubrations announce her intention—*The Factory Boy*, etc.; and she treats her subject cleverly, no doubt, but coarsely, literally, and vulgarly—not so much with vulgarity of manner, but by an appeal to the vulgar prejudices and vulgar cant which animate the ignorant and narrow-minded of every grade.[21]

Clearly evident in these attacks was the fear that a dramatic presentation such as Mrs. Trollope's might have some effect upon the nation's lawmakers. And, while it might be difficult to prove a direct relationship, Mrs. Trollope's book was an important contribution to the the repeal of the bastardy clauses of the New Poor Law. While most of the new legislation remained largely intact until after the First World War, in 1844, the House of Commons passed the "Little Poor Law," which once again gave unwed mothers the right to bring suit against putative fathers in Petty Sessions, subject to corroborative evidence of paternity.[22]

Even more daring than Mrs. Trollope's frank treatment of Jessie's plight was the book's instrument of reform and exposure, another strong and unconventional woman, Martha Maxwell, to whose story that of Jessie Phillips is inextricably tied. Depicted as "an odd girl," an "eccentric, and, in some sort, whimsical young lady," Martha Maxwell learns about the bastardy clauses from her father, with whom she discusses Jessie's case.

> Setting aside the obvious and horrible injustice of thus making one responsible for a fault committed by both, let us look . . . at the wisdom,

justice, and humanity of the choice which has selected the woman as the
sacrifice. . . . How is it with the wretched woman? Alas, poor wretch!
she is the victim of her lover . . . the victim of the short-sighted policy of
her country, which, while hoping (vainly) to save a few yearly shillings
from the poor-rates, has decreed that a weak woman . . . who has
committed this sin shall atone for it by being trampled in the dust,
imprisoned in a workhouse with her wretched offspring till driven from it
to seek food for both by labour, that the most respectable part of her own
sex refuse her upon principle! . . . And how fares it the while with the
privileged seducer? Why, he, *being of the sex which makes the laws,* is so
smugly sheltered by them that there is no earthly reason whatsoever why
he should not go on in the course he has begun, and thank the gods that he
is not a woman. [pp. 203–4]

Martha emerges as Mrs. Trollope's staunch defender of women's
rights. She does not reject Jessie, and after the murder of the baby, she is
one of the few to believe in Jessie's innocence. The *Athenaeum* bitterly
summarized Martha's part in the plot, concluding with a clear attack
on Mrs. Trollope's woman characters in general.

A young lady (Martha Maxwell), who has been sought in marriage by
Jessie's seducer, becomes acquainted with this passage of his adventures,
accepts him (in jest), and forces a written promise of marriage from him
(in jest), in the Quixotic hope of shaming or terrifying him into doing
justice to the ruined maiden. Nay, more, to work out her delicate scheme
of benevolence, she takes another young unmarried man into her
confidence, acquaints him with the Squire's offence in full, consults him on
the feasibility of her expedient, and ends by marrying him! We must add,
too, that while poor Jessie is dying of her shame, and Martha Maxwell
benevolently busy in comforting her, that eccentric young lady is
described as finding "great amusement" in "the innumerable tricks and
seemingly playful caprices" by which she keeps the villain on the rack.
*Mrs. Trollope has done much in enlightening the circulating library world
as to the manner in which her sex can act, but this last display of feminine
ingenuity out-Barnabys Barnabyism!*[23]

As with other reviews, Mrs. Trollope was not moved by such criticism.
Indeed, in the next few years, she would return repeatedly to the theme
of "female ingenuity," and her novels voiced for her age the emerging
feminine consciousness.

In November 1843, when all the installments of her novel were
complete, Mrs. Trollope set out for what she anticipated would be a
year's residence in Florence. But her travels extended over the next
seven years, during which she moved regularly between Penrith and
Florence. In the autumn and winter, she stayed in Italy, heading north

when spring came to see Cecilia, the grandchildren, Anthony, and her other friends and family. Never again did she make permanent residence in the land of her birth.[24]

During this period of busy social activity and travel, she produced a steady stream of best-sellers, light romantic fictions well calculated to please her readers. All these novels were in the main stories of marrying and giving in marriage, loose-jointed composites of what the *Spectator* called "courtships and dinners in country-houses, flirtations at fêtes and the opera, and the intrigues of maneuvering mothers and aunts." Their heroes and heroines were conventional, and despite a variety of interesting obstacles, true love always triumphed. Designed to amuse and divert, such books were often "bidden to country-houses for the entertainment of Christmas guests," for, as one reviewer noted, while often improbable and even extravagant, they "will not be found bores." In them, Mrs. Trollope maintained her firm command of the palpable real world, imbuing all she touched with what the *Dublin Review* called "a *gusto*—a lingering enjoyment of all the good things of this life, which is quite enthusiastic."[25] She knew her world "thoroughly—oh thoroughly," in the words of one of her characters, and in her novels she rendered the good dinners, the sets of diamonds and opera-boxes, the well-appointed houses, carriages, and fantastic apartments. She knew also its secret sins, pettinesses, pretentiousness, and social climbers, struggling to attach themselves to the great ones of society. To her ability to suffuse these rather ordinary, even third-rate novels with pervasive, energetic realism and a light satiric touch, Mrs. Trollope owed much of her popularity.

But in the decade of the 1840s, following her work on *Jessie Phillips*, Mrs. Trollope's novels began to change. While her heroines continued to fulfill themselves successfully in marriage, the subplots tended to stress the difficulties that determined, and even moderately intelligent and willful girls encountered in their marital ventures. All these novels included a series of strong, exciting women, an interest she had pursued from her three comic Barnaby books through her social reform fiction in which women were the vehicles of change and rejuvenation. Now, as she produced the light romances then in demand, she suited herself by drawing her favorite kind of female characters as fortune hunters, villainesses, sirens, and unhappy wives. Outsiders to the main story, they could be blessedly exempt from the exigencies of the sentimental main plot.

Of these various types, the most successful was the fortune hunter, a character traditionally subject to scorn and low humor, but in Mrs. Trollope's hands, women of considerable talent and intelligence, for whom the reader learns to feel compassion and admiration. Driven by

social constraints and economic necessity, these women pursue men in
an occupation Mrs. Trollope renders variously as degrading, boring, and
in every way beneath their abilities. An early example appeared in *The
Laurringtons* (1844) in Charlotte Mastermann, whose name tells her
story. A penniless outsider, she captures the spoiled darling heir, as
insipid and weak a man as she is a strong and daring woman. And even as
Mrs. Trollope's deepest interest lay with this character and not with her
romantic heroine, so too did the reviewers find themselves oddly
fascinated. The *Athenaeum* appreciatively called Miss Mastermann "as
artful and fashionable a shrew as ever sold herself for an establishment
and took out the sacrifice in tormenting her buyer."[26] Once married,
Charlotte dominates her husband's life, contriving "to rule with a rod,
very considerably stronger than the stoutest iron, the heroic heart and
the steadfast will of the great chieftain of the Laurrington race without
encountering the slightest opposition from any one." With undisguised
pleasure, the author asked: "Are there no individuals among the lords of
creation who can recognise their own history here?" (2:78)

Young Love, a novel of the same year, continued the pattern. This
time the foolish hero excapes entrapment (but only barely) by the
heartless, bored, and profligate Amelia Thorwold. Not the average gold
digger, Amelia longs for excitement as well as security. When her
conquest of young Alfred proves too easy, she resolves to try instead for
a former lover, in cleverness, roguery, and general amorality more her
equal. Playing a dangerous double game, she uses each man to make the
other jealous, artfully assuming the weak and delicate image to which
men seemed so ready to capitulate.

> The most pathetic actress that ever lived could scarcely have spoken these
> sentences in a more touching manner than Miss Thorwold. She appeared
> to weep, but it was gentle, not violent weeping; the former being sure to
> touch and melt the heart of man, and the latter to revolt and harden it.
> [2:147–48]

She and Lord William elope, but he quickly deserts her, leaving Amelia
to return undaunted to the hapless Alfred. How she almost succeeds in
marrying him as well, failing only at the last moment, provides most of
the excitement of the third volume. Moved by the lady's desperate
pluck, the reader feels regret when all her hopes finally come to naught.[27]

In *The Lottery of Marriage* (1849), the accomplished female sharper
again fails, this time because of mistaken identities, by marrying the
wrong (penniless) cousin.[28] But this intelligent lady is not impeded, as
was Amelia Thorwold, by any illusions about loving the man she
pursues. She is simply tired to death

with this eternal labour, and eternal failure! . . . I certainly was a little subject to love fits some dozen years ago or so, but my intellectual constitution has improved and developed itself marvellously of late years, and I have no longer any such stuff in my thoughts. [1:73]

Mrs. Trollope was distressed by the severe limitations imposed upon women who, it seems must marry or starve. As yet unable to suggest other solutions, she continued in these novels her search, begun as early as *Domestic Manners*, for ways to express the unique position of women in a world of limited goals.

In *The Attractive Man* (1846), she made her strong woman a villain. The action of the novel was solidly set in the small country environment that Mrs. Trollope handled so well, complete with the ubiquitous dinner parties, balls, and even the new gentleman in the neighborhood who proves to be, alas, no Mr. Knightley, but Theodore Vidal, a desperate fraud, in search of marrying a fortune. The book's really interesting character is Lucy Dalton, a penniless girl adopted by the wealthy father of the tale's true heroine as her companion. When Mary Clementson prepares to enter society at seventeen, Lucy realizes that her time at the great house is almost up. There she has developed some showy acquirements of her own, and she has also learned to be dishonest and devious. She represented, in her own words, "the lowly-born, the dependent, the penniless" (2:99). While a more conventional and proper young lady would have dutifully prepared for an existence as a governess (such as Jane Austen's Jane Fairfax), Lucy determines to survive without capitulating to that dreary fate. She surpasses even Vidal in diabolical cleverness and recognizes herself "superior to him in innate power and indomitable strength of character" (3:130–31). It is her idea that Vidal marry Mary Clementson for the money and afterward continue their secret relationship. When her mother overhears the plot, Lucy forcibly commits her to a madhouse! Of course the lovers fail, for Victorian morals had to be served, but Mrs. Trollope's depiction awakens appreciation for Lucy's audacity and sympathy for the problems of dependent women. Although the author punishes Lucy with failure, she cannot resist having Mary Clementson kindly grant Lucy a small pension at the end. Even a shred of independence is no inconsiderable achievement.

The reviewers were compelled to notice Mrs. Trollope's evolving interest in such deviant female types and concluded that she had really gone too far. The *Literary Gazette* was particularly troubled:

The Attractive Man is not an attractive novel. On the contrary, it is repulsive; and especially as regards the portraiture of the females, of all ages, stations, and descriptions. . . . The bloom is off the fairest and freshest of them; and the others are more seriously blemished, from slighter defects to corruption at the very core. . . . It is positively disagreeable, and almost disgusting, to read three volumes in which the development of emotions and passions in the breasts of women affords nothing more refreshing to human nature than such weaknesses, follies, vices, and crimes. Heaven forbid that we should not consider the whole to be a false and malicious libel![29]

Lucy's immorality left the reviewers at a loss for adjectives, let alone motivations. The *Literary Gazette* called her "an unprincipled fiend at seventeen," and *John Bull* was admittedly puzzled: "It is impossible to believe so much matured profligacy could have existed in a country girl of seventeen or eighteen." But women liked and understood the book in spite of such reviews. Harriet Garnett, who knew the problems of the single woman with a small income in early Victorian society, praised *The Attractive Man* and strongly recommended it to her sister.[30]

But once successfully married and in positions of some security, women's problems were not over. In a society where marriage ushered in domestic confinement, idleness, and intellectual stagnation, some women sought other outlets for their energies. Mrs. Trollope had earlier depicted the exotic, sensual woman. In *The Attractive Man*, she included Lady Sarah Monkton, a beautiful recumbent, whose whole life "was passed in ceaseless endeavours to inspire passion." Her most prevalent occupations were "dressing, dancing, sleeping, and reading French novels. Flirting must not be named in addition to these, because it could no more be classed as a separate and distinct occupation, than breathing might be. She was always flirting, or making ready to flirt." Such a life was exciting for awhile, "but the worst part of the business is the sort of dying life that follows, if these innocent assassins of the peace of mankind have not the good fortune to expire, like other pretty flowers, when their bloom is past" (1:131). When love is a woman's whole world, what is left, Mrs. Trollope wondered, when beauty fades?

Still another novel of these years explores the theme of fading beauty.[31] Although *The Three Cousins* (1847) studies "the three great classes into which mortal ladies are divided—one being a maid, one a wife, and one a widow" (1:i), respectively eighteen, thirty-four, and fifty-two, Mrs. Trollope is primarily interested in the oldest of the three, who has lived by her wit, coquetry, and "that masterly management of colours and of textures by means of which a woman can make herself look as bewitchingly lovely in a well-lighted drawing-room as she had when she was still 18" (2:12–13). She works hard to preserve a youthful appearance, and Mrs. Trollope affectingly renders her, as she wearily undresses after an evening's efforts, performing her nightly ablutions before the impartial and devastating mirror. Despite "great resources in an intellect that was never for an instant at a loss for expedients, in perseverance that was never wearied, in courage that was never daunted" (2:2–3), she must find security through marriage to one of the book's ineffectual males, despite a frank lack of feeling for "the bright vision himself" (2:161).

Fortune hunters, villains, seductresses, aging beauties, young maidens of seventeen—they share a common plight. To survive, they must please men and achieve marriage in a difficult world. To succeed, they must behave with discipline, inner fortitude, and a soldier's strength. Gradually, these stories that centered on achieving marriage revealed instead nagging and unsolved problems. The reader forgot rather rapidly the inevitable comings-together of the various star-crossed lovers, and remembered instead the valiant and desperate women who failed. *John Bull*, which admittedly took up "any work by Mrs. Trollope, with the certainty of being pleased," tried to characterize the particular kind of celebrity that she had won in these years, noting that, "her own sex she seems to have studied with profound attention," uncomfortably regretting her repeated interest in "the heartless woman of the world [and] all the elaborate devices by which artificial manners are made to represent natural impulses."[32]

Indeed, throughout these novels of the 1840s, Mrs. Trollope entered her story to speak in behalf of those women who seemed most reprehensible, foolish, or puzzling, painstakingly explaining to her readers their situations.

> Women are often accused, and often with justice, of being artful; but nobody seems to remember, when this is predicated of them as a fault, that, were it otherwise, they must often be guilty of another fault . . . that most painful of all accusations, a want of delicacy. Poor souls! How may they safely steer their course between the two?[33]

To this valid question, the mores of Victorian society provided no viable answer. Repeatedly, Mrs. Trollope insisted that women are forced by society to conceal natural impulses. In yet another history of an unhappy marriage and the duties of a wife toward a tyrannical husband (*Town and Country*),[34] the author frequently intruded with knowledgeable comments about the nature of women: "It is by no means uncommon to see women more true than frank. Many very excellent persons of both sexes are so; but I am of opinion that this is oftener found in females than in males" (1:151). Since women were often forced to capitulate, conceal their feelings, or be frustrated, they needed a natural outlet which those in power did not require.

> It is a great mistake, to say to women, when under strong emotion of any kind, "*Don't cry!*" for it is by much the best thing they can do. It is a part of their nature, and a very kindly part, too; and though long teaching, or a very sturdy disposition, may enable some of us to do without this indulgence, we all do a vast deal better with it; that is to say, when circumstances are such as to make a truly feminine heart require this truly feminine relief. [1:151–52]

Because of the role of women in society, female attention to dress was similarly explained by Mrs. Trollope as being a necessity and not a frivolous pastime:

> As well might an ambassador be called silly for throwing all the amenity possible into his manner when approaching the sovereign from whom he hopes to obtain some valuable advantage. A woman believes, and often truly believes, that dress increases her attractions; and her tactics would be very defective if she neglected it. [*Three Cousins*, 2: 159–60]

Yet even while these devices helped women cope in a male-dominated world, they were, finally, pitiful. Mrs. Trollope frequently sympathized with coquettes who were foolish in the eyes of the men they tried to captivate. "Poor woman," she wrote once of such a lady, "What would her feelings have been could she have read his heart" (*Lottery of Marriage*, p. 52). Her deepest compassion went out to the unhappily married. More than once, the author's voice spoke pointedly on this subject.

> Without meaning to be in the slightest degree uncivil to the lords of the creation, I certainly think that the demise of a husband may occasionally be felt rather as a relief than as an infliction by his widow. Neither is it absolutely unnatural, or impossible, that the death of a wife may, in like manner, produce less of sorrow than of thankfulness. But it is rarely that the condition of a widower can be so obviously improved as that of a widow by such an event. A fretful, or in any way troublesome wife passes off the scene, and her surviving spouse will probably lead a much more happy life without her; but the whole manner of his existence, his place, and power, his social and domestic importance, can scarcely undergo so great a change as it is common enough to see displayed in the case of a well-endowed widow, who has not been much indulged in the exercise of free will whilst she remained a wife.[35]

In the metamorphosis of maid, to wife, to widow, the last state was best of all. How shocking the intrusive voice of these novels must have seemed, running like a subversive undercurrent beneath the conventional events of the story. It permeated the whole, repeatedly accounting for the actions of women, detailing their secret thoughts and dilemmas, transcribing their inner lives. In the last analysis, the most fascinating personage in all these novels, most of them not important by any aesthetic or literary/historical standards, is the author's voice on behalf of her women.

In *Jonathan Jefferson Whitlaw* and in *Jessie Phillips*, Mrs. Trollope had taken up the cause of the exploited woman, black and white. Here was an issue with which she could truly identify, and it helped gain her celebrity as a troublesome reformer. The *Athenaeum* sarcastically called her the "Rebecca of Novel-writers" and recollected "the raptures expressed, in the announcements of this novel *(Jessie Phillips)*, at the prospect of the Poor Laws being 'arranged' by the same truth-telling and powerful writer as had attacked American Democracy and Slavery." A minor episode in that book might well have been the author's comment on her own evolution. "This is quite new, Mrs. Buckhurst," one character remonstrates. "I never expected that I should live to see you turn Radical." What follows is pure Frances Trollope: "Live a little longer, Mr. Lewis," replied the old lady, returning his smile, "And you may chance to see the very staunchest old Tories among us turn Chartist." While Mrs. Trollope herself certainly never became a Chartist or took up arms in riot or sedition, she did become a quiet revolutionary of sorts. As Rosina Bulwer, her friend and interesting example of downtrodden womanhood, was to dub her, she was truly a "pioneer of feminism."[36]

14

Contentment, Change, and Loss

I have indeed suffered, more than I can express,
more even than I expected.

IN THE spring of 1844 Anthony announced his engagement to Rose
Heseltine, a Rotherham bank manager's daughter whom he had met in
Ireland. In May Mrs. Trollope returned from Florence to inspect her
prospective daughter-in-law and attend the marriage on 11 June.
Afterwards, the whole family gathered for a summer visit with the
Tilleys at Carlton Hill. Rose Trollope recalled her early impressions of
her famous mother-in-law and the loving reception the old woman gave
to the girl who was to make Anthony such a satisfactory wife. In her
sixty-fifth year, Mrs. Trollope was still full of energy.

> There was no one more eager to suggest, and carry out the suggestions, as
> to mountain excursions, picnics, and so forth. And she was always the life
> and soul of the party with her cheerful conversation and her wit. She rose
> very early and made her own tea, the fire having been prepared over
> night—(on one occasion I remember her bringing me a cup of tea to my
> room, because she thought I had caught cold during a wet walk in the
> mountains)—then sat at her writing-table until the allotted task of so many
> pages was completed; and was usually on the lawn before the family
> breakfast-bell rang, having filled her basket with cuttings from the rose-
> bushes for the table and drawing-room decorations.[1]

Anthony told his mother that he was working on the manuscript of a first
novel with an Irish setting. There was a brief flurry when he seemed to
have misplaced it, but at last Mrs. Trollope learned from Rose that all
was well. "I rejoice to hear that Anthony's manuscript is found, and I
trust he will lose no *idle* time, but give all he can, without breaking in
upon his professional labours, to finish it." Anthony is somewhat less than
fair in recounting that his mother "did not give me credit for the sort of
cleverness necessary for such work," for certainly this letter was
encouraging.[2] That she worried about the possible effect upon his post

office duties was simply her good sense and also her recollection, not so long distant, of his desperate days in London. She was pleased to see him so much the solid citizen, with job and wife, and would not have liked to see him lose all he had earned.

She herself was working on *The Robertses on Their Travels*, which was serialized and published in 1846. It was a delightful satire on the traveling English, of whom she, of course, had made a prominent one. Mrs. Trollope sketched the insolent manners and impropriety of the Roberts family in adventures she had culled from her personal experience. *John Bull* reported that in spite of Mrs. Trollope's claim to have taken care to prevent recognition and avoid personal satire, she had "not quite succeeded," and some people professed to know "some of the originals." The book proved to be one of her most popular and least controversial novels, full of "out-of-the-way difficulties" and the usual quota of dangers. The manner was happy, "with great drollery and liveliness," albeit one reviewer found the author, as ever, somewhat "too fond of painting the darker side of human nature."[3]

At Carlton Hill Mrs. Trollope had again found her daughter pregnant and her delicate health

> but so, so. She cannot walk without suffering so much from fatigue that I content myself with taking her to a bench near the sea, and sitting there till I think she has inhaled a sufficient quantity of *iodine*.[4]

That winter, after she and Tom had returned to Florence, Cecilia was delivered of her first boy. The Garnetts reported that she was "as well as possible, and very happy, for her three girls made her wish for a boy; Mrs. Trollope too will be pleased at the birth of a grandson." Indeed, she delightedly heard the news and was reading John Tilley's letter when her Italian man-servant entered the room. "I wish you could have seen his terrified countenance" she told Cecilia. "The tears, I know, were running down my cheeks, and I know, also, that I was indulging in a broad grin,—so that I suspect Luigi thought I was seized with sudden phrensy." When Mrs. Trollope explained the cause, he "seemed to think it reasonable enough; and uttered the words '*Maschio? Bene!*' as if (conceited he-thing!) he thought the ecstasy perfectly well accounted for."[5] And while she continued to work hard at her novels, she found time to send "Miss Frances Trollope Tilley" a "night cap and a shift" for her doll, explaining that it "is all that I have had time to make." She who had hemmed sheets and read Dante at twenty-nine continued to exercise and treasure both the domestic and the intellectual side of her rich nature.

When the winter was over, and the alarming Florentine floods had subsided, Mrs. Trollope again planned a visit to her daughter. First, she met with Colburn, with whom she settled upon two novels and a volume of traveling sketches. After visiting friends at Clifton, she proceeded to Carlton Hill. There she found her daughter once again with child. Anthony and his wife as well as Henry Milton and family were guests. Undeterred by the festive atmosphere of family reunion, she began the writing of these novels, trusting that if her health continued to be good, "enabling me to get up at four o'clock every morning," she should be able to accomplish the task. Still, such a feat was "less easy to do . . . in a house surrounded by company, than it would be without it."[6]

That summer Anthony entrusted his mother with the completed manuscript of *The Macdermots of Ballycloran.* She agreed not to look at it before giving it to a publisher. The apprehensive Anthony fancied that he

> could see in the faces and hear in the voices of those of my friends who were around me at the house in Cumberland—my mother, my sister, my brother-in-law, and, I think, my brother—that they had not expected me to come out as one of the family authors. There were three or four in the field before me, and it seemed to be almost absurd that another should wish to add himself to the number. . . . I would perceive that this attempt of mine was felt to be an unfortunate aggravation of this disease.[7]

Once again, Anthony did not do justice to his mother's concern, for she in fact undertook to get the novel read and accepted. She would hardly have performed such a task if she shared the indifference to his literary future that so many commentators have read into this celebrated passage from Anthony's autobiography. Mrs. Trollope was relieved to see that her youngest son had come through his time of depression and illness to solid respectability and even literary creation. She knew what inner discipline was needed to sustain two such differing careers and could only have been pleased to see Anthony so much in command of himself and his future.

By the end of September she returned to Florence where she and Tom plunged into the usual round of parties and socializing. They established themselves in new quarters in the Via del Giglio and in the winter of 1845–1846 "entertained a great deal, and received at her dinner-parties and soirees, emphatically the best society that Florence had to boast." They enjoyed amateur theatricals and even a costume ball, to which they went dressed in garb peculiarly at odds with their truest selves, Tom as a jester, and Mrs. Trollope as a sedate Quakeress. Later Tom's second wife speculated on the source of Mrs. Trollope's unquestionable popularity.

> She was not a famous sayer of witty things; she had no reputation of former beauty, which often arouses an interest of curiosity; she did not trade upon an audacious self-assertion and disregard of other people's claims and feelings . . . she was not wealthy; and although she was a successful writer of books, she did not hold a pre-eminent position in literature. But she had admirable good sense, much genuine humour, great knowledge of the world, a quick appreciation of others' gifts, and, above all, a character of the most flawless sincerity, and a warmly affectionate heart.[8]

After her customary spring visit to Penrith in 1846, Mrs. Trollope set off on a tour in the Tyrol, Bohemia, and Silesia, accompanied by her son and some friends. Their destination was Graffenberg, where Tom planned to take the popular cold water cure. Utilizing traveling experiences in her accustomed fashion, she produced two volumes of sketches, entitled *Travels and Travelers*. She described the cure, clever but not scientific, and King Ludwig's Valhalla on the Danube with its 160 busts of great men like Keppler, Mozart, and Dürer, a sight required for "all who do not intend to die and be buried, without having any idea how beautiful a marble hall may be." The rest of the volumes were filled with stories, some of murders and acquitals of the innocent, adventures with drunken coachmen, contraband trade between Switzerland and Austria, and midnight passages through the Mont du Chat. She visited Rousseau's favorite residence Les Charmettes, and impudently traced his faults to a bad childhood.[9]

Her exhilaration when on the road knew no bounds. She was astonished that so many other people found traveling difficult, for she was an inveterate rambler, who proudly detailed her "habitual punctuality," as she rose at five each day, a practice which "has so often enabled me and mine to go farther and see more within a given space of time than most people. I believe I have boasted rather often of this wakeful virtue already, but I do it without scruple. . . ."[10] Indeed, for her, travel had become an expression of religious feeling. As she recalled the sheer physical loveliness of places like the Lake of Bourget, she thanked whatever sustaining and restorative power had created the world in which she took such intense delight.

> It is good for us all to know how bounteous the God of nature has been in decorating the habitation in which he has ordained that man shall dwell during his threescore and ten years of mortal life; it is good that we should

be told of it, if accident prevents our full acquaintance with the fact by means of our own experience.

She welcomed "long days of wandering enjoyment" and was willing always to pay "the trifling exertion which it requires to leave your bed a little before you are quite tired of it" to procure them. She who habitually began her days before the nights had ended frequently described the effects of the rising sun, "the gradual illumination of that indescribable, rose-coloured light," greeting each day of her traveling life with a *joie de vivre* all her own. As she rose early to climb those Italian hills, Frances Trollope was sixty-seven years old.[11]

In the new year appeared *Father Eustace: A Tale of the Jesuits*, Mrs. Trollope's contribution to that popular nineteenth-century genre, the anti-Jesuit novel.[12] In 1845, John Henry Newman had embraced Roman Catholicism, and in 1850 the Catholic episcopacy was restored in England. The Oxford Movement and Roman Catholicism in general were regarded by many Englishmen with almost hysterical fear and suspicion. Mrs. Trollope's book was an attack upon the Society of Jesus, upon its traditionally devious intrigues, and most of all, upon its unquestioning obedience to a superior. It was a cloak and dagger story of a sort she had not indulged in since *The Abbess*; the plotting was outrageous, and the characters, particularly the Jesuits, were stereotypes of sinister evil. The book had its titillating aspects, for Father Eustace, disguised as a country gentleman and charged with converting the rich and lovely heroine to Catholicism, instead falls in love with the fair Juliana; their encounters and the prospect of stolen kisses between a young girl and a priest provided some exciting moments for nineteenth-century readers.

Mrs. Trollope took the subject seriously and frequently interrupted her story with lectures on the dangers of Catholicism, devoting much space to Father Eustace's interviews with his superior, where, in a florid style, the author made clear her position on such religious authority.

> The elder Jesuit looked down upon his younger victim with a sinister smile. He saw that [Father Eustace] was still a slave; and knew that . . . there would be no danger of his breaking his chains, although they should drag him into the lowest depths of misery, and sin, so long as his spirit remained thralled by . . . his vow of absolute unquestioning obedience. [3:189-90]

But such subject matter crippled Mrs. Trollope's satiric, humorous style. The *New Monthly Magazine* noted the change:

Mrs. Trollope has . . . seldom been less herself—that is to say, lightly descriptive, biting, and epigrammatic—she is here neither frivolous nor humorous, she seems to have felt that she had a great and very serious subject in hand, and she labours in the development of the great struggle between religion, obedience, and passion, with an earnestness of purpose. . . .

The materials she had in hand, suggested another critic, demanded "for their perfect development, a vivid fancy, a strong imagination, a stern and gloomy enthusiasm, a power over the passions, such as Mrs. Radcliffe would have brought to the task. Mrs. Trollope's is essentially a practical mind, shrewd, observant, and tied down to the realities of this world."[13]

In April 1847, she left Florence for England, for the usual purposes: business with publishers, arrangements for new novels, and a visit with the Tilleys and the Anthony Trollopes. This time she arrived to find notices of Anthony's first novel, *The Macdermots of Ballycloran.* Despite his typically self-denigrating comment that "the book was not only not read, but was never heard of," reviews had appeared in several journals. Most of them noted strong affinities between his work and that of his mother. *Howitt's Journal* advised its readers to order the new novel at their circulating libraries; if it be, "as is said, by the son of Mrs. Trollope, then the son assuredly inherits a considerable portion of the mother's talent." *Douglas Jerrold's Shilling Magazine* thought the writer had obviously "inherited a keenness of observation and power of narrative." The *Spectator* suspected Mrs. Trollope's assistance, finding the subject such as "Mrs. Trollope herself might have chosen, or advised," but believed that Anthony's work was superior to that of his mother: "There is . . . more of mellowness in the composition of Mr. A. Trollope, and less of forced contrivance in the management of his story, than the fluent lady has ever displayed. . . ." Only the *Athenaeum* demurred, calling the novel "unfortunate only in the name of its author; who comes before the public with the disadvantage of *not being* the popular writer for whom careless readers might have mistaken him." One thing was clear: his mother's reputation was a mighty force with which he would have to reckon. Perhaps this is the reason Anthony preferred to forget the notices of his first novel.

That year, Mrs. Trollope published another book herself, *The Three Cousins*, which "met with a great deal of favour." For ten more years, she continued to produce her yearly quota of novels; for Anthony, thirty-five years of writing remained. Between them, if one reckons from the number of publications, they would dominate the field of English fiction for half a century.[14]

Once again she prepared for a tour, this time to Germany and Switzerland, and described her ambitious itinerary to a friend:

> Our present plan is to leave London on 13th July and steam up the Rhine, visiting Heidleberg enroute—to pass ten days at Baden-Baden, and then to proceed to Schiffhausen, and so on by sundry picturesque ins and outs, over the Helvio Pass down to the Lake of Como—From thence to Venice where Trollope is to meet his learned friends in Congress—and thence home by the last week in September.

She felt safe to be leaving Cecilia, who seemed, in the light of her many confinements, "on the whole better than . . . expected." By now a fifth little Tilley, Edith Diana Mary, had been added to the brood. Mrs. Trollope testily noted that her daughter's rapid succession of pregnancies was not "likely to contribute to the strength of a delicate woman." Still, she loved the grandchildren, "very nice little creatures, and all well both in mind and body—and this is some little consolation for their having come upon us so rapidly."[15]

Then, in August, John Tilley anxiously sent word to his mother-in-law that the doctors had ordered Cecilia to spend two years in Italy to recover her failing health. At once, Mrs. Trollope broke off her trip, sending Tom to fetch Cecilia and herself heading for home. By September, they were united at Florence, whence Cecilia had arrived "looking very pale and ill, and evidently very weak." Although "the doctors . . . had declared that Mrs. Tilley's lungs were not touched," Mrs. Trollope was alarmed because she had seen such confident medical judgments proven wrong before. She set to work at once to make the stay as happy as possible, knowing that Cecilia's separation from her family surely "preyed on her mind," even though her daughter never complained about the absence of "her beloved husband and children."[16] When doctors suggested that even the Florentine winter would be too severe, Mrs. Trollope dutifully took an apartment in Rome. Cecilia's recovery seemed increasingly doubtful.

Other changes loomed before her. Tom, her companion and friend of a lifetime, had expressed his intention to marry Theodosia Garrow, an intelligent and cultured girl and a friend of the Brownings. It was a step of which Mrs. Trollope heartily approved, and she generously offered the young people a home "as long as she should live," for the violent objections and "terrible scenes" of Theo's father had soured the prospective union. In Mr. Garrow's view, Tom possessed nothing more than "the prospect of a strictly bread-and-cheese competency at the death of my mother, and 'the farm which I carried under my hat,' as somebody calls it." As Tom recalled later:

The marriage was not made with the full approbation of my father-in-law; but entirely in accordance with the wishes of my mother, who simply, dear soul, saw in it, what she said, that 'Theo' was, of all the girls she knew, the one she should best like as a daughter-in-law.[17]

During the mild Roman winter, Cecilia remained "much the same," looking "very well, but . . . very weak," but the doctors hoped "that the warm weather will make a very favorable difference." Even while caring for her daughter, the novel writing went on apace: as 1848 opened, Harriet Garnett advised Julia to "read Mrs. Trollope's last novel—*Town and Country*—it is extremely pretty, and very liberal." Mrs. Trollope complained to Tom, "If I had paper, I would forthwith begin [another novel]. . . . but here the paper is a baiocco per sheet and is moreover most abominably bad." The task of writing seemed necessary to her peace of mind and inner well-being. If she was to remain strong for what she feared lay ahead, she could not let go.[18]

She did not forget Tom's troubles, sending her love frequently to "dear Theo," and once asking for "a copy of her lines on the Coliseum." She even succeeded in persuading Mr. Garrow to let Theodosia join Mrs. Trollope and Cecilia in Rome, where a deep affection grew between the two young women. An old family friend visiting Rome described her encounters with the party.

I delighted in Rome—and all the interesting antiquities. My first drive was to the Coliseum where the Pope happened to drive also. Mrs. Trollope and I were presented together and her, I suppose by this time, daughter-in-law. Her Tom was engaged to Miss Garrow—a very clever and agreeable person. Poor Mrs. Tilley I think very delicate.

And indeed, by the time Julia Pertz received this letter, Tom Trollope was a married man. The ceremony took place on 3 April 1848 in the British minister's chapel at Florence.[19] The Garnetts could not hide their surprise at the news.

Miss Garrow has no fortune at present, but is an only child, and will have something at her parents' death. She will be able also to make money as an author, and has already published several poems successfully. The marriage is a very good one for Tom, and I am pleased at the great pleasure it gives his mother. He will I am sure make an excellent husband, for he has been and is a most devoted son. He has been in the best society at Florence, and his manners are much improved,—still I wonder that so distinguished a girl as Theodosia Garrow, who is just 29, should have taken a fancy to him. I think the mother must be as great an attraction as the son, and to live with her may be a great inducement in the young lady's mind.[20]

Never one of Tom's admirers, Harriet found it difficult to account for his marriage in any other terms. It is a delightful and amusing tribute to Harriet's unbounded admiration for her old friend.

Now all Mrs. Trollope's surviving children were married and established. But Cecilia was failing fast. In 1848 all attempts to effect a cure in Italy were given up; on the first day of May, Cecilia started for England alone. The Garnetts, living at Brighton near the family of Mrs. Trollope's brother, heard the news of her return. She was

> so weak that she is carried from her bed to a sofa. Chambers who saw her said her case was hopeless. She was to set out Friday for a sheltered sea coast in Lancashire, Lytham, where she would find her children. Her husband met her in London, and had the sad task of telling her that her eldest child Fanny is said by the medical men to be in a deep decline,—she had been confined to one room the whole winter, and like her mother, grows every day weaker. Cecilia bore this calamity with great fortitude, and is quite aware of her own danger, and composed. How hard to leave a husband she is devotedly attached to, and four young children, without counting her poor little Fanny, who will perhaps go before her. She did not know what her mother would do for the summer, and Mrs. Trollope is quite unconscious of Cecilia's danger, and Mrs. Milton says she cannot last long as every day she grows visibly weaker. . . . My heart bleeds for them all.[21]

Cecilia accepted the inevitable, composed herself, and directed her husband to write her mother the truth about her condition. That July, one of the doctors prescribed a remedy that produced a temporary relief, but Cecilia herself was not deceived.

> She does not share these hopes, and says she regrets the amelioration because the pain will be greater to her friends at her death. She has prepared her husband herself for this event, and behaves with the noblest fortitude and resignation—expressing no pang at all she quits,—yet no woman ever loved a husband and children more fervently than she does. Mr. Tilley had written to Mrs. Trollope that if she wished to see Cecilia again she must come immediately to England.

Following her temporary improvement, the doctors had pronounced Cecilia's case "less serious than was supposed"; Harriet remarked, "How little medical men seem to know of complaints! The two most eminent ones declared she had but a few days to live on her return from Italy."[22] Buoyed by these hopes, the old mother decided to remain in Italy for the winter. Then, in February, the picture again changed. Anthony rushed to Kensington from Ireland to see his dying sister, and the Garnetts were sure that Mrs. Trollope would be "much shocked" by Cecilia's condition. "What a blow for her," wrote Harriet, for Mrs. Trollope "was not at all aware of Cecilia's danger," and in her advanced age could hardly be expected to brave the tumultuous revolutions that paralyzed Europe for a trip to see her dying daughter.[23]

But Mrs. Trollope had already set out from Italy, on the long and solitary journey, truly "a dismal trial to my strength of all kinds." She arrived on 10 March, exhausted but grateful to find she had not been too late, writing Tom of "the unspeakable consolation of finding my darling Cecilia had again rallied." She prepared for her fourth and last deathbed vigil, marked as were the others, by tireless nursing, watching, and the ever alloted number of daily pages. At seventy, this ordeal would be the most difficult of all. Cecilia was able to converse with her mother and welcome her, "as if in perfect health." Yet no deceptions were practiced on the old lady, and she was immediately told, "there is *no* hope!" Yet even while this "dreadful sentence" was pronounced with conviction, she told Tom "there are moments when it is difficult to believe."[24]

As Cecilia lay on her early deathbed, her children cared for by friends and relatives, her grief-stricken husband anxiously watching, the anguished old mother waited too, even while she sought again to find the circumstances to continue her ritual of writing. She worried lest the upset household prevent her from continuing her regular and stringent schedule. She told Tom:

The difficulty of finding a quiet half-hour here to write, is incredibly great. Sometimes I feel in absolute despair on the subject. John Tilley is *very* kind, but he has no power to help it. Cecilia sleeps in the back drawing-room, and has the doors open day and night into the other, so I cannot work there. At night (the only quiet time), although I am sorely tired, I *would* try, had I fire. But this I cannot have, because the fire in my room is laid for the morning, which is the only moment I can command.

In the midst of things, she even received Colburn, who, although civil, reminded her that she "was a little behind [her] time." Twice he muttered that he was ready to make another engagement upon the same terms, and she promised to talk about it when she was finished with the work at hand. She fretted: "But when will this be? To write more than a page at a time, is pretty nearly impossible. And even so, I scarcely know what I am writing."[25]

In April, Cecilia worsened. John Tilley tried to take care that Mrs. Trollope would not be disturbed at night, but often he did not lie down at all, and she only for an hour or two. By day, Cecilia's state required "constant, unremitting watchfulness." Mrs. Trollope found her daughter's "patience, her trusting confidence in the fate that awaits her, and her tender thoughtfulness for every one . . . more beautiful and more touching" than she could describe. She was eager to hear news from Tom and Theodosia, needing "some gilding over the future" to "bear the heavy sorrows of the present." She told Theo, "It is the saddest scene that ever mother watched."

> Her poor dear devoted husband never leaves her side when not forced away by official duty. It is piteous to watch him hanging over her. Little Fanny is getting better, I hope. The other poor unconscious little things seem well. The boy is enchanting.[26]

On 10 April, Cecilia died. Mrs. Trollope told Tom, "the last month has been the most suffering period of my existence." The blows were falling in rapid succession, for she also heard that her brother Henry was seriously ill. She told Rose Trollope, "I have indeed suffered more than I can express, more even than I expected."[27]

With determination, she set about interesting herself in the living, especially Rose and Theo, "the only daughters now left me." She wrote Rose of her gratitude that Anthony had arrived in time to see his sister once more:

> Sad as the scene was, I almost wish you could have witnessed her departure. She was like an angel falling asleep in happy certainty of awakening in Heaven. I am very *very* glad my dear Anthony saw her on her death bed—The impression left on his mind, however painful at the moment of receiving it, will remain with him for-ever, more as consolation, than sorrow.

Her major concern, however, was the remaining Tilley children. When Anthony and Rose took little Edith to live with them, Mrs. Trollope was particularly appreciative: "God bless you for all your kindness to her, my dear daughter! We shall none of us ever forget it."[28] She and John Tilley engaged a day governess for the other children, thus leaving the family's evenings "free from the annoyance of a stranger, whom one would wish to make comfortable, without exactly knowing how to set about it." Only after seeing to these arrangements did Mrs. Trollope visit the Garnetts, who had recently lost their mother. The old friends anxiously desired a reunion before Mrs. Trollope returned to Italy, and she told Tom that the change of air and scene would do her good. "I would willingly make my absence longer, were it not that I do not like to leave my dear good son-in-law alone." As always, she refused to concede defeat.

By degrees, I dare say, we shall emerge from the deep seclusion in which I
have, of necessity, been living for the last nine or ten weeks. . . . Yes,
dear Tom, I love to look forward *still*. And hitherto the habit of doing so
has not often led to disappointment.[29]

After a week with the Garnetts, she felt "greatly, *wonderfully* better."
To her own surprise, she began to eat again. She took hope that little
Fanny Tilley could be saved, even while she could not deny "that the
chances are against us." That summer Harriet reported, "There can be
no hope for little Fanny Tilley,—poor child she is evidently in a decline,
but is gay and happy—so like her mother." While Mrs. Trollope had
been away, another blow fell. In May, the first of the little grandchildren
died, the only son, Arthur. He had been "the most interesting of the
children," as Harriet told Julia:

Mrs. Trollope doted on him and will be very sorry. Poor child!—he was
doomed from his birth, and so I fear are the two that remain,—of Fanny
there is not a shadow of hope, and Edith, who is in Ireland, and was born
when her mother was in a deep decline, cannot live I think. Anne it is
possible may be saved, for she is darker and more like the Tilley family.
Tilley will probably have another family to supply their loss. A man does
not grieve long for wife or children, yet no man ever loved a wife better
than he did Cecilia, and she was most tenderly attached to him. The
medical men who attended her all said they had never seen as fond and
devoted a husband.[30]

The Anthony Trollopes, fearing that these sad events might prove too
much for the old lady, invited her to visit them in Ireland, at Mallow.
There, Rose took her mother-in-law on walking tours in splendid Irish
scenery. Once again Mrs. Trollope was revived by her insatiable interest
in what she saw around her. Rose reported:

We took her to Killarney, with which she was enchanted. Lord Kenmare's
park especially delighted her. She walked through the gap of Dunlo as
easily as if she had been twenty-nine instead of sixty-nine! And was
delighted with young Spellan, the bugler. In the evening we had old
Spellan the piper introduced with his bagpipes into our sitting-room—at
first to her dismay. But soon tears were rolling down her cheeks from the
pathos of his music.

One day we put her on one of Bianconi's cars running to Glengariff, after
much protest on her part against the ramshackle looking machine.
Presently, however, after a few jerks, and a dozen 'Niver fear, yer honour!'
from Mick the driver, she almost persuaded herself that she would rather
travel through Ireland in that way than any other![31]

Afterwards, Mrs. Trollope left Ireland to visit her sister. Her channel crossing was "a nasty rolling passage," but she assured her "dear Rose" that she was "marvelously well." In spite of all she had suffered, her constitution and spirits seemed as strong as ever. Indeed, "her Irish excursion, and Anthony's wife and children" had been the elixir she needed.

> I most really and truly do feel thankful for the great enjoyment in all ways which this dear visit has given me—And as much as one may venture at my age to look forward to any thing, I shall indulge myself by looking forward to a repetition of it.

She never tired of travel or walks, and her letter to Rose closed in a characteristic manner. "The weather is bright—and the sea looks beautiful from [Mary's] windows . . . and so we are going to take a ramble."[32]

But further trials were in store. That autumn, little Frances Trollope Tilley, to the end "gay and happy," was dead. Even long after there had been no hope, the child, according to Harriet's report, sustained "very high spirits and enjoys life very much." Soon, the third grandchild Cecilia also died, and a few months later Henry Milton was gone. As Harriet remarked, "Poor Mrs. Trollope will feel this deeply, for she loved her brother very much."[33] These losses would finally sever Mrs. Trollope's ties with England and the past. To complete the rupture, John Tilley, looking about him to shore up the ruins of his household, was about to take another wife. He had made his wife a deathbed vow to marry her cousin. Harriet told Julia:

> Mr. Tilley would have been married by this time but for little Cecilia's death, but as soon as decency allows, he will marry Miss Partington, a friend and cousin of his late wife, who almost lived with them during her lifetime. Of course this will not render his house agreeable to Mrs. Trollope, and she will reside with Tom and his wife at Florence,—this I regret very much on our account,—her society was such a pleasure to us.[34]

Later, in 1852, when this second wife herself died, leaving a boy of three weeks old, Tilley hardly felt her loss, for he had never been an attentive husband to Marianne Partington:

> His love was buried with poor Cecilia, and Marianne, tho' an amiable was not an attractive woman, and he married her from devotion to his wife's wishes. He was so devoted to Cecilia during her long illness, never leaving

her for an hour that he could possibly help, feeding her and watching over her like a fond mother to a baby, that Marianne must have felt the difference, for she had lived much with them.

In the midst of these trials, Mrs. Trollope continued her writing, in order to complete the two novels she had promised to Colburn for 1850. In July she delivered the manuscript of *The Old World and the New*, written during these psychologically exhausting losses. At the very least, the book is a testimony to her powers of concentration and recuperation.[35]

In terms of plot, it was her most extraordinary melodrama, requiring of its readers more than the usual willing suspension of disbelief. An English family, forced by financial problems, emigrates to America and settles in Mrs. Trollope's old haunt, the Cincinnati area of Ohio, where despite many obstacles, they build a fine house and create a new way of life. In this familiar retelling of the confrontation of two cultures, Mrs. Trollope again introduced her familiar prejudices—spitting, the nasal twang of American speech, judges who believe slavery is the only refined way of life, evangelical preachers, and the pretentiousness of American art, illustrated by the *Monongeheliad*, widely hailed as "the most remarkable poem in the language" (2:284). But her satire is blunt-edged when compared to that of *Domestic Manners*, and for the first time Mrs. Trollope implies that in time the United States will "catch up" with Europe. Thus this set of English travelers decide to stay in the end. Mrs. Trollope's farewell to the country whence sprang her fame was beneficent and mild.

Almost simultaneously, she completed her second novel of the year, *Petticoat Government*, a romantic story indistinguishable from her numerous efforts to rule the circulating libraries.[36] Upon her return to Italy, she stayed at Pau, awaiting the result of Tom and Theo's house-hunting in Florence. Now, as she mulled over her life, her recent and terrible losses, and the future that lay before her, new conceptions revolved in her fertile imagination. She was entering her seventies. Stripped of close family, her beloved daughter and most of the Tilley grandchildren dead, her two surviving sons married, she created still another innovation, her last: a curious series of novels unabashedly glorifying independent strong women. From the vicarage at Heckfield, through the wilds of the American Midwest, to the luxury of the Florentine villa to which she would soon proceed, Mrs. Trollope knew that she had "made it" on her own, and in these last works, in a disguised and fanciful autobiography, she celebrated herself and sang the story of her own courageous soul: the triumphant feminine.

15

The Triumphant Feminine

*I have always thought and felt that I was not quite
an ordinary character.*

IN MARCH 1850 Tom and Theo bought a house in Florence at the
northwestern angle of the Piazza della Indipendenza and christened it
the Villino Trollope. That May, when preparations were complete,
Mrs.Trollope joined them. There, she completed her last series of
novels, centering upon a group of heroines whose most obvious quality
was their sturdy, even aggressive independence and whose most
frequent trial was confronting tyrannical fathers or coping with
marriages to weak or evil men. From the comical widow Barnaby
through the desperate fortune hunters of the forties, she had focused
on the position of women. But these latter-day heroines, unlike her
humorous or peripheral portrayals of triumphant women, emerged
victorious in ways strikingly disregardful of the proprieties and goals
around which most Victorian ladies shaped their lives.

While *Second Love* (1851), like most other novels of its kind and
period, concludes with a happy marriage, the bulk of its three volumes
concerns the trials attendant upon three unhappy unions.[1] One takes
place between a clever woman and a man neither her intellectual nor her
moral equal. She, "the sworn-to-be-obedient wife of a man who often
required the practice of such a faculty in his helpmate," learned soon to
keep "the spirit of truth, which was an essential part of her
nature . . . as carefully concealed in her breast, as an incendiary keeps
his dark lantern in his bosom" (1:134). Another of the book's marriages is
undertaken out of pity, and the last is a loveless match between a young
woman and an elderly man. Throughout, the ladies are strong and
dominant, their men stupid pawns. Release comes not because of female
submission or patient resignation to a malicious fate; indeed, Mrs.
Trollope frquently intrudes upon her story to criticize the notion of
passive obedience by wives or daughters. Ultimately, those who
preserve inner integrity, struggling actively against bad situations, are
rewarded by the death or disappearances of their respective spouses.

240

Mrs. Trollope's next novel explored the consequences of feminine obedience in some detail, and its plot perfectly exemplified her theme of the triumphant feminine.[2] *Mrs. Mathews* (1851) is the story of a woman who leads a happy single life, even as she passes "the extremest limit of young-maidenism." Later, she confides to her diary that a woman's "very highest prime and vigor of existence" comes only after the age of thirty. "No female reaches her period of greatest power till she has passed her girlish bloom" (1:1 ff.). Even as two more decades pass, Mary King has no desire to marry and exults in her maturity. Here is certainly a new subject for a novel, but alas, given the prejudices of the time, single happiness cannot last.

When she turns fifty, her old father wonders "what would become of her and her money, when she should no longer have any man belonging to her." He is "strongly convinced that men, and not women, should have the management of money." Mrs. Trollope, who had so admirably administered the financial affairs of her family ever since the collapse at Harrow, depicted this anxiety as an amusing if dangerous masculine prejudice, for "it might have been difficult to find any individual of any sex, or of any age, or in any situation of life, more perfectly capable of taking efficient care of their own concerns than was Mary King" (1:21). Her father's arguments are a curious if touching example of what has subsequently been identified as male chauvinism.

> You will want a husband to look after your concerns, Mary. . . . Who will be able and proper to sign the receipts for rent? Who will write to order in wine? Who will say when the drains of the home pastures ought to be looked to?—And oh Mary! Mary! Who will sit at the side of the fire with you through the long winter evenings? Indeed, indeed you will break my heart, my dear child, if you go on to the last saying that you will not be married. [1:37–38]

To meet the wishes of her dying father, Mary agrees to wed his old friend and confidant, Mr. Mathews, but she is undeceived about future prospects.

> She saw her position exactly as it was,—and, such as it was, she did not like it. She did not like the idea of belonging to any man;—though, to say the truth, Mr. Mathews was very little, if at all, disagreeable to her, in the character of an owner and master, than any other man would have been. [1:46]

She consents only on terms that insure complete independence. Accepting his bride's claim that she could not be "passively obedient to anyone," Mr. Mathews grants her a separate allowance of £500 a year and the right to dispose of her own property. She also insists upon the privacy of a section of the house for her own use, a practice Mrs. Trollope advocated for all her female readers:

> I would strongly recommend to any of my fair readers, about to enter the holy state of matrimony, that they should at first setting off act upon the same principle that Mrs. Mathews did; namely, that they should begin as they intend to go on. Had she not done this she might have found it very difficult at a later period to have established such a system of liberty as to the disposal of her own time as she subsequently enjoyed. . . . [1:114–15]

But after her father's death, Mr. Mathews is transformed. Belligerently calling himself "master of the house," he takes over its management. He consorts with vulgar people, forgers and criminals, but through a singular series of complicated events, Mrs. Mathews finally prevails and saves her independence. Mr. Mathews even makes a new will, returning everything to his wife, after which he conveniently dies. This facile resolution does not detract from the serious subject matter of this astonishing fable, illustrating the power of independent women if they would but perceive it. The tough Mary King Mathews conquers singlehandedly. The single mistake of her life had been capitulation to her father's wishes, and the moral came clearly through to Mrs. Trollope's readers. Could she have imagined a more revolutionary story for 1851, the year of the Great Exhibition, with its emphasis on female domesticity?

In the following year, Mrs. Trollope published *Uncle Walter* (1852), an unusual assault on the polite conventions of society, particularly those surrounding the rites of marriage.[3] The unusual man of the title is in his seventies and returns to England after years in the Australian backwoods, provokingly ignorant of the way marriages are made "nowadays." Her heroine is a young girl with independent ideas, who even before the appearance of her Uncle Walter has separated herself from the life of her family, in that "room of one's own" which ladies of a later period found so indispensable. She reads Ruskin's *Seven Lamps* and Froude's *Nemesis of Faith*; no sweet young thing is Kate. At dinner, she holds her own in lively theological discussions and debates on the morality of good architecture. She immediately takes a liking to her big, bluff uncle, and mutual sympathy emerges when he learns that Kate's parents are determined to marry her off to a naive, awkward, but rich young lord, in no way a proper companion or her intellectual equal. The two conspire to achieve her union with a penniless but more intelligent and worthy man.

The book contains a number of humorous scenes involving the ritual of arranging marriages and Mrs. Trollope's most outrageous fortune hunter, the enterprising Mrs. Fitzjames, who pursues her game undaunted by the unfortunate accident of being already married. After a series of complications, including the appearance of the suitor's disreputable identical twin about whom, it seems no one has ever heard, entailing a confusion conveniently carrying the reader into the third volume, Uncle Walter emerges as the fairy godfather, settling all his money on his brother's children, provided her parents permit Kate to select the husband of her choice.

In addition to the story of a woman's search for independence amid restricting social conventions, the novel presents Mrs. Trollope's most interesting dissection of the method by which people hide their base motives and sordid compromises: the elevated rhetoric of polite society. Here, she framed a conclusion toward which she had long been working: polite language is the facade erected by a selfish and insincere world. The "decency" she had so often been charged as offending was in fact the most hypocritical word of all:

> The key to this language is simply putting words indicative of the generous, the noble, and the great, in order to express thoughts shabby, dirty, and little. It is a figure of speech which furnishes immense resources; and it may also be said, that in the present state of society, *decency* could scarcely exist without it. [1:133]

The central issue of the book focuses on the family's insistence that financial considerations dominate the selection of a proper husband for Kate. Only Uncle Walter—who has lived away from society for so long—is bewildered and asks Kate's brother for clarification:

> "Am I to understand then, Henry, that you too are of opinion that it is the wish of your father and mother to coerce the affections of their daughter, in order to give them an opportunity of selling her?" "My dear uncle! what very shocking words you use," cried the young cynic. "I declare," he continued, affectedly casting down his handsome eyes, "that it seems to me to be positively indecent to speak of such things. There is no refinement, no delicacy in your language, Uncle Walter, so that it is almost unintelligible to polite organizations." [1:303-4]

Society, Henry insists, does not impose conditions, it only educates men and women to accept them:

You are doing our social system an injustice. My sister Kate's education may have been somewhat neglected in this respect, but as a general rule, I must protest that the young ladies intended for the market, are carefully and admirably trained to prepare them for it. I can assure you, uncle, that our practice in that respect puts the method of the Constantinople dealers to shame. There the fair ones, we are told, do shrink painfully from the exhibition made of them, and evidently dislike the *trotting out*. But with the superior methods of training for our market, the pretty creatures are fully as anxious for the sale, as the seller. [1:305]

When Uncle Walter inquires whether the lady's affections should play any part, his nephew dismisses this "very dangerous doctrine." As the discussion intensifies, the characters gradually strip their language of subterfuge. For Walter, such a view of marriage is indistinguishable from prostitution. He wonders

that the same society which thinks no language strong enough to upbraid the degraded creature who sells herself, when the price paid is to save her from starvation, should smile upon and approve the very same act, when not the necessaries, but the luxuries of life are the legalized payment? [1:310]

Walter's frankness prompts a reply in kind, bringing Mrs. Trollope back to the theme of her first literary effort, a clumsy poem to Almighty Cant, the goddess of the contemporary world. Now thirty-five years later, she completed her analysis of the linguistic pillars of polite society, as Henry replies:

You appear to me to be altogether incapable of appreciating the enormous value of cant. It is quite a vulgar error to suppose that the principal or most valuable effect of cant is to deceive others. This is very far from being the case. Those born and bred under its influence, not only speak, but think cant; and it is quite certain that they must do so in order to speak it well. It is like a foreign language. To speak French well, you must think in French. In fact, it is this alone that makes our actual system of society possible. All crooked paths are made to look straight, and the rough places not only plain, but very particularly smooth. By the aid of its omnipotent eloquence, all the infamies committed among us are concealed even from the actors in them; and if the said actors do not appear absolutely holy, they at all events appear perfectly decent. Trust me, Uncle Walter, you will be held as an unwelcome intruder into this part of the terraqueous globe, if you persist in rudely tearing down the delicate and graceful veil which cant throws over us. Respectable people will, for the most part, be quite ready to declare that your language is that of a very dangerous libertine. [1:310-11]

Over her long writing life, Mrs. Trollope seemed to many "an unwelcome intruder," and "respectable people," while they no longer considered her a "dangerous libertine," continued to characterize her books as coarse and vulgar.

One reviewer of *Uncle Walter,* while admitting that "Mrs. Trollope could not . . . write a dull story if she were to try," found fault with its severity. *John Bull* noted a predominance of mercenary or hypocritical characters and complained that "a future historian of England might fairly conclude that in the first half of the nineteenth-century all the mothers of England were hireling matchmakers, and all her Clergy hunters after place, money, and popularity, mere worldings and profligates." The *Literary Gazette* thought the novel was written "with more than her usual coarseness and bad taste." The *Athenaeum* agreed, protesting against this depiction of still another "and probably the coarsest— of Mrs. Trollope's coarse, unscrupulous, scheming widows."[4]

By the standards of its time, there were grounds for calling *Uncle Walter* coarse. It contained her most unprincipled fortune hunter, a woman considerably "deteriorated in character" from the constant need to use her charms to remain financially solvent. The *Athenaeum* asked openly:

> Now we put it to Mrs. Trollope whether such are the fitting materials and the fitting *dramatis personae* to be offered as the elements of light fiction, under the guarantee of a lady's penmanship, for the entertainment of her sex.

Compelled to include lengthy and representative passages in this review, this critic proceeded to excerpt one of the fortune hunter's amorous adventures, while politely apologizing to the "lady readers," whom he confidently hopes would "make no further acquaintance with Mrs. Fitzjames and her doings than they may derive from our columns." The reviewer concluded by finding Mrs. Trollope's coarseness all-pervasive and exceedingly repetitive.

> The whole thing is very dreary:—and 'Uncle Walter' reads like a disagreeable recollection of 'Widow Barnaby' with scraps of the 'Vicar of Wrexhill' scattered throughout it. *Toujours perdrix* will tire any appetite; and 'Barnaby' roasted as a 'widow'—*fricassed* as 'Widow Married'—and then hashed as 'Barnaby in America'— will scarcely tickle the palate when her bones are 'deviled' (in every sense) as Mrs. General Fitzjames.

In her old age, Mrs. Trollope had not lost one whit of her tendency to

shock and offend critics who still attempted to preserve the "fairyland of
fiction" from the harsh truths of the contemporary world.

But she had not used coarse language; she did not enjoy the company
of vulgar people, and she did not glorify baseness in speech or action.
Her goal was always that men, and latterly women, should perceive the
cant that deprived their lives of true nobility. Her life's ambition was
precisely that which her heroine Kate attains in this novel. Helped by
Uncle Walter, she learns "to know real right from real wrong more
clearly than I ever did before."

Mrs. Trollope's next novel, *The Young Heiress* (1853), is an
improbable melodrama with a shocking plot. Her heroine has lived
many years as the mistress of a turbulent, Rochester-like character, who
treats her badly. She bears him a son, whom he rears with his legitimate
daughter, but when he decides to remarry, he roughly and crudely tells
his mistress that their love-making days are over although she may stay
on as his servant. Meekly she accepts, while secretly vowing revenge.
Eventually, she poisons her erstwhile lover, and after three adventure-
packed volumes, secures the family money for her son, who has
meanwhile distinguished himself in India. Leaving a written confession
to her crime, for which her son had become the primary suspect, Sarah
dies, but her son can now return to England and claim bride and fortune.
While the novel's pattern resembles the other productions of Mrs.
Trollope's last period in featuring a dominant female character, it is a
distinctly inferior book as a whole.[5]

The following year, she completed a work whose provocative title
clearly indicates its focus: *The Life and Adventures of a Clever Woman*
(1854).[6] Charlotte Morris is Mrs. Trollope's most indomitable heroine, a
motherless seventeen year old, who soon outgrows her governesses.
Thereupon, her wealthy, indulgent father takes a London apartment so
that both can see the social world. Charlotte begins a daily journal, in
whose pages she promises to tell her "follies and blunders," as well as her
"most flattering triumphs." Although "not, perhaps, absolutely beautiful," she is handsome and well-dressed enough to make her own way.
Marriage may become necessary, but her ultimate goal is more
grandiose: "If I can manage to get myself recognised as the possessor of
fortune, fashion, and talent, I shall be perfectly satisfied with my lot"
(1:99). She strives to become "a conspicuous and admired leader in
society" (1:190). Like her creator, she is "strong enough to bear a good
deal of fatigue. . . . No woman, I conceive, could ever succeed in
attaining to the position to which I aspire, were her constitution, either of
mind or body, weak" (1:220).

Nevertheless, she subsequently becomes Mrs. Cornelius Folkstone, but only in response to the realities of life for women. Had she not married, she writes in her journal

> my brilliant position in society would have been speedily converted, in the eyes of the world, into that of a disappointed old maid. This would have impeded, not to say destroyed, my still upward progress in society. I knew this, and I determined upon becoming a wife instead of an old maid, with the same decision of purpose which I have manifested upon every other occasion. [2:190]

Detached and logical, she remains undeceived about her motives and pretends to feel neither love nor respect for the man upon whom she eventually settles.

From the day of her marriage, however, her history proceeds toward catastrophe. Her husband soon reveals the typical male conceptions of his time, flattering himself

> that he knew the world and "the sex" too well, for any danger to exist that property settled on a wife could fail, in one way or another, to become the property of her husband. He had made himself familiar, in theory at least, both with kissing and cuffing, and no man could have a more implicit confidence in any law, than he had in that which says, "What belongs to my wife, is mine; what belongs to me, is my own." [3:127]

But Mrs. Trollope's tale shows that such methods fail with a truly "clever" woman. Charlotte is undeceived by her husband's romantic approaches.

> Idiot! Did he really believe that I could be taken in by his precious mixture of kisses and coaxing? Did he really think that I would welcome his enchanting caresses one moment, and borrow a little money from my father for him the next? Let him go on—I am quite ready for him. . . . I have always thought and felt, that I was not quite an ordinary character. [3:228]

Realizing that a power struggle is underway, she revels in her superiority, even anticipating the conflict with "something very like pleasure."

> Most women, I believe, having discovered with a certainty, beyond the reach of any reasonable doubt, that they had married a lowminded, money-seeking villain, stead of a gentleman, would feel broken-hearted, broken-spirited, and altogether blighted, and wretched for life. But how different is my condition. . . . This precious husband of mine has sold

himself for the shadow of wealth, of which he will never, never, never touch the reality. . . . Poor man! He has met with one too powerful both in mind and position for him to cope with! Perhaps when he is fully aware of this, he may grow humble. [3:228 ff.]

Finally, Mr. Folkstone tries force. It was time, he thought

to throw off the troublesome mask of civility which he had hitherto worn, and tell her in plain English that, as long as he lived, her settlement was a farce, for that there was no law, nor gospel either, which could prevent his locking her up, and keeping her upon bread and water till she obeyed his commands. [3:244]

When she resolves to leave him, he overcomes her physically and locks her up. Until she capitulates, she will remain his prisoner. Throughout her ordeal, Charlotte bears up remarkably well, regretting only "that she could not record it in her journal" (3:278). Eventually help arrives, and in the end Folkstone conveniently dies. Subsequently, Charlotte spurns two offers of marriage and continues in that state of blessed singleness with which her admiring creator had rewarded her. She records her struggle for "maisterye" and triumph in her journal:

It is so common to hear of the tyranny of fathers and husbands! And yet it seems to me as certain as that the sun is in Heaven, that fathers, and husbands too, may be managed with the greatest ease, if women would but set their wits a little more steadily to work upon the business. My own case seems to me to furnish a very fair specimen of what may be done by a little forethought and good management. [2:179]

Such had been Mrs. Trollope's message ever since she had angered the Americans when she told their women that should they "ever discover what their power might be, and compare it with what it is, much improvement might be hoped for."

Two more novels followed: *Gertrude* (1855), and *Fashionable Life in Paris and London* (1856). [7] In these Mrs. Trollope expanded her theme: once women had learned they need not live only for marriage, they could adapt to life quite successfully. The novels provide several ways. In *Gertrude*, a woman learns to live for her daughter and her library. In *Fashionable Life*, the heroine longs to do something in the world, and after traveling extensively, she decides to live in Paris and invites a female friend, who can bring rank and influence to the establishment, to join her. The author comments:

If all people set about carrying out their own arrangements, and their own intentions, in as business-like and rational a manner as did the female co-partnership I am describing, there would be much fewer disappointments in life. [1:242]

Eventually, two more women join the group, making the little society almost perfect, a female paradise. As a whole, however, the novel, like its predecessor, reveals a distinct decline. It is largely a pastiche of seances, mesmerism, Roman Catholic conversions, wicked guardians, and social class snobbery. After it was finished, Mrs. Trollope wrote no more.[8]

16

Endings

*I am in truth grown most woefully idle, and worse still,
most woefully lazy, and this symptom is both new and
disagreeable to me.*

MRS. TROLLOPE enjoyed her Florentine life immensely and settled into a
regular routine. In the autumn and winter she stayed in the Villino
Trollope, surrounding herself with parties and theatricals; once she
delighted her friends with a riotous portrayal of Mrs. Malaprop. She met
the Brownings, through their friendship with Theo, and proudly
watched as Tom steadily produced his volumes of Italian history: *The
Girlhood of Catharine de' Medici, The Life of Filippo Strozzi, Paul the
Pope and Paul the Friar,* and *A Decade of Italian Women.*[1] In addition,
he wrote a score of novels, mostly on Italian subjects. Moreover,
Anthony's novels regularly found their way to her reading table: *The
Kellys and the O'Kellys* (1848), *La Vendé* (1850), and *The Warden*
(1855). In 1856, *Barchester Towers* was complete. Whether or not by
May of 1857, when the latter was finally published, she was able to read
and appreciate this first great achievement of her youngest son is
unfortunately unclear. One hopes she was.

There were great picnics in these days, often in the park of the grand
duke. Mrs. Trollope also made the seven-mile climb to a magnificent
view of the Arno and joined in a three-day excursion to Vallombrosa. In
summer, she left the young people in Florence and traveled to the Baths
of Lucca, partly out of a desire for a cooler climate, partly to give the
couple some time to themselves. By the summer of 1852, the frail Theo
was pregnant.[2] Mrs. Trollope loved her house in Florence, "one pleasant
feature of which," she wrote, "is a large garden, where we literally sit
under the shade of our orange-trees," but even more the land itself held
her. As she told her old friend Mary Russell Mitford:

There is a most delicious sort of harmony in the whole landscape, which
enchants me beyond all I have ever looked upon; and this, as I take it, is
owing to the purity of the light, and the surpassing and intense blueness of
the sky. Our blue is not like your blue; it is deeply dark, though as clear as

250

limpid water. Claude, and Claude alone, gives some idea of this. . . . As to our scenery, Switzerland, Germany, ay, and England too, can often show *much* finer. But for the *effect*, and its power of bewitching the eye, it is magical!

The intrepid wanderer had finally come to rest. Miss Mitford congratulated her upon a well-earned happiness "domestic and social . . . and the blessings of bodily health and mental vigor" that she obviously still enjoyed. Mrs. Trollope was truly "the joy and ornament" of her large circle.[3]

Mrs. Trollope followed the revolutionary events that had so recently transpired in Italy, telling Harriet Garnett that "the rapid improvement of the people is inconceivable." A liberal herself, always at odds with her more conservative sister, Harriet was delighted to hear that Mrs. Trollope had reverted to her old opinions:

She writes with as much ardour on the subject as our warmest liberals could do,—and is in reality a good liberal herself. When I congratulated her on the change, she said, "I should be sorry to live and not be able to improve with the times. My eyes are now thank Heaven open."

Indeed, she had come full circle. During the revolutions of 1848, she read the poet Charles Mackay and was enchanted. Her favorite lines expressed the sentiments which had prompted her, long ago, to seek the new world of America:

> There's a good time coming, boys,
> A good time coming
> We may not live to see the day,
> But Earth will glisten in the ray
> Of the good time coming.[4]

When Anthony tried to interest her in meeting them at the Great Exhibition of 1851, she declined. She did not love such displays, claiming wryly that "she should be crushed in the crowd." In truth, she had no desire to return to England, and Harriet did not wonder "at her not liking to live in this dear, aristocratical, selfish land."[5]

In 1852, she received word that Julia Garnett Pertz was dead. Her husband wrote Mrs. Trollope:

You my dear friend who knew her so intimately and possessed her love and gratitude like very few, under whose hospitable roof our loving hearts were united to each other for ever, you feel what a blessed life has been mine, and you will feel my present bereavement.

The Pertz children were grown, and the lonely widower added:

> In my solitary hours I have been looking through letters and papers kept
> by my beloved Julia. Amongst them one has particularly touched me,
> where you write in May 1827 to Julia that her letter written about me
> showed that she loved me—the letter I carried to you from Paris. Now I
> should be very grateful to you my dear friend, if you would be so kind to
> communicate to me her letters kept by you, particularly that one; I should
> value them as most precious relics, since they are the genuine and beautiful
> expression of her pure elevated generous lovely being.

But alas, Mrs. Trollope could not comply:

> Some of my most cheerful and most happy hours have been passed in her
> dear society, and I shall remember her, and all her charming qualities till I
> cease to remember any thing. My wandering habits have been such, and,
> at the same time, my correspondence has been so large, that I many years
> ago came to the resolution of keeping *no letters whatever*—and this
> resolution I have adhered to so strictly that I have not a single letter in my
> possession, excepting one or two recent ones which are still unanswered.[6]

In 1853, Tom's child was born; they named her Bice, the Tuscan
nickname for Beatrice. That April, Anthony and Rose came to Florence
to see the new baby, and Rose again was favorably impressed by her
mother-in-law's hearty energies.

> She took me about everywhere, and explained everything to me. And she
> made me happy by a present of an Italian silk dress. She also gave me a
> Roman mosaic brooch, which had been a present to her from Princess
> Metternich during her stay in Vienna. It is a perfect gem.

Mrs. Trollope kept her own whist-table, and the dazzled Rose thought
her "the most charming old lady who ever existed." Her sturdy
independence made her original, and Rose could detect "nothing
conventional about her," while she hastened to explain that Mrs.
Trollope was

> perfectly free from the vice of affection; and was worlds asunder from the
> "New Woman" and the "Emancipated Female" School. I do not think she
> had a mean thought in her composition. She was lavishly generous as
> regards money; full of impulse, not free from prejudice—but more often
> in *favour* of people than otherwise,—but once in her good books, she was
> certain to be true to you. She could say a sarcastic word, but never an ill-
> natured one.[7]

Her novels continued to be popular, and some were reissued in cheaper editions. Mary Russell Mitford, herself not fond of "the present race of novel-writers," found her old friend's work interesting. "In spite of her terrible coarseness, [she] has certainly done two or three marvelously clever things." She was a "most elegant and agreeable woman," Miss Mitford reminisced. "I have known her these fifty years; she must be turned of seventy, and is wonderful for energy of mind and body."[8]

She continued to interest herself in her new granddaughter, whom she described to Anthony as "a species of prodigy."

> She wants three months of being two years old, and already contrives to talk fluently of most earthly affairs. Her musical propensities are, without joke, or exaggeration of any kind, really wonderful. Whatever tune she wishes her mother to play she *hums* with sufficient accuracy to make her wishes perfectly understood. No opera dancer ever danced more exquisitely in time and as to pictures of all kinds her comprehension, and the delight she receives from them is quite unlike any thing I ever saw in one so young. . . . *De plus* she really is very pretty.[9]

All the loving and spoiling she had hoped to end her days expending on the little Tilleys poured out now on Bice. She loved, too, to hear about Harry and Fred, Anthony's two boys, and when they were old enough, enjoyed receiving notes from them.

She began to take a disturbing interest in spiritualism, a fascination upon which Rose later blamed her serious decline in health. She had invited one practitioner of this mysterious art to the Villino Trollope in the winter of 1845, having found his conversation on the subject of spiritual visitations edifying. She was anxious to understand what she called the "semi-spiritual state," once explaining the reasons behind her stubborn faith in the occult:

> One gentleman in large practice told me that he had almost constantly perceived in the last stage of pulmonary consumption a manifest brightening of the intellect; and children at the moment of passing from this state to that which follows it will often (as I well know) speak with a degree of high intelligence that strongly suggests the idea that there are moments when the two conditions *touch*. That the region next above us is occupied by the souls of men about to be made perfect, I have not the shadow of a doubt. The puzzling part of the present question is this . . . why do we get a dark and uncertain peep *now* at a stage of existence from which philosophy has so long been excluded? And I am inclined to say in reply, 'be patient, and be watchful and we shall all know more anon.'[10]

Nearing the end of her long life, for the first time her thoughts turned backwards to dwell on those she had lost: Arthur, Henry, Emily, Thomas Anthony, Cecilia, the Tilley grandchildren. Her once bright and worldly intellect was shadowed by these preoccupations.

In 1885 she fulfilled an old plan, meeting Anthony and Rose at Venice. Afterwards, she returned with them to London, where she met and admired another famous medium, inviting him back to the Villino Trollope, whence transpired many more seances. In her last novel, she included several depictions of seances, mostly in a favorable light. In the summer following the publication of *Fashionable Life*, she seemed ready to stop, letting the literary flame pass to her youngest son, to whom she wrote:

> Age eighty (minus not quite three), Thermometor eighty (plus rather more than four) must be accepted as an excuse my very dear Anthony both by you and my highly valued new correspondent [her grandson] for not having acknowledged your very precious *packet* earlier. I am in truth grown most woefully idle, and worse still, most woefully *lazy*, and this symptom is both new and disagreeable to *me*. But the degree of activity of which I have been wont to boast, and on which I have so often been complimented might have been accounted in my very best days as positive *idleness* to what you manifest. Tom and I agree in thinking that you exceed in this respect any individual whom we have ever known or heard of—and I am proud of being your mother—as well for this reason as for sundry others. I rejoice to think that you have considerably more than the third of a century to gallop through yet before reaching the age at which I first felt inclined to cry halte la![11]

For Frances Trollope, suffering and decline were manifested in an inexplicable lethargy and a sudden loss of the resilient energy that had carried her through her long life and writing career. To her letter to Anthony, Tom appended a line: "My mother is pretty well, though weak, and it is impossible not to see that the last year has made a greater change in her than ever any one year did before. She does not suffer in any way but from inability to exert herself." It was to be her last trial, perhaps her most difficult of all. Her growing senility seemed a mystery to Tom: "Why did the mind perish before the body?" he asked himself. Always indefatigable both physically and mentally, Mrs. Trollope was finally tired.[12]

She wrote brief notes to Anthony's sons and was pleased to hear from little Harry that his "dear Papa and Mama had talked to you about me, and had made you understand, notwithstanding our being so far apart, that you had a grandmama, and you were right in thinking that it would give her great pleasure to receive a letter from you." She sent the boy a gold sovereign, admonishing him cautiously not to spend it all at once, "for that would be foolish, but to be ready upon any occasion when you might want to spend a little more money than usual." The last letter she ever wrote (unfortunately undated) is almost a fragment, whose brevity and halting awkwardness tell more than words can say that the marvellous pen would soon be completely still.

My darling Anthony:
You ask me to write—I and my pen have been so long divorced that I hardly know how to set about it—But you ask me to write and therefore write I will—though I have no news to tell you more fresh than that I love you dearly—I should like to see you again but can hardly hope it! God bless you my dear, dear Son! Your loving mother
Frances Trollope[13]

Her strong constitution preserved her seven more years until 6 October 1863, when she died peacefully at the age of eighty-four. She was buried in Florence, in "the beautiful little cemetery on which the Apennine looks down," by her beloved son and lifelong companion Thomas Adolphus, who had served her faithfully to the end. He fulfilled even his last promise to her—opening a vein in her arm after her death, for she had latterly entertained a curious dread of being buried alive. He composed the epitaph for her gravestone, a learned Latin farewell.

Franciscae Trollope
quod mortale fuit
Hic jacet
Divinae autem particulae aurae
Memoria nullum marmor quaerit
Apud Stapleton
In Agro Somerset, Anglorum
A.D. 1780 nata,
Florentiae
Tusculum A.D. 1863
nacta est.[14]

But Frances Eleanor Trollope's admiring biography of her mother-in-law contained a more appropriate epitaph, one which has greater meaning for all who quest with time on their hands and dissatisfaction in their hearts and confusion in their minds about "life styles" and "fulfillment." She wrote:

She was honest, courageous, industrious, generous, and affectionate;
. . . those qualities enabled her to surmount difficulties, to overcome

sorrow, to endure harsh judgments, and to inspire the faithfullest friendship and love.

That, I think, is the lesson of Frances Trollope's life.[15]

On her personal character, little more needs to be added. Her son Tom called her "the happiest-natured person I ever knew—happy in the intense power of enjoyment, happier still in the conscious exercise of the power of making others happy. . . ." Anthony spoke of "the mixture of joviality and industry which formed her character," finding in that curious combination her most distinctive quality. "Even when she was at work," he recalled, "the laughter of those she loved was a pleasure to her." Indeed, her sense of humor was exquisite, even while her powers of satire were devastating.

She loved people; all her life she surrounded herself with family and friends. But in the main, like so many other women of her time, the world of her closest intimates was primarily female. In youthful years she was close to her selfless spinster aunt, Fanny Bent, and the Winchester schoolmaster's daughter, Marianne Gabell. Later, in London, she entertained Mrs. Edwards the bookseller's widow and Mrs. Bartley the actress, who bestowed free tickets upon Mrs. Trollope and her family and spoke to the great John Murray on her behalf. Her Harrow friend Lady Dyer subsequently married a German nobleman, whose Bamberg castle was offered to Mrs. Trollope as a refuge from her various troubles. With some women, she shared her sorrows, anxieties, and joys, confident that they had experienced similar emotions. She corresponded with Madame Fauche, the consul's wife at Bruges, with whose marital difficulties she deeply sympathized. In America, she followed the tragic fortunes of Frances Wright's younger sister Camilla, and later, in Paris, briefly championed the cause of Rosina Bulwer. She was forever fascinated by Frances Wright. As a famous author, and even before, she was part of the supportive network of female literary friendships, primarily exemplified in her circle by Mary Russell Mitford and Letitia Landon. Abroad, she socialized with Lady Sevestre and Lady Normandy. Her other illustrious female friends included the Princess Melanie, Metternich's wife, Madame Récamier, and Madame de Chateaubriand.

Her emotional ties with two sisters were deep and lasting. She remained in close touch and correspondence with Harriet Garnett and Julia Garnett Pertz over a lifetime. These associations with literary, cultured, and intellectual women were an important part of her complex life. Their shared experiences and mutual affections helped shape her novelist's vision. To her female friends, Frances Trollope was unique and central. When she left England forever, the letters of Harriet Garnett continued to express deep regrets about the departure of this incomparable friend.[16]

To all her surviving children, she successfully proved mother, friend, and literary inspiration. Tom described his mother as the "inseparable companion of so many wanderings in so many lands," and Anthony stressed her perfect heart and complete "power of self-sacrifice." There are those who can make us conscious of what they are doing and suffering for us: of these, Mrs. Trollope was not one. When the family watched their mother toiling away at her novels, nursing the sick and dying, and managing during the hard times at Bruges, they sometimes felt a sense of helplessness and guilt, which her manner quickly dispelled. As Anthony wrote:

> Now and again there would arise a feeling that it was hard upon my mother that she should have to do so much for us, that we should be idle while she was forced to work so constantly; but we should probably have thought more of that had she not taken to work as though it were the recognised condition of life for an old lady of 55.[17]

Indeed, perhaps the most unique feature of her career is the age at which she began it. Her life offers, as Anthony noted, "great encouragement to those who have not begun early in life, but are still ambitious to do something before they depart hence." Mrs. Trollope accomplished a great deal, beginning in her fifth decade and leaving her mark on English literature. Her nature was a pioneering one, both in her life and in all her thirty-four novels and five travel books. In many areas of the evolving fictional art in the nineteenth century she was the first to tread, anticipating the achievements of other writers and by her experiments influencing them and the course of fiction across the century. Her novels were often, in one way or another, path-breaking, setting a tone of realism, satire, and social consciousness. She was among the first to explore contemporary social problems as subject matter for popular fiction, using American slavery, evangelical excesses, child labor, and the plight of the fallen woman in best-selling novels. Over the next hundred years such problems became the proper matter for fiction, and due respect must be paid to the woman who first braved critical wrath for her onslaughts upon "the fairyland of fiction." The taste of the age had settled it that the novel should elevate and purify: Mrs. Trollope showed that it could reflect, expose, sometimes castigate, with equally moral and beneficial effects.

She also deserves a place in the history of English literature for her achievement in writing perhaps the most popular and controversial book of travels ever to appear, *The Domestic Manners of the*

Americans. Finally, she invented and developed a new kind of heroine in an age where treatment of the female was uniformly genteel and delicate. Her ladies were strong, independent, ingenious, and "vulgar"; they prepared the way for more complex and balanced literary approaches to women, free from traditional stereotypes and taboos.

The critics often called her coarse and vulgar. Her daughter-in-law marvelled at her rough treatment at the hands of the critics:

> Those who demand for women's work a fair field and no favour—could certainly not have complained that Mrs. Trollope was treated with any contemptuous indulgence by reason of her sex. The critics, big and little, who disliked her writings, belaboured them as heartily as though she had been a man—perhaps even a little more heartily. . . . to a flattering point of ruthlessness.[18]

Nevertheless, she became one of the most popular authors of her day. Of that she was always proud. Whenever she endured attacks in the reviews, she often remarked, "It will only help the sales go on." Detachment and objectivity she had mastered under stern and difficult conditions. Her life was marked to the end by those qualities which she gave to many of her heroines: great strength, inner resourcefulness, a firm sense of independence, and great pride in her accomplishments as a woman.

Perhaps the best way to conclude an account of this life is to tell a tale of the good old times, before Mrs. Trollope's worst troubles had come upon her. In April 1832 *Domestic Manners* made her at once famous and solvent. With her newly earned gains, she sent her son Henry off on a geological and antiquarian jaunt to the southwest of England, visiting his Exeter cousins and wandering through Devon and Cornwall. He collected stones and specimens, climbed over rocks and caves, brandishing his hammer and pocketing "one half of Low Clifford's property." He told his "most venerable and much venerated she parent" of the beautiful natural sights he beheld. Once, catching a glimpse of the distant hills above Ottery, on which the sun was shining in striking contrast to the gloominess of the nearer range, he could not stifle a cry: "Oh mother, how I longed for you as I gazed on all that passed beneath my feet."

When he reached Buckfast Abbey, the finest old ruin in the western county, he went to see it but was told he could not without the permission of a Captain White, who resided on the spot. The dirty and dishevelled Henry sent in his name, begging admittance. At once, the gallant captain came out himself, and in Henry's words,

> Not only showed me the mines but asked me to dine, took me to his

dressing room where I washed and shaved and put on a coat and waistcoat of his.

Henry's explanation for this royal reception was both amusing and touching. "To your fame, oh illustrious mother, do I owe this honor—this dinner—not to mention ruins, tea, conversation, and cake."[19]

How she must have enjoyed that letter! She had never asked for fame, though she had won it. All she sought was that her talents and industry might sustain the needs of those who depended upon her strenuous efforts. Dinner, tea, conversation, and cake—all this and more, *she* had provided. More than any other woman of her time, she exemplified in her life and works the triumphant feminine.

Abbreviations Used in the Notes

AT	Anthony Trollope, *An Autobiography* (1883).
BrM	British Museum, the Bentley Papers.
FET	Frances Eleanor Trollope, *Frances Trollope: Her Life and Literary Work from George III to Victoria*, 2 vols. (1895).
FWC	Frances Wright Collection, letters owned by Dr. Cecilia Payne-Gaposchkin and currently housed in the Houghton Library, Harvard University.
GLC	Greater London Council, Muniments of Lord Northwick (Acc. 76).
GPC	Garnett-Pertz Collection, letters owned by Dr. Cecilia Payne-Gaposchkin and currently housed in the Houghton Library, Harvard University.
HSP	Historical Society of Pennsylvania.
JMA	John Murray Archives.
MRM	*The Friendships of Mary Russell Mitford as Recorded in Letters from Her Literary Correspondents*, edited by Alfred Guy L'Estrange, 2 vols. (1882).
Notebooks, IULL	Three notebooks of Frances Trollope, Indiana University, the Lilly Library.
NYPL	New York Public Library, the Henry W. and Albert A. Berg Collection, Astor, Lenox and Tilden Foundations.
NYPL-MS	New York Public Library, Manuscripts and Archives Division, Astor, Lenox and Tilden Foundations.
PCP	The Morris L. Parrish Collection, Princeton University Library.
TAT	Thomas Adolphus Trollope, *What I Remember* (1888).
TCP	The Robert H. Taylor Collection, Princeton University Library.
UCLA	University of California, Los Angeles, Dept. of Special Collections, Research Library, Collection 712: Trollope Family Papers.
UIU	University of Illinois, Urbana, manuscript material of Anthony Trollope and letters, journals, and other manuscripts of members of the Trollope family, Rare Book Room, University Library.

Notes

CHAPTER ONE

1. *Gentleman's Magazine*, February and March 1780, meteorological weather diary for previous year.

2. Information from Dr. G. V. Bennett, Librarian, New College, Oxford. The quotation is from Warden Sewall, who only occassionally added such personal notes to the official record. The second quotation is from Rosamund Bayne-Powell, *English Country Life in the 18th Century*, p. 85. Cf. Tindal Hart, *The Country Priest in English History*, and *The 18th Century Parson*, passim.

3. William Milton, *Documents and Facts relating to the original propositions and plans now carrying into effect for the . . . improvement and enlargement of the Port and Harbour of Bristol, stated in a letter to a friend*, London (1806); and William Milton, *Essay on the subject of converting the Port of Bristol into a Floating Harbour, addressed in the year 1791 to the Incorporated Society of Merchant Venturers of that City*, London (1812).

4. Thomas Adolphus Trollope, *What I Remember*, pp. 13–14 (hereafter cited as TAT). For the inventions, see *Gentleman's Magazine*, January 1814, p. 38; and May 1818, p. 406. For similar activities by country parsons, see Hart, *Country Priest*, p. 72.

5. According to records at Heckfield Vicarage, William Milton was in residence from September 1774 through September 1775, and again from October 1776 through September 1777. Thereafter, he was not present except for a rare visit until August 1801. A hired curate served in his place. Evidence compiled from the registers by Mrs. Isla Brownless, wife of the present vicar of Heckfield. From the nearest computation available (1838), it appears that with fees, the living was worth about £400 a year. It has been necessary to go into these details precisely because the modern biographers of Mrs. Trollope have invented fictional recreations and passed them off as factual accounts. The first offender was Eileen Bigland (*The Indomitable Mrs. Trollope*, 1954), whose book opens with a rhapsodic picture of Frances Milton's youth at Heckfield. The rest of the book is largely worthless, on a par with this distortion. Inexplicably, in a recent retelling of Mrs. Trollope's story (*The Life, Manners and Travels of Fanny Trollope: A Biography*, 1978), Johanna Johnston has outdone even Miss Bigland. Her book is flawed by fanciful conversations ("How is the bazaar?"), inaccurate information (Frances Wright's husband was never her assistant at New Harmony), misspellings (Madame Fauche becomes Mrs. Fanche), garbled sources and even incorrect titles of Mrs. Trollope's novels (*Blue Belles of England* in this account is transformed into a "Scottish Novel," and retitled after the popular song!). Mrs. Trollope has not been well served by her modern biographers.

6. For Henry Milton, See A. G. K. L'Estrange, *The Life of Mary Russell Mitford, Told by Herself in Letters to Her Friends*, 2:84; and Arthur Lucas, *John Lucas: Portrait Painter*, pp. 3, 62, and 109. Records of the marriage and baptisms come from registers in St. Augustine's, St. Michael's, and St. Thomas's Churches, Bristol.

7. Information from Mrs. Isla Brownless, wife of the present vicar of Heckfield.

8. Hart, *18th Century Parson*, p. 42. Cf. Bayne-Powell, *English Country Life*, p. 85.

9. Anthony Trollope, *An Autobiography*, p. 21 (hereafter cited as AT).

10. Mrs. Mitford to Mary Russell Mitford, 14 November 1802, in A. G. K. L'Estange, *The Friendships of Mary Russell Mitford as Recorded in Letters from Her Literary Correspondents*, pp. 8–9 (hereafted cited as MRM).

11. Mary Russell Mitford to Frances Trollope, 1 August 1852, Morris L. Parrish Collection, Princeton University Library (hereafter cited at PCP). This letter shows clearly that Frances Milton was not familiar with Heckfield or Swallowfield (Miss Mitford's village) until her father moved there permanently in 1802. The account in the beginning of the study by Lucy Poate Stebbins and Richard Poate Stebbins (*The Trollopes: The Chronicle of a Writing Family*) is pure fancy.

12. Frances Eleanor Trollope, *Frances Trollope: Her Life and Literary Work from George III to Victoria*, 1:10 (hereafter cited as FET).

13. See n. 1, chap. 2.

14. See TAT, p. 41; and AT, pp. 11–12. In 1808, Thomas Anthony seems to have been moderately rich in his own right. Two years earlier, he had inherited nearly £1,700 from his father and was in possession of property estimated to be worth £6,000, including certain freehold in Lincoln's Inn and leasehold on Keppel Street. Information from Last Will and Testament of the Reverend Anthony Trollope, Public Record Office (hereafter cited as PRO), Prob. 11/1453, and the marriage settlement, 23 May 1809, discussed below in n. 20.

15. These letters have a curious history, as Thomas Adolphus tells the story: "Some years ago, not many years I think after my mother's death, an anonymous stranger sent my brother Anthony a packet of old letters written by my mother to my father shortly before and shortly after their marriage. He never was able to ascertain who his benevolent correspondent was, nor how the papers in question came into his possession." TAT, p. 158. The letters are now in the Robert H. Taylor Collection at Princeton University Library (hereafter cited as TCP) and were used with the kind permission of Mr. Taylor.

16. Thomas Anthony Trollope to Frances Milton, 19 July, 23 September, and 2 October 1808, and her reply, 23 September 1808, TCP. Portions of some of these courtship letters have been printed in FET, and Michael Sadleir, *Trollope, A Commentary*.

17. Thomas Anthony Trollope to Frances Milton, 1 November 1808, TCP, and FET, 1:20.

18. Frances Milton to Thomas Anthony Trollope, 2 November 1808, TCP.

19. Frances Milton to Thomas Anthony Trollope, 2 and 6 December 1808, TCP.

20. Thomas Anthony Trollope to Frances Milton, 8 December 1808, and Frances Milton to Thomas Anthony Trollope, 9 December 1808, TCP. The issue of the marriage settlement was taken very seriously, especially because Thomas Anthony stood to inherit the rich estates of his uncle Adolphus Meetkerke. Thus, on 23 May 1809, Thomas Anthony Trollope settled £6,000 upon his wife, and in return she renounced all rights she might have in common law to real or personal property that her husband owned or might gain. Mr. Trollope raised this money by selling his freehold property in Lincoln's Inn and his leasehold on property in Kepel Street. The money raised was placed in trust with three trustees, Thomas Partington (apparently a brother or relative of the second Mrs. Milton), William Taunton (apparently a friend of Thomas Anthony Trollope) and Henry Milton, Frances's brother. Marriage Settlement, Gloucestershire Records Office, D34/9/94. In addition, Mr. Milton apparently made a settlement upon his daughter, but I have not been able to establish the amount. It must have been handsome, however, and was apparently equal to what he gave to his son on his marriage. The settlement is mentioned in William Milton's Last Will and Testament, Public Record Office, Prob. 11/1694/241–42.

21. Thomas Anthony Trollope to Frances Milton, 8 December 1808, and Frances Milton to Thomas Anthony Trollope, 9 December 1808, TCP. This issue becomes a standing joke with them. On 28 February 1809, Thomas Anthony wrote Frances Milton: "The success of the coach I now find is past all doubt, and the inhabitants of Reading begin to murmur & threaten to rise and pull the town about their ears or do some other loyal and patriotic act if the scheme be not immediately and generally adopted. I admire this zeal which must be attended with the best of consequences; except that I begin to think that your pin money will swell beyond all reasonable bounds—but this must be provided against with settlements. Otherwise it might really [be] mischievous." Frances Milton wrote Thomas Anthony on 1 March 1809: "I really think I must engage, if you behave well, to allow you a thousand a year or so, out of my coach-receipts. I know this is a trifling compared with what I shall receive, but then I think I shall be expected to drive a few patent coaches of my own and that you know will be expensive," TCP.

22. Thomas Anthony Trollope to Frances Milton, 5 December; Frances Milton to Thomas Anthony Trollope, 6 December; and Thomas Anthony Trollope to Frances Milton, 8 December 1808, TCP. The first letter is incorrectly marked "November."

23. Frances Milton to Thomas Anthony Trollope, 10 January 1809, TCP.

24. Frances Milton to Thomas Anthony Trollope, 26 February, and his reply, 28 February 1809, TCP.

25. Thomas Anthony Trollope to Frances Milton, n.d. [mid-February]; Frances Milton to Thomas Anthony Trollope, 26 February; Thomas Anthony Trollope to Frances Milton, 28 February; Frances Milton to Thomas Anthony Trollope, 16 March 1809, TCP.

26. Frances Milton to Thomas Anthony Trollope, 2 May, and his reply, 4 May 1809, TCP.

27. The first quotation is from Frances Milton to Thomas Anthony Trollope, 9 December 1809. The second is Thomas Anthony Trollope to Frances Milton, 4 March 1809, TCP. Waiting for a letter, Frances had complained: "Hope delayed maketh the heart sick," and Thomas Anthony Trollope thought she had stopped writing in retaliation. Frances Milton to Thomas Anthony Trollope, 26 February 1809, TCP.

28. Thomas Anthony Trollope to Frances Milton, 9 March; Frances Milton to Thomas Anthony Trollope, 9 March; Thomas Anthony Trollope to Frances Milton, 21 March, and her reply, 22 March 1809, TCP.

29. Frances Milton to Thomas Anthony Trollope, 9 April 1809, TCP.

30. Frances Milton to Thomas Anthony Trollope, 2 May, and his reply, 4 May 1809, TCP.

31. Frances Milton to Thomas Anthony Trollope, 7 May 1809, TCP.

32. Frances Milton to Thomas Anthony Trollope, 14 May 1809, TCP.

33. Thomas Anthony Trollope to Frances Milton, 11 May 1809, TCP. Sir John Trollope was the eldest brother of Thomas Anthony's father. The male line of this family died out in the twentieth century, and the title then passed to a grandson of Anthony Trollope and great-grandson of Thomas Anthony and Frances Trollope.

34. Thomas Anthony Trollope to Frances Milton, 15 May 1809, TCP.

35. Frances Milton to Thomas Anthony Trollope, 18 May 1809, TCP.

36. Frances to Thomas Anthony Trollope, 18 and 20 July 1809, TCP.

37. Thomas Anthony to Frances Trollope, 10 August 1810, TCP.

38. Frances to Thomas Anthony Trollope, 12 August 1810, TCP.

39. Because of inaccuracies in previous accounts, it may be helpful to include the full particulars known of these births. Thomas Adolphus was born on 29 April 1810 and

baptized on 19 December 1810; Henry was baptized on 11 November 1811; Arthur William was born on 31 August 1812 and baptized on 18 November 1812; Emily was apparently born on 8 December and died the next day. She was buried on 10 December 1813; Anthony was born on 24 April 1815 and baptized 18 May 1815. All of these births were in London, and the records are from the Bishop's Transcripts for St. George's Parish, Bloomsbury, currently housed in the County Record Office, London. Cecilia Frances was baptized on 19 February 1817; and the second Emily was baptized on 29 July 1818. These last two children were apparently born in Harrow, and the records are from the Bishop's Transcripts for the Parish of Harrow-on-the-Hill, currently housed in the Middlesex Records Office, London.

40. TAT, p. 3.

41. *Ibid.*, p. 7. For general information on life at Keppel Street, see *ibid.*, pp. 1–19.

42. *Ibid.*, p. 6. Fanny Bent was the daughter of Mary Gresley Milton's sister. Frances Trollope remained close to her cousin Fanny and her half-sister Mary all her life.

43. *Ibid.*, pp. 16, 18.

CHAPTER TWO

1. See Thomas Anthony Trollope to Frances Milton, 1 November 1808, TCP; and TAT, pp. 43–44. In the first decade of the century, less than 15 percent of the English families had an annual income of more than £50, and less than 3 percent earned more than £200 a year. See P. K. O'Brien, "British Incomes and Property in the early Nineteenth Century," *Economic History Review* 12 (1959): 267.

2. Anthony Trollope, *Orley Farm*, pp. 8–9. For Anthony's admission that he had modeled his fictional farm house upon his parents' house, see AT, p. 21.

3. Muniments of Lord Northwick, deposited in the Greater London Council (hereafter cited as GLC). The original agreement between Trollope and Lord Northwick is dated 13 October 1813 and is in a box of uncatalogued material. Information is also from survey and maps of 1806, ACC 643/2nd dep., and ACC 79/60. New indentures were drawn up in 1819 when the new house was built. See ACC 76/59 and ACC 76/620.

4. See Frances to Thomas Anthony Trollope, 12 August 1810, TCP; and TAT, pp. 7 ff.

5. There is uncertainty about the date of the move. Sadleir (*Trollope*) says 1816, and Thomas Adolphus (TAT, p. 40) says 1818, but in a letter to Anthony's son Henry late in 1886 (while writing his memoirs) Thomas Adolphus asked for help in fixing·the date, for he himself was not sure. See Thomas Adolphus Trollope to Henry Trollope, 13 December 1886, University of Illinois Library at Urbana, A 63767, "Anthony Trollope, manuscript material, also letters, journals, and other manuscripts of members of the Trollope family" (hereaftrer cited as UIU). The Poor Rate Books for Keppel Street show that Trollope's house was empty in 1815, and another occupant appears for 1816 through 1819. This information, coupled with Anthony's baptism in London in May 1815, supports the conclusion that the Trollopes probably moved to Harrow in 1815. The Poor Rate Books for St. George's, Bloomsbury, are currently located at the Holborn Library, London.

6. For the Meetkerke situation, see TAT, p. 44. The information that the idea originated with Lord Northwick is found in Thomas Anthony Trollope to Lord Northwick, 15 November 1833, GLC, ACC 76/2346. In the area south of his great park at Harrow-on-the-Hill, a number of splendid houses had recently been built. Trollope's mansion

would continue the semicircle formed by the Hermitage, the Butts, the Mount, and Sudbury House.

7. In the original agreement of 13 October 1813 (GLC, uncatalogued material), Lord Northwick suggested the £3,000 figure for the house. The agreed-upon reduction of £240 would cover a thirty-year mortgage at 5 percent—a common rate for the times. With this reduction, Trollope's annual rent for the farm was £420, which eventually rose to £447 once the new acres were secured for a proper garden and approach to the new house. Both of his sons, apparently, misunderstood the arrangements, for they criticized their father on this point. See AT, p. 6; and TAT, p. 43. Their story has been accepted by all commentators. See Sadleir, *Trollope*, p. 53 ff.; James Pope-Hennessy, *Anthony Trollope*, pp. 37–38; and Stebbins and Stebbins, *Trollopes*, p. 15. Indeed, the latter account places the blame inexplicably on Frances. Most recently, C. P. Snow has repeated all the old stories in his biography, *Trollope: His Life and Art*, and Johanna Johnston (*Fanny Trollope*) has retold the tale with the addition of fictionalized dialogue and careless misinformation.

8. Frances Trollope to Lord Northwick, 21 February 1819, GLC, ACC 76/1578. This quotation and all subsequent quotations of Crown copyright records in the Greater London Council appear by permission of the Controller of H. M. Stationery Office. For the background of the disputes and the various problems encountered, see Thomas Anthony Trollope to Lord Northwick, 12, 13, 16, 18, 21, and 28 February 1819, GLC, ACC 76/1573, /1574, /1575, /1576, /1577, /1579.

9. In the 1805 survey of the area of Illots Farm (that is, eight years *before* Trollope rented it), one of the fields is already called "Julians." GLC, ACC 76/565.

10. For the Meetkerke disaster, see TAT, p. 47. The quotation is from Thomas Anthony Trollope to Lord Northwick, 12 February 1820, Vaughan Library, Harrow School, Harrow-on-the-Hill. The new expenses are described in Thomas Anthony Trollope to Lord Northwick, 15 November 1833, GLC, ACC 76/2346. There has been general confusion about the naming of the houses at Harrow, which my new material has now clarified.

11. Drury festivites are from Frances Trollope to Mrs. Drury, n.d., University of California, Los Angeles, Collection 712, Trollope Family Papers (hereafter cited as UCLA). Other quotations from Anna W. Merivale, *Family Memorials*, p. 238 (diary entry for 11 February 1822).

12. MS with Anthony's explanatory note: "My mother's lines on the burial of Lord Bryon's illegitimate daughter." The copy appears to have been made by Anthony himself in 1834, and he has added extensive notes: UIU.

13. "Salmagundi Aliena," UIU. Of this stanza Anthony wrote: "Cunningham the vicar— he may well be called 'mild-eyed'—a man almost worshipped by the low church at Harrow—very unpopular with the gentry and much feared by the poor—a most despicable hypocrite—a gentleman-like man with very pleasing manners and a sweet voice. I used to talk to Cunningham a good deal at one time, and he always used to be very civil to me. But he is a cringing hypocrite—& the most confounded liar, and would give his eyes to be a bishop. . . ." A more laudatory account of the Rev. John William Cunningham (vicar of Harrow from 1811 until his death in 1861) can be found in the pamphlet "Cunningham of Harrow," by Agnes L. Wyatt. In addition to her detestation of evangelical piety, Mrs. Trollope probably disliked Cunningham for his success. It was he who rented their Julians in 1820.

14. "Salmagundi Aliena," UIU. Anthony concludes his commentary: "There is much wit in the lampoon and it is interesting to me from a variety of causes."

15. Given the declining prices, Trollope found it difficult to meet his annual rents. Later he wrote that in seventeen years his produce had never sufficed to pay the rent. GLC, ACC 76/2274. For a general discussion of the situation, see J. S. Cockburn and T. F. T. Baker, eds. *A History of the County of Middlesex*, 4:228 ff. The prices of the times are discussed in the *Economist*, 13 July 1974, pp. 62–63.

16. See TAT, pp. 62–65; and FET, 1:90–91. *The Vicar of Wrexhill* (1837) is discussed below, pp. 150 ff. Mrs. Trollope later claimed that there were "at least a dozen different originals" who have been named for her vicar. "I need hardly tell you," she wrote her son, "that it is no portrait of Mr. Cunningham—and as for the very unjust assertion that I have quarrelled with him, I will only say that if I *had* I would never have written the book at all, for fear this very thing should be said of me." Frances Trollope to Thomas Adolphus, n.d., PCP. While perhaps not intentional, the similarities are pronounced.

17. "The Righteous Rout, or Signs of the Times," MS, UIU. Surviving from the same period is another little play entitled "Almacks, or the Alarm," MS, UIU. In this short drama, the plot turns on the inability of the ladies to get the men to come to a ball and thereby secure wives and sweethearts. There is also a lengthy poem that survives from about the same period, "A Receipt to Make a Vulgus," satiric advice on how to write a suitable Latin poem: MS, UIU.

18. See Merivale, *Family Memorials*, p. 238.

19. John Garnett to Gen. Horatio Gates, 4 May 1796, Gates Collection, New York Historical Society, p. 150.

20. John Garnett to Gates, 16 December, 1798 and Anna Maria Garnett to Mrs. Gates, 12 April 1799, Gates Collection, pp. 133, 150.

21. Information on the Garnett family from Georg H. Pertz's unpublished memoir of his wife, the former Julia Garnett. This document is in the possession of Dr. Cecilia Payne-Gaposchkin, Julia Garnett Pertz's great-granddaughter, who is a world-renowned astronomer and was the first woman chairman of a Harvard department.

22. Information from the Pertz memoir. Subsequently, Mrs. Trollope thanked Julia and her mother for their letters from America, none of which have survived, and she referred on occasions to Julia's oldest sister, Anna Maria Garnett, as "the oldest friend I have in the world." I have been unable to find any confirmation of this friendship, but as the only Garnett to stay in America, where she married a Mr. Stone and ran a school, Anna Maria would prove a true friend to Mrs. Trollope during her troubles in the United States. Mrs. Garnett and her three daughters, Frances, Harriet, and Julia settled in Paris. The son Henry, about whom little is known, died in 1826, an outcast from his family, who considered him something of a libertine.

23. Frances Wright, *Course of Popular Lectures . . . with Three Addresses on Various Public Occasions* (1820), p. 7. Information on her life is from William Randall Waterman, *Frances Wright*; A. J. G. Perkins and Theresa Wolfson, *Frances Wright: Free Enquirer: The Study of a Temperament;* and Margaret Lane, *Frances Wright and the "Great Experiment."*

24. Frances Wright, *Views of Society and Manners in America* (1821), p. 71. Cf. the views expressed by Robina Craig Millar (Frances and Camilla Wright's friend) to Julia and Harriet Garnett, 21 June 1820, shortly after Miss Wright's return: "In the natural, moral and political features of your great and growing country, she has found objects to fill & gratify her capacious—her magnificent mind!—and in you she has met objects of esteem & affection she hardly believed to exist." This letter is part of an extremely rich and extensive correspondence between Frances Wright and members

of the Garnett family, made available to the author by the kind generosity of Dr. Cecilia Payne-Gaposchkin. These letters have subsequently been housed at the Houghton Library at Harvard University. They will be cited as the Frances Wright Collection (hereafter FWC). Selections have been edited by Dr. Gaposchkin and recently published: Cecilia Helena Payne-Gaposchkin, "The Nashoba Plan for Removing the Evil of Slavery: Letters of Frances and Camilla Wright, 1820–1829," *Harvard Library Bulletin* 23 (1975): 221–51, 429–61.

25. Frances Wright to Julia and Harriet Garnett, October 1820, FWC.

26. Lane, *Frances Wright*, pp. 12 ff., and Merivale, *Family Memorials*, p. 238.

27. TAT, p. 65.

28. Frances Wright to Lafayette, 16 July and 29 December 1821, Lafayette Papers, MSS f-303 and 304, University of Chicago. Cf. discussion in Lane, *Frances Wright*, pp. 15 ff.

29. Unless otherwise noted, all the remaining quotations in this chapter are from Frances Trollope's handwritten account, which her son Anthony found and entitled "My mother's Journal of a Visit to La Grange." This MS and a number of other letters and journals were acquired by the University of Illinois in 1953 from Miss Muriel Rose Trollope, Frances Trollope's great-granddaughter and her last descendant in England to bear the family name.

30. Frances Trollope to her son Thomas Adolphus, n.d. [1825], cited in FET, 1:58: "When you are next at home I shall insist upon your going with me to the National Gallery. It begins to be well worth seeing and *I* begin to be anxious to find out whether you are likely to enjoy the pleasure which a good picture is capable of bestowing. To me the love of pictures has been through life a source of very great pleasure, and I heartily wish it may become so to you." This letter is from a large collection of letters that Frances wrote to her oldest son over a period of more than forty years. Although quoted frequently in Frances Eleanor Trollope's study of her mother-in-law, these letters have apparently been lost. They are the single large collection which I have been unable to examine. Their importance is seen from a remark by Frances Eleanor Trollope to Richard Bentley, 23 December 1894: "I cannot refrain from saying that, high as my respect for 'the Mammy' (as we always spoke of her *en famille*) has been ever since I first heard or knew anything of her, it has been enormously increased by my perusal of these family papers. . . . I do not think that one would find in many families, a son who preserved the bulk of his mother's letters covering a period of nearly forty years! There are letters from Mrs. Trollope to her eldest son at Winchester written in 1824, seventy years ago." Printed in Robert H. Taylor, "The Trollopes Write to Bentley," *Trollopian* 3 (1948): 214.

31. Stanley T. Williams, ed., *Journal of Washington Irving, 1823–24*, p. 42. Inexplicably Williams misinterprets this entry to conclude that Mrs. Trollope was the "tall thin talking woman," when it is clearly Miss Wright. Later, Irving read Mrs. Trollope's work on America and used some of its material in his own book on the American West. See S. T. Williams, *Life of Washington Irving*, 1:258; and 2:38. The remarks of General Lafayette are reported in Frances Wright to Frances Trollope, 17 September 1823, UCLA. I have been unable to find Lafayette's letter to Frances Wright.

CHAPTER THREE

1. FET, 1:55–57.

2. Frances Trollope to Julia Garnett, 6 August 1824. This is from an extremely large

collection of letters from family and friends to Julia Garnett, who in September 1827 married the German historian Georg Heinrich Pertz and moved to Hanover and later Berlin. Julia Garnett Pertz faithfully kept all the letters sent to her over the next twenty-five years; these valuable documents were preserved in the family and are now owned by Cecilia Payne-Gaposchkin, Julia's great-granddaughter. Through the generous and enthusiastic cooperation of Dr. Gaposchkin, I have enjoyed full access to these superb documents, which will be cited as the Garnett-Pertz Collection (hereafter GPC).

3. Frances Wright to Julia Garnett, 4 December 1825, FWC.

4. "Our theatre," she wrote in July 1826, "is made in our drawing-room and the object of it was to improve the French pronunciation of our children by getting up scenes from 'Molière.' " Frances Trollope to Mary Russell Mitford, in MRM, 1:167-68.

5. Frances Trollope to Mary Russell Mitford, n.d., but June and summer 1826, MRM, 1:159-60, 164. For Mary Russell Mitford, see W. J. Roberts, *Mary Russell Mitford: The Tragedy of a Blue Stocking*, pp. 112-23.

6. See John Francis McDermott, "Mrs. Trollope's Illustrator: Auguste Hervieu in America (1827-1831)," *Extrait de la Gazette des Beaux-Arts*, March 1958, pp. 169-90.

7. Frances Trollope to Mary Russell Mitford, 22 April 1827, MRM, 1:168-69.

8. Frances Trollope to Mary Russell Mitford, 10 June 1827, PCP.

9. For favorable views of this project, see Edd Winfield Parks, "Dreamer's Vision: Frances Wright at Nashoba," *Tennessee Historical Magazine* 2d Series, 2 (1932): 75-86; and O. B. Emerson, "Frances Wright and Her Nashoba Experiment," *Tennessee Historical Quarterly* 6 (1947): 291-314. For a more critical view, see William H. and Jane H. Pease, "A New View of Nashoba," *Tennessee Historical Quarterly* 19 (1960): 99-109. See also the documents published in Gaposchkin, "Nashoba," *passim.*

10. Quoted in Mrs. Millar to Julia Garnett, 2 September 1826, FWC.

11. Frances to Thomas Adolphus Trollope, May 1825, cited in FET, 1:78. Bad weather left the wheat mildewed and spoiled nearly seven-eighths of the hay crop. In the next year, Trollope complained that he could make no profit even from his sheep: GLC, ACC 76/1799, /1800, /1818.

12. TAT, pp. 41-42. Much later, writing to Harriet Garnett (7 December 1828), Frances Trollope made explicit reference to her husband's intolerable temper: "He is a good, honourable man—but his temper is dreadful—every year increases his irritability—and also its lamentable effect upon the children": GPC. Although it was never diagnosed in his lifetime, it appears as if Mr. Trollope was suffering from a brain tumor.

13. Frances Trollope to Julia Garnett, 17 May 1827, GPC. In 1824 Julia had visited the Trollopes at Harrow. Frances Wright to Julia Garnett, n.d. [1824], FWC. For the general atmosphere, see FET, 1:97.

14. Frances Trollope to Julia Garnett, 17 May 1827, GPC.

15. Georg Heinrich Pertz to Frances Trollope, 2 November 1852, GPC. The earlier quotation is from the Pertz memoir.

16. Miss Wright's exposition of these noble ideas is found in a fragment of a letter to Sismondi, n.d., FWC: "It is the moral condition of the race of color which engages me—it is to prepare the two colors for the coming change. It is to kill prejudice in the white man by raising the black man to his level. It is by offering not the mere theory, but the practice of equality beneath the roof of Nashoba and presenting a first

example of union and brotherhood whose influence may perhaps extend beyond the little boundary of our acres until—who knows? It may be—by the whole population . . . ."

17. Frances Trollope to Julia Garnett, 17 May 1827, GPC. Mrs. Trollope makes no mention of her opinions on free love. The letter, however, is missing its last page, where she may have added something similar to her later strong objections.

18. James Mylne (professor at Glasgow College and great-uncle to the Wright sisters) to Julia Garnett, 12 August FWC; and Julia Garnett to Sismondi, 3 September 1827. The Garnett-Pertz Collection contains a large number of letters from Sismondi. Julia herself had earlier been tempted to join Frances Wright but had drawn back at the scandalous rumors. Her sister Harriet had, however, determined to go, and Julia even leased a house in Paris in order to block her family's inclination to return to America with Miss Wright. Information contained in Mrs. Millar to Julia Garnett, 2 June 1827, and Harriet Garnett to Julia Pertz, 12 December 1827, GPC.

19. Robert Dale Owen to Frances Wright, 25 August 1827, Frances Wright Letters, The University of Chicago Library.

20. Mary Shelley to Frances Wright, 12 September 1827, copy of letter in Julia's handwriting, FWC. Perkins and Wolfson (*Wright*, p. 176) say this letter is lost.

21. Frances Wright to Mary Shelley, 15 September 1827, copy of letter in Julia's handwriting, FWC. This copy does not totally correspond with that printed in Perkins and Wolfson, *Wright*, pp. 176–77.

22. Frances and Thomas Anthony Trollope to Madame and Monsieur Monod, 5 March 1827, Dreer and Gratz Collection, The Historical Society of Pennsylvania (hereafter cited as HSP). Henry Trollope boarded with the Monods during his months in Paris.

23. Frances Trollope and Frances Wright to Harriet Garnett, 8 October 1827, GPC. Mrs. Trollope's hopes that Harriet would accompany them to Nashoba were blocked by Julia's efforts. See n. 18, above.

24. See AT, pp. 11–13: "I wish I could give some adequate picture of the gloom of that farmhouse."

25. Frances Trollope to Harriet Garnett, 7 December 1828, GPC. This explanation seems correct, since in her first letter after leaving Nashoba, she explained her decision to leave in the same way: "I certainly do not believe that it was her [Fanny Wright's] intention to deceive me, when she gave such a discription [*sic*] of her Nashoba, as induced us to fix upon it as a residence for a year or two during which, from motives of economy, we had decided upon residing abroad," Frances Trollope to Charles Wilkes, 14 February 1828, Cincinnati Historical Society.

26. AT, p. 19. Italics added.

27. Marianne Skerret to Julia Pertz, September 1828, GPC.

28. Lafayette to Charles Wilkes, 8 November 1827, Lafayette Papers, Manuscript Division, Library of Congress. The original letter is not accurately reproduced in Perkins and Wolfson, *Wright*, pp. 180–81.

29. Mary Garnett (mother) to Julia Pertz, 26 October; Mary and Harriet Garnett to Julia Pertz, 27 November 1827, GPC. In the latter, Mrs. Garnett adds: "She has told her Harrow friends by a note after she left it, that it is a visit [to] her friends the Wilkes, Nashoba, to see Niagara, place her children at school & return with her husband in 1 or 2 years. But the gossip of Harrow will tell perhaps another story. . . . In short it passes all comprehension as to the motive. It must be a very strong one to induce a woman to give up the comforts of all the society she has hitherto at least respected."

30. Mary Garnett to Julia Pertz, 20 November 1827, GPC. The earlier quotation is Harriet Garnett to Julia Pertz, 12 December 1827, GPC.

31. Frances Wright to Harriet Garnett, 20 March 1828, FWC. This letter demolishes those commentators—of whom Sadlier is the most prominent—who insist that Mr. Trollope originated the idea. See Sadlier, *Trollope*, p. 71: "Unluckily Frances Wright preached the perfection of America to Thomas Trollope also, until in the obscure depths of that gloomy gambler's mind an astounding idea took root."

32. Writing nearly a year after the departure, Mrs. Trollope's close London friend, Marianne Skerret told Julia: "I feel now that there is but little hope for Mrs. Trollope's return. . . . It looks like a settlement there. . . . I regret what they have done but I don't think less affectionately of them. I wish to see them all again (excepting one, I can't say I want to see Mr. Hervieu back)." September 1828, GPC.

33. There is at least full unanimity in erring on this point. Of the family members, Anthony is closest to the truth, but he only guesses at Miss Wright's influence and insists the chief purpose was to set up Henry in business (AT, pp. 19-20). Thomas Adolphus is vague and guarded, shielding the image of his beloved mother to the last, while his second wife, Frances Eleanor, who knew nothing directly, concocts a completely incorrect story that Mrs. Trollope sailed in order to "settle sundry preliminaries" before Thomas Anthony joined them in the speculation. See TAT, p. 108; and FET, 1:99. Subsequent commentators—blithely spinning tales with no factual foundation—have sometimes disagreed on whether it was Frances or Thomas Anthony who was really the instigator. Mrs. Trollope comes out the winner—and a self-appointed reformer of American manners as well as daring entrepreneur—in Stebbins and Stebbins, *Trollopes*, pp. 29-30; and William H. Hildreth, "Mrs. Trollope in Porkopolis," *Ohio State Archaelogical and Historical Quarterly* 58 (1949): 35. Mr. Trollope is singled out in Allen C. Clark, "The Trollopes," *Columbia Historical Society Records* 27-28 (1937): 81; Pope-Hennessy, *Trollope*, pp. 43-44, and, as noted, Sadleir *Trollope*, p. 62. In his flawless style, Sadleir summarized all, however, when he concluded that the Trollopes' goals were clear: "Success would be immediate; profits immense. The family fortunes would be made." Johnston, (*Fanny Trollope*), despite access to the recently published documents clarifying this issue, continues to insist that "there is no direct evidence as to whether it was Fanny or her husband and who first thought of a venture in America." Fn. 8, p. 220.

34. Frances Trollope and Frances Wright to Julia Pertz, 26 December 1827, GPC.

35. Frances Trollope, *Domestic Manners of the Americans* (Donald Smalley ed.), p. 28. All further references, cited parenthetically in the text, are to this edition. This passage, of course, was written four years after the events described. The letter with the vividly expressed opinions was written less than a year after the trip to Nashoba. Frances Trollope to Harriet Garnett, 7 December 1828, GPC.

36. Frances Trollope to Harriet Garnett, 7 December 1828, GPC (for the first quotation). The second is from Frances Trollope to Charles Wilkes, 14 February 1828, Cincinnati Historical Society, Cf. FET, 1:107. During Frances Wright's absence from Nashoba Richeson Whitby, one of the trustees she had left behind, had married the unfortunate Camilla Wright, after apparently raping her.

37. Unsigned article [Timothy Flint], "Travellers in America, etc.," *Knickerbocker or New York Monthly Magazine* 2 (1833): 288. From Miss Wright's comments to him. General Lafayette clearly assumed that Mrs. Trollope had come to stay for a long period. Lafayette to Charles Wilkes, 8 November 1827, Lafayette Papers, Library of Congress.

38. Cited in Perkins and Wolfson, *Wright*, p. 190. All my efforts to find this journal have failed.

39. Frances Trollope to Charles Wilkes, 14 February 1828, Cincinnati Historical Society. For Henry's presence at New Harmony, there are no records, but the files of the Workingmen's Institute are incomplete, and scholars do not have access to the Owen family papers. That he was there is attested to in Robert Dale Owen to Frances Wright, 21 September 1827, Wright Papers, University of Chicago.

40. Frances Trollope to Charles Wilkes, 14 February 1828, Cincinnati Historical Society. Wilkes must have forwarded an account of this to the Garnetts, but without the reference to Miss Wright's health. See n. 41.

41. Harriet and Mary Garnett to Julia Pertz, 30 March 1828, GPC.

42. Harriet Garnett to Julia Pertz, 7 April 1828, GPC.

43. Frances to Thomas Adolphus Trollope, 4 May 1828, cited in FET, 1:111–13. None of Mrs. Trollope's letters to her husband for this period have survived, but apparently some were not lost in transit and were delivered.

44. For her public account, see Trollope, *Domestic Manners*, pp. 30–31; her private version is found in Frances Trollope to "my beloved boys at Winchester," 14 March 1828, cited in FET, 1:107. For Cincinnati in 1827, see William Bullock, *Sketch of a Journey through the Western States of North America . . . with a Description of the New and Flourishing City of Cincinnati by Messrs. B. Drake and E. D. Mansfield* (1827); and Richard C. Wade, *The Urban Frontier: Pioneer Life in Early Pittsburg, Cincinnati, Lexington, Louisville and St. Louis (1964).*

45. Cincinnati *Gazette*, 28 March 1828.

46. Information from Walter B. Hendrickson, "The Western Museum Society of Cincinnati," *Scientific Monthly* 63 (1946): 70–71; Elizabeth R. Kellogg, "Joseph Dorfeuille and the Western Museum," *Journal of the Cincinnati Society of Natural History* 22 (1945): 3–29. For Dorfeuille and his researches on parasitical insects, see William Newham Blane, *An Excursion thru the United States and Canada during the years 1822-23 by an English Gentleman*, p. 126. Hervieu's advertisement is found in the Cincinnati *Gazette*, 8 April 1828.

47. For listing of the museum's advertisements, see Donald Smalley's introduction to his 1949 edition of *Domestic Manners*, p. xxvi. Previous quotation from TAT, p. 122. For Hiram Powers in Cincinnati, see TAT, pp. 122–23; his subsequent meeting with Mrs. Trollope is from FET, 2:11–12.

48. Cincinnati *Gazette*, 12 April 1828.

49. Frances Trollope to Charles Wilkes, 18 June 1828, PCP.

50. Frances to Thomas Adolphus Trollope, 30 June 1828, cited in FET, 1:114. Hervieu's subsequent sketches were a startling innovation in the travel-book genre, which had hitherto limited illustrations to grand etchings of monuments, scenic views, and great historical figures. At Mrs. Trollope's suggestion, Hervieu drew a series of cartoons showing the manners of the Americans. They have not been properly appreciated, and McDermott's comment ("Hervieu," p. 196) is typical: "These sketches have the same acid-sour quality that distinguished Madam Vinegar's *Domestic Manners*, and like that book distort, not by false statement but by deliberate selection of the less attractive aspects of American life." It does seem strange that illustrations should be criticized because they attempt to follow the tone of the book!

51. TAT, pp. 122–23. Wade (*Urban Frontier*, p. 261) correctly attributes the idea to Mrs. Trollope.

52. Cited in Smalley's footnotes to *Domestic Manners*, p. 63, n. 2. Although Wade (*Urban Frontier*, p. 261) correctly suggests that most western cities had a counterpart to the Western Museum, he fails to point out that none ever had an exhibition based on Dante, Mrs. Trollope only visited Cincinnati.

53. Edward Deering Mansfield, *Personal Memories, Social, Political and Literary* (1879), pp. 183-84. Cf. another account in William H. Venable, *Beginnings of Literary Culture in the Ohio Valley* (1891), p. 315.

54. Both quotations are from Trollope, *Domestic Manners*, pp. 62-63.

CHAPTER FOUR

1. Harriet Garnett to Julia Pertz, 19 August 1828, GPC.

2. Frances Trollope to Harriet Garnett, 27 April 1828, GPC.

3. Camilla Whitby to Harriet Garnett, 20 November 1828, FWC.

4. The first quotation is from Frances Trollope to Lafayette, 23 April 1829, Lafayette Papers, Cornell University Library. Here she adds: "Mr. Owen, the father, is at present in this city, having been engaged in a long public controversy with a clergyman here, in which it has been his object to prove that there is no God. Mr. Owen is, in my opinion, a poor weak ignorant man, believing himself a prophet as firmly as Mahomet did." The later quotations are from Trollope, *Domestic Manners*, pp. 67-69, 153.

5. See Daniel Aaron, "Cincinnati, 1818-1838: A Study of Attitudes in the Urban West," (Ph.D. diss., Harvard University, 1942), p. 405; and Kathryn Kish Sklar, *Catherine Beecher: A Study in American Domesticity*, p. 109.

6. Elias Pym Fordham, *Personal Narrative of Travels in Virginia, Maryland, Pennsylvania, Ohio, Indiana, Kentucky; and of a Residence in the Illinois Territory: 1817-1818*, pp. 192-93. The earlier quotation is from Walter Stirling to George Harrison, 20 July 1832, HSP.

7. Alexis de Tocqueville, *Democracy in America*, Part Two, Book 3, chap. 41. Cf. his witty remarks on the seclusion of American women in a letter to his sister, 8 June 1831, printed in George W. Pierson and Dudley C. Lunt, *Tocqueville in America*, pp. 95-96.

8. Mrs. Trollope noted (*Domestic Manners*, p. 39) the "number of free Negroes who herd together in an obscure part of the city, called little Africa." By 1829, these numbered nearly 10 per cent of the population, but by 1834, nearly two-thirds of them were forced to leave the hostile city. See Sklar, *Beecher*, pp. 132-33, and Wade, *Urban Frontier*, p. 225.

9. For the quotations on Mrs. Trollope in Cincinnati, see an unsigned review of *Domestic Manners*, in *Illinois Monthly Magazine* 2 (1832): 506; and in *Cincinnati Mirror and Ladies' Parterre* 1 (1832): 188. For the issue of Mrs. Trollope's manners, see Clara Longworth de Chambrun, *Cincinnati: The Queen City*, p. 145. The cult of domesticity is discussed in Barbara Welter, "The Cult of True Womanhood: 1820-1860," *American Quarterly* 18 (1966): 151-74; and Carroll Smith Rosenberg, "Beauty, the Beast, and the Militant Woman: A Case Study in Sex Roles and Social Stress in Jacksonian America," *American Quarterly* 23 (1971): 562-84.

10. Frances to Thomas Adlophus Trollope, n.d., cited in FET, 1:118. The author erred in placing this letter after the visit of the husband. Moreover, this letter conclusively shows that Mrs. Trollope had not originally planned to settle in Cincinnati. Had she done so, she would certainly have secured letters to prominent people there, and

especially from Lafayette, whose relations with Mr. Neville are described by Ophia P. Smith, in "Joseph Tasso," *Ohio State Archeological and Historical Quarterly* 56 (1947): 22. In writing his letter of introduction, Lafayette expressed surprise that Mrs. Trollope was still in Cincinnati, for he had been told "that it was [her] intention to move with family to New York." Lafayette to Frances Trollope, 11 November 1828, Benjamin Franklin Collection, Yale University.

11. Harriet Garnett to Julia Pertz, 15 July 1828, and Sophia Hay to Julia Pertz, 25 May 1828, GPC. Cf. the clear statement in Mary and Harriet Garnett to Julia Pertz, 1 July 1828, GPC: "We spoke much to [Macready] of Mrs. Trollope. He [had] tried every argument to dissuade her from her plan. She listened and then said it is too late. Her husband goes in August to New York for her."

12. Frances Trollope to Harriet Garnett, 27 April 1828, GPC. Mr. Trollope (accompanied by the eldest son Thomas Adolphus) left England on 31 August 1828, and after a stormy crossing lasting thirty-eight days in steerage passage on the *Corinthian* and an overland trip through the American Northeast, arrived in Cincinnati in October 1828. Mrs. Trollope must have already made extensive plans for her project, for the deed to the property on Third Street near Broadway was executed on 20 January 1829. Mr. Trollope paid $1,665 for the land with a mortgage held by a local businessman Nicholas Longworth. He had come to America to carry out the transaction because of the laws prohibiting married women from owning or disposing of property. For details, see TAT, pp. 109-11, and Hamilton County Court House, Deed Book 30, p. 209. Mr. Trollope must have left Cincinnati almost immediately, for after a leisurely tour of the eastern United States, he was back in England by March 1829, to raise money for building the bazaar from his wife's inheritance.

13. Frances Trollope to Harriet Garnett, 7 December 1828, GPC.

14. See information and prospectus printed in *The Cincinnati Directory and Commercial Advertiser for the Year 1829*, pp. 175 ff.

15. Having resided in the city for almost a year, Mrs. Trollope was certainly aware of the location of the commercial district and chose her lot precisely because she had other purposes in mind. The misunderstanding of these purposes explains the faulty interpretations found in Carl Abbott, "The Location and External Appearance of Mrs. Trollope's Bazaar," *Journal of the Society of Architectural Historians* 29 (1970): 256-60, with a map and exact measurements of the distances. Similar misunderstandings pervade the unsigned review of *Domestic Manners* in *Illinois Monthly Review*, August 1832, p. 511; and Russell A. Griffin, "Mrs. Trollope and the Queen City," *Mississippi Valley Historical Review* 37 (1950): 289-302.

16. Frances Trollope to Harriet Garnett, 27 April 1828, GPC. Descriptions are from the 1829 *Cincinnati Directory*. A recent study demonstrates some similarities between the bazaar and a museum in London but is wrong in assuming that Mrs. Trollope could have learned about Egyptian architecture only from that building. See Clay Lancaster, "The Egyptian Hall and Mrs. Trollope's Bazaar," *Magazine of Art* 43 (1950): 94-99. The flaws in Cincinnati architecture are discussed in Ralph L. Rusk, *The Literature of the Middle Western Frontier*, 1:37-38. For a sample of contemporary critical comments, compare: "A more absurd compound of every species of architecture never entered the head of any architect. . . . This building is as ill-adapted for a bazaar as for a dwelling-house": C.D. Arfwedson, *The United States and Canada in 1832, 1833, and 1834*, 2:130. "This bazaar is the great deformity of the city. Happily, it is not very conspicuous, being squatted down among houses nearly as lofty as the summit of its dome": Harriet Martineau, *Retrospect of Western Travel* (1838), 2:54. "The order under which [the bazaar] must be classed is . . . *preposterous*. They call it 'Trollope's Folly' ": Captain Frederick Marryat, *Diary in*

America (1839), p. 261. "The most remarkable object in Cincinnati . . . is a large Graeco-Moresco-Gothic-Chinese looking building—an architectural compilation of prettiness of all sorts, the effect of which is eminently grotesque": [Thomas Hamilton], *Men and Manners in America by the author of Cyril Thornton* (1833), pp. 169–70. For a later, more favorable verdict, see Venable, *Literary Culture*, p. 355: "There is a good deal of romance, poetry, and pathos associated with this same quaint and curious arabesque, Egyptesque, oriental, Gothic, bazarre Bazaar. Marvelous it rose, hard by the Beautiful River, with balconies looking out toward the Kentucky hills." Today, the bazaar has been replaced by a no less preposterous superhighway leading to the equally ecclectic Riverfront Stadium.

17. Venable, *Literary Culture*, pp. 355–56; and *Cincinnati Directory*, pp. 176–77. For Mrs. Trollope's aesthetic appreciation of the location, see *Domestic Manners*, p. 41: "Deep and narrow watercourses, dry in summer, but bringing down heavy streams in winter, divide these hills into many separate heights, and this furnishes the only variety the landscape offers for many miles round the town. The lovely Ohio is a beautiful feature wherever it is visible, but the only part of the city that has the advantage of its beauty is the street nearest to its bank."

18. Pope-Hennessy, *Trollope*, p. 43. Descriptive quotations from *Cincinnati Directory*, p. 177; and Venable, *Literary Culture*, p. 356.

19. While in Cincinnati, Captain Marryat learned the general reputation of Mrs. Trollope in that city: "It is fair to us," he quotes a native Cincinnatian as saying, "that it should be understood that when Mrs. Trollope came here, she was quite unknown, except inasmuch as that she was a married woman, travelling without her husband. In a small society . . . it was not surprising, therefore, that we should be cautious about receiving a lady who, in our opinion, was offending against *les bienséances*. Observe, *we do not accuse Mrs. Trollope of any impropriety*; but you must be aware how necessary it is, in this country, to be regardful of appearances, and how afraid every one is of their neighbor." Marryat, *Diary*, pp. 261–62.

20. Frances Trollope to Julia Pertz, 22 August 1831, GPC.

21. See Cincinnati *Gazette*, 17 October 1829; and an unsigned review of *Domestic Manners* in *Cincinnati Mirror*, 1 (1832): 188.

22. Cincinnati *Gazette*, 23 November, 19 and 25 December 1829. Apparently reflecting the "national attitude in microcosm," Cincinnati exhibited "considerable public prejudice against the arts," Aaron, "Cincinnati," pp. 381, 388.

23. Frances Trollope to Julia Pertz, 22 August 1831, GPC.

24. Information from Thomas Anthony Trollope's legal deposition, 31 March 1830, PCP; and Longworth & Blachly vs. Thomas A. Trollope, March 1834, Hamilton County Court House, Deed Book 49, p. 450. The original cost of the land ($1,665) was covered by a mortgage held by Nicholas Longworth. After returning to England, Trollope sent $2,000 in cash for the building and subsequently a shipment of goods reportedly worth $4,000, but which may have cost him as little as $2,000. Thus the total investment was between $4,000 and $6,000—a large sum for those days, but only a fraction of the loss suggested by most commentators. Aaron ("Cincinnati," p. 300) claims it was $17,000; Stebbins and Stebbins (*Trollopes*, p. 39), and Hildreth ("Porkopolis," p. 35) come up with $20,000; and the most recent, Griffin ("Queen City," p. 300) reckons $24,000! None of these authorities cites sources, and they seem to delight in escalating the amount the Trollopes lost in Cincinnati. Apparently the source for their investment was Frances's own money—inherited from her father. In 1827, shortly after Mr. Milton's will was probated, Thomas Anthony purchased a packet of lands in Newland called The Hardings. He sold it in 1829 for a sum of

£1,380 (and a neat profit of nearly £430). Since Thomas Anthony's own fortunes in Harrow were so bad in these years, this deal could only have been carried out with the money Frances inherited from her father (details from D34/IX/95 and 96. County Record Office, Gloucester). Thus all the money for the bazaar came from Mrs. Trollope herself.

25. All quotations from Frances Trollope to Julia Pertz, 12 March 1830, GPC.

26. *Ibid.*

27. Diary of Thomas Adolphus Trollope, 19 April 1830, cited in FET, 1:126. For Thomas Adolphus' assessment, see TAT, p. 205.

28. Hamilton, *Men and Manners*, 2:171–72.

29. Frances to Thomas Adolphus Trollope, April 1830, cited in FET, 1:127. She wrote of similar plans to the Garnetts: Harriet Garnett to Julia Pertz, 11 April 1830, GPC.

30. Frances Trollope to Julia Pertz, 12 March 1830, GPC.

31. The earlier quotation is from Frances Trollope to Mary Russell Mitford, 20 January 1829, MRM, 2:193. The three notebooks are in the possession of Indiana University, the Lilly Library, which graciously permitted me to use them. On the inside of the first appears: "H. Trollope, a series of Portfolios." Mrs. Trollope has scribbled remarks and rent receipts over Henry's writings. The second notebook is marked: "T. A. Trollope, Win. Coll. Alumn. 1827." Mrs. Trollope has again written over this inscription. Upside down and beneath, she has recorded: "The innumerable butterflies that people the air in summer look like a bed of tulips on the wing." She was obviously trying to work up a more "sublime" style. The third slim book is inscribed "H.T.," with the initials "T.A.T., March 25, 1825," written over it. Under this, Mrs. Trollope has added the words of Thomas Moore on America: "Where bastard freedom moves / Her fustian flag in mockery over slaves." Most of this third notebook is taken up with a lengthy review of Sir Walter Scott. Hereafter, these will be cited as Notebooks, IULL.

32. Frances Trollope to Julia Pertz, 12 March 1830, GPC.

33. Frances Trollope to Mary Russell Mitford, 28 July 1830, in MRM, 1: 220. For the book, see Captain Basil Hall, R. N., *Travels in North America in the years 1827 and 1828* (1829), which rapidly went through three editions. It was reviewed in the Cincinnati *Gazette*, 21 November 1829, while Mrs. Trollope was still in the city.

34. Notebooks, IULL. For the meeting with the publisher, see also Frances Trollope to Mary Russell Mitford, 28 July 1830, in MRM, 1:220.

35. Notebooks, IULL. The earlier quotation is from Frances Trollope to Mary Russell Mitford, 28 July 1830, in MRM, 1:220. Italics added.

36. Quotation is from Frances Trollope to Mary Russell Mitford, 29 May 1831, in MRM, 1:227. The widely held contention that Mrs. Trollope wanted the book to sell and therefore deliberately wrote an anti-American tract is best presented by Ada B. Nisbet, "Mrs. Trollope's *Domestic Manners*," *Nineteenth Century Fiction* 4 (1949–50): 319 ff. Although Mrs. Trollope denied her book had been influenced by Captain Hall, her decision to turn the notebooks into a published account followed her reading of his book. Subsequently, she added sections that were not in her notes and in these she followed Hall's topical arrangement. The nature of her spontaneous notes, however, determined the uniqueness of *Domestic Manners*. Cf. Frances Trollope to Mary Russell Mitford, 28 July 1830, in MRM, 1:221.

37. Walter Stirling to George Harrison, 20 July 1832, HSP. The phrase about the need to visit Niagara is from Frances to Thomas Adolphus Trollope, late summer 1830, cited in FET, 1:129–30. This was an ironic misjudgment; the Cincinnati sections are

undoubtedly the strength of the book. The second half is a more conventional account, characterized by formal information transmitted in a stilted and unnatural style. See Helen Heineman, "Frances Trollope in the New World: *Domestic Manners of the Americans," American Quarterly* 21 (1969): 551 ff.

38. Frances to Thomas Adolphus Trollope, late summer 1830, in FET, 1:131; and Frances Trollope to Julia Pertz, 18 April 1831, GPC.

39. Frances Trollope to Julia Pertz, 22 August 1831, GPC. The earlier quotation is from Trollope, *Domestic Manners*, p. 294.

40. The first quotation is Frances Trollope to Julia Pertz, 18 April 1831, GPC. The second is Frances Trollope to Mary Russell Mitford, 29 May 1831, in MRM, 1:226-28.

41. See the discussion of the general situation in J. S. Cockburn and T.F.T. Baker, *A History of the County of Middlesex*, pp. 228 ff. His plight had nothing whatsoever to do with some foolish act on his part, but the over-spending on the house and the investment in Cincinnati now compounded his problems.

42. Thomas Anthony Trollope, Thomas Hill, Joseph Perry, and Thomas Hottsdon to John Lord Northwick, 17 December 1830, GLC ACC 76/2273.

43. See Thomas Anthony Trollope to Lord Northwick, 27 December 1830; Quilton (the local agent) to Lord Northwick, 28 December 1830, 1 and 24 January 1831; Thomas Anthony Trollope to Lord Northwick, 5, 20, and 24 January 1831; Henry Trollope to Lord Northwick, 16 January 1831; and Lord Northwick to Quilton, 16 January 1831, in GLC, ACC 76/2277-2281, 2284-2286. Thomas Anthony's letters pathetically tried to persuade Lord Northwick to take into account his past faithfulness: "When you shall have taken into consideration, my lord, the great, I may say the unexampled pressure of the times as affecting the hay farmer; the heavy and almost ruinous losses I have sustained, particularly during the last two years; and that during the long period of seventeen years all my rents have been paid . . . I am still induced to think that your lordship will not permit my present default . . . which from the necessity of the times has been common to all (or most of) your tenants in this place, to deprive me of that bounty . . . nor turn to your own benefit not my unwillingness but my absolute inability of paying the rent." Thomas Anthony Trollope to Lord Northwick, 20 January 1831, GLC, ACC 76/2284.

44. Frances Trollope to Julia Pertz, 22 August 1831, GPC.

45. *Ibid.*

46. Frances Trollope to Mary Russell Mitford, 16 September 1831, in MRM, 1:228.

47. Information from Frances Trollope to Mary Russell Mitford, 16 September 1831, in MRM, 1:228; and Frances Trollope to Julia Pertz, 25 November 1831, GPC. For the "sacred den," see FET, 1:152.

48. Frances Trollope to Julia Pertz, 25 November 1831, GPC.

49. *Ibid.* The earlier quotation is Frances to Thomas Adolphus Trollope [autumn 1831], cited in FET, 1:143.

50. Frances Trollope to Harriet Garnett, 7 December 1828; and Frances Trollope to Julia Pertz, 25 November 1831, GPC.

51. Frances Trollope to Julia Pertz, 25 November 1831, GPC; and Hervieu to Thomas Adolphus, cited in FET, 1:138-39. During the needy times following their return from America, Mrs. Trollope tried to find Hervien patronage with her London friends and with Mary Russell Mitford, who commissioned him to do her portrait. But Hervieu earned his most enduring fame as Mrs. Trollope's illustrator; her novels and travel books proved the ideal medium for the young Frenchman's talents. From

his unconventional caricatures of American life in *Domestic Manners* to his brooding scenes of slavery in *Whitlaw*, Hervieu was an invaluable collaborator. His pictures were charged with originality and the same idealism that had led him to America where he had supported the friend whose family had fallen on such unaccountably bad times. Hervieu led a double artistic life, counterpointing his satiric book illustrations with conventional exhibitions of classical scenes (Sappho imploring Venus from the Leucadian Rock, Thermopylae, Love and Folly, An Offering to Venus) and romantic tributes to Byron, the idol of the age. In his time, this orphan boy who had been sentenced to prison as a dangerous radical and who had been forced to sell his food to buy colors exhibited forty-seven paintings in the Royal Academy and at the British Institute and was elected a member of the Society of Fine Arts at Lille. When he married a Swiss girl in 1842, he passed out of Mrs. Trollope's story.

52. Frances Trollope to Julia Pertz, 22 March 1832, GPC.

CHAPTER FIVE

1. Mrs. Trollope's rough draft for a preface, IULL, printed in the Smalley edition of *Domestic Manners*, Appendix A, pp. 431–42.

2. Flint's observation is from "Travellers," pp. 286–87.

3. Frances to Thomas Adolphus Trollope, cited in FET, 1:167.

4. Samuel Clemens, *Life on the Mississippi*, p. 392.

5. For an examination in more detail of the differences in the two halves of the book, see Heineman, "Frances Trollope," pp. 551 ff.

6. After Mrs. Trollope, all foreign travelers considered it necessary to devote a substantial part of their books to the role of women in the United States. See Page Smith, *Daughters of the Promised Land*, pp. 77–93. By her own analysis, Mrs. Trollope determined the importance of this subject in any discussion of America. The quotation, which was not included in her travel book, is from the Notebooks, & is printed in the Smalley edition of *Domestic Manners*, Appendix A, p. 422.

7. Wright, *Society and Manners*, pp. 218–19.

8. Hall, *Travels*, 3:149–50, 152.

9. Una Pope-Hennessy, ed. *The Aristocratic Journey: Being the Outspoken Letters of Mrs. Basil Hall, written during a Fourteen Months' Sojourn in America*, pp. 121, 125, 198, 230.

10. Long after Mrs. Trollope had written her book, Harriet Martineau enlarged upon the theme: "While woman's intellect is confined, her morals crushed, her health ruined, her weakness encouraged, and her strength punished, she is told that her lot is cast in the paradise of women; and there is no country in the world where there is so much boasting of the 'chivalrous' treatment she enjoys. . . . She has the best place in stagecoaches; when there are not chairs enough for everybody, the gentlemen stand; she hears oratorical flourishes on public occasions about wives and home and apostrophes to women; she has liberty to get her brain turned by religious excitements, that her attention may be diverted from morals, politics, and philosophy; and, especially, her morals are guarded by the strictest observance of propriety in her presence. In short, indulgence is given her as a substitute for justice." Harriet Martineau, *Society in America* (1837), pp. 105–6. These were precisely the points that Mrs. Trollope made a half-dozen years earlier.

11. For confirmation of Mrs. Trollope's analysis concerning the exclusion of women from

the vital activities of the community, see Ethel Peal, "The Atrophied Rib: Urban Middle-Class Women in Jacksonian America," *passim*. For the accuracy of Mrs. Trollope's conclusions, see Rosenberg, "Beauty," 562 ff.

12. Elizabeth Sandford, *Woman in her Social and Domestic Character* (1831), p. 173.

13. Cf. Martineau, *Society*, 3:132, on the boredom and uselessness of such lives.

14. Cf. the similar views expressed later by Harriet Martineau (*Society*, p. 118): "But the prosperity of America is a circumstance unfavorable to its women. It will be long before they are put to the proof as to what they are capable of thinking and doing; a proof to which hundreds, perhaps thousands of Englishwomen have been put by adversity, and the result of which is a remarkable improvement in their social condition, even within the space of ten years."

15. For purity as the essential feminine virtue, see Welter, "Cult of True Womanhood," p. 154. Cf. the excellent discussion of the exaggerated expectations for women in Duncan Crow, *The Victorian Woman*, pp. 27 ff.

16. Unsigned review of *Domestic Manners*, in *Illinois Monthly Magazine* 2 (1832): 519–20.

17. Unsigned reviews of *Domestic Manners*, in *New Monthly Magazine* 35 (1832): 452; and *Edinburgh Review* 55 (1832): 487–88. Stirling to Harrison, 20 July 1832, HSP.

18. Unsigned reviews of *Domestic Manners*, *New Monthly Magazine* 35 (1832): 452; *Athenaeum*, no. 231 (1832): pp. 204–6.

19. *Edinburgh Review*, 55 (1832): 522; *New Monthly Magazine*, 35 (1832): 450; and unsigned review of *Domestic Manners*, in *Gentleman's Magazine* 102 (1832): 346.

20. Unsigned review of *Domestic Manners*, in *North American Review* 78 (1833): 9–10.

21. *Edinburgh Review* 44 (1832): 487–88; *North American Review* 78 (1833): 2.

22. *Illinois Monthly Magazine* 2 (1832): 506.

23 Unsigned Review of *Domestic Manners* in *American Quarterly Review* 12 (1832): 130.

24. *New Monthly Magazine* 35 (1832): 453; Flint, "Travellers," pp. 286–87; *North American Review* 78 (1833): 5, 1.

25. *Illinois Monthly Magazine* 2 (1832): 505–6, 520.

26. The charge is from Sadlier, *Trollope*, p. 87.

27. Trollope, *Domestic Manners*, pp. lxxvii–lxxviii.

28. Unsigned review [Basil Hall] of *Domestic Manners*, in *Quarterly Review* 47 (1832): 39–80; and unsigned review of *Domestic Manners*, in *Fraser's Magazine* 5(1832): 336–50.

29. See conclusion of Smith, *Daughters*, p. 92.

30. Frances Trollope to Julia Pertz, 22 March 1832, GPC.

31. TAT, p. 162; FET, 1:171; and Sadleir, *Trollope*, p. 78. Money was still short, however, and she could not afford to send a copy of her book to Harriet. Harriet Garnett to Julia Pertz, 7 April 1832, GPC.

32. FET, 1:156.

33. Most of the reviews were bad. *New Monthly Magazine*, 35 (1832): 452, found the book indecent, coarse, with a prurient style of innuendo and description "inconsistent with delicacy." *Literary Gazette* (1832), p. 262, found its woman's view "one sided." *Gentleman's Magazine* 102 (1832): 346, considered it "vulgar," and the *Edinburgh Review* 55 (1832): 496, believed the whole thing an attack upon the Reform Bill: "If

she uncovers the nakedness of our Transatlantic children, it is out of pure alarm for the English constitution."

34. Mary Garnett to Julia Pertz, 3 May 1832; Harriet Garnett to Julia Pertz, 19 May 1832; Lafayette to Harriet Garnett, 14 June 1832; and Sismondi to Julia Pertz, 2 December 1832, in GPC. The original of the Lafayette letter is now owned by the Lafayette Society of America. Frances Trollope to Mary Russell Mitford, 23 April 1832, in MRM, 1:233.

35. Frances Trollope to Mary Russell Mitford, 23 April 1832, in MRM, 1:234.

36. Frances to Thomas Adolphus Trollope, 31 May 1832, FET, 1:167.

37. Frances to Thomas Adlophus Trollope, n.d. [1832], FET, 1:161.

38. *Ibid.*, 164, 167.

39. Frances Trollope to Julia Pertz, 1 and 9 February 1832, GPC.

40. Frances Trollope to Julia Pertz, 27 June 1832, GPC.

41. Basil Hall to Frances Trollope, 17 May 1832, UCLA. Mrs. Trollope believed that Whittaker should have made an additional settlement because of the extraordinary success of *Domestic Manners*, which had sold more than 2,200 copies. By the terms of their agreement, Mrs. Trollope was entitled to nothing beyond her original £400. "This must pay him well," she wrote Miss Mitford, "but I suppose it is all right." Frances Trollope to Mary Russell Mitford, 23 April 1832, MRM, 1:233.

42. Frances to Thomas Adolphus Trollope, ca. July 1832, cited in FET, 1:169-70.

43. Frances Trollope to Georgina [?], n.d. [1832], TCP.

44. Frances Trollope, *The Refugee in America*, 3 vols. (1832). All further references, cited parenthetically in the text, are to this edition. In addition to her experiences in America, Mrs. Trollope apparently tried to model her fiction upon that of Sir Walter Scott, whom she greatly admired. While still in Cincinnati, she had written an extensive review/appreciation of his works, filling one of her notebooks with comments on his "exquisitely villainous" characters. See Notebooks, IULL. For an evaluation of *The Refugee*, see Sadleir, *Trollope*, p. 89.

45. See *The Refugee*, 1:19, 30-32, 78, 84, 89 ff., 119. Cf. *Domestic Manners*, pp. 92-93. For Mrs. Trollope's comment on the conviction of Americans that theirs was also a superior literature, see *The Refugee*, 2:112.

46. *The Refugee*, 2:101 ff. In an earlier letter, Mrs. Trollope described Hervieu's similar reaction to Nashoba: "I think I never saw a man in such a rage. He wept with passion and grief mixed"; quoted in Smalley's introduction to *Domestic Manners*, p. xviii.

47. *The Refugee*, 2:103-5.

48. Frances Trollope to Julia Pertz, 16 February 1833, GPC. Information about the review of *Our Village* is from Mary Russell Mitford to Frances Trollope, 18 September 1831 (County Borough of Reading Public Library), and Frances Trollope to Mary Russell Mitford, 27 December 1832, MRM, 1:243-44.

49. Unsigned review of *The Refugee*, in *Quarterly Review*, 48 (1832): 508.

50. Basil Hall to Frances Trollope, 21 January 1833, and n.d. UCLA.

51. Unsigned review of *The Refugee*, in *Westminster Review*, 18 (1833): 213. In its review of her next novel, the *Spectator* reflected upon the achievements of her first: "*The Refugee* bore evident marks of being compounded of materials from the nearest circulating library; but still it had something in it that every body could not write. It was necessary to have been beyond the sea; it was necessary to possess a certain smart talent of observation, properly prepared with a discreet quantity of

exaggeration. America had plainly been seen by the 'old woman'; though it was clear that she had worn a pair of spectacles of a hugely magnifying power, and with not a few flaws in the glass." *Spectator* 6 (1833): 526.

CHAPTER SIX

1. Frances Trollope to Julia Pertz, 16 February 1833, GPC. For her earlier reading of Mrs. Radcliffe, see Frances Milton to Thomas Anthony Trollope, 6 December 1808, TCP.

2. Frances Trollope, *The Abbess: A Romance*, 3 vols. (1833). All further references, cited parenthetically in the text, are to this edition. Quotation is from 1:172. For Mrs. Trollope's own intense fear of such a death, see below, chap. 16. Frances Eleanor Trollope thought *The Abbess* "quite out of her usual manner," but comparable with many popular novels of its time and class." FET, 2:184. For these literary products, see J. M. S. Tompkins, *The Popular Novel in England, 1770-1800*, pp. 268 and 280.

3. Unsigned review of *The Abbess*, in *Spectator* 6 (1833): 526-27. See also reviews in *Literary Gazette* (1833), p. 360, and *John Bull* (1833).

4. Unsigned review of *The Refugee*, in *Westminster Review* 28 (1833): 208-227.

5. Harriet Garnett to Julia Pertz, February [1833], and Frances Trollope to Julia Pertz, 16 February 1833, GPC.

6. Frances Trollope to Julia Pertz, 16 February 1833, GPC.

7. Frances Trollope to Julia Pertz, 23 August 1833, GPC. The planned trip is described in Frances Trollope to Mrs. Bartley, 23 May 1833, PCP..By November the MS was not even half ready for the press. Frances Trollope to Julia Pertz, 14 November 1833, GPC.

8. Frances Trollope to Julia Pertz, n.d. [Spring 1834], GPC.

9. *Ibid.*; and Frances Trollope to John Murray, 14 December 1833 and 14 January 1834, John Murray Archives (hereafter cited as JMA).

10. Frances Trollope to John Murray, February 13, 1834, JMA.

11. Frances Trollope to Julia Pertz, n.d. [Spring 1834], GPC.

12. Frances Trollope to John Murray, 6 March 1834, JMA.

13. Frances Trollope to John Murray, 17 March 1834, JMA.

14. Frances Trollope to Julia Pertz, n.d. [Spring 1834], GPC.

15. Quotation is Lord Northwick to his agent Quilton, 24 November 1833, GLC, ACC 76/2349A. Other information contained in Quilton to Lord Northwick, 1 October and 22 November 1833, and Northwick to Quilton, 24 November and undated, 1833, GLC, ACC 76/2342, /2348, /2349B, /2349C. For the general distress, see Quilton to Lord Northwick, 26 and 30 November and 23 December 1833. Mr. Trollope's payment is discussed in Quilton to Northwick, 9 and 10 December 1833, GLC, ACC 76/2350, /2351, /2360, /2355-56.

16. Frances Trollope (from Bruges) to Julia Pertz, 13 July 1834, GPC.

17. Quotation is from Quilton to Lord Northwick, 27 and 30 December 1833. Information on rents is from Quilton to Lord Northwick, 9 January and 16 February 1834, GLC, ACC 76/2361, /2362, /2363, /2364.

18. In November 1833, the Hamilton County Court of Common Pleas approved seizure if default continued. Nicholas Longworth obtained a court order on 13 January 1834. The appraisal took place on 15 January, the public sale on 18 February 1834. The

purchaser was, of all people, Nicholas Longworth, Mrs. Trollope's friend who, in the words of one commentator, "is more widely known as a real estate entrepreneur . . . than as a patron of the arts." In this case, he seems to have been the only one to profit from the bazaar. Ironically, he later subsidized Hiram Powers when the latter began a sculpturing career in Florence and again crossed paths with Mrs. Trollope. See Hamilton County Court House, Deed Book 49, p. 450, and for Longworth, Louis Leonard Tucker, "Cincinnati: Athens of the West, 1830–1831," *Ohio History* 75 (1966): 20.

19. Quilton to Lord Northwick, 16 April 1834. Earlier quotation is from Quilton to Lord Northwick, 3 April 1834. Both letters mention that they enclose letters from Mr. Trollope, but these have apparently not survived. GLC, ACC 76/2374, /2372.

20. Quilton to Lord Northwick, 18 April 1834, GLC, ACC 76/2375. Another enclosure from Mr. Trollope has apparently been lost. For Henry Milton's actions, see FET, 1:199.

21. Quilton to Lord Northwick, 21 April 1834, GLC, ACC 76/2376. The agent added: "Mr. Trollope has been borrowing money of Coln. Grant and nearly all the little stock and furniture he has, he has made over to him in way of payment." This was apparently the story Mrs. Trollope used to save her possessions.

22. AT, pp. 23–24.

23. Quilton to Lord Northwick, 26 April 1834, GLC, ACC 76/2377.

24. Frances Trollope to John Murray , 22 April 1834, JMA.

25. Harriet Garnett to Julia Pertz, 7 May 1834, GPC.

26. AT, pp. 23–24.

27. Frances Trollope to Julia Pertz, 13 July 1834, GPC.

28. AT, p. 21.

29. Frances Trollope to Colonel Grant, 3 June 1834, PCP.

30. First quotation is from Frances Trollope to John Murray, 22 July 1834, JMA. The second is from Frances Trollope to Mrs. Bartley, 30 July 1834, PCP.

31. Mary Garnett to Julia Pertz, n.d. [postmark, 26 December 1834], GPC. The exchange with the publisher is Frances Trollope to John Murray, 20 January 1835, cited in FET, 1:226.

32. AT, pp. 24–25.

33. Frances to Thomas Adolphus Trollope, n.d. cited in FET, 1:223–24, 227–28. Henry's illness is discussed in Frances Trollope to Dr. Edwin Harrison, 17 October 1834, PCP.

34. Frances Trollope, *Tremordyn Cliff*, 3 vols. (1835). All further references, cited parenthetically in the text, are to this edition.

35. Frances to Thomas Adolphus Trollope, 23 December 1834, cited in FET, 1:227–28. Cf. TAT, p. 174.

36. Unsigned reviews of *Tremordyn Cliff*, in *Spectator* 8 (1835); *Athenaeum*, no. 411 (1835), pp. 692–93; *Literary Gazette*, no. 972 (1835), pp. 563–64; and the London *Times*, 17 September 1835, p. 3.

37. Frances Trollope to Richard Bentley, 24 June 1835, TCP.

CHAPTER SEVEN

1. Geoffrey Trease, *The Grand Tour*, p. 238.

2. See the twelve books (including *The Englishwoman in Egypt* by Mrs. Poole, and

Journal of a Yacht Voyage to Texas by Mrs. Houston) reviewed together under the title "Lady Travellers," in *Quarterly Review* 76 (1845): 98–137; and the eight other books all published within the same year that were reviewed along with Mrs. Trollope's *Belgium and Western Germany* in an article entitled "German Tourists," in *Westminister Review* 22 (1835): 510–20.

3.   Unsigned review of Monro, *A Summer Ramble in Syria*, in *London and Westminster Review* 25 (1836): 103–37. Cf. Sir Francis Head, *Rough Notes taken during some Rapid Journeys across the Pampas and among the Andes* (1826); Sir Francis Head, *Bubbles from the Brunnens of Nassau by an old man* (1834); Anna Jameson, *Visits and Sketches at Home and Abroad*, 4 vols. (1833) and Anna Jameson, *Slight Reminiscences of the Rhine, Switzerland, and a corner of Italy* (1834).

4.   Unsigned review of Monro's Tartar trip, in *Westminister Review* 25 (1836): 103–37.

5.   See Dr. Abraham Eldon, *The Continental Traveller's Oracle; or Maxims for Foreign Locomotion*, 2 vols. (1828); and William Howitt, *German Experiences addressed to the English; both stayers at home and goers abroad* (1844). In the latter book, the author addressed such problems as where to buy firewood without being charged high prices.

6.   Unsigned review of *Belgium and Western Germany*, in *New Monthly Magazine* 41 (1834): 505.

7.   Frances Trollope, *Paris and the Parisians in 1835*, 2 vols. (1836). All further references cited parenthetically in the text, are to this edition. Mrs. Trollope wrote this account in the form of travel letters; quotation is from letter 27.

8.   Unsigned review, of *Belgium and Western Germany*, in *Spectator* 7 (1834): 684 ff. For an analysis of "writers who travel," see V. S. Pritchett, "The Writer as a Traveler," *New Statesman and Nation* 51 (1956): 693–94.

9.   Although the Garnetts were not impressed with the event and told Mrs. Trollope not to go, they knew better: "I think it more probable she will come," Harriet Garnett to Julia Pertz, 24 June 1833, GPC.

10.   Frances Trollope, *Belgium and Western Germany*, 2 vols. (1834). All further references cited parenthetically in the text, are to this edition. Diary of Thomas Adolphus Trollope, n.d., cited in FET, 1:197; Frances Trollope to Julia Pertz, 23 August 1833, GPC; and Frances Trollope to John Murray, 15 October 1833, JMA.

11.   Sir Arthur Brooke Faulkner, *Visit to Germany and the Low Countries in the years 1829, 1830, and 1831*, 2 vols. (1833). Sending a portion of her manuscript to the publisher in early 1834, she added: "I also send Sir Arthur Brooke Faulkners abominable volumes—I scratched and marked these very freely when I first read them but should have done so with more care, if I had thought at the time of sending them to you." Frances Trollope to John Murray, 13 January 1834, JMA. Cf. Head, *Bubbles*, pp. 502–3.

12.   See Faullker, *Visit to Germany*, 1:152 ff. Mrs. Trollope's description of the students is in *Belgium and Western Germany*, 1:150: "Hair, long and exquisitely dishevelled; throats bare with collars turned back almost to the shoulders; with here a miniature beard, curiously trimmed into a perfect triangle; and there moustaches long, thin and carefully curled, might be seen repeated in one knot after another thru the whole length of the room. "Ironically, the dullest part of the book is her account of Hanover, where she visited her dear Julia and had Dr. Pertz provide statistics about students, professors, and German universities (2:224 ff.). In her letter announcing their plans, she was obviously vexed that it would be a working-visit: "We are just going to see sights—so odious my dear Julia." Frances Trollope to Julia Pertz, 23 August 1833, GPC.

13. Unsigned review of *Belgium and Western Germany*, in *Westminister Review* 22 (1835): 518. Mrs. Trollope herself uses the phrase "in issimo" (1:294).

14. Trollope, *Belgium and Western Germany*, 1:48-52; 2:156, 60, 62.

15. Unsigned review in *Spectator* 7 (1834): 684.

16. Unsigned review in *New Monthly Magazine* 41 (1834): 505, *Belgium and Western Germany* was also reviewed with Faulkner's *Visit to Germany* in an unsigned article, in *Literary Gazette*, no. 913 (1834), p. 491-93. Cg. unsigned reviews in *Quarterly Review* 58 (1837): 326; and *Athenaeum*, nos. 35/and 36 (1834), pp. 529-31, 618-20.

17. Frances Trollope to John Murray, 22 July 1834, JMA. This letter ends: "Were this to happen, your kind hint as to the form should not be forgotten."

18. The terms of the contract for *Tremordyn Cliff* gave Mrs. Trollope £250, and if the sale reached 950 copies, she would receive an aditional £100. Memoranda of agreements between Frances Trollope and Richard Bentley, 10 and 28 March 1835, British Museum (hereafter cited as BrM), ADD 46612 f., 150, 156.

19. Mary Garnett to Julia Pertz, 27 April 1835, GPC.

20. Mary Garnett to Julia Pertz, 15 July 1835, GPC. For the Garnetts, who were in some financial trouble, Mrs. Trollope's success was phenomenal: "Mrs. Trollope in *coining* money literally," Mrs. Garnett commented.

21. Frances Trollope to John Murray, 20 July 1835, JMA.

22. Frances Trollope to Richard Bentley, 5 October 1835, PCP. From the start, she had objected to the proposed length, writing to the publisher to propose 330 pages for each volume. She also was concerned lest he hold her to the contract to write a book that "treated in a similar manner" to *Domestic Manners* the subject of Paris. "My hope is that I shall be able to produce two light and lively volumes—but the *manner* can hardly be exactly similar." Frances Trollope to Richard Bentley, n.d. [March 1835], TCP.

23. Frances Trollope to Richard Bentley, 24 June 1835, TCP.

24. Mrs. Trollope had completed the first volume of *Paris* in late October; the second was briefly delayed by the death of her husband. At the very end, the publisher asked for more material to fill up the pages, but she refused. Frances Trollope to Richard Bentley, 21 October 1835, and n.d. [November 1835], TCP. On 23 November 1835 she renegotiated the method of payment, receiving £100 in cash and the remainder in six and twelve months. BrM, ADD 46612, f. 157.

25. Trollope, *Paris*, letters 33, 58, 27.

26. *Ibid.*, letters 78, 5, 34, and 45.

27. Unsigned review of *Paris*, in *Literary Gazette*, no. 987 (1836), p. 5.

28. Trollope, *Paris*, letter 42.

29. Unsigned review of *Paris*, in *Spectator* 9 (1836): 40-41.

30. Mary Garnett to Julia Pertz, 15 July 1835, GPC.

31. *Quarterly Review* 76 (1845): 98-137.

32. Frances Trollope to Richard Bentley, 21 October 1835, TCP.

33. Frances Trollope to John Murray, 7 November 1835, JMA.

34. Harriet Garnett to Julia Pertz, 22 November 1835, GPC.

35. Harriet Garnett to Julia Pertz, 22 November and 19 December 1835, GPC.

36. Harriet Garnett to Julia Pertz, 12 January 1836, GPC; and Anthony to Thomas Adolphus Trollope, January 1836, cited in FET, 1:248.

37. Frances to Thomas Trollope, n.d., cited in FET, 1:250. The MS introduction has apparently been lost.

38. Anthony to Thomas Adolphus Trollope, n.d. [12 February 1836], cited in FET, 1:259. Earlier quotation, Mary Russell Metford to Frances Trollope, 20 February 1836, Boston Public Library, by courtesy of the Trustees.

39. Frances Trollope to Richard Bentley, 28 March 1836, TCP.

40. Memorandum of an agreement between Frances Trollope and Richard Bentley, 27 April 1836, BrM, ADD 46612, f. 240.

41. Cecilia had been sent off to enjoy the country air. "She has suffered much lately, and though *not ill*, would I think derive great benefit from change of air and scene." Frances Trollope to John MacGregor 23 March 1836, HSP. Cf. Harriet Garnett to Julia Pertz, 23 June 1836, GPC.

42. Frances Trollope to Julia Pertz (Stuttgart) , 2 August 1836, GPC.

43. Mary Garnett to Julia Pertz, 14 August 1836, GPC.

44. Frances Trollope to Julia Pertz (Vienna), 17 January 1837, TPC.

45. Frances Trollope to John Murray (Vienna), 3 December 1836, JMA. Earlier quotation is Frances Trollope to Julia Pertz, 17 January 1837, TCP.

46. Frances Trollope to Princess Metternich, 20 January 1837, PCP.

47. Frances Trollope to Richard Bentley (Vienna), 27 February 1837, TCP.

48. Frances Trollope to Julia Pertz, 17 January 1837; and Harriet Garnett to Julia Pertz, 13 May 1837, GPC.

49. Frances Trollope, *Vienna and the Austrians: with some account of a Journey through Swabia, Bavaria, the Tyrol, and the Salzbourg*, 2 vols. (1838). All further references cited parenthetically in the text, are to this edition.

50. Unsigned review of *Vienna and the Austrians*, in *Spectator* 11 (1838): 209-10.

51. Trollope, *Vienna and the Austrians*, 1:155, 169, 184–86, 241 ff., 265.

52. *Ibid.*, 2:291, 353. Review is from the *Spectator*, 11 (1838): 210.

53. Frances to Thomas Adolphus Trollope, 12 and 27 September 1837, PCP.

54. Frances Trollope to Richard Bentley, 5 December 1835, and 13 August 1837, TCP.

55. Frances Trollope to Richard Bentley, 15 December 1837, TCP.

56. Charles Buller, Jr., to Richard Bentley, 10 October 1837, PCP.

CHAPTER EIGHT

1. The quotation is from Clara H. Whitmore, *Woman's Work in English Fiction from the Restoration to the Mid-Victorian Period*, p. 234.

2. Frances Trollope, *The Life and Adventures of Jonathan Jefferson Whitlaw: or Scenes on the Mississippi*, 3 vols. (1836). All further references, cited parenthetically in the text, are to this edition. Cf. Richard Hildreth, *The White Slave: or Memoirs of Archy Moore*, preface to the 1855 edition, pp. xxi ff.; and Harriet Beecher Stowe, *Uncle Tom's Cabin: or Life among the Lowly* (1851). Mrs. Trollope wrote the novel in order to raise money for another tour. In December 1835, she signed an agreement with Richard Bentley, by which she would receive £250 for the three-volume novel. Should sales reach 1,200 copies, she would receive an additional £100. The agreement carried an unusual addendum; Hervieu would provide fifteen etchings, for which he would receive £75. The book was to be ready for publication in four months, March 1836. Memorandum of agreement, 26 December 1835, BrM, ADD 46612, f. 201.

Earlier, she and Bentley agreed to a new schedule of payments for *Paris and the Parisians*: BrM, ADD 46612, f. 157.

3. A good discussion of the prevailing forms of fiction, from which the quotation is taken, is George H. Ford, *Dickens and His Readers: Aspects of Novel-Criticism since 1836*, pp. 33 ff. Ford naturally stresses Dicken's contributions.

4. Unsigned review of *Jonathan Jefferson Whitlaw, Athenaeum*, no. 453 (1836), pp. 462–463. Cf. discussion of the Newgate novel in Robert A. Colby, *Fiction with a Purpose: Major and Minor 19th Century Novels*, pp. 8 ff.

5. William Makepeace Thackeray, review of Lever's *St. Patrick's Eve*, in *Morning Chronicle*, 3 April 1845, and earlier quotation from his review of Benjamin Disraeli, *Sybil*, in *Morning Chronicle*, 13 May 1845, printed in Gordon N. Ray, ed., *William Makepeace Thackeray's Contributions to the "Morning Chronicle,"* pp. 71, 86.

6. For Mrs. Trollope's earlier interest in the white man's treatment of the Indians, see *Domestic Manners*, p. 221.

7. C. Maria Child, ed., preface to Linda Brent's *Incidents in the Life of a Slave Girl* (1861).

8. FET, 1:252 ff. See unsigned reviews of *Jonathan Jefferson Whitlaw*, in the *Spectator* 9 (1836): 634–35; *Literary Gazette*, no. 1015 (1836), pp. 420–22; and *Athenaeum*, no. 453 (1836), pp. 462–63.

9. Unsigned review of *The Vicar, Athenaeum*, no. 517 (1837), p. 708. Cf. unsigned review in *Westminster Review* 28 (1838): 115: "We might declare that she chose the loathsome organic disease of the Southern States of America for the subject of a novel, partly to gratify her Yankee-phoebia, and partly for the profit to be reaped by those who minister coarse excitement to the mob of readers. But in a spirit of charity, we will give her credit for motives more philanthropic and less paltry. . . . [*The Vicar*] is written with as hearty and thorough-going a *gusto* for what is repulsive and horrible as if its authoress had drunk of the witch broth . . . which she had so recently anathematized as being the inspiration of MM. Hugo, Balzac, etc."

10. Frances Trollope, *The Vicar of Wrexhill*, 3 vols. (1837). All further references, cited parenthetically in the text, are to this edition. Much later, the clerical novel with a focus on female religious folly and reprehensible clergymen became more frequent and dominant. Vicars who "lead ladies up the garden" and clerics who seduce parish girls are commonplace in novels after 1856. See excellent discussion in Margaret Maison, *Search Your Soul, Eustace: A Survey of the Religious Novel in the Victorian Age*, pp. 84 ff. Mrs. Trollope's interest in this aspect of clerical life goes back to her days in Harrow and America. See *Domestic Manners*, p. 276.

11. Unsigned review of *The Vicar, Examiner*, no. 1548 (1837), p. 628.

12. Unsigned review of *The Vicar in Athenaeum*, no. 517 (1837), p. 708.

13. William Makepeace Thackeray, review of *The Vicar*, in *Fraser's Magazine* 17 (1838): 83.

14. *Ibid.*, 79 ff.

15. Unsigned reviews of *The Vicar* in the *Examiner*, no. 1548 (1837), p. 628; *Fraser's Magazine*, p. 81; and the London *Times*, 25 October 1837.

16. Frances Trollope to Richard Bentley, 15 December 1837, TCP. In her broad study, Inga-Stina Ewbank calls Mrs. Trollope a woman "driven to writing because of financial distress" and thus "inevitably anxious to 'give them what they want.'" She is further described as having "a finger on the pulse of the public and an eye on the seller's market, rather than gifts or inclinations in any one particular literary

direction." Such criticism is unfair for two reasons. It overlooks the fact that Mrs. Trollope's incredible range included many genres in which she introduced innovative and daring themes, which won her more criticism than approbation, and which opened for greater development fields that she had been the first to explore. Moreover, this criticism implies that a "finger on the pulse of the public" is somehow a disgrace, yet all great writers—and above all her contemporary Charles Dickens— have searched for this same pulse. See Inga-Stina Ewbank, *Their Proper Sphere: A Study of the Brontë Sisters as Early Victorian Female Novelists*, chapter 1.

17. Frances to Thomas Adolphus Trollope, two letters, n.d. [November and December 1837], cited in FET, 1:287 ff.

18. Frances Trollope to Julia Pertz, 26 January 1838, GPC. Information on her book is from Frances Trollope to Richard Bentley, 10 February 1838, TCP.

19. Frances to Thomas Adolphus Trollope, 17 May 1838, PCP. Cf. FET, 1:299.

20. Frances Trollope to Richard Bentley, 21 and 29 May 1838, TCP. She offered to "furnish a novel in November next, and another in the month of May following for £700 each for the copyright—or £600 on delivery of the MS and £100 more after the sale of 1450 copies, with a further £100 after the sale of 2000—leaving the ultimate copyright with my family." Her long delayed novel on Vienna finally appeared late in 1838: Frances Trollope, *A Romance of Vienna*, 3 vols. (1838).

21. Thomas Adolphus Trollope to Richard Bentley, 18 September 1838, TCP. There is some confusion as to the date of Cecilia's marriage. Although Thomas Adolphus and his wife (TAT, p. 278, and FET, 1:300) give the day as 11 February 1839, contemporary letters clearly place the marriage in August. See Mary Garnett to Julia Pertz, 22 August 1838, GPC.

22. Anna Drury to Mrs. Anthony Trollope, n.d., cited in FET, 2:260-61.

23. Frances to Thomas Adolphus Trollope, n.d., cited in FET, 1:288-90.

24. R. H. Barham to Richard Bentley, 26 November 1838, Berg Collection, New York Public Library (hereafter cited as NYPL). The last quotation is from an unsigned review of *The Widow Barnaby*, *Athenaeum*, no. 584 (1839), pp. 9-10.

CHAPTER NINE

1. Frances Trollope, *The Widow Barnaby*, 3 vols. (1838). All further references, cited parenthetically in the text, are to this edition. The Thackeray quotation is from Frank W. Chandler, *The Literature of Roguery*, 2:453. This excellent book completely misses Mrs. Trollope's contributions to the genre. Daniel Defoe's *Moll Flanders*, of course, centered on a female picara, but it appeared more than a century earlier and portrayed a very different kind of woman. The widow is respectably middle class.

2. Thackeray's comment is from his review of *Jerome Paturot*, in *Fraser's Magazine*, 28 (1843): 350. The next sentence contains his praise for Mrs. Trollope noted below. The last quotation is from an unsigned article, "Female Novelists: Part V, Mrs. Trollope," *New Monthly Magazine* 96 (1852): 25.

3. Frances Trollope, *The Barnabys in America: or Adventures of the Widow Wedded*, 3 vols. (1843), 1:2-3. All further references, cited parenthetically in the text, are to this edition.

4. Within a year, *The Widow Barnaby* had appeared in a cheap, popular edition, becoming vol. 81 in Bentley's series that sold at six shillings. The sequel to this successful novel was ready within ten months: Frances Trollope, *The Widow Married: a Sequel to the Widow Barnaby*, 3 vols. (1840). All further references, cited

parenthetically in the text, are to this edition. The third and final novel in the series appeared in 1843. Like many of Mrs. Trollope's novels, these were translated into French, and even mounted on the boards. See *Examiner*, no. 1721 (1841), pp. 54–55.

5. Frances Trollope to Mary Russell Mitford, 2 August 1837, in MRM, 2:26.

6. Mrs. Barnaby, briefly Mrs. O'Donagough and then Mrs. Major Allen, changes her name frequently before returning triumphantly—and at her husband's request—to the name of Barnaby at the end of the third novel. Quotations from *The Widow Barnaby*, 2:87, and 1:146.

7. As previously noted, all of Frances Trollope's own money and that which she and her husband had inherited from her father had been lost in the Cincinnati venture. Intact, however, was the marriage settlement that Thomas Anthony had provided. Writing to Julia in 1834 at the nadir of the family fortune, in exile in Belguim to avoid prosecution, Mrs. Trollope exclaimed: "My settlement (oh! what a blessed thing is a settlement!) affords an income sufficient to support us in perfect comfort here." Frances Trollope to Julia Pertz, 13 July 1834, GPC.

8. Flint, "Travellers," pp. 290–91.

9. Unsigned reviews of *The Widow Barnaby*, *Spectator* 12 (1839): 15; and *Athenaeum*, no. 584 (1839), pp. 9–10.

10. Unsigned review of *The Widow Barnaby*, in the London *Times*, 24 January 1839.

11. Unsigned article, "Modern Novelists—Great and Small," *Blackwood's Edinburgh Magazine* 77 (1855): 355–56. For an analysis of the change in the fictional treatment of women, which does not, however, evaluate Mrs. Trollope's contributions, see Robert Palfrey Utter and Gwendolyn Bridges Needham, *Pamela's Daughters, passim*.

CHAPTER TEN

1. Frances Trollope, *The Life and Adventures of Michael Armstrong, the Factory Boy* (1840). All further references, cited parenthetically in the text, are to this edition. This novel appeared first in monthly parts, from 26 February 1839, with plates by Hervieu, R. W. Buss, and Thomas Onwhyn. In 1840, both a three volume and a one volume edition appeared. For the backgrounds, see W. H. Chaloner, "Mrs. Trollope and the Early Factory System," *Victorian Studies* 4 (1960): 159–66. Although admitting that "at the opening of the 'hungry '40's' [Mrs. Trollope] is one of the first to make fiction of industrial problems," Mrs. Ewbank insists on attributing this breakthrough to Mrs. Trollope's "eye on the seller's market." Ewbank, *Proper Sphere*, p. 14. The quotation is from FET, 1:303.

2. For information about and the public interest in Manchester, see Asa Briggs, *Victorian Cities*, pp. 90, 93, 116. Charles Dickens also visited the city (in 1838–1839) but could not bring himself to use the materials until much later. See Edgar Johnson, *Charles Dickens: His Tragedy and Triumph*, 1:225. Thomas Carlyle also visited Manchester, for *Past and Present*. For Mrs. Trollope's intentions, see FET, 1:301.

3. TAT, pp. 280–81.

4. FET, 1:301; TAT, p. 281. For the Blincoe memoir, see A. E. Musson, "Robert Blincoe and the Early Factory System," *Derbyshire Miscellany* 1 (1958): 111–17.

5. See Chaloner, "Trollope," pp. 165–66, and TAT, p. 282. For Stephens, see J. T. Ward, "Revolutionary Tory: The Life of J. R. Stephens," *Transactions of the Lancashire and Cheshire Antiquarian Society, passim*. For Oastler, see Cecil Driver, *Tory Radical: The Life of Richard Oastler, passim*.

6. TAT, p. 280. For her visits, see *Bradford Observer*, 21 March 1839. The conditions are well described in Briggs, *Victorian Cities*, p. 147. For the accuracy of her observations, see J. T. Ward, *The Factory Movement, 1830-1955, passim*; and J. L. and Barbara Hammond, *Lord Shaftesbury, passim*. Only Chaloner's rather superficial article ("Trollope," pp. 159 ff.), suggests that Mrs. Trollope erred in her conclusions.

7. R. H. Horne, *New Spirit of the Age* (1844), pp. 141–42. Cf. Benjamin Disraeli, *Sybil or the Two Nations*, and its discussion in Briggs, *Victorian Cities*, pp. 98–99, and Kathleen Tillotson, *Novels of the 1840's*, pp. 119 ff. Despite Mrs. Trollope's efforts, most critics consider Disraeli's work the first such novel. As in other matters, the fact that Mrs. Trollope was a woman prevented many of her contemporaries from taking her seriously,.

8. Tillotson, *Novels*, p. 122. The earlier quotation is from fragment of a letter by Frances Trollope, n.d., printed in FET, 1:301.

9. Mary Russell Mitford to Elizabeth Barrett, 3 January 1840, in L'Estrange, *Life*, 2:217.

10. Harriet Martineau, "A Manchester Strike," *Illustrations of Political Economy* (1834), pp. 134–36; Charlotte Elizabeth [Tonna], *Helen Fleetwood* (1841), serialized in *The Christian Lady's Magazine* during 1839 and 1840. According to Margaret Dalziel (*Popular Fiction 100 Years Ago: An Unexplored Tract of Literary History*, p. 145), most contemporary fiction stated or implied that poverty was the fault of the poor. And P. J. Keating (*The Working Classes in Victorian Fiction*, pp. 228 ff.) explicitly includes Mrs. Trollope as one of the popular novelists who insist that the causes of the evil were "vicious employers and overseers [who] are sadists" and whose removal would solve everything. Valid as such criticisms may be for other novelists of the period, they do not apply to Mrs. Trollope, whose analysis and solution were entirely different.

11. Trollope, *Michael Armstrong* 2:164–65. Even before the book appeared, popular agitators linked the questions of slavery and child labor. Informing its readers of Mrs. Trollope's forthcoming book, *The Northern Star* wrote on 2 March 1839: "Mrs.Trollope is about to enter the lists with Boz in a monthly illustrated publication to be called *Michael Armstrong, the Factory Boy*. . . . This announcement has given rise to a good deal of speculation as to how this celebrated authoress will treat so interesting a subject. We have heard that it is her intention to lend the whole power of her vigorous pen to the great object of THE EMANCIPATION OF OUR WHITE NEGROES. The lash of her satire has already been felt by the slave owner on the other side of the Atlantic, and if her pen be wielded with similar ability on the present occasion, her subject is one which will ensure to her the most eager attention from many thousands of her countrymen. The cheap form of publication, so much in vogue at present, has been, we think, most judiciously chosen for the work."

12. For comparison with Dickens, see the unsigned review of *Oliver Twist*, in *Quarterly Review* 64 (1839): 90. Unsigned review of *Michael Armstrong*, in *New Monthly Magazine* 57 (1839): 286. For discussion of serialization, see Tillotson, *Novels*, pp. 25 ff.; and John Butt, "The Serial Publication of Dicken's Novels: *Martin Chuzzlewit* and *Little Dorrit*," in Ian Watt, ed., *The Victorian Novel: Modern Essays in Criticism*, pp. 70–82.

13. *Northern Star*, 2 March 1839.

14. First is the unsigned review of *Michael Armstrong*, *Athenaeum*, no. 615 (1839), p. 589. The second is from *New Monthly Magazine* 57 (1839): 286.

15. In *Michael Armstrong* (2:164), Mrs. Trollope herself warned the public: "Let none

dare to say this picture is exaggerated, till he has taken the trouble to ascertain by his own personal investigation that it is so." For confirmation, see William Rathbone Greg, "An enquiry into the state of the manufacturing population and the causes and cures of the evils therein existing" (1831), reprinted by Kenneth E. Carpenter, ed., *The Ten Hours Movement in 1831 and 1832;* and Frederick Engels, *The Condition of the Working Class in England,* ed. W. O. Henderson and W. H. Chaloner, pp. 111 ff. For Dickens, see Johnson, *Dickens,* 1:225.

16. For the history of this particular print, see Chaloner, "Trollope," p. 166.

17. John Brown, *A Memoir of Robert Blincoe . . .* (1832), reprinted in Carpenter, *Ten Hours Movement.* For the background, see J. T. Ward, "The Factory Movement," in *Popular Movements ca. 1830–1850,* p. 57: "The hostility of many agricultural communities and the demographic revolution together encouraged the adoption of a recruitment policy fraught with hazards . . . . Hard pressed Poor Law authorities would welcome opportunities of reducing both parochial rates and personal responsibilities by sending cartloads of pauper and orphan children to the North."

18. *Cf.* Blincoe, *Memoir,* p. 32, and Trollope, *Michael Armstrong,* 3:154.

19. Blincoe, *Memoir,* p. 44 Cf. Trollope, *Michael Armstrong,* 2:159. Similar conditions of roving pigs and workers eating rotten and decaying food thrown to these animals are described in Engels, *Conditions,* pp. 80–86, and *Weekly Dispatch,* 5 May 1844.

20. Blincoe, *Memoir,* pp. 34–35, and Trollope, *Michael Armstrong,* 2: 236–37, 243.

21. Blincoe, *Memoir,* p. 35.

22. TAT, pp. 281–82. For Parson Bull, see J. C. Gill, *The Ten-Hours Parson: Christian Social Action in the Eighteen-Thirties,* pp. 21 ff.

23. M. A. Stodart, *Hints on Readings for Young Ladies,* cited in Ewbank, *Proper Sphere,* p. 38. I have been unable to locate a copy of this book.

24. Unsigned article, "Gallery of Literary Characters, Part XLI, Miss [Letitia Elizabeth] Landon," in *Fraser's Magazine* 8 (1833): 433.

25. Edward Bulwer-Lytton's review, "Lady Blessington's Novels," in *Blackwood's Edinburgh Review* 67 (1838): 349; and unsigned article, "Living Literary Characters, Part X, Miss Mitford," in *New Monthly Magazine* 32 (1831): 367. In her study of the Brontës, Mrs. Ewbank (*Proper Sphere,* pp. 41 ff.) found them atypical because they refused to restrict themselves to domestic and social concerns—women's proper sphere. Neither had Mrs. Trollope. Mrs. Ewbank also mentions that the most frequent criticism of the Brontë novels was that they were "coarse," the very word always used in reviews of Mrs. Trollope.

26. Horne, *Spirit,* p. 141.

27. *Bolton Free Press,* 22 February 1840, cited in Chaloner, "Trollope," p. 165. In August 1839, the Rev. J. R. Stephens had been sentenced to eighteen months imprisonment for using seditious and inflammatory language. Cf. similar criticism in the unsigned review of *Michael Armstrong, Athenaeum,* no. 615 (1839), p. 589.

28. Unsigned review of *Michael Armstrong* in the *Athenaeum,* no. 165 (1839), pp. 587–90.

29. For a discussion of this novel, see below chapter 13, pp. 211 ff.

CHAPTER ELEVEN

1. Frances Trollope to Charles Colburn, 17 June 1839, MS and Archives Division, New York Public Library (hereafter cited as NYPL-MS). She received 800 guineas for *Michael Armstrong,* and this became her standard rate. Proudly she wrote her

brother: "Colburn was here last night—and Tom settled with him (for I escaped the job by *retiring* to dress for a party) for two novels to be written as early as suits my convenience for which I am to receive *eight hundred guineas each.*" Frances Trollope to Henry Milton, 9 March 1839, PCP.

2. TAT, pp. 284–87.

3. See FET, 1:303. Dr. Elliotson's resignation is noted in the London *Times*, 7 January 1839. Apparently, she had already completed the July and August installments of *Michael Armstrong* (then appearing in serial form), probably in order to make her summer visit easier.

4. Frances Trollope to Julia Pertz, 26 September 1839, GPC. Cf. TAT, p. 298.

5. TAT, pp. 300, 322–23.

6. Frances Trollope to Richard Bentley, 21 May 1838, describing her new idea as "a special subject, which I believe I manage best, and . . . called *Tempers.*" The quotation about her surprise at its popularity is from Frances Trollope to Cecilia Tilley, 23 March 1840. Both letters in TCP.

7. Frances Trollope, *One Fault: A Novel*, 3 vols. (1839). All further references, cited parenthetically in the text, are to this edition. For an evaluation of the popular reluctance to discuss failing marriages, see Dalziel, *Popular Fiction*, pp. 113, 120.

8. Frances Trollope to Harriet Garnett, 7 December 1828, GPC.

9. TAT, p. 205. Cf. Anthony's recollection: "The worst curse of all was a temper so irritable that even those whom he loved best could not endure it." AT, pp. 27, 13.

10. Cited in Dalziel, *Popular Fiction*, p. 117.

11. Unsigned reviews of *One Fault*, Spectator 12 (1839): 1138–39; and *Literary Gazette*, no. 1193 (1839), pp. 754–55.

12. Frances Trollope to Julia Pertz, 26 September 1839, GPC. Tom was to travel with Hervieu by another route and meet Anthony and his mother in Paris somewhat later.

13. Harriet Garnett to Julia Pertz, 4 December 1839, GPC.

14. Mary Garnett to Julia Pertz, 8 March 1840. Earlier quotation is Harriet Garnett to Julia Pertz, 10 January 1840. Both letters in GPC.

15. Frances Trollope to Cecilia Tilley, 23 March 1840, TCP; and Frances Trollope to Julia Pertz, 24 May 1840, GPC. For her stay in Paris, see also FET, 1:307–11. She even tried to help General Pepe publish his book on Italy; see Frances Trollope to unknown correspondent, December 1839, NYPL-MS.

16. Frances Trollope to Cecilia Tilley, 23 March 1840, TCP; and Frances Trollope to Julia Pertz, 24 May 1840, GPC.

17. Frances Trollope, *The Ward of Thorpe Combe*, 3 vols. (1841). All further references, cited parenthetically in the text, are to this edition.

18. Unsigned reviews of *The Ward*, in *John Bull* 22 (1842): 153 (italics added); *Athenaeum*, no. 754 (1842), p. 312; and *Literary Gazette*, no. 1315 (1842), p. 229.

19. Unsigned review of *The Ward* in the *Athenaeum*, no. 754 (1842), p. 312.

20. Harriet Garnett to Julia Pertz, 12 June 1840, GPC.

21. Unsigned article, "Female Novelists, Part V, Mrs. Trollope," *New Monthly Magazine* 96 (1852): 19. Cf. unsigned review, *John Bull* 20 (1840): 536.

CHAPTER TWELVE

1. AT, p. 44

2. AT, pp. 38–43.

3. AT, pp. 45, 63. In a letter to her daughter, Mrs. Trollope chatted about her brother's attempt at fiction that had appeared this year, a novel called *Rivalry*. Frances to Cecilia Tilley, 23 March 1840, TCP. While reviewers found the novel promising, they claimed it was often what one by his sister never was—tame and commonplace. One reviewer in particular claimed that while it was "of Mrs. Trollope's school," the novel lacked "the breadth and vigour" of her humor and talent at caricature. Unsigned review of *Rivalry*, *New Monthly Magazine* 59 (1840): 136–37.

4. Frances Trollope to Rosina Bulwer, n.d. [July 1840], printed in Louisa Deve, *Life of Rosina, Lady Lytton*, p. 195.

5. Quotations from Stebbins and Stebbins, *Trollopes*, pp. 101–2. The authors use this incident to mock Mrs. Trollope's concern for Anthony.

6. Frances Trollope, *Charles Chesterfield; or the Adventures of a Youth of Genius*, 3 vols. (1841); and Frances Trollope, *The Blue Belles of England*, 3 vols. (1842). All further references, cited parenthetically in the text, are to these editions. She published this latter work with Saunders and Otley and thereby aroused the ire of her regular publisher, Charles Colburn. For discussion of this incident, see below, p. 206.

7. FET, 2:265.

8. The character of Marchmont became so well-known that Plumer Ward, a popular author, used him to represent all book-reviewers: "the illustrious Marchmont, a jewel in modern satire, who can review a book without reading it." Cited in Sadleir, *Trollope*, p. 100. Sadleir uses this story to illustrate Mrs. Trollope's status, "even among the intellectuals."

9. AT, p. 105.

10. Thomas Hay Sweet Escott, *Anthoy Trollope: His Public Services, Private Friends, and Literary Originals*, p. 33. The earlier quotation is from AT, p. 25.

11. Cf. Trollope, *Chesterfield, 2:104*–5; and Anthony Trollope, *The Way We Live Now*, 2 vols. (1875). By starting her career at 53, Mrs. Trollope had avoided the temptation to use personal charms to advance her professional life and much preferred sending her faithful Tom to dicker and discuss. See Frances Trollope to Henry Milton, 9 March 1839, PCP.

12. Cf. Trollope, *Blue Belles*, 2:159–60, 194 ff.; and Anthony Trollope, *Barchester Towers*, 3 vols. (1857).

13. Cf. Trollope, *Blue Belles*, 2:169–70, 234, 300–301; and Anthony Trollope, *The American Senator*, 3 vols. (1877).

14. Frances Trollope to Cecilia Tilley, 23 March 1840, TCP. Earlier quotations are from Frances Trollope to Cecilia Tilley, n.d., cited in FET, 1:314; and Harriet Garnett to Julia Pertz, 10 January 1840, GPC.

15. Frances Trollope to Cecilia Tilley, 23 March 1840, TCP; Frances Trollope to Julia Pertz, 24 May 1840, and Harriet Garnett to Julia Pertz, 12 June 1840. GPC. In the latter, Harriet added: "Cecilia is again with child which her mother regrets very much." Subsequently, Mrs. Trollope reported that her granddaughter was "the most beautiful one she has ever seen." Harriet Garnett to Julia Pertz, 29 November 1840, GPC.

16. Frances Trollope to Rosina Bulwer, 3 July 1840, printed in Devey, *Lady Lytton*, pp. 196–98. Information also from Michael Sadleir, *Bulwer: A Panorama, I. Edward and Rosina, 1803–1836*, pp. 368 ff.; Rosina Lytton Bulwer to Frances Trollope, 20 July 1840, UCLA; and Lady Lytton Bulwer, *Budget of the Bubble Family* (1840), introduction.

17. Frances Trollope to unknown correspondent, 17 October 1840, PCP. Information

also from TAT, p. 257; and Frances Trollope to unknown correspondent, 26 March 1840, PCP. According to TAT, p. 260, Anthony Trollope later took one of these girls in as his housemaid at Waltham.

18. Frances Trollope to Richard Bentley, 21 August 1840, TCP.

CHAPTER THIRTEEN

1. Frances Trollope, *Hargrave: or the Adventures of a Man of Fashion*, 3 vols. (1843). All further references, cited parenthetically in the text, are to this addition. For the controversy with Colburn, see the account in FET, 1:322-25.

2. Unsigned review of *Hargrave*, *Athenaeum*, no. 806 (1843), pp. 333-34.

3. Harriet Garnett to Julia Pertz, 5 April 1841, GPC. For the long postponed Italian trip, see TAT, p. 325; and FET, 1:325.

4. Frances Trollope to Richard Bentley, 19 February 1842, TCP. Frances Trollope, *A Visit to Italy*, 2 vols. (1842).

5. Unsigned review of *A Visit to Italy*, *Athenaeum*, nos. 781 and 782 (1842), pp. 884-86, 906-9.

6. Harriet Garnett to Julia Pertz, 24 March, 6 April, and 4 May 1842, GPC. According to FET, 2:16, Mrs. Trollope moved into her new house on 23 July 1842.

7. TAT, pp. 327-29.

8. Presentation volume with note from Frances Trollope to Lady Musgrave, 21 November 1842, University of Michigan Library. Quotations are from Frances Trollope to Mary Russell Mitford, 16 December 1842, in MRM, 2:78-79. When Mr. Mitford died, friends raised a subscription for his daughter, and Frances Trollope contributed. See L'Estrange, *Life*, p. 265.

9. Mrs. Stone to Julia Pertz, n.d. [1842], GPC. Second quotation from Harriet Garnett to Julia Pertz, 17 November 1842, GPC.

10. Charles Dickens to Frances Trollope, 16 December 1842, NYPL.

11. TAT, pp. 299-300.

12. Thomas Adolphus to Henry Trollope, 26 June 1883, UIU. Earlier quotations cited in FET, 2:15. According to the same source, Mrs. Trollope accepted poor terms from Colburn for *The Barnabys in America* because she needed cash for the house.

13. Harriet Garnett to Julia Pertz, 18 September 1843, GPC. Her departure date can be established from the cancellation of her subscription to the *Quarterly*, 17 November 1843, PCP.

14. Frances Trollope, *Jessie Phillips: A Tale of the New Poor Law*, appeared in monthly parts beginning 31 December 1842. In 1843, it was published in three volumes as *Jessie Phillips: A Tale of the Present Day*. Subsequent references to this work, cited parenthetically in the text, will be to the one-volume edition of 1844. I have been unable to find any explanation of the change in the sub-title. Advertisement for *Jessie Phillips* is from the *Northern Star*, 31 December 1842.

15. For the background to the new law, see Driver, *Oastler*, pp. 269 ff., and the contemporary analyses discussed in Mark Blaug, "The Myth of the Old Poor Law and the Making of the New," *Journal of Economic History* 23 (1963): 151-84; and Mark Blaug, "The Poor Law Report Reexamined," *Journal of Economic History*, 24:229-45. Generally, while showing the inadequacies of the old law, Blaug criticizes the methods used to create the new one.

16. Quotation is from advertisement for *Michael Armstrong*, in *Morning Chronicle*, 9

March 1840. For background, see M. E. Rose, "The Anti-Poor Law Agitation," in Ward, *Popular Movements*, p. 80 ff.; and Nicholas C. Edsall, *The Anti-Poor Law Movement 1834–44, passim*. Mrs. Trollope was particularly impressed by the sermons she heard delivered by the Rev. Joseph Raynor Stephens while in Manchester. These are reported in the *Northern Star*, 9 and 16 March 1839. Cf. TAT, p. 282. An example of the style of these sermons would be helpful:

> There is more blood upon the door steps of that parish office behind this market-place—there is more blood upon the door steps of that parish office—more blood upon the door steps of every parish office in England, of every workhouse, and of every foundling hospital—there is more blood on the door steps of these houses, which ought to be houses of mercy, sanctuaries to which the poor and the destitute can fly for refuge—there is more blood on the door steps of these houses than ever was shed on the field of Waterloo. . . .

> There is more blood on the walls of yonder mills in Ashton—and in every other town where the factory system has reared its hateful head, and sent down its hellish smoke and fire upon the people—there is more blood upon these factories, than ever was shed in the time of the civil wars in England. . . .

> I believe that these national sins, that these national murders, will have to be visited by God with an awful retribution upon the nation.

In the conclusion of this sermon, preached on 16 March 1839, Stephens touched upon the plight of single young girls and may well have provided Mrs. Trollope with the seed of her future novel:

> Does God send us . . . Guardians to take that young maiden—because she has no father or mother, because she has no brother to stand up for her—to take that young maiden, and put her into a machine, which they call a "holdfast," . . . and apply the shears, and crop off her curls, and locks from her head, that she would almost rather die than lose? That is done under the New Poor Law.

17. The phrase about workhouses as prisons is from Gill, *Ten-Hours Parson*, p. 158. For her examples, see Trollope, *Jessie Phillips*, pp. 1–3, 50, 55, 116–17. The celebrated passage about conditions for the new workhouses in the New Poor Law reads:

> It is necessary that the pauper should be relieved, not by giving him money or goods to be spent or consumed in his own house, but by receiving him into a public establishment. But a public establishment, if properly arranged, necessarily secures to its inmates a larger amount of bodily comfort than is enjoyed by an ordinary independent labourer in his own dwelling. For example, an inmate of a well-appointed union workhouse lives in rooms more spacious, better ventilated, and better warmed; his meals are better and more regularly served; he is more warmly clad, and he is better attended on in sickness than if he were in his own cottage. . . . The only expedient, therefore, for accomplishing the end in view, which humanity permits, is to subject the pauper inmate of a public establishment to such a system of labour, discipline, and restraint as shall be sufficient to outweigh, in his estimation, the advantages which he derives from the bodily comforts which he enjoys. This is the only mode, consistent with humanity, of rendering the condition of the pauper less eligible than that of the independent labourer; and upon this principle the English Union workhouses have been organized. [Cited in Thomas Mackay, *A History of the English Poor Law*, 3:283–84.]

18. In her novel, Mrs. Trollope ever maintained that the New Poor Law was simply "part of a body of class legislation based on selfishness and [middle] class interest" (p. 219). In her excellent study, "How Cruel was the Victorian Poor Law?" *Historical Journal* 11 (1968): 365–71, Ursula Henriques fully supports Mrs. Trollope on this point.

19. Frances Trollope to unknown correspondent, 27 February 1843, HSP.

20. For details of the new provision, see Ursula Henriques, "Bastardy and the New Poor Law," *Past and Present* 37 (1967): 103–29. This provision caused much debate, and at one point Bishop Philpotts of Exeter, a strong opponent of the measure, rose in the House of Lords to point out that in the Commissioner's Report, fathers of illegitimate children were always called "unfortunate persons," yet the mothers were denounced in terms of "vice." *Ibid.*, p. 113.

21. Unsigned reviews of *Jessie Phillips*, in *John Bull* 23 (1843): 732; and (in a joint review of *Martin Chuzzlewit*) *Spectator* 16 (1843): 17–18.

22. Henriques, "Bastardy," p. 119. For later treatments of similar themes, see Mrs. Gaskell, *Ruth* (1853); and the character of Hetty in George Eliot, *Adam Bede* (1859).

23. Unsigned review of *Jessie Phillips*, Athenaeum, no. 835 (1843), pp. 956–57.

24. Between 1844 and 1850, Mrs. Trollope wrote twelve multi-volume works, including eight romantic novels, two travel books, an anti-Jesuit story, and her final novel of American life.

25. Unsigned review of *The Laurringtons*, *Athenaeum*, no. 842 (1843), p. 1107; *Spectator* 16 (1843): 1237; and *Dublin Review* 15 (1843): 530–46.

26. Frances Trollope, *The Laurringtons: or Superior People*, 3 vols. (1844). All further references, cited parenthetically in the text, are to this edition. Unsigned review in the *Athenaeum*, no. 842 (1843), p. 1107. For an earlier example of this type of character, see Margaretta Hartley, in Trollope, *Blue Belles*.

27. Frances Trollope, *Young Love: A Novel*, 3 vols. (1844). All further references, cited parenthetically in the text, are to this edition. The similarities between the life of Amelia and Anthony's compelling fortune hunter Arabella Trefoil have been mentioned before. Both mother and son found their artistic sympathies curiously engaged by these desperate ladies on the hunt for security as well as affection. The combination seemed a difficult one for women to achieve in the nineteenth-century marriage market.

28. Frances Trollope, *The Lottery of Marriage: A Novel*, 3 vols. (1849). All further references, cited parenthetically in the text, are to this edition.

29. Frances Trollope, *The Attractive Man*, 3 vols. (1845). All further references, cited parenthetically in the text, are to this edition. Unsigned review of *The Attractive Man*, *Literary Gazette*, no. 1501 (1845), pp. 700–701.

30. Harriet Garnett to Julia Pertz, 3 December 1845, GPC. Unsigned reviews of *The Attractive Man* in *Literary Gazette*, no. 1501 (1845), p. 701; and in *John Bull* 25 (1845):739.

31. Frances Trollope, *The Three Cousins*, 3 vols. (1847). All further references, cited parenthetically in the text, are to this edition.

32. Unsigned review of *The Three Cousins*, in *John Bull* 27 (1847): 344.

33. Trollope, *Young Love*, 2:204–5.

34. Frances Trollope, *Town and Country: A Novel*, 3 vols. (1848). All further references, cited parenthetically in the text, are to this edition. This novel was subsequently reissued as *Days of the Regency* (1857), much to the annoyance of Anthony, who feared that his mother might seem "in league with the publishers in palming off old

novels." Anthony to Frances Trollope, 27 January 1859, cited in FET, 2:283–84.

35. Frances Trollope, *The Young Countess: or Love and Jealousy*, 3 vols. (1848), 1:3. All further references, cited parenthetically in the text, are to this edition. This novel too was reissued, under the title *Love and Jealousy* (1860).

36. Trollope, *Jessie Phillips*, p. 112; and unsigned review in the *Athenaeum*, no. 835 (1843), pp. 956–57. For the dual nature of the protest movement, see Mark Hovell, *The Chartist Movement*, pp. 79 ff. The last quotation is cited, without source, in Sadleir, *Trollope*, p. 107.

CHAPTER FOURTEEN

1. Rose Heseltine Trollope's memoir of her mother-in-law, n.d., cited in FET, 2:39.

2. Frances to Rose Heseltine Trollope, 7 August 1844, TCP, and AT, p. 63.

3. Frances Trollope, *The Robertses on Their Travels*, 3 vols. (1846). All further references are to this edition. Unsigned reviews of *The Robertses*, in *John Bull* 26 (1846): 247; and *Gentleman's Magazine* 26 (1846): 179.

4. Frances to Rose Heseltine Trollope, 7 August 1844, TCP.

5. Frances Trollope to John Tilley, January 1845, printed in FET, 2:60–61; and Harriet Garnett to Julia Pertz, 5 January 1845, GPC.

6. Frances to Thomas Adolphus Trollope, n.d., cited in FET, 2:52. Information also in Harriet Garnett to Julia Pertz, 5 January and 11 June 1845, GPC.

7. AT, pp. 63–64.

8. FET, 2:55. Earlier quotations from pp. 54, 58.

9. Frances Trollope, *Travels and Travelers: A Series of Sketches*, 2 vols. (1846). All further references, cited parenthetically in the text, are to this edition.

10. Trollope, *Travels*, 1:50–51, and 2:69–70.

11. *Ibid.*, 1:50 ff. Earlier quotation is from 2:293–94.

12. Frances Trollope, *Father Eustace: A Tale of the Jesuits*, 3 vols. (1847). All further references are to this edition. For a convenient summary of this popular genre, see the chapter entitled, "The Wicked Jesuit and Company," in Maison, *Search your Soul, Eustace*, pp. 169–82, and Robert Lee Wolff's chapter entitled, "The Catholics and Their Friends and Enemies," in *Gains and Losses* pp. 27–107, esp. pp. 38–40.

13. Unsigned reviews of *Father Eustace*, in *New Monthly Magazine* 79 (1847): 135; and in *John Bull* 27 (1847): 11.

14. Anthony's statement is found in AT, p. 65. Anthony Trollope, *The Macdermots of Ballycloran*, 3 vols. (1847). For the reviews of *Macdermots*, see Donald Smalley, ed., *Trollope: The Critical Heritage*, 548–52. For the reception of *The Three Cousins*, see FET, 2:79.

15. Frances Trollope to unknown correspondent, 25 June 1847, PCP.

16. Harriet Garnett to Julia Pertz, 12 December 1847, GPC. For the doctor's opinion, see FET, 2:96.

17. TAT, p. 379, and FET, 2:107.

18. Frances to Thomas Adolphus Trollope, 10 February 1848, PCP. The earlier quotation is from Harriet Garnett to Julia Pertz, 3 January 1848, GPC.

19. Lucy Gilbert to Julia Pertz, 13 April 1848, GPC.

20. Harriet Garnett to Julia Pertz, n.d. [1848], GPC.

21. Harriet Garnett to Julia Pertz, 30 May 1848, GPC.

22. Harriet Garnett to Julia Pertz, 22 October 1848, GPC.

23. Harriet Garnett to Julia Pertz, 19 and 25 February 1849, GPC.

24. Frances to Thomas Adolphus Trollope, 11 March 1849, FET, 2:140–41.

25. *Ibid.*, p. 141.

26. Frances to Thomas Adolphus Trollope, 2 April 1849, FET, 2:142.

27. Frances to Rose Heseltine Trollope, 20 April 1849, TCP; and Frances to Thomas Adolphus Trollope, 14 April 1849, FET, 2:144.

28. Frances to Rose Heseltine Trollope, 20 April 1849, TCP.

29. Frances to Thomas Adolphus Trollope, 9 May 1849, FET, 2:145–46.

30. Harriet Garnett to Julia Pertz, 26 May 1849, GPC. Earlier quotation is Harriet Garnett to Julia Pertz, 12 August 1849, GPC.

31. Rose Heseltine Trollope's memoir, cited in FET, 2:161–62. Mrs. Trollope was actually seventy at the time.

32. Frances to Rose Heseltine Trollope, 15 August 1849, TCP. The additional information is from Harriet Garnett to Julia Pertz, 12 and 26 August 1849, GPC.

33. Harriet Garnett to Julia Pertz, 20 January 1850, GPC. Earlier quotations from Harriet Garnett to Julia Pertz, 12 and 26 August 1849, GPC.

34. Harriet Garnett to Julia Pertz, 6 May 1850, GPC.

35. Frances Trollope, *The Old World and the New: A Novel*, 3 vols. (1849). Earlier quotation is Harriet Garnett to Julia Pertz, 6 January 1852, GPC.

36. Frances Trollope, *Petticoat Government: A Novel*, 3 vols. (1850).

CHAPTER FIFTEEN

1. Frances Trollope, *Second Love, or Beauty and Intellect: A Novel*, 3 vols. (1851). All further references to this group of novels, cited parenthetically in the text, are from these editions.

2. Frances Trollope, *Mrs. Mathews, or Family Mysteries*, 3 vols. (1851).

3. Frances Trollope, *Uncle Walter: A Novel*, 3 vols. (1852).

4. Unsigned reviews of *Uncle Walter*, in *John Bull* 33 (1852): 396; *Literary Gazette*, no. 1873 (1852), p. 906; and *Athenaeum*, no. 1305 (1852), pp. 1169–70.

5. Frances Trollope, *The Young Heiress: A Novel*, 3 vols. (1853).

6. Frances Trollope, *Life and Adventures of a Clever Woman*, 3 vols. (1854).

7. Frances Trollope, *Gertrude, or Family Pride*, 3 vols. (1855); and Frances Trollope, *Fashionable Life: or Paris and London*, 3 vols. (1856).

8. This last novel does contain one interesting character, Monsieur Roche, a mysterious entrepreneur who almost cheats the ladies by having them invest money in a shady, nonexistent firm. Although it all turns out well, Roche seems to be a precursor of Melmotte in Anthony Trollope's *The Way We Live Now* (1875).

CHAPTER SIXTEEN

1. TAT, pp. 419–20. Titles from TAT, p. 417.

2. This fact occasioned Anthony's spirited letter on the advantages of having children, 5 October 1852, printed in FET, 2:242–43.

3. Frances Trollope to Mary Russell Mitford, April 1852, in MRM, 2:96–98; and Mary Russell Mitford to Frances Trollope, 1 August 1852, PCP.

4. Harriet Garnett to Julia Pertz, 12 December 1847, and 24 April 1848, GPC.

5. Harriet Garnett to Julia Pertz, October 1848, and 29 December 1851, GPC.

6. Georg Heinrich Pertz to Frances Trollope, 2 November 1852; and Frances Trollope to Georg Heinrich Pertz (Florence), 14 November 1852, GPC. This last sentence is not exactly true, for Mrs Trollope had kept all of the letters from her son Thomas Adolphus. Unfortunately, these are now lost.

7. Rose Heseltine Trollope's memoir, n.d., cited in FET, 2:244.

8. Mary Russell Mitford to Mrs. Hoare, autumn 1852, cited in L'Estrange, *Life*, 2:315–17. Although her last new work appeared in 1856, at least five of her previous novels were subsequently reissued: *The Lottery of Marriage* (1862); *Town and Country* (1857); *The Vicar of Wrexhill*, (1860); *The Widow Barnaby* (1860); *The Young Countess* (1860).

9. Frances to Anthony Trollope, 17 December 1854, TCP. Beside the sentences which suggest that his nineteen-month-old daughter talks fluently, Tom has added "!!!! T.A.T." and next to the suggestion that she dances as exquisitely as a ballerina, he has again noted "!!!"

10. Frances Trollope to Monsieur Jarvis, 31 December 1854, Beinecke Rare Book and Manuscript Library, Yale University.

11. Frances to Anthony Trollope, 8 July 1856, TCP. Information also from FET, 2:256.

12. Thomas Adolphus to Anthony Trollope, 8 July 1856, TCP.

13. Frances to Anthony Trollope, n.d., TCP. The earlier letter is Frances to Henry Trollope Esq., 8 July 1856, TCP.

14. The translation of the epitaph reads: "Here lies what was mortal of Frances Trollope—but her special spirit is divine, and her memory seeks no marble monument. Born in Stapleton in Somerset, England, A.D. 1780, she came to rest in Florence, Tuscanny, A.D. 1863." TAT, p. 302. Perhaps the fun-loving Frances would have preferred the epitaph which a flip critic wrote for her in 1843:

    > I Mrs. Trollope
    > Made these vols. roll up;
    > And when Heaven shall take my soul up,
    > My works will fill a big hole up.   [*Literary Gazette*, no. 1366 (1843), p. 182.]

15. FET, 2:301.

16. The author is currently working on a study of several of these 'hidden lives' based on this collection of unpublished letters. See also Carroll Smith-Rosenberg, "The Female World of Love and Ritual: Relations between Women in 19th Century America," *Signs: Journal of Women in Culture and Society* 1 (1975): 1–29.

17. AT, p. 24.

18. FET, vol. 1.

19. Henry to Frances Trollope, 9 and 24 August 1832, TCP.

Bibliography

.I. MANUSCRIPT SOURCES

The impetus for undertaking a fully researched biography of Frances Milton Trollope began with my discovery of thirty letters from Mrs. Trollope to Julia Garnett Pertz. Although these comprise only a small portion of a huge correspondence preserved by Julia Garnett Pertz, which her great-granddaughter Dr. Cecilia Payne-Gaposchkin graciously permitted me to use, they showed how many of the established accounts of Mrs. Trollope were erroneous; indeed, these errors have been repeated in all published references to her. I therefore decided to attempt to reconstruct her life from contemporary letters, thus rescuing her reputation from recent biographers. Throughout my book, I have made frequent reference to the Garnett-Pertz Collection, comprising weekly or bi-monthly letters from the Garnett family to Julia over a span of twenty-five years and letters from numerous friends and acquaintances. In addition, the same collection contains invaluable letters from Frances and Camilla Wright to Julia Pertz, selections of which Dr. Gaposchkin has now published in the *Harvard Library Bulletin*. The entire collection forms a unique historical record of the thoughts and actions of a circle of women from 1820 to 1852. I am currently working on a complete study of this representative circle and the friendships they treasured. The collection is currently housed in the Houghton Library, Harvard University but is not as yet open to scholars. Once again I acknowledge my enormous debt of gratitude to Dr. Gaposchkin, whose generosity has helped make this book more than just another superficial account.

Concerning Mrs. Trollope's own correspondence, I have succeeded in locating nearly 250 unpublished letters. Her daughter-in-law, Frances Eleanor Trollope, apparently had access to all the letters in the possession of family members when she wrote her two-volume biography in 1895. A great deal of my initial research involved locating the present whereabouts of this correspond-ence in order to reexamine it for this biography. I was aided by Mr. Robert Cecil, the grandson of Bice Trollope (Mrs. Charles Stuart-Wortley), the only child of Thomas Adolphus. After an exhaustive search, Mr. Cecil ruefully concluded that practically no Trollopiana was left in England. The extant letters are now nearly all in the United States. Thomas Adolphus, Mrs. Trollope's eldest son, left all his papers, including those of his mother, to his second wife, Frances Eleanor. Upon her death in 1913, instead of giving the papers to the lineal family—the descendant of Thomas Adolphus's daughter by a previous marriage and thus into the Cecil family, she willed all her effects to her sister, Ellen Lawless Ternan who, after her relationship with Charles Dickens, had married the Rev. George Wharton Robinson. When Mrs. Robinson herself died in 1914, she bequeathed all her possessions to a daughter, Gladys Eleanor Robinson Reece and a son Geoffrey Wharton Robinson. In 1960, the latter sold his holdings

299

to the University of California at Los Angeles, where they form the heart of Collection 712, Trollope Family Papers. In 1974, Princeton University bought the remaining Trollope papers in the possession of Mrs. Reece. They joined a huge collection of Trollopiana which Morris L. Parrish had carefully assembled over the years. Apparently purchased from numerous sources and not from family members, the Parrish collection contains a large number of letters from and to Mrs. Trollope. Another private collector, Robert H. Taylor, has assiduously gathered an impressive number of Mrs. Trollope's letters, including the interesting courtship correspondence, whose mysterious reappearance in 1869 is recounted by Anthony in his *Autobiography*. Anthony subsequently gave the papers to his brother, and in 1892, Frances Eleanor Trollope returned them to Anthony's son Henry Merivale, who apparently sold them.

Thus the bulk of the correspondence (most, but not all of which was available to Frances Eleanor Trollope) is currently housed at UCLA (seventeen letters); in the Morris L. Parrish Collection at Princeton (seventy letters); and in the Robert H. Taylor Collection at Princeton (thirty-eight letters from Mrs. Trollope and forty-three letters in the courtship correspondence). In addition, all three collections have a number of important letters to Mrs. Trollope, particularly from General Lafayette, Charles Dickens, Basil Hall, and her son Henry. The principal missing collection is the correspondence of forty years from Mrs. Trollope that her son Thomas Adolphus lovingly preserved. Inexplicably, this rich source has apparently disappeared without a trace, although a number of letters from Mrs. Trollope to Thomas Adolphus are found in the Morris L. Parrish collection. Missing also are the letters from Mrs. Trollope to her daughter Cecilia Tilley, mentioned by Bradford Booth as being in the possession of the family. All efforts to reach the family and learn of their present location have been in vain.

In addition to the material available to Frances Eleanor Trollope, I have located a number of other manuscripts and fragments gathered by Anthony. These eventually passed to his granddaughter Muriel Rose Trollope, who died in 1953. Shortly before her death, through Professor Gordon N. Ray and on the advice of Michael Sadleir, Anthony's biographer, she sold the papers in America. Although the bulk of the material consists of letters to Anthony's son, Henry Merivale, from his father, mother, and brother, the collection also includes manuscripts of Mrs. Trollope's early literary efforts. They are currently housed as the Anthony Trollope collection at the University of Illinois Library, Urbana, Illinois.

Particularly helpful are documents that detail Mrs. Trollope's relations and negotiations with her publishers. Ms. Virginia Murray gave me access to the twenty-two letters from Mrs. Trollope to John Murray in 1833–35. These communications, which throw new light on her life in Bruges, are housed in the John Murray Archives. The extensive correspondence with the publisher Richard Bentley is contained in the Robert H. Taylor Collection at Princeton, and the records of Mrs. Trollope's contracts are from the Bentley papers in the British Museum. Individual letters are dispersed in a variety of libraries and depositories. Full description of their location is given in the footnote citations.

Finally, mention should be made of the important correspondence between Thomas Anthony Trollope and John Lord Northwick concerning the ill-fated farm at Harrow and the mansion house built there by the Trollopes. From them I have been able to reconstruct accurately the complex financial story. These documents are part of the Muniments of Lord Northwick, owned by the Greater London Council and housed at the Greater London Record Office.

II. WORKS BY FRANCES TROLLOPE
(Listed chronologically)

The Domestic Manners of the Americans. With illustrations by A. Hervieu. 2 vols. London: Whittaker, Treacher, 1832. Reprinted, Donald Arthur Smalley, ed. New York: Alfred Knopf, 1949.

The Refugee in America: a Novel: 3 vols. London: Whittaker, Treacher, 1832.

The Mother's Manual: or Illustrations of Matrimonial Economy. An Essay in Verse. With illustrations by A. Hervieu. 1 vol. London: Treutel and Würtz and Richter, 1833.

The Abbess: A Romance. 3 vols. London: Whittaker, Treacher, 1833.

Belgium and Western Germany in 1833: including Visits to Baden-Baden, Wiesbaden, Cassel, Hanover, the Harz Mountains, etc. etc. 2 vols. London: John Murray, 1834.

Tremordyn Cliff. 3 vols. London: Bentley, 1835.

Paris and the Parisians in 1835. With illustrations by A. Hervieu. 2 vols. London: Bentley, 1836.

The Life and Adventures of Jonathan Jefferson Whitlaw: or Scenes on the Mississippi. With illustrations by A. Hervieu. 3 vols. London: Bentley, 1836.

The Vicar of Wrexhill. With illustrations by A. Hervieu. 3 vols. London: Bentley, 1837.

Vienna and the Austrians. With illustrations by A. Hervieu. 2 vols. London: Bentley, 1838.

A Romance of Vienna. 3 vols. London: Bentley, 1838.

The Widow Barnaby. 3 vols. London: Bentley, 1839.

The Widow Married: A Sequel to The Widow Barnaby. With illustrations by R. W. Buss. 3 vols. London: Colburn, 1840.

The Life and Adventures of Michael Armstrong, the Factory Boy. With illustrations by A. Hervieu, R. W. Buss, and T. Onwhyn. Published in twelve monthly numbers from 1 March 1839 to 1 February 1840 by Colburn. First book edition in 3 vols. London: Colburn, [December] 1839, and in a one-volume edition [March, 1840].

One Fault: a Novel. 3 vols. London: Bentley, 1840.

Charles Chesterfield: or the Adventures of a Youth of Genius. With illustrations by "Phiz." 3 vols. London: Colburn, 1841.

The Ward of Thorpe Combe. 3 vols. London: Bentley, 1841.

The Blue Belles of England. 3 vols. London: Saunders and Otley, 1842.

A Visit to Italy. 2 vols. London: Bentley, 1842.

The Barnabys in America: or Adventures of the Widow Wedded. With illustrations by John Leech. 3 vols. London: Colburn, 1843.

Hargrave: or the Adventures of a Man of Fashion. 3 vols. London: Colburn, 1843.

Jessie Phillips: a Tale of the Present Day. With illustrations by John Leech. Published in eleven monthly parts from 31 December 1842 to 30 November 1843 by Colburn as *Jessie Phillips: a Tale of the New Poor Law*. First book edition in 3 vols. London: Colburn, 1843, and in a one-volume edition, 1844.

The Laurringtons: or Superior People. 3 vols. London: Longman, Brown, Green and Longmans, 1844.

Young Love: a Novel. 3 vols. London: Colburn, 1844.

The Attractive Man. 3 vols. London: Colburn, 1846.

The Robertses on their Travels. 3 vols. London: Colburn, 1846.

Travels and Travelers: a Series of Sketches. 2 vols. London: Colburn, 1846.

Father Eustace: a Tale of the Jesuits. 3 vols. London: Colburn, 1847.

The Three Cousins. 3 vols. London: Colburn, 1847.

Town and Country: a Novel. 3 vols. London: Colburn, 1848.

The Young Countess: or Love and Jealousy. 3 vols. London: Colburn, 1848.

The Lottery of Marriage: a Novel. 3 vols. London: Colburn, 1849.

The Old World and the New: a Novel. 3 vols. London: Colburn, 1849.

Petticoat Government: a Novel. 3 vols. London: Colburn, 1850.

Mrs. Mathews, or Family Mysteries. 3 vols. London: Colburn, 1851.

Second Love, or Beauty and Intellect: a Novel. 3 vols. London: Colburn, 1851.

Uncle Walter: a Novel. 3 vols. London: Colburn, 1852.

The Young Heiress: a Novel. 3 vols. London: Hurst and Blackett, 1853.

The Life and Adventures of a Clever Woman. Illustrated with Occasional Extracts from her Diary. 3 vols. London: Hurst and Blackett, 1854.

Gertrude: or Family Pride. 3 vols. London: Hurst and Blackett, 1855.

Fashionable Life: or Paris and London. 3 vols. London: Hurst and Blackett, 1856.

Variant Titles

Lynch Law. *1857* reissue of *The Life and Adventures of Jonathan Jefferson Whitlaw* [1836].

The Ward. Reissue of *The Ward of Thorpe Combe* [1841].

Days of the Regency. 1857 reissue of *Town and Country* [1848].

III. PUBLISHED BOOKS AND ARTICLES

Aaron, Daniel. "Cincinnati, 1818–1838: A Study of Attitudes in the Urban West." Ph.D. dissertation, Harvard University, 1942.

Abbott, Carl. "The Location and External Appearance of Mrs. Trollope's Bazaar." *Journal of the Society of Architectural Historians* 29 (1970): 256–60.

Altick, Richard D. *The English Common Reader: A Social History of the Mass Reading Public 1800–1900*. Chicago: University of Chicago Press, 1957.

Arfwedson, C. D. *The United States and Canada in 1832, 1833, and 1834.* 2 vols. London: Bentley, 1834.

Atwater, Caleb. *A History of the State of Ohio, Natural and Civil*. Cincinnati: Glezen & Shepard, 1838.

Bayne-Powell, Rosamund. *English Country Life in the 18th Century*. London: John Murray, 1935.

Blane, William Newham. *An Excursion thru the United States and Canada during the years 1822–23 by an English Gentleman*. London: Baldwin, Cradock & Jay, 1824.

Blaug, Mark. "The Myth of the Old Poor Law and the Making of the New." *Journal of Economic History* 23 (1963): 151–84.

Blaug, Mark. "The Poor Law Report Reexamined." *Journal of Economic History* 24 (1964): 229–45.

Brent, Linda. *Incidents in the Life of a Slave Girl* (1861). Edited by C. Maria Child. New York: Harcourt Brace, 1973.

Briggs, Asa. *Victorian Cities*. New York: Harper & Row, 1963.

Brown, John. "A Memoir of Robert Blincoe." In *The Ten-Hours Movement in 1831 and 1832*. Edited by Kenneth E. Carpenter. New York: Arno Press, 1972.

Bryant, P.H.M. *Harrow*. London: Blackie and Son, Ltd., 1936.

Bullock, William. *Sketch of a Journey through the Western States of North America . . . with a Description of the New and Flourishing City of Cincinnati by Messrs. B. Drake and E. D. Mansfield*. London: Morgan, Lodge and Fisher, 1827.

Butt, John. "The Serial Publication of Dickens's Novels: *Martin Chuzzlewit* and *Little Dorrit*." In *The Victorian Novel: Modern Essays in Criticism*. Edited by Ian Watt, pp. 70–82. New York: Oxford University Press, 1971.

Chaloner, W. H. "Mrs. Trollope and the Early Factory System." *Victorian Studies* 4 (1960): 159–66.

Chambrun, Clara Longworth de. *Cincinnati: the Queen City*. New York: C. Scribner's Sons, 1939.

Chandler, Frank W. *The Literature of Roguery*. 2 vols. Boston: Houghton Mifflin, 1907.

The Cincinnati Directory and Commercial Advertiser for the Year 1829. Cincinnati: Robinson and Fairbank, 1829.

Clark, Allen C. "The Trollopes." *Columbia Historical Society Records* 37–38 (1937): 79–100.

Clemens, Samuel [Mark Twain]. *Life on the Mississippi.* New York: Sagamore Press, 1957.

Cockburn, J. S., and T.F.T. Baker, eds. *A History of the County of Middlesex,* vol. 4. London: Oxford University Press, 1971.

Colby, Robert A. *Fiction with a Purpose: Major and Minor 19th Century Novels.* Bloomington: Indiana University Press, 1967.

Cowell, Joseph. *Thirty Years Passed Among the Players in England and America.* New York: Harper and Bros., 1844.

Crow, Duncan. *The Victorian Woman.* London: George Allen & Unwin, 1971.

Dalziel, Margaret. *Popular Fiction 100 Years Ago: An Unexplored Track of Literary History.* London: Cohen and West, 1957.

Devey, Louisa. *Life of Rosina, Lady Lytton.* London: Swan Sonnenschein, Lowry & Co., 1887.

Driver, Cecil. *Tory Radical: the Life of Richard Oastler.* New York: Oxford University Press, 1946.

Dunbar, Janet. *The Early Victorian Woman: Some Aspects of Her Life 1837–1857.* London: George G. Harrap & Co., 1953.

Edgeworth, Maria. *The Modern Griselda: a Tale.* London: Hunter and Baldwin, Cradock, and Jay, 1819.

Edsall, Nicholas C. *The Anti-Poor Law Movement 1834-1844.* Manchester: Manchester University Press, 1971.

Eldon, Abraham. *The Continental Travelers' Oracle; or Maxims for Foreign Locomotion.* 2 vols. London: Colburn, 1828.

Emerson, O. B. "Frances Wright and Her Nashoba Experiment." *Tennessee Historical Quarterly* 6 (1947): 291–314.

Engels, Frederick. *The Condition of the Working Class in England.* Edited and translated by W. O. Henderson and W. H. Chaloner. New York: Macmillan, 1958.

Escott, Thomas Hay Sweet. *Anthony Trollope: His Public Services, Private Friends and Literary Originals.* London: John Lane, 1913.

Ewbank, Inga-Stina. *Their Proper Sphere: A Study of the Brontë Sisters as Early Victorian Female Novelists.* London: Scandinavian University Books, 1966.

Faulkner, Sir Arthur Brooke. *Visit to Germany and the Low Countries in the Years 1829, 1830 and 1831.* 2 vols. London: Bentley, 1833.

Flint, Timothy. "Travellers in America, etc." *Knickerbocker, or New York Monthly Magazine* 2 (1833): 283–302.

Ford, George H. *Dickens and His Readers: Aspects of Novel-Criticism since 1836.* Princeton: Princeton University Press, 1955.

Ford, Henry A., and Kate B. Ford. *History of Cincinnati, Ohio, with Illustrations and Biographical Sketches.* Cleveland: L. A. Williams & Co., 1881.

Fordham, Elias Pym. *Personal Narrative of Travels in Virginia, Maryland,*

Pennsylvania, Ohio, Indiana, Kentucky; and of a Residence in the Illinois Territory, 1817–1818. Cleveland: Arthur H. Clark Co., 1906.

Gill, J. C. *The Ten-Hours Parson: Christian Social Action in the Eighteen-Thirties.* London: S.P.C.K., 1959.

Greg, William Rathbone. "An inquiry into the State of the Manufacturing Population and the Causes and Cures of the Evils therein Existing." London, 1831. In *The Ten-Hours Movement in 1831 and 1832.* Edited by Kenneth E. Carpenter. New York: Arno Press, 1972.

Greve, Charles T. *Centennial History of Cincinnati and Representative Citizens.* 2 vols. Chicago: Biographical Publishing Co., 1904.

Griest, Guinevere L. *Mudie's Circulating Library and the Victorian Novel.* Bloomington: Indiana University Press, 1970.

Griffin, Russell A. "Mrs. Trollope and the Queen City." *Mississippi Valley Historical Review* 37 (1950): 289–302.

Hall, Basil. *Travels in North America in the Years 1827 and 1828.* Edinburgh: Cadell & Co., 1829.

[Hamilton, Thomas]. *Men and Manners in America by the Author of Cyril Thornton,* 2 vols. Edinburgh: William Blackwood, 1833. Reprinted (2 vols. in one). New York: Augustus M. Kelley, 1968.

Hammond, J. L., and Barbara Hammond. *Lord Shaftesbury.* London: Harcourt, Brace & Co., 1923.

Hart, A. Tindal. *The Country Priest in English History.* London: Phoenix House, 1959.

———. *The 18th Century Country Parson (circa 1689–1830).* Shrewsbury: Wilding & Son Ltd., 1955.

Head, Sir Francis. *Bubbles from the Brunnens of Nassau by an Old Man.* Brussels: Hauman & Co., 1840.

———. *Rough Notes taken during some Rapid Journeys across the Pampas and Among the Andes,* 1826. Reprinted. Carbondale: Southern Illinois University Press, 1967.

Heineman, Helen. "Frances Trollope in the New World: *Domestic Manners of the Americans.*" *American Quarterly* 21 (1969): 544–59.

———. "Frances Trollope's *Jessie Phillips*: Sexual Politics and the New Poor Law," *International Journal of Women's Studies* 1 (January 1978), 60–80.

———. "Starving in that Land of Plenty: New Backgrounds to *Domestic Manners of the Americans.*" *American Quarterly* 24 (1972): 643–60.

Hendrickson, Walter B. "The Western Museum Society of Cincinnati." *Scientific Monthly* 58 (1946): 66–72.

Henriques, Ursula. "Bastardy and the New Poor Law." *Past and Present,* no. 37 (July 1967), pp. 103–29.

———. "How Cruel Was the Victorian Poor Law?" *Historical Journal* 11 (1968): 365–71.

Hildreth, Richard. *The White Slave; or Memoirs of Archy Moore.* New York: Miller, Orton and Mulligan, 1856.

Hildreth, William H. "Mrs. Trollope in Porkopolis." *Ohio State Archaeological and Historical Quarterly* 58 (1949): 35-51.

Holyoake, George Jacob. *Life of Joseph Raynor Stephens: Preacher and Political Orator*. London: Williams and Norgate, 1881.

Horne, R. H. *New Spirit of the Age*. New York: J. C. Riker, 1844.

Houghton, Walter E. *The Victorian Frame of Mind 1830-1870*. New Haven: Yale University Press, 1957.

Hovell, Mark. *The Chartist Movement*. Manchester: Manchester University Press, 1925.

Howitt, William. *German Experiences addressed to the English: both stayers at home and goers abroad*. London: Longman, Brown, Green, and Longmans, 1844.

Jaeger, Muriel. *Before Victoria: Changing Standards and Behaviour 1787-1837*. London: Chatto and Windus, 1956.

Jameson, Anna. *Visits and Sketches at Home and Abroad*. New York: Harper and Bros., 1834.

Johnson, Edgar. *Charles Dickens: His Tragedy and Triumph*. 2 vols. New York: Simon and Schuster, 1952.

Johnston, Johanna. *The Life, Manners, and Travels of Fanny Trollope: A Biography*. New York: Hawthorn Books, Inc. 1978.

Keating, P. J. *The Working Classes in Victorian Fiction*. London: Routledge & Kegan Paul, 1971.

Kellogg, Elizabeth R. "Joseph Dorfeuille and the Western Museum." *Journal of the Cincinnati Society of Natural History* 22 (1945): 3-29.

"Lady Travelers," *Quarterly Review* 76 (1848): 98-137.

Lancaster, Clay. "The Egyptian Hall and Mrs. Trollope's Bazaar." *Magazine of Art* 43 (1950): 94-99.

Lane, Margaret. *Frances Wright and the "Great Experiment."* Manchester: Manchester University Press, 1972.

L'Estrange, Rev. Alfred Guy, ed. *The Friendships of Mary Russell Mitford as Recorded in Letters from Her Literary Correspondents*. 2 vols. London: Hurst and Blackett, 1882.

————. *The Life of Mary Russell Mitford, told by Herself in Letters to Her Friends*. 2 vols. New York: Harper and Bros., 1870.

Lucas, Arthur. *John Lucas: Portrait Painter, 1828-1874*. London: Methuen and Co., Ltd., 1910.

Lytton-Bulwer, Lady. *The Budget of the Bubble Family*. Paris: Baudry's European Literature, 1840.

Mackay, Thomas. *A History of the English Poor Law*. 3 vols. New York: G. P. Putnam's Sons, 1900.

Maison, Margaret. *Search Your Soul, Eustace: A Survey of the Religious Novel in the Victorian Age*. London: Sheed and Ward, 1961.

Mansfield, Edward Deering. *Personal Memories, Social, Political and Literary*, *with Sketches of Many Noted People, 1803-1843*. Cincinnati: Robert Clarke & Co., 1879.

Marchand, Leslie A. *The Athenaeum: A Mirror of Victorian Culture*. University of North Carolina Press, 1941.

Marryat, Frederick. *Diary in America*. London: 1839. Reprinted, Jules Zanger, ed. London: Nicholas Vane, 1960.

Martineau, Harriet. *Illustrations of Political Economy*. Vol. III, *A Manchester Strike*. London: Charles Fox, 1834.

————. *Retrospect of Western Travel*. New York: Harper and Bros., 1838.

————. *Society in America*. 3 vols. London: Saunders and Otley, 1837.

McDermott, John Francis. "Mrs. Trollope's Illustrator: Auguste Hervieu in America (1827-1831)." *Extrait de la Gazette des Beaux-Arts* (March 1958): pp. 169-90.

Merivale, Anna W. *Family Memorials*. Exeter: Thomas Upward, 1884.

Mesick, Jane Louise. *The English Traveler in America*. New York: Columbia University Press, 1922.

Mews, Hazel. *Frail Vessels: Woman's Role in Women's Novels from Fanny Burney to George Eliot*. London: Athlone Press, 1969.

Milton, William. *The Danger of Traveling in Stage Coaches; and a Remedy proposed to the consideration of the Public*. London and Reading: Privately printed, 1810.

————. *Documents and Facts relating to the original propositions and plans now carrying into effect for the . . . improvement and enlargement of the Port and Harbour of Bristol, stated in a letter to a friend*. London: Privately printed, 1806.

————. *Essay on the subject of converting the Port of Bristol into a Floating Harbour, addressed in the year 1791 to the Incorporated Society of Merchant Venturers of that City*. London: Privately printed, 1810.

————. "Letter to the Editor." *Gentleman's Magazine*, January 1814, p. 38, and May 1818, p. 406.

Mitford, Mary Russell. *Our Village*. London: Macmillan, 1893.

"Monro's *A Summer Ramble in Syria*." *The London and Westminster Review* 25 (1836): 103-37.

Musson, A. E. "Robert Blincoe and the Early Factory System." *Derbyshire Miscellany* 1 (1958): 111-17.

Nevins, Allan. *America Through British Eyes*. Gloucester, Mass: Peter Smith, 1968.

Nicholls, Sir George. *A History of the English Poor Law*. 3 vols. London: 1854. Reprinted. New York: Augustus M. Kelley, 1967.

Nisbet, Ada B. "Mrs Trollope's *Domestic Manners*." *Nineteenth Century Fiction* 4 (1949-50): 319-24.

O'Brien, P. K. "British Incomes and Property in the early 19th Century." *Economic History Review* 12 (1959): 255-67.

Parks, Edd Winfield. "Dreamer's Vision: Frances Wright at Nashoba." *Tennessee Historical Magazine*, 2d series, 2 (1932): 75–86.

Payne-Gaposchkin, Cecilia Helena. "The Nashoba Plan for Removing the Evil of Slavery: Letters of Frances and Camilla Wright, 1820–1829." *Harvard Library Bulletin* 23 (1975): 221–51, 429–61.

Peal, Ethel. "The Atrophied Rib: Urban Middle-Class Women in Jacksonian America." Ph.D. dissertation, University of Pittsburgh, 1970.

Pease, William H., and Jane H. Pease. "A New View of Nashoba." *Tennessee Historical Quarterly* 19 (1960): 99–109.

Perkins, A. J. G., and Theresa Wolfson. *Frances Wright, Free Enquirer: The Study of a Temperament*. New York: Harper and Bros., 1939.

Pierson, George W., and Dudley C. Lunt. *Tocqueville in America*. New York: Doubleday, 1959.

Pope Hennessy, James. *Anthony Trollope*. Boston: Little Brown and Co., 1971.

Pope-Hennessy. Una. *Three English Women in America*. London: Ernest Benn Ltd., 1929.

———. ed. *The Aristocratic Journey: Being the Outspoken Letters of Mrs. Basil Hall, written during a 14 months Sojourn in American 1827–1828*. New York: G. P. Putnam's Sons, 1931.

Pritchett, V. S. "The Writer as a Traveler." *The New Statesman and Nation* 51 (1956): 693–94.

Roberts, David. "How Cruel Was the Victorian Poor Law?" *Historical Journal* 6 (1963): 97–106.

Roberts, W. J. *Mary Russell Mitford: the Tragedy of a Blue Stocking*. London: Andrew Melrose, 1913.

Rosa, Mathew Whiting. *The Silver-Fork School: Novels of Fashion Preceding Vanity Fair*. New York: Columbia University Press, 1936.

Rose, M. E. "The Anti-Poor Law Agitation." In *Popular Movements ca. 1830–1850*. Edited by J. T. Ward. New York: MacMillan, 1970.

Rosenberg, Carroll Smith. "Beauty, the Beast and the Militant Woman: A Case Study in Sex Roles and Social Stress in Jacksonian America." *American Quarterly* 23 (1971): 562–84.

Rusk, Ralph L. *The Literature of the Middle Western Frontier*. 2 vols. New York: Columbia University Press, 1925.

Sadleir, Michael. *Bulwer: A Panorama*. Vol. 1, *Edward and Rosina*. Boston: Little, Brown and Co., 1931.

———. *XIX Century Fiction: a Bibliographical Record Based on his own Collection*. 2 vols. Los Angeles: University of California Press, 1951.

———. *Trollope: a Commentary*. New York: Farrar, Straus and Co., 1947.

Sandford, Elizabeth. *Woman in her Social and Domestic Character*. 5th ed. Boston: Otis, Broaders & Co., 1843.

Skinner, John. *The Journal of a Somerset Rector; parochial affairs of the parish of Camerton, 1822-1832.* Edited by H. Coombs and A. N. Box. London: John Murray, 1930.

Sklar, Kathryn Kish. *Catherine Beecher: A Study in American Domesticity.* New Haven: Yale University Press, 1973.

Smalley, Donald. *Anthony Trollope: The Critical Heritage.* New York: Barnes and Noble, 1969.

──────. ed. *The Domestic Manners of the Americans by Frances Trollope.* New York: Alfred Knopf, 1949.

Smith, Ophia P. "Joseph Tosso, the Arkansaw Traveler." *Ohio State Archaeological and Historical Quarterly* 56 (1947): 16-45.

Smith, Page. *Daughters of the Promised Land.* Boston: Little, Brown & Co., 1970.

Snow, C. P. *Trollope: His Life and Art.* New York: Charles Scribner's Sons, 1975.

Stebbins, Lucy Poate and Richard Poate Stebbins. *The Trollopes: the Chronicle of a Writing Family.* New York: Columbia University Press, 1945.

Stodart, M. A., *Female Writers: Thoughts on their Proper Sphere and on their Powers of Usefulness.* London: R. B. Seeley and W. Burnside, 1842.

Stowe, Harriet Beecher. *Uncle Tom's Cabin; or Life among the Lowly.* Boston: John P. Jewett and Co., 1851.

Taylor, Robert H. "The Trollopes Write to Bentley." *The Trollopian* 3 (1948): 87-88, 201-14.

Thackeray, William Makepeace. *Contributions to the "Morning Chronicle."* Edited by Gordon N. Ray. Urbana: University of Illinois Press, 1955.

Thomson, Patricia. *The Victorian Heroine: A Changing Ideal 1837-1873.* London: Oxford University Press, 1956.

Tillotson, Kathleen. *Novels of the 1840's.* London: Oxford University Press, 1954.

Tocqueville, Alexis de. *Democracy in America.* New York: Schocken Books, 1961.

Tompkins, J. M. S. *The Popular Novel in England, 1770-1800.* Lincoln: University of Nebraska Press, 1961.

[Tonna, Mrs] *Helen Fleetwood by Charlotte Elizabeth.* 5th ed. New York: Charles Scribner, 1852.

Trease, Geoffrey. *The Grand Tour.* London: Heinemann, 1967.

Trollope, Anthony, *The American Senator.* 3 vols. London: Chapman & Hall, 1877.

──────. *An Autobiography.* 2 vols. Edinburgh: 1883. Reprint (2 vols. in one). London: Oxford University Press, 1961.

──────. *Barchester Towers.* 3 vols. London: Longman, 1857.

──────. *The Macdermots of Ballycloran.* 3 vols. London: Newby, 1847.

──────. *Orley Farm.* 3 vols. London: Chapman & Hall, 1862.

──────. *The Way We Live Now.* 2 vols. London: Chapman & Hall, 1875.

Trollope, Frances. A complete chronological listing of her published works is found in Part II of this Bibliography, pp. 302–303.

Trollope, Frances Eleanor. *Frances Trollope: Her Life and Literary Work from George III to Victoria*. 2 vols. London: Bentley & Son, 1895.

Trollope, Thomas Adolphus. *What I Remember*. New York: Harper & Bros., 1888.

Tucker, Louis Leonard. "Cincinnati: Athens of the West, 1830–1831." *Ohio History* 75 (1966): 10–25.

Tuckerman, Henry T. *America and Her Commentators, with a Critical Sketch of Travel in the United States*. New York: Charles Scribner, 1864.

Utter, Robert Palfrey, and Gwendolyn Bridges Needham. *Pamela's Daughters*. New York: Macmillan, 1936.

Venable, William H. *Beginnings of Literary Culture in the Ohio Valley*. Reprinted. New York: Peter Smith, 1949.

Wade, Richard C. *The Urban Frontier: Pioneer Life in Early Pittsburgh Cincinnati, Lexington, Louisville, and St. Louis*. Chicago: University of Chicago Press, 1964.

Ward, J. T. *The Factory Movement, 1830–1855*. London: Macmillan, 1962.

———. "The Factory Movement." In *Popular Movements ca. 1830–1850*. Edited by J. T. Ward. London: Macmillan, 1970.

———. "Revolutionary Tory: the Life of Joseph Raynor Stephens of Ashton-Under-Lyne (1805–1879)." *Transactions of the Lancashire and Cheshire Antiquarian Society* 68 (1958): 93–116.

Waterman, William Randall. *Frances Wright*. New York: Columbia University Press, 1924.

Welter, Barbara. "Anti-Intellectualism and the American Woman: 1800–1860." *Mid-America* 48 (1966): 258–70.

———. "The Cult of True Womanhood: 1820–1860." *American Quarterly* 18 (1966): 151–74.

Whitmore, Clara H. *Woman's Work in English Fiction: From the Restoration to the Mid-Victorian Period*. New York: G. P. Putnam's Sons, 1910.

Williams, Stanley T. *Life of Washington Irving*. 2 vols. New York: Oxford University Press, 1935.

———. ed. *Journal of Washington Irving* (1823–1824). Cambridge, Mass: Harvard University Press, 1931.

Wolff, Robert Lee. *Gains and Losses: Novels of Faith and Doubt in Victorian England*. New York: Garland Publishing, Inc., 1977.

Wright, Frances. *Course of Popular Lectures . . . with Three Addresses on Various Public Occasions*. New York: The Free Enquirer, 1829.

———. *Views of Society and Manners in America*. Reprinted. Ed. Paul R. Baker. Cambridge, Mass: Harvard University Press, 1963.

Young, G. M., ed. *Early Victorian England: 1830–1865*. 2 vols. London: Oxford University Press, 1934.

IV. LIST OF PERIODICALS CITED

American Quarterly Review
Athenaeum
Blackwood's Edinburgh Magazine
Bradford Observer
Cincinnati Advertiser and Ohio Phoenix
Cincinnati Chronicle and Literary Gazette
Cincinnati Gazette
Cincinnati Mirror and Ladies' Parterre
Dublin Review
Edinburgh Review
Examiner
Fraser's Magazine
Gentleman's Magazine
Illinois Monthly Magazine
John Bull
Knickerbocker, or New York Monthly Magazine
Literary Gazette and Journal of the Belles Lettres (titles vary)
Morning Chronicle
New Monthly Magazine
North American Review
Northern Star and Leeds General Advertiser (titles vary)
Quarterly Review
Saturday Evening Chronicle and General Literature, Morals and Arts
    (Cincinnati)
Spectator
London *Times*
Weekly Dispatch
Westminster Review

312

Index

Baedeker, Karl, 121–122.
Bazaar, The Cincinnati, 59–68, 95, 113, 273–74.
Bent, Fanny, 18, 115, 264.
Bent, Mary, 18, 264.
Bentham, Jeremy, 30.
Bentley, Richard, Publisher, 119–20, 129–36, 141–42, 153, 155–56, 204, 207, 283, 284, 286.
Beyle, Henri (Stendhal), 32.
Blincoe, Robert, 177–79.
Bull, Parson, of Brierly, 180, 185, 212.
Bulwer, Rosina, Lady Lytton, 193, 203–05, 225.
Buss, R.N., Illustrator, 167.
Byron, George Gordon, Lord, 23–24, 172, 200.

Caldwell, Dr., 60.
Campbell, Rev. Alexander, 60.
Chateaubriand, Madame de, 205.
Clark, Mary, 193.
Clyde, Charles, 4.
Clyde, Mrs. Mary Milton, 4, 6, 11, 238.
Colburn, Henry, Publisher, 155, 186, 194, 206, 211, 228, 235, 239, 289–90.
Constant, Benjamin, 32, 40.
Cook, Thomas, 121.
Cooper, James Fenimore, 32, 40.
Cunningham, Rev. John William, 25–26, 265, 266.

Dickens, Charles, 131, 158–60, 171–74, 209–10, 286–87.
Disraeli, Benjamin, 171.
Doherty, John, 170.
Dorfeuille, Joseph, 53, 55–59, 73, 271.
Drury, Anna, 155.
Drury, Henry, 130.
Drury Family, 24, 26.
Dyer, Lady, 18, 70.

Edgeworth, Maria, 8, 97, 152.
Elliotson, Dr. 186, 198, 204, 290.
Ellis, Mrs. Sarah Stickney, 6, 191.

Fauche, Mrs., 114.
Faulkner, Sir Arthur Brooke, 110, 125, 282.
Flint, Timothy, 50, 80.
Freeling, Mrs. Francis, 117, 196.
Fry, Elizabeth, 97.

Gabell, Marianne, 5, 101, 103.
Garnett, Fanny (Frances), 28.
Garnett, Harriet, 28–30, 42, 45–6, 48, 62–3, 69, 74, 101, 109, 134, 136–7, 189, 193, 195, 207–09, 211, 233–38, 250.
Garnett, Henry, 28, 266.
Garnett, Mrs. Mary, 5, 28–32, 38, 40, 47, 52, 70, 101, 109, 115, 118, 129, 133–37, 139, 192, 195, 203, 207–08, 227, 233–34, 236.
Garnett, John, 3, 27–29.
Garrow, Joseph, 232–33.
Gates, General Horatio, 27.
Gore, Mrs. Catherine, 158, 168.
Grant, Colonel, 114–15, 281.

Hall, Captain Basil, 71–2, 76–7, 79, 82, 86, 93, 102–03, 105–06, 163.
Hall, Mrs. Basil, 86.
Hamilton, Captain, 69, 73, 95, 101.
Hay, Sophia, 28.
Head, Sir Francis, 122, 125, 282.
Hervieu, Auguste, 39–40, 48–55, 57, 61, 65–70, 73–4, 78, 80, 94, 100, 104, 109, 115, 128, 133, 137–38, 140–41, 173, 176, 208, 270–71, 276–77, 279.
Hildreth, Richard, 143.
Horne, R.H., 171.

Irving, Washington, 31–2, 35, 100, 267.

Jameson, Anna, 122, 282.

Kater, Captain Henry, 101.
Kean, Charles, 38–39.

Lafayette, General Marie Joseph, Marquis de, 30, 32–5, 38, 40, 47, 55, 62, 65, 67, 69, 73, 101.
Landon, Letitia Elizabeth, 183–84.
Leech, John, Illustrator, 167,211.
Lewis, Matthew Gregory ("Monk"), 107.
Longworth , Nicolas, 113, 273–75, 280–81 .

Macready, William Charles, 38–9, 41, 273.
Marryat, Captain Frederick, 157, 273–74.
Martineau, Harriet, 109, 171.
Meetkerke, Adolphus, 8, 11, 16, 19, 20–21, 23, 262.
Mérimée, Prosper, 32.
Merivale Family, 24, 265.

Metternich, Prince Clemens von, 138–40, 154.
Metternich, Princess Melanie, 138–40, 252.
Milman, Lady, 103.
Milton, Henry (Harry), 4–5, 7, 16, 28, 30, 114–15, 117, 197, 228, 234, 236, 238, 262, 290–91.
Milton, Mrs. Henry, 234.
Milton, Mrs. Mary Gresley, 4–5.
Milton, Mrs. Sarah Partington, 5, 7, 10, 12, 16, 21.
Milton, Rev. William, 3–7, 12–13, 17, 27–8, 37, 261.
Mitford, Mary Russell, 6, 38–40, 70, 72, 74, 76, 101, 105, 109, 135, 171, 184, 209, 250–51, 253, 276.
More, Hannah, 97, 152.
Murray, John, Publisher, 100, 110–11, 115, 117, 119, 121, 129, 134.
Mylne, Dr. James, 43, 260.

Nashoba, 40–41, 43–51, 59–60, 73, 85, 101, 104, 173, 268–69.
New Harmony, Indiana, 40–41, 51–52, 60, 101.
Northwick, John Lord, 19, 21–23, 75, 109, 112–16, 264–65, 276, 280–81.
Nott, Dr., 5, 18.

Oastler, Richard, 170, 177, 184–85, 212.
Okey Sisters, 198, 204.
Owen, Robert, 40, 44, 60, 97.
Owen, Robert Dale, 40, 44.

Pepe, General Guglielmo, 18, 32, 193, 290.
Pertz, Georg Heinrich, 42–4, 251–52, 268.
Pertz, Mrs. Julia Garnett, 28–30, 37–8, 42–5, 49, 62, 68–70, 74, 76–8, 100–04, 109, 116, 134, 136, 138–39, 154, 187, 193, 203, 208–09, 233, 237–38, 251–52, 268.
Powers, Hiram, 53, 56–57, 281.

Radcliffe, Ann, 107, 231.
Recamier, Madame, 193, 205.

Sandford, Elizabeth, 91, 191.
Saunders and Otley, Publishers, 206.
Shelley, Mary, 44–45.
Siddons, Mrs. Sarah, 18.
Sismondi, J.C.L. Simonde de, 32, 40, 101.
Spurzheim, Dr., 60.
Stephens, Joseph Raynor, 170, 177, 184, 185, 212, 289, 293.
Stodart, Miss M.A., 183, 191.
Stone, Mrs. Anna Maria Garnett, 69–70, 72, 74, 84, 209, 266.

Stowe, Harriet Beecher, 143–45, 147.

Thackeray, William Makepeace, 144, 152, 157–58, 285.
Tilley, John, 155, 187, 210, 226–27, 231–36, 238.
Tilley, Mrs. Cecilia Trollope, 17, 37, 47, 49, 76, 101, 112, 114–15, 117, 135–37, 139, 141, 155, 187, 193, 195, 197, 203, 207–08, 211, 219, 227, 232–36, 284, 291.
Tilley, Children of John and Cecilia, 192.
  Frances Trollope Tilley, 196, 203, 207, 227, 234, 236–38, 291.
  Arthur Tilley, 227, 237.
  Cecilia Tilley, 238.
  Anne Tilley, 237.
  Edith Diana Mary Tilley, 232, 236–37.
Tilley, Mrs. Marianne Partington, 238.
Tocqueville, Alexis de, 61, 272.
Tonna, Charlotte Elizabeth, 172, 288.
Trollope, Anthony, 17, 19, 21, 23–5, 46–7, 76, 101, 111, 114–15, 117–18, 129, 134–35, 141, 154–55, 159, 186, 192, 196–205, 208, 211, 219, 226, 228, 231, 234, 236–38, 250–55, 257, 294, 296.
Trollope, Mrs. Anthony (Rose Heseltine), 226, 236–38, 252, 254.
Trollope, Children of Anthony and Rose.
  Harry Trollope, 253–54.
  Fred Trollope, 253.
Trollope, Arthur William, 17, 23, 37, 46, 112.
Trollope, Emily I, 17, 20.
Trollope, Emily II, 17, 21, 37, 47, 49, 112, 114, 134–35.
Trollope, Frances Milton, Residences and Travels, in chronological order:
  Bristol, 4–5.
  Heckfield, 6–7, 10–16, 261–16.
  London (Courtship), 7–16
  Illots Farm (Harrow), 20.
  Julians (Harrow), 21–23.
  Julian Hill (Harrow), 24–5, 37–46, 103–09, 112–15.
  France, 27–32, 45.
  La Grange (Lafayette's Home), 33–36, 267.
  Harrow Weald, 46–7, 75–7, 100–103.
  Nashoba, 46–51.
  Cincinnati, 51–69.
  Washington, 69–74.
  Bruges, 115–17, 133–34.
  Hadley, 134–36, 140–42, 154.
  Vienna, 136–40.
  London, 154–56, 186–88, 192, 198–201.

Manchester, 169–71, 174–75.
Carlton Hill (Penrith), 187–88, 192, 196, 203–05, 207–10, 292.
Paris, 192–95.
Italy, 207, 210–11, 218–19, 227–28, 230–34, 236, 238–40.
England, 218–19, 226–28, 231, 235–36, 254.
Germany, 229–31.
Ireland, 237–38.
Villino Trollope (Florence), 240, 250–55.
Trollope, Frances Milton, Works, (shortened titles) arranged in alphabetical order:
The Abbess (1833), 107–09, 157, 230.
The Attractive Man (1846), 221–22.
The Barnabys in America (1843), 161–65, 210.
Belgium and Western Germany in 1833 (1834), 118, 123–29, 140.
The Blue Belles of England (1842), 198–203, 206.
Charles Chesterfield (1841), 198–203, 206, 291.
The Domestic Manners of the Americans (1832), 69, 71–2, 76–101, 103–04, 109, 121, 129, 135, 142, 145, 160, 163–64, 167, 169, 221, 239, 258.
Fashionable Life (1856), 248–49, 254.
Father Eustace (1847), 230–31.
Gertrude (1855), 248.
Hargrave (1843), 206.
Jessie Phillips (1843), 185, 211–19, 225, 292–93.
Jonathan Jefferson Whitlaw (1836), 136, 142–50, 157, 164, 225.
The Laurringtons (1844), 220.
The Life and Adventures of a Clever Woman (1854), 246–48.
The Lottery of Marriage (1849), 220–21, 224.
Michael Armstrong (1839), 169–86, 192, 211–12, 287–89.
Mrs. Mathews (1851), 241–42.
The Old World and the New (1849), 239.
One Fault (1840), 154, 169, 186–92.
Paris and the Parisians in 1835 (1836), 131–36.
Petticoat Government (1850), 239.
The Refugee in America (1832), 77, 102–06, 109, 142, 157, 160.
"The Righteous Rout" (1823), 26, 266.
The Robertses on their Travels (1846), 227.

A Romance of Old Vienna (1838), 140, 142, 154.
"Salmagundi Aliena" (1822), 24–25, 265.
Second Love (1851), 240.
The Three Cousins (1847), 222–24, 231.
Town and Country (1848), 223–24, 233.
Travels and Travelers (1846), 229–30.
Tremordyn Cliff (1835), 109, 118–19, 129–31, 134, 136, 157.
Uncle Walter (1852), 242–46.
The Vicar of Wrexhill (1837), 120, 131, 136, 150–53, 157, 285.
Vienna and the Austrians (1838), 136–40, 142.
A Visit to Italy (1842), 136, 207–09.
The Ward of Thorpe Combe (1841), 194, 204.
The Widow Barnaby (1839), 156–68, 171.
The Widow Married (1840), 160–61, 165–67, 169, 186, 192.
The Young Countess (1848), 225, 295.
The Young Heiress (1853), 246.
Young Love (1844), 220.
Trollope, Henry, 17, 37, 45–47, 49, 51, 53, 55, 62–3, 66, 68, 76, 101, 109, 112, 115–20, 128, 135, 197, 259.
Trollope, Sir John, 15, 263.
Trollope, Thomas Adolphus, 16–18, 23, 37, 41, 45–6, 52–3, 55, 62, 68, 76, 78, 80, 101–02, 110, 115, 117–20, 129–30, 134, 137–41, 153–55, 169–71, 180, 186, 188–89, 192–93, 197, 204, 207–08, 210–11, 227–29, 232–36, 240, 250, 252–56, 263.
Trollope, Mrs. Thomas Adolphus (Theodosia Garrow), 232–33, 236, 240, 250.
Trollope, Child of Thomas Adolphus and Theodosia,
Bice (Beatrice) Trollope, 252–53, 297.
Trollope, Mrs. Thomas Adolphus (Frances Eleanor Ternan), 100, 169, 229, 255.
Trollope, Thomas Anthony, 3, 7–25, 27, 34, 36, 41, 46–9, 52, 59, 62–3, 66–8, 74–5, 78, 112–16, 129–30, 133–34, 189, 192, 197, 268.
Trollope, Villino, 240, 250, 253, 254.
Twain, Mark (Samuel Clemens), 82.

Western Museum of Cincinnati, 53–58.
Whitehouse Farm (New Jersey), 27–9, 41.

Whittaker and Treacher, Publishers, 40, 76, 103, 110, 119, 135.

Wilkes, Charles, 27, 35, 51, 55, 66.

Wordsworth, William, 186.

Wright, Camilla (Mrs. Richeson Whitby), 29-30, 44, 270.

Wright, Frances (Mme D'Arusmont), 28-32, 35-8, 40-41, 43-51, 59, 60, 71, 85, 97, 266-67.